Why Minorities Play or Don't Play Soccer

Soccer, the most popular mass spectator sport in the world, has always remained a marker of identities of various sorts. Behind the façade of its obvious entertainment aspect, it has proved to be a perpetuating reflector of nationalism, ethnicity, community or communal identity, and cultural specificity. Naturally therefore, the game is a complex representative of minorities' status especially in countries where minorities play a crucial role in political, social, cultural or economic life. The question is also important since in many nations success in sports like soccer has been used as an instrument for assimilation or to promote an alternative brand of nationalism. Thus soccer was appropriated to strengthen national identity during Nazi dominance in pre-Second World War Germany while Jewish teams in pre-Second World War Europe were set up to promote the idea of a muscular Jewish identity. Similarly, in apartheid South Africa, soccer became the game of the black majority since it was excluded from the two principal games of the country – rugby and cricket. In India, on the other hand, the Muslim minorities under colonial rule appropriated soccer to assert their community-identity. In the USA or in certain African countries, the game has provided a means for minority ethnic communities to construct their unique cultural identity. Similarly, soccer in contemporary Britain has been appropriated to fight racism, forge cultural resistance and integrate the minorities. Yet again the game can provide autonomous space to women – traditionally considered to be minority participant and spectator – to assert their identity.

The book examines why in certain countries, minorities chose to take up the sport while in others they backed away from participating in the game or, alternatively, set up their own leagues and practised self-exclusion. The book examines European countries like England, Ireland, Germany and Denmark, the USA, Africa, Australia and parts of Asia including Israel and India.

This book was previously published as a special issue of *Soccer and Society*.

Kausik Bandyopadhyay, an Associate Editor of *Soccer and Society,* teaches History at West Bengal state University, Barasat, India. A former Fellow at the Maulana Abul Kalam Azad Institute of Asian Studies, Kolkata, Bandyopadhyay is the author of *Playing Off the Field: Explorations in the History of Sport* (Kolkata: Towards Freedom, 2007) and *Playing for Freedom: A Historic Sports Victory* (New Delhi: Standard Publishers, 2008); co-author of *A Social History of Indian Football: Striving to Score* (London: Routledge, 2006); issue editor of Asia Annual 2008: *Understanding Popular Culture* (New Delhi: Manohar, 2010) and co-editor of *Fringe Nations in World Soccer* (London: Routledge, 2008).

Why Minorities Play or Don't Play Soccer

A Global Exploration

Edited by Kausik Bandyopadhyay

Routledge
Taylor & Francis Group

LONDON AND NEW YORK

First published 2010 by Routledge
2 Park Square, Milton Park, Abingdon, Oxon, OX14 4RN

Simultaneously published in the USA and Canada
by Routledge
270 Madison Avenue, New York, NY 10016

Routledge is an imprint of the Taylor & Francis Group, an informa business

© 2010 Taylor & Francis

Typeset in Times New Roman PS by Value Chain, India

British Library Cataloguing in Publication Data
A catalogue record for this book is available from the British Library

ISBN10: 0-415-49714-0
ISBN13: 978-0-415-49714-5

CONTENTS

Abstracts   ix

1   Introduction: minorities and the global game
    Kausik Bandyopadhyay   1

2   Forgotten fields? Centralizing the experiences of minority ethnic men's football clubs in England
    Daniel Burdsey   8

3   Playing games with 'race': understanding resistance to 'race' equality initiatives in English local football governance
    Jim Lusted   26

4   North or South? Darron Gibson and the issue of player eligibility within Irish soccer
    David Hassan, Shane McCullough and Elizabeth Moreland   44

5   Deutschland über Alles: discrimination in German football
    Christos Kassimeris   58

6   The dream of social mobility: ethnic minority players in Danish football clubs
    Sine Agergaard and Jan Kahr Sørensen   70

7   The promise of soccer in America: the open play of ethnic subcultures
    Derek Van Rheenen   85

8   Association football to fútbol: ethnic succession and the history of Chicago-area soccer since 1920
    David Trouille   99

9   No single pattern: Australian migrant minorities and the round ball code in Victoria
    Roy Hay and Nick Guoth   127

10   In search of an identity: the Muslims and football in colonial India
    Kausik Bandyopadhyay   147

11   Colonial legacy, minorities and association football in Kenya
    Wycliffe W. Simiyu Njororai   170

12   Not just for men: Israeli women who fancy football
    Amir Ben-Porat   187

Index   201

Sport in the Global Society – Contemporary Perspectives

Series Editor: Boria Majumdar

Why Minorities Play or Don't Play Soccer
A Global Exploration

Sport in the Global Society – Contemporary Perspectives

Series Editor: Boria Majumdar

The social, cultural (including media) and political study of sport is an expanding area of scholarship and related research. While this area has been well served by the Sport in the Global Society Series, the surge in quality scholarship over the last few years has necessitated the creation of *Sport in the Global Society: Contemporary Perspectives*. The series will publish the work of leading scholars in fields as diverse as sociology, cultural studies, media studies, gender studies, cultural geography and history, political science and political economy. If the social and cultural study of sport is to receive the scholarly attention and readership it warrants, a cross-disciplinary series dedicated to taking sport beyond the narrow confines of physical education and sport science academic domains is necessary. Sport in the Global Society: Contemporary Perspectives will answer this need.

Other Titles in the Series

Australian Sport
Antipodean Waves of Change
Edited by Kristine Toohey and Tracy Taylor

Australia's Asian Sporting Context
1920s and 19330s
Edited by Sean Brawley and Nick Guoth

'Critical Support' for Sport
Bruce Kidd

Disability in the Global Sport Arena
A Sporting Chance
Edited by Jill M. Clair

Diversity and Division – Race, Ethnicity and Sport in Australia
Edited by Christopher J. Hallinan

Documenting the Beijing Olympics
Edited by D. P. Martinez

Football in Brazil
Edited by Martin Curi

Forty Years of Sport and Social Change, 1968-2008
"To Remember is to Resist"
Edited by Russell Field and Bruce Kidd

Global Perspectives on Football in Africa
Visualising the Game
Edited by Susann Baller, Giorgio Miescher and Raffaele Poli

Global Sport Business
Community Impacts of Commercial Sport
Edited by Hans Westerbeek

Governance, Citizenship and the New European Football Championships
The European Spectacle
Edited by Wolfram Manzenreiter and Georg Spitaler

Reviewing UK Football Cultures
Continuing with Gender Analyses
Edited by Jayne Caudwell

Soccer in Australia
Fencing Off the World Game
Edited by Christopher J. Hallinan and
John Hughson

South Africa and the Global Game
Football, Apartheid and Beyond
Edited by Peter Alegi and Chris
Bolsmann

Sport – Race, Ethnicity and Identity
Building Global Understanding
Edited by Daryl Adair

Sport and the Community
Edited by Allan Edwards and David
Hassan

Sport, Culture and Identity in the
Land of Israel
Edited by Yair Galily and Amir Ben-
Porat

Sport in Australian National Identity
Kicking Goals
Tony Ward

Sport in the City
Cultural Connections
Edited by Michael Sam and John E.
Hughson

The Changing Face of Cricket
From Imperial to Global Game
Edited by Dominic Malcolm, Jon
Gemmell and Nalin Mehta

The Flame Relay and the Olympic
Movement
John J. MacAloon

The Making of Sporting Cultures
John E. Hughson

The Politics of Sport
Community, Mobility, Identity
Edited by Paul Gilchrist and Russell
Holden

The Politics of Sport in South Asia
Edited by Subhas Ranjan Chakraborty,
Shantanu Chakrabarti and Kingshuk
Chatterjee

Who Owns Football?
The Governance and Management of the
Club Game Worldwide
Edited by David Hassan and Sean Hamil

Why Minorities Play or Don't Play
Soccer
A Global Exploration
Edited by Kausik Bandyopadhyay

Abstracts

Forgotten fields? Centralizing the experiences of minority ethnic men's football clubs in England
Daniel Burdsey

This essay provides a socio-historical analysis of British Asian and black men's amateur football clubs in England. It argues that, from their early development to the present day, they have been far more than simply sites of recreation and leisure, for they have taken on vital social functions in terms of fighting racism, forging cultural resistance and integrating the wider community. The essay critiques dominant football histories and contends that, due to their failure to centralize the issues and problems facing minority ethnic players and teams (as well as those of other oppressed groups), the processes through which the game is reported, represented and documented reproduce the racism and white privilege intrinsic to the sport itself. The remainder of the essay examines the experiences of minority ethnic football clubs in post-war England. First, the analysis traces key phases and occurrences in the development of clubs, leagues and federations, and demonstrates how the rationale for/implications of these changes can only be fully comprehended if contextualized within the racial politics – both parliamentary and popular – of these respective time periods. Second, it examines the rise of identity politics and shifting political approaches to multiculturalism, and discusses how these have impacted on the identities and membership of minority ethnic clubs. It concludes with a discussion on the rapidly transforming demographics of multiethnic Britain and the implications that this will have for amateur football.

Playing games with 'race': understanding resistance to 'race' equality initiatives in English local football governance
Jim Lusted

Sport continues to play a prominent role in debates around the inclusion and exclusion of minority groups in Britain. Despite its legacy of racist chanting and abuse in the professional game, English soccer is now increasingly promoted by the British government and the English Football Association (FA) as having a central role to play in challenging racism and increasing the involvement of ethnic minorities in British civic society. This essay attempts to begin to account for the – often problematic – experiences of ethnic minorities in the grass roots game by focusing on those who organize and control local football. Particular attention is paid to the amateurist origins of County Football Associations (CFAs) that emerged in Victorian Britain and continue to inform decision making and the priorities at these associations. It focuses on how those in positions of power at this level – Council Members – are coming to terms with the increasingly diverse nature of their playing population. It uses research undertaken at five CFAs across England that elicited the opinions of those within CFAs with regard to the FA's 'Sports Equity Strategy'. This new FA document requires CFAs to take positive action to increase the involvement of ethnic minorities across their local game, including within the CFAs themselves. The essay also discusses some of the reasons why many members of CFAs have difficulty in supporting such race equality initiatives. It explores the ways in which *racialized* narratives become particularly relevant in understanding such resistance. It is argued that the difficulties faced by ethnic minorities in English local football are better understood when analyzing the complex ways that 'race' is employed to legitimize the positions of those currently in charge of the game.

North or South? Darron Gibson and the issue of player eligibility within Irish soccer
David Hassan, Shane McCullough and Elizabeth Moreland

The issue of player eligibility in Irish soccer is a controversial one. When given the opportunity, players born in Northern Ireland should represent that country at senior international level. However, talented footballers from the Catholic community in Northern Ireland are defecting to the Republic of Ireland in ever increasing numbers. Motivated by a range of factors, from socio-political beliefs to sporting pragmatism, these players benefit from a degree of laxity within FIFA's regulations dealing with eligibility in the international arena. This issue has been given particular focus in recent times following the high-profile defection of Manchester United's Darron Gibson from Northern Ireland to the Republic of Ireland. Gibson's decision was especially noteworthy as he failed to meet any of the criteria deemed necessary to permit such a move. This essay examines the role of the key actors in this process, which has resulted in Northern Ireland, a country with a limited pool of suitable personnel at this level, losing some of its most talented players to its neighbour and one of its fiercest rivals.

Deutschland über Alles: discrimination in German football
Christos Kassimeris

Considering that the reunification of Germany demanded that present-day German society adjusts to the new political realities and an all-expansive European Union, by means of integrating the populations of a previously divided nation, the emergence of neo-Nazi groups soon after the fall of the Berlin Wall did not facilitate the relevant process of transition. On the contrary, it made certain that the fascist past of Germany was exposed, just as the socio-political differences caused by the country's division were reflected. Given the capacity of football to strengthen national identity, this essay explores the extent of manipulation the popular game had to endure during the Nazi regime's stay in power and then assesses racial discrimination in German football in its present form, as well as the role of the extreme right.

The dream of social mobility: ethnic minority players in Danish football clubs
Sine Agergaard and Jan Kahr Sørensen

The purpose of this essay is to inquire into the prospects of social mobility among young ethnic minority males who are at the start of their career in Danish football clubs. The essay is based on a local field study which involved interviews with 10 talented ethnic minority players, and eight coaches and club leaders in two ethnic minority clubs, three clubs that we refer to as transit clubs, and one premier league club in a Danish provincial city. Bourdieu's concepts are used to describe the players' chances of social mobility and the observed disparity between the prospects for ethnic minority players from a ghetto area and those from other parts of the city. According to Bourdieu, the players compete not only for a position in a particular football team but also for an improvement in their position within a stratification system (in this case, the field of football). The analysis shows that the possibility of social mobility is here dependent on whether the players' physical capital is acknowledged and converted into cultural, social and economic capital.

The promise of soccer in America: the open play of ethnic subcultures
Derek Van Rheenen

This essay juxtaposes the perceived lack of success of professional soccer in the United States with the nation's rich history of ethnic and amateur soccer. It argues how soccer as ethnic subculture has provided a means for minority ethnic communities to construct a unique cultural identity while becoming a part of an emerging multicultural nation. In evidence of this more complex and nuanced process of cultural assimilation, the essay chronicles the rise of the Greek-American Athletic Club in the San Francisco Soccer Football League (SFSFL), the oldest American soccer league in continuous existence. Perhaps reflective of other urban ethnic soccer clubs and the immigrant communities supporting their team, the San Francisco Greek-Americans initially recruited players solely from their own community. Over time, however, the team began to recruit players based on their competitive potential rather than their ethnic heritage. With a mixture of non-Greek foreign-born and US-born players, the San Francisco Greek-Americans made the Bay Area Hellenic communities proud by becoming one of the most dominant amateur soccer teams in the history of the SFSFL and the United States.

Association football to fútbol: ethnic succession and the history of Chicago-area soccer since 1920
David Trouille

Prompted by the underappreciated position of sports in sociological research, this essay examines the interconnections between the development of professional and amateur men's soccer in Chicago and theoretical understandings of minority, race, ethnicity, immigration, integration, and urban relations. Through archival research, interviews, and ethnographic fieldwork, including participation in a local ethnic league, the author was able to reconstruct and analyze the largely undocumented history of men's soccer in Chicago. By uncovering the ways in which soccer teams and leagues have exhibited patterns of ethnic succession, the essay demonstrates the continued relevance of this sociological theory, through its application to neglected social institutions like soccer leagues and for non-spatial conceptions of urban ethnic communities. In addition, it explores the symbolic and substantive functions performed by the soccer teams and leagues as sites for the construction and maintenance of collective ethnic identities. The study covers the period from 1921 to the present.

No single pattern: Australian migrant minorities and the round ball code in Victoria
Roy Hay and Nick Guoth

Association football in Australia has served a multiplicity of changing purposes for migrant minorities since the mid-nineteenth century. Some individuals and groups embraced the game as an important element of cultural identification and distinction; others used it as one of a number of means of finding a way into some areas of Australian society; and yet others have shunned the game as being un-Australian. Some migrants played the game, but had no further involvement, while others used the game as a means of entry into 'mainstream' Australian society. A few used the code for political purposes. By examining the experience of three migrant groups in Victoria, some of the common generalizations about migrants and football can be shown to be less than firmly grounded.

In search of an identity: the Muslims and football in colonial India
Kausik Bandyopadhyay

This essay deals with soccer's burgeoning communal encounter in India from the 1930s, which began to erode football's overwhelming status as an instrument of cultural nationalism. It intends to show that this trend can be meaningfully explained only in terms of socio-political and economic life of India in the 1930s. The unhealthy clash between the Hindu *bhadrolok* dominated Indian Football Association and the Mohammedan Sporting Club, representative of the minority Muslim community, often played a critical role in this unhealthy contest, creating possibilities of communalization of sport in the 1930s and 1940s. This communal conflict in Indian football also explains why the first Indian team Mohun Bagan's victory of the IFA Shield in 1911 is still perceived as a greater nationalistic triumph than Mohammedan Sporting Club's five straight Calcutta Football League titles between 1934 and 1938. Mohammedan's success had a visibly mixed impact on Indian footballing society. For the majority of the *minority* Muslims, Mohammedan Sporting Club had become a symbol of identity and confidence all over India. In fact, while the contribution of the Mohammedan

Sporting Club in making the Muslim League popular in Bengal was not insignificant, the Muslim League also played an important role in promoting the club. On the other hand, the factors influencing the gradual marginalization of the club from the Indian sporting scenario in the 1940s also throws light on the association between minority politics, communalism and sport in the Indian context. As the essay argues, it was the oppositional perception of identity of two communities in a tense socio-political context of Bengal, which led to the fracture of footballing nationalism from the 1930s.

Colonial legacy, minorities and association football in Kenya
Wycliffe W. Simiyu Njororai

Kenya is a country that has a good reputation earned through her sportsmen and women, especially the athletes in middle and long distance running. However, it is association football (soccer) that attracted the imagination of the nation as the number one sport. To understand the context of football in Kenya, one should have an idea of the country's ethnic composition, geographical/regional distribution and colonization. For much of Kenya's history, her 42 ethnic groups were loose social formations, fluid and constantly changing. In the late nineteenth and early twentieth centuries British colonial rule solidified ethnic identities among Kenya's people. Colonial administrators associated ethnic groups with specific areas of the country by designating areas where only people with a particular ethnic identity could reside. This pattern of ethnically based settlement and regionalism has persisted in Kenya since it became independent. Given the regionalization of the different ethnic groups, it was easy for football to follow a similar pattern. A deeper look at the evolution of football in the country places the minority and regional orientation in contra distinction to the dominant political class who had no time for the sport. Post-colonial legacies underpinning the popularity of association football include ethnicity, regionalism, athletic ethic and the formalization of narrowly based football administrative structures that curtailed innovation and entrepreneurship. In this essay, 'minority' is conceptualized as ethnic groups having a distinctive presence within a society yet having little political power relative to other groups. Analysing the Luhya and Luo from a minority perspective, the essay shows how they solidified their ethnic identity and nationalism through football clubs, thereby dominating the game in the country to date. Additionally, the support for ethnic teams is analyzed using the Psychological Continuum Model (PCM) which explains the awareness, attraction, attachment and team allegiance of the Luhya to AFC Leopards and Luo to Gor Mahia football clubs.

Not just for men: Israeli women who fancy football
Amir Ben-Porat

This essay deals with the minority participant and spectator in the global game from the perspective of gender. Taking the participatory fandom of the Israeli female spectators as a case study, it argues that the increasing presence of women at football matches has assumed enormous significance in challenging the male hegemony over the game. Albeit being independent and committed fans, the relationship of Israeli women to football is intermediated by the gender effect. The essay interrogates three basic questions relating to female fans: becoming a football fan, fandom as a way of life, and the relative autonomy of behaviour in the stadium. While admitting the fact that women enjoy only relative autonomy in football fandom, it concludes that football no longer remains 'just for men' as the game provides autonomous, albeit relative, space for women to assert their identity and commitment in the football stadium.

Introduction: minorities and the global game

Kausik Bandyopadhyay

Department of History, West Bengal State University, Barasat, India

Soccer, the most popular mass spectator sport in the world, has always remained a marker of identities of various sorts. Behind the façade of its obvious entertainment aspect, it has proved to be a perpetuating reflector of nationalism, race, ethnicity, religion, community or communal identity, gender and cultural specificity. Naturally, therefore, the game could become a complex representative of minorities' status, especially in countries where minorities play a crucial role in political, social, cultural or economic life. The question is also important since success in soccer has often been used as an instrument for assimilation or to promote an alternative brand of nationalism. Thus Jewish teams in pre-Second World War Europe were set up to promote the idea of a muscular Jewish identity. Similarly, in apartheid South Africa, soccer became the game of the black majority since they were excluded from the two principal games of the country – rugby and cricket. In India, on the other hand, the Muslim minorities under colonial rule appropriated soccer to assert their community-identity.

Who is a minority has different meanings in different regions. Within states, contestation over recognition of specific minority groups has been a persistent problem. Minorities themselves employ different terminologies to identify their groups. According to C.L. Lennox, the challenges are twofold: 'on the one hand, it has proved difficult to take a predominantly European concept of national minority and to translate it to other regions given the differences in social and political history. On the other hand, states have resisted recognition of certain groups as minorities as a tactic to avoid duties to respect minority rights.'[1] In very general terms, a minority group may be defined as 'a subordinate group whose members have significantly less control or power over their lives than members of a dominant or majority group' and experience 'a narrowing of opportunities (success, education, wealth etc) that is disproportionately low compared to their number in the society'.[2]

Studies on minorities in the realm of sport have to date mostly concentrated on ethnicity and race as categories representing minority status in society.[3] While these two factors predominate in the articulation of minority position in various societies, such a linear understanding of minority representation in the world of sports tends to limit our view of sporting contestations and competitions to a great extent. Social categories of religion, gender, class or community also shape the participatory behaviour of a minority group in different parts of the world. The patterns of manifestation and articulation of these social categories through soccer raise the important question of the possibility of social *inclusion/exclusion* that the game, both as a cultural practice and social institution, can afford to achieve.[4] It is within the everyday realm that one may find the micro-enactment of inclusion/exclusion, group definition and minority identity.[5] On the other hand, at the level of application, there have been sincere attempts to enhance 'the lives of at-risk youth in minority communities' through soccer.[6]

This volume seeks to examine why in certain countries, minorities chose to take up soccer while in others they backed away from participating in the game or, alternatively, set up their own leagues and practiced self-exclusion. It looks at European countries such as England, Ireland, Denmark and Germany, along with the USA, Kenya, Israel, India and Australia. While it is admitted that ethnic and racial factors are of paramount significance in undertaking any interdisciplinary effort to study the role of minorities in sport, it is important to *explore* and *include* the other markers of minority status including religion, gender or community into the widening field of discourses on the subject. Hence, rather than following the conventional practice of putting the entire emphasis on ethnicity or race, the present volume makes an effort to bring in religion, community and gender as determinants of minority status in soccer. It therefore attempts to make a nuanced contribution to the ever-growing literature on the subject from an interdisciplinary and comparative perspective.

The volume unfolds with a socio-historical analysis of amateur football clubs of British Asians and black men in England. These clubs, according to Daniel Burdsey, are far more than simply sites of recreation and leisure and have taken on vital social functions in terms of fighting racism, forging cultural resistance and integrating the wider community. Critiquing the dominant football histories which mostly ignore the issues and problems facing minority ethnic players and groups, he contends that the processes through which the game is reported, represented and documented reproduce the racism and white privilege intrinsic to the sport itself. Examining the experiences of minority ethnic football clubs in post-war England, Burdsey contextualizes amateur football in the wider context of racial politics, with the sport increasingly becoming a site for political and cultural resistance. While the chapter concentrates exclusively on men's football, it admits that many of the issues, problems and tensions faced by minority male players are also mirrored in the women's game. Finally, it tries to analyse the impact of the rise of identity politics and shifting political approaches to multiculturalism on the identities and membership of minority ethnic clubs.

Jim Lusted's essay, 'Playing games with "race"', emphasizes the leading role football continues to play in discussions around the politics of 'race' and social integration in European nation states, particularly in debates around the inclusion and exclusion of minority groups in Britain. Admitting the efforts of the British government and the English Football Association (FA) in promoting soccer's central role in challenging racism and increasing the involvement of ethnic minorities in British civic society, Lusted unravels the experiences of ethnic minorities at the grass roots or local level of the game, pointing in particular to the often discriminatory attitude of the County Football Associations towards British ethnic minorities. By using the results of research undertaken at five County Football Associations, the essay argues that the FA's recent attempt to ensure football's accessibility to all communities across England by adopting the *Ethics and Sports Equity Strategy* has met with challenges as well as resistances which reflect a scepticism amongst local sports power elite towards adopting race equality initiatives into the local game. Hence, concludes Lusted, to effect sustainable and meaningful involvement of ethnic minorities in such English leisure settings, the structural relations between local governing bodies and their ethnic minority participants need to change fundamentally.

The treatment of Irish soccer by David Hassan, Shane McCullough and Elizabeth Moreland in the context of a traditional rivalry between Northern Ireland and the Republic of Ireland brings to focus the varied representations of minority sentiments on the field of soccer. The apparent tensions between the two rival governing bodies of the game, as the authors show, reflect in reality a clash of sectarian, political and national priorities, embedded in the history of subjugation of Northern Ireland at the hands of the British state and the subsequent partition of Ireland in 1922. Focusing upon the issue of player selection and eligibility at international level, the essay offers an analysis of the sporting and political tensions surrounding soccer in modern-day Northern Ireland. Taking the case of the high-profile defection of Manchester United's Darron Gibson from Northern Ireland to the Republic of Ireland, it explains the recent trend of defection of young talented players from Northern Ireland to the Republic of Ireland in terms of a number of interlocking issues including religious identity, family ties, political affiliations, personal and national identities and sporting pragmatism. As the essay points out, the critical role of FIFA in the process has served only to exacerbate an already troublesome relationship between soccer's governing bodies.

Christos Kassimeris concentrates on the nature of racist discrimination in German football and tries to decipher a continuity between the Nazi appropriation of football in the 1930s and the neo-Nazi manipulation of the game in the 1990s. He argues that football's instrumentality in the construction of a collective *national* identity in Nazi, post-Second World War and post-Unification Germany went hand in hand with racial discrimination in German football. According to him, Germany's hosting of the World Cup in 2006 attracted special attention because of the continuing acts of racism in the German game. Describing such acts as a 'disturbing phenomenon', Kassimeris urges all the pertinent actors to take action to combat racism along with nationwide anti-racism campaigns and relevant acts of legislation.

Sine Agergaard and Jan Kahr Sørensen inquire into the prospects of social mobility among young ethnic minority males who are at the start of their career in Danish football clubs. On the basis of a local field study involving interviews with young players, coaches and leaders of clubs affiliated as 'ethnic minority', 'transit' and 'premier league' in a Danish provincial city, the authors go on to enumerate the challenges facing young male football players from ethnic minority backgrounds, living in both the ghetto area as well as other parts of the city, who would like to become professional footballers. Using Bourdieu's classical social theory of concepts of field, habitus and capital, the essay attempts to analyse whether the players have their football skills acknowledged and converted into the fundamental forms of cultural, social and economic capital that altogether enhance their social recognition. Examining the prevailing conditions of soccer in Denmark, Agergaard and Sørensen conclude that the dream of social mobility that drives so many ethnic minority talents, particularly those from low socio-economic conditions, is not likely to be fulfilled in Danish football clubs. However, with the growing number of football migrants and the increasing presence of ethnic minority players, the Danish clubs might soon have to think of developing their management strategies to accommodate the ethnic minority players in a multicultural context.

Soccer in America has always remained at the margins of the country's mainstream sporting and popular cultural arena. This marginalization of American soccer along with the perceived lack of success of the professional game has allowed the sport to retain a certain richness of cultural and historical expression, particularly in soccer's juxtaposition with American dominant sports. In such context, Derek Van Rheenen examines soccer's potential as ethnic subculture to redefine the dominant notion of sport as an agent of social assimilation and mobility. Chronicling the rise of the Greek-American Athletic Club in the San Francisco Soccer Football League (SFSFL), the oldest American soccer league in continuous existence, Rheenen argues how soccer as ethnic subculture has provided a means for minority ethnic communities to construct a unique cultural identity while becoming a part of an emerging multicultural nation. However, with increased competition and the blurring of lines between amateurism and professionalism, which has significantly altered the process of player recruitment and volunteerism, a clear process of team and league assimilation, resulting in a more general process of ethnic assimilation and integration in San Francisco, has been on the ascendance in American soccer. Thus, concludes Rheenen, rather than a tale of promise unfulfilled, the San Francisco Football Soccer League, and American soccer in general, has provided an open terrain for new ethnicities to play and compete for cultural space in an emerging nation.

David Trouille's study of the history of the Chicago-area soccer since 1920 examines the interconnections between the development of professional and amateur men's soccer in Chicago and theoretical understandings of minority, race, ethnicity, immigration, integration and urban relations in the wider perspective of sociological research. Employing the theory of ethnic succession as an analytical tool, the essay also points to the sociological importance of the soccer teams and leagues over time – an imprint and legacy that has mostly been ignored. Specifically, it examines the ways in which soccer teams and leagues have repeatedly exhibited patterns of ethnic succession and filled important symbolic and substantive functions, including the fostering and maintenance of ethnic identities and communities. In doing so the essay critically traces the development of Chicago-area soccer from its popular peak in the 1920s to the present day, thereby retrieving the rich yet neglected history of soccer in the Chicago area over the past nine decades.

Soccer in Australia has been unique in the sense that the game there has remained a powerful vector of, and space for, minority representation and contestation. Roy Hay and Nick Guoth draw attention to the diverse appropriation of the game by migrant minorities in Australia. While some individuals and groups embraced the game as an important element of cultural identification and distinction, others used it as a means of entry into 'mainstream' Australian society. While a few used the code for political purposes, others have shunned the game as being un-Australian. By examining the experience of three migrant groups in Victoria – Scots, Croatians and the Dutch, the authors have found some of the common generalizations about migrants and football to be less than firmly grounded. It is therefore argued that soccer helped some immigrants to come to terms with Australian society, albeit in differing ways. Football in Australia, conclude Hay and Guoth, has served a multiplicity of changing purposes for migrant minorities since the mid-nineteenth century.

Bandyopadhyay's essay on Muslim participation in football in colonial India brings to light soccer's burgeoning communal encounter in Bengal from the 1930s against the backdrop of the socio-political and economic life of the region in a decade of turmoil. While trying to explore and analyse the key factors precipitating such communal conflict in Indian football, it also explains why in contrast to Mohun Bagan's victory against East Yorkshire Regiment in the IFA Shield final in 1911, still perceived as the greatest nationalistic triumph on sporting field in colonial India, five straight Calcutta Football League titles by the Mohammedan Sporting Club, representative of the minority Muslim community, between 1934 and 1938, have not been given due recognition in the social history of colonial India. The essay, dwelling on the impact of Mohammedan's success on Indian footballing society and Indian Football Association's critical relations with the club, draws attention to the transition of Indian football from a nationalist force to a communal cauldron during the tense socio-political context of the 1940s, and thereby throws light on the association between minority politics, communalism and sport in the Indian context.

The theme of diversified representation of ethno-regional minorities in sport gets concentrated focus in Njororai Wycliffe W. Simiyu's discussion on Kenyan football. The regionalization of different ethnic groups, a legacy of colonial rule, according to Simiyu, has helped football to follow a similar pattern of development in the country. Conceptualizing 'minority' as ethnic groups having a distinctive presence within a society yet having little political power relative to other groups, Simiyu analyses the footballing success and dominance of the politically marginalized Luhya and Luo ethnic groups in the light of a multiplicity of colonial legacies such as regionalization, urbanization, schooling, Christianity, divide and rule as well as political and demographic status as minorities. The appropriation of football as a symbol of ethnic solidarity, social cohesion and national identity becomes evident in the strong identification of Luhya and Luo with AFC Leopards and Gor Mahia football clubs respectively as also in the formers' attraction, attachment and allegiance to those clubs. Using the Psychological Continuum Model (PCM), the author underlines the deep and passionate fan base of the two ethnic-based football teams that dominated the football landscape in Kenya.

Any understanding or analysis of minority participation in sport/soccer remains incomplete without a proper appreciation of women's role as participants and spectators. Amir Ben-Porat's essay 'Not just for men: Israeli women who fancy football' redresses this imbalance. Taking the participatory fandom of the Israeli female spectators as a case study, it argues that the increasing presence of women at football matches has assumed enormous significance in challenging the male hegemony over football, which has over time constantly relegated women to a minority status. While Ben-Porat admits that the relationship of Israeli women to football continues to be intermediated by subtle gender effect, he forcefully argues that women in Israel have attained a certain amount of autonomy as independent and committed fans, thereby asserting their identity and invading the traditionally hegemonized domain of men.

The role of minorities in sport constitutes a fast developing area of research in the history and sociology of sport, more so because football has long been a site which articulates the complexities and diversities of minority sentiments in societies across the world. In view of the complexities of minority position in sport in general and soccer in particular in different parts of the globe, it is easy to comprehend that a single volume can only scratch the surface. However, going beyond the conventional paradigm of concentrating on ethnicity and race as the *only* viable markers of minority position in sporting spaces, it offers a more holistic perspective of looking at minority life and culture through the lens of soccer, thereby paving the way for further and fuller coverage of the significant issues revealed through minority attitudes to, and participation in, the game.

Why Minorities Play or Don't Play Soccer is thus an interdisciplinary effort designed to respond to the growing interest in the subject in different parts of the world. As has already been mentioned, it intends to make a viable contribution to the growing body of literature on the subject. It also intends to address the changing ways of representing minorities in the world's most popular spectator sport. More importantly, the essays in the volume concentrate on exploring the relationships between the national, regional and local in the history of minority participation in the game in the countries studied. James Walvin once suggested, 'more emphasis needs to be placed on local studies without losing sight of the broader context'.[7] As the work has tried to weave the microcosms of local and regional histories into the macrocosm of national studies, it is expected to generate future forays into more specialized regional and local studies. Such forays could also be able to address more specifically Walvin's notion that 'general structures do indeed have a place, but they will inevitably be subjected to the qualifications of specific and local peculiarities.'[8] While this volume has raised a few issues and addressed a few questions with regard to minority participation in soccer, more studies, I expect, will follow to supplement this effort.

Notes

1. Lennox, 'Who Is A Minority?'
2. See http://academic.udayton.edu/race/01race/minor01.htm.
3. A few such examples include Jarvie, *Sport, Racism and Ethnicity*; Verma, *Winners and Losers*; Mayer, *Jews and the Olympic Games*; Sorek, *Arab Soccer in a Jewish State*; Kugelmass, *Jews, Sports*; Burdsey, *British Asians and Football*; Back, Crabbe and Solomos, *The Changing Face of Football*.
4. An instructive discussion on football and social exclusion in the British context has been offered in Wagg, *British Football and Social Exclusion*.
5. For more layers on this, see Collins, Collins and Kay, *Sport and Social Exclusion*.
6. For example, Minority Soccer Development (MSD), a non-profit organization based in USA, is committed to doing so through community-based programmes. Established in January 2009, the MSD is dedicated to their goal of 'advancing futures, building communities, and transforming lives' through soccer. It hopes to be a positive and powerful tool for social change in the US and Latin America. See for details http://www.minoritysoccer-dev.org.
7. Walvin, 'Sport, Social History', 10.
8. Ibid.

References

Back, Les, Tim Crabbe, and John Solomos. *The Changing Face of Football: Racism, Identity and Multiculture in the English Game.* Oxford: Berg, 2001.

Burdsey, Daniel. *British Asians and Football: Culture, Identity and Exclusion.* London: Routledge, 2007

Collins, Michael Frank, Mike Collins, and Tess Kay. *Sport and Social Exclusion.* London: Routledge, 2003.

Jarvie, Grant. *Sport, Racism and Ethnicity.* London: Routledge, 1991

Kugelmass, Jack. *Jews, Sports and the Rites of Citizenship.* Champaign, IL: University of Illinois Press, 2007.

Lennox, C.L. 'Who Is A Minority? Interests and Identities in the International Protection Regime for Minorities'. Paper presented at the Annual Meeting of the International Studies Association, San Diego, California, March 22, 2006.

Mayer, Paul Yogi. *Jews and the Olympic Games: Sport – A Springboard for Minorities.* London and Portland, OR: Valentine Mitchell, 2004

Sorek, Amir. *Arab Soccer in a Jewish State: the integrative enclave.* Cambridge: Cambridge University Press, 2007.

Verma, Gajendra. *Winners and Losers: Ethnic Minorities in Sport and Recreation.* London: Routledge, 1994

Wagg, Stephen. *British Football and Social Exclusion.* London: Routledge, 2004.

Walvin, James. 'Sport, Social History and the Historian'. *The British Journal of Sports History* 1, no. 1 (1984): 5–13.

Forgotten fields? Centralizing the experiences of minority ethnic men's football clubs in England

Daniel Burdsey

Chelsea School, University of Brighton, Eastbourne, UK

Introduction

The metaphorical 'road to Wembley' – the colloquial term used to refer to clubs' progression towards the English FA Cup Final – is widely recognized as one of the most prestigious and exciting in the world of elite men's football. Far fewer people are aware that the competition actually begins, with the involvement of small amateur and semi-professional clubs, a full nine months before the May final. Yet it was on a late summer afternoon in August 2007, in the tournament's 'extra preliminary round', that one of the most socially significant FA Cup ties of recent years took place.

Widespread academic and popular acknowledgement of the role that football plays in the articulation of ethno-cultural identities (in both a local and a global sense) means that such attributions no longer generate – or, it could be argued, deserve – the attention that they once did. However, this fixture, between Sporting Bengal and London APSA at Mile End Stadium, in the London Borough of Tower Hamlets, was unquestionably a watershed for English football: it was the first ever FA Cup match to be played between two predominantly British Asian clubs.[1] The impact of the tie was reflected not simply in the excitement generated in the respective local communities, but also by the fact that the BBC and Sky Sports sent their cameras along to cover the fixture, including brief highlights in their results round-ups and magazine programmes – something usually unheard of for games at this level. On this occasion the honours went to Pakistani APSA, who won the replay after a closely fought, drawn first encounter with their Bangladeshi rivals.

Neither of the teams possessed pretensions of progressing far beyond this stage of the competition – in fact APSA were eliminated in the following round – but, in essence, that has never been their rationale for participation. Instead, for the players, clubs and supporters that turned out to cheer them on, it is more a case of continuing to represent their respective communities in the public sphere, and maintaining their efforts in trying to gain inclusion in a sporting culture that has traditionally discriminated against them and has prevented them from gaining access to professional level.[2] As APSA chairman Zulfi Ali states, 'bringing inner London communities together and providing hope for future young Asian stars is the real goal we intend to achieve'.[3] The involvement of British Asian clubs in one of the nation's primary sporting institutions is an indication of how far minority ethnic football clubs and organizations have progressed in the 60 years of post-Second World War migration, and is also reflective of the inroads that these communities have made in other aspects of society. However, this must not obfuscate the fact that the journey has frequently been, and continues to be, a difficult one – often characterized by racism on the field and discrimination within the game's structures and institutions. What these clubs have achieved is thus even more notable in the context of the adversity and opposition they have faced in simply trying to gain inclusion in the national sport.

Same old stories? the silencing of minority ethnic voices in dominant football histories

As the African proverb goes, 'Until lions have their own historians, tales of the hunt will always glorify the hunter'. This adage is customarily a useful point of departure when teaching students about racism and minority ethnic football histories on the undergraduate 'Football Cultures' module at the University of Brighton. Its application to both the scholarly study and media representation of sport remains particularly pertinent, and consequently it represents a useful analogy in explaining to students that racism and the privileges that accrue from embodying whiteness are not confined to the structures and regulations of sport itself; they are also reproduced in the processes through which sport is reported, represented and documented. In other words, what is traditionally read and learnt about sport has been written by members of dominant groups; it has focused on the communities, collectivities and institutions to which they belong or identify with; and, like all hegemonic narratives, it has given preference to material and discourses that exemplify and maintain their interests, statuses and positions of power.

Yet, in making such observations it is important to point out that it is not simply a matter of what is included, but about what is left out as well. As Riordan states, it is equally 'important to bear in mind the kinds of sports and movements that have been *excluded* by society's ruling institutions'.[4] To this crucial point, we might add 'players, clubs and communities'. Apropos of this, dominant narratives of English football are guilty of not only prioritizing and normalizing the experiences of certain groups (primarily white, heterosexual, able-bodied men), but also of ignoring, marginalizing and problematizing those of others. Whilst the growing influence of feminist, post-colonial and, more recently, Critical Race Theory perspectives in social scientific accounts of sport means that investigative lenses are gradually being opened up to recognize the experiences of subordinate groups, it remains the case that most dominant histories of the national game are 'whitewashed'. Minority ethnic communities have been systematically denied the opportunity to contribute to hegemonic analyses and thus they have not been allocated the status of authoritative voices.[5] As a result, the experiences and stories of minority ethnic players and clubs remain very much a 'hidden' history.[6]

Consequently, the impression that many people are left with is that minority ethnic involvement in English football is simply a post-1970s addendum and the preserve of the professional game. The fact that the first black professional footballers, Arthur Wharton and Walter Tull, played as far back as the late nineteenth century, never fails to astound the uninitiated, yet is of little surprise when one considers that their stories have, until recently, been erased from the nation's footballing past.[7] Likewise, the experiences of minority ethnic (and female) players have been wholeheartedly ignored by football's *literati* in the 'post-Fever Pitch'[8] proliferation of writing on the amateur game.

Whilst it would be incorrect to state that the experiences of minority ethnic amateur clubs and players are ignored by the media completely, they are habitually portrayed through a white, male journalistic gaze, and usually framed within one of the following modes of reportage: as stereotypical caricatures, possessing religio-cultural attributes and engaging in practices that inhibit participation, such as the wearing of certain clothing or fasting during the Muslim month of Ramadan; as powerless victims of racism without the ability to (try to) resist their oppression; or as unworthy of sophisticated investigation, with the focus instead placed on trivial, off-field issues, such as players' occupations or the frequency of a common surname within the playing squad at a particular club. Female players receive even less coverage, with any references to British Asian girls and women trivialized through the ubiquitous link to Gurinder Chadha's *Bend It Like Beckham* movie. Most problematically, racism rarely warrants a mention in these accounts, sustaining the pervasiveness of claims of meritocracy and 'colour-blind'[9] recruitment and selection policies in the game.

In a broader sense, an examination of otherwise comprehensive, general historical portrayals of minority ethnic communities in Britain by the likes of Fryer, Ramdin and Visram reveal no mention of the game at amateur level whatsoever, let alone its socio-political role.[10] This oversight is illuminated by the prominence attached to football in other, more specific accounts, particularly those based around photography and/or oral history.[11] Furthermore, the internet, with its more egalitarian sense of participation in terms of producing and accessing material, is becoming a valuable resource in subverting this situation. Unable to gain publishing contracts or to have their voices heard within governing bodies, aspects of the anti-racist football movement and the media, a number of minority ethnic football clubs are beginning to tell their own stories, offering rich, detailed oral histories and photo galleries on their websites.[12]

However, those of us in the academy who investigate and write about sport need also to play our part. Research into the sporting experiences of minority ethnic groups must attempt to overcome the silencing of these players and aim to centralize their experiences, attitudes, opinions and aspirations. As Hylton points out, when analysing social spheres, such as sport, which are characterized by unequal power relations and the marginalization of minority ethnic groups, we must 'ensure that those issues stay at the centre of [our] investigations or lens, rather than at the comfortable rim'.[13] Key to achieving these objectives is the use of life history and storytelling approaches, for they possess the potential to help us 'uproot the dysconscious racism or uncritical and distorted ways of thinking about race that have led to tacit acceptance of the dominant White norms and privileges'.[14]

Outline of the essay

This essay aims to centralize the experiences and achievements of, and the issues and problems facing, minority ethnic football clubs. Its explicit focus is nevertheless limited in three main ways. First, and perhaps most obviously, the analysis concentrates on amateur and semi-professional levels of English football. Compared to the professional sphere, they remain significantly under-researched but, as Williams points out, 'looking only at the role of *professional* clubs in England … and to look only at *fans* of those clubs is to touch on barely the thin surface of the wider football community'.[15] More pertinently, it can be argued that it is in amateur football that the politics of race are most explicit, with the sport being used by minority ethnic youngsters as a setting where they can engage in processes of political and cultural resistance.[16]

Second, this essay concentrates predominantly on teams representing British Asian and black communities. The term 'British Asian' is used here to refer to the heterogeneous communities who trace their ancestry to, or who migrated themselves from, the Indian subcontinent, i.e. India, Pakistan or Bangladesh. The term 'black' is used to describe the diverse groups of people in Britain of sub-Saharan African or African-Caribbean heritage.[17] Not only do these groups form the largest minority ethnic populations in Britain[18] and represent the most established in terms of length of settlement, but they have also had the most substantial involvement in organized amateur football. However, they are by no means the only minority ethnic groups involved in amateur football in Britain. To claim otherwise simply does not stand up to scrutiny given the rapidly changing demographics of multiethnic Britain, and reproduces the selective amnesia and marginalization of minority groups that characterize many dominant accounts. The latter part of this chapter therefore turns the focus towards these other, 'new', migrant populations, including refugees and other displaced peoples. Furthermore, the clubs and organizations cited in this account are merely exemplars and it is not suggested that they are more important or significant than those that have been left out.

Third, as problematic as the racial biases of dominant football histories has been the absence of research into the position of females within minority ethnic football cultures. This essay apologetically reproduces this state of affairs. It examines men's football exclusively as the focus is predominantly on the *historical* role of clubs, leagues and federations. Whilst many of the issues, problems and tensions faced by minority ethnic male players are mirrored in the women's game,[19] similar institutions are presently under-developed in the latter sphere. Notwithstanding this, the experiences of female players must be fundamental to any future research agenda on race and football.

This essay is divided into two broad sections: first, a loosely diachronic, socio-historical examination of key phases and issues in the development of British Asian and black football clubs, and the ways that their members have sought to resist racism in the game and wider society; and second, an analysis of how the rise of identity politics and shifting political approaches to multiculturalism have impacted on the identities and membership of minority ethnic clubs. It concludes with a discussion on the rapidly transforming demographics of multiethnic Britain and the implications that this will have for amateur football.

British Asian and black men's amateur football clubs: from post-war to present

Elsewhere I have argued that the establishment and early development of British Asian men's football clubs need to be contextualized within the social climate facing migrants in the immediate post-migration phase and that, consequently, sociological analyses must take into account the racial politics – both parliamentary and popular – of this era.[20] This position is reaffirmed in this broader account of minority ethnic involvement in English amateur football, which similarly seeks to position the experiences of clubs within the wider trajectories of race relations in British society. This is not to suggest that all developments in the game, the activities and avenues pursued by individual clubs, or the roles they have adopted are purely responses to wider social issues. Yet the contention is that many clubs represent far more than just football teams and that this significance can only be fully elucidated if the wider context is taken into consideration. Similarly, this essay does not claim that football played or plays the same – if, indeed, any – role in the post-migratory and current lives of all British Asian and black communities, but argues that it embodies a far greater social function than is widely acknowledged or has been documented.

The early-post migration years

The establishment of British Asian and black men's football clubs can be traced back almost as far as the post-war mass migrations from the Indian subcontinent and the Caribbean themselves. As substantial migrant communities established themselves across urban Britain during the 1950s and 1960s, clubs such as Albion Sports (Bradford), Coventry Sporting, Guru Nanak (Gravesend), Guru Nanak and Highfield Rangers (both Leicester), Paak United (Nelson), Punjab United and Punjab Rovers (both Wolverhampton), and Supna (Leicester) soon followed suit. Excluded from professional football and the bulk of amateur venues, it was urban green spaces such as Hackney Marshes in London and Victoria Park in Leicester that provided the settings for these teams to participate. Football was far more than simply a popular leisure activity though, for the game played an important social role for the groups of men who – due to the fact that settlement was originally seen as a temporary, working venture – made up the vast majority of early migrants. For many of these men, football took up a large proportion of their social lives, with participation facilitating contact with friends, family and workmates who, as a result of processes of chain migration, had often emigrated from the same village or area. It is important to point out that, in the early stages of development, a team did not necessarily equate to a club. As most migrants originally predicted that migration would be short-lived and eventually reversed once sufficient capital had been generated, there was no need to put substantial structures in place. However, as these sojourns began to turn into settlements for the vast majority, it became necessary to implement more formal club set-ups and to organize competitions.

Football did not simply enable social interaction between friends and kin as, through the creation of tournaments, there was also the opportunity to meet and form allegiances with migrants in other parts of the country. Much of this was arranged under the auspices of trade unions, such as the Indian Workers' Association, which recognized the potential for using sport as a means of cementing ethnic and class solidarities.[21] For British Asian communities, this function was provided by the Shaheed Uddam Singh Games.[22] Held in locations such as Gravesend, Southall, Coventry and Derby they included kabaddi, wrestling, hockey and volleyball, as well as football, forming 'distinct masculinized sites in which men, young and old, indulged themselves in sportive and other hedonistic pursuits, notably the excessive consumption of alcohol'.[23] Whilst girls and women were present, their role was limited to that of supporters and providers of nourishment, reflecting the wider, cross-cultural marginalization of females in sporting spaces.

The wider integrative role of football was originally limited, however, for, contrary to the desires of many migrants to interact with other groups, they were excluded – parallel to other social institutions and spaces – from white-dominated mainstream teams, leagues and facilities. One solution was the formation of their own clubs and teams, with matches often confined – for reasons of logistics as well as safety – to friendlies against other members of their communities or in specially organized competitions. Yet inadequate infrastructure and insufficient numbers of organized teams were hampering the ambitions of many players and clubs. Participation in regular competitive football could, therefore, only be achieved by breaking into the ranks of mainstream leagues. This frequently proved to be a hazardous endeavour though, with players, supporters and local residents often encountering racist abuse and physical violence. Clubs could rarely rely on match officials or league committees to punish the offenders, with many of them complicit in these acts of discrimination.

The opposition and resentment shown towards these new clubs from within the white amateur football fraternity arose because the former were perceived to represent a challenge to their power and dominance in the game, but it also reflected wider racist and anti-immigration discourses amongst sections of the indigenous white population. These exemplified a shift in Western Europe during the latter half of the twentieth century from cruder biological racisms, which revolved explicitly around phenotypical characteristics and racial hierarchies, to the notion of cultural racism, the key tenet of which was the idea of cultural difference and the degree to which minority ethnic groups were believed to conform to, and assimilate into, the norms and values of 'traditional' domestic life. Fuelled by politicians such as Enoch Powell and an associated increasing prominence of neo-fascist groups such as the National Front and the British Movement, migrant groups from the Indian subcontinent and the Caribbean were believed to represent a threat to jobs, housing and the social cohesion of the nation. Social spheres, such as sport and leisure, were prime areas in which the subsequent racist backlash took place.

Minority ethnic clubs subsequently adopted a hugely important, but extremely difficult, role, trying to integrate players and members of the wider community into British society whilst, at the same time maintaining a sense of identity and upholding cultural traditions – all in the face of widespread racial exclusion. A further factor added to the equation was the small matter of trying to achieve success on the pitch. Yet, in certain settings, this complex and potentially contradictory manoeuvre was (at least partially) achieved. Indeed, the paradoxical racial politics of football meant that whilst the amateur game frequently replicated the prejudices and exclusion of other aspects of society, it also provided minority ethnic players with the chance to achieve (contingent) inclusion by offering the opportunity to demonstrate their abilities, physical competencies and masculine identities. These latter aspects were particularly pertinent for British Asian players, for a perceived lack of physicality and masculinity (along with the possession of alternative cultural values) has historically been a central component of the western racial discourses through which they have been Othered and positioned as antithetical to the cultures of English football.[24] Cross-cultural interaction was not confined to the pitch though, as corollary aspects of the amateur football experience, such as the post-match trip to the pub, also played a part in this process.[25]

Football, black youth and cultural resistance

Whilst Britain's minority ethnic communities share a common location as oppressed groups and the recipients of racism, they have at times been subjected to specific racial discourses and stereotypes. Thus, while black communities have traditionally been regarded as possessing greater cultural similarities to the white mainstream and as representing less of a threat to traditional values than South Asian migrants, they have been Othered and problematized in other ways. For instance, as the children of post-war Caribbean migrants reached adolescence during the 1970s, not only did they find themselves faced with structural discrimination in the education system and the labour market, but young males also became the target of a moral panic over allegations of their involvement in street mugging.[26] As a result, they were routinely forced to endure oppressive surveillance, often unjustified stop-and-search procedures, and frequent violent harassment by the police. Unrest between young black men and the police erupted at the 1976 Notting Hill Carnival in West London, and in parts of Birmingham, Bristol, Leeds, Liverpool and London in 1981 and 1985. This alienation was augmented by the systematic marginalization and closure of black cultural and leisure spaces, which had come to be associated, in the popular imagination, with danger and criminality.[27]

In this context, football clubs came to play an important role for young black men in latter twentieth-century Britain. Whilst the game's inherent popularity was key, it is also crucial to acknowledge that sport was one of the few public leisure activities in which young black men were sanctioned to participate and gather in large numbers. The combination of the residual racial stereotype that African-Caribbeans are genetically predisposed to achieve sporting success, and dominant post-Scarman[28] political rhetoric that purported that the mass provision of sport facilities was the solution to assuaging inner-city tensions and mediating the putative excesses of black masculinity, meant that amateur football became one of the few arenas in which young black men were able to form their own organizations without direct interference from white authorities.

Carrington's seminal study of sport, race and social space demonstrates how sport clubs responded to this situation.[29] Whilst his focus is cricket – the Caribbean Cricket Club (CCC) of Leeds, to be precise – the similarities with football are apparent. Carrington highlights how the CCC represents an important social space for its members and a means of forming group solidarities. Applying Hesse's notion of 'white governmentality',[30] he describes the ways that black bodies are controlled, regulated and subject to surveillance in public spaces and then, drawing on Sivanandan's 'communities of resistance',[31] shows how the CCC facilitates resistance to, and protection from, racism as well as the celebration of cultural heritage and engagement in traditional activities. Carrington demonstrates how the CCC truly embodies the status of community institution in that it is seen to represent Chapeltown – the district in which the club is based and home to most of the city's black communities – by both the club members themselves and the local white population.[32]

Dominant processes of racialising specific urban landscapes are also central to the context for the development of two prominent black football clubs: Highfield Rangers and Almithak. Based in Leicester and Liverpool respectively, they are situated in districts that have historically been labelled dangerous, deviant and criminal simply because of their sizeable black communities. Located in Highfields, Rangers were formed by Caribbean migrants during the 1970s – a period which witnessed significant support for the neo-fascist National Front party in the city[33] – and have subsequently gone on to become one of the most important and well-known minority ethnic institutions in Leicester. One member places Rangers' social significance in the context of the marginalization and suppression of the city's other black cultural institutions in the early post-migration epoch. He states that, 'I think, during the early days, Highfield Rangers was a very important part of the black community. The only real thing that the Afro-Caribbean community had were the football teams.'[34] Another player reiterates this, arguing that 'Rangers speaks for the black people within Highfields, the main focus of Highfields'.[35] Whilst other minority ethnic clubs possess names that are ostensibly more directly related to their ethnic or religious identities, the choice of Highfield Rangers has actually proved equally explicit due to the associations, in the local imaginary, of the area with black people and blackness.[36]

The Highfield Rangers story is one of both footballing success and community empowerment, but it also exemplifies the wider minority ethnic football experience in that it is a tale of enduring racism from opponents, discrimination from officials and governing bodies, and barriers to their progression in terms of facility provision. Detractors also exist in the city's black community itself, with the club facing criticism for their political conservatism and their failure to use their position as a springboard for activism.[37] However, this stance needs to be placed in the wider context of the pressures placed on minority ethnic players and clubs to underplay their alterity in order to gain inclusion in various aspects of the game.[38] During the 1990s the club made great upward strides within the amateur football pyramid and now compete in the Premier Division of the Leicester Senior League. Rangers were also the starting point for Dion Dublin and Emile Heskey, black players who went on to forge successful professional careers and win England caps. Yet, as is the case with many of the clubs mentioned in this essay, the relationship between Rangers and the city's professional club, Leicester City, has been tenuous and problematic, and has not led to a breakthrough of local minority ethnic talent into their ranks.

Almithak were established in the 1980s in Toxteth, south Liverpool or, more specifically, the Liverpool 8 postal district. The area houses the vast majority of the minority ethnic population in a city which is home to Europe's oldest black community (dating as far back as at least the 1700s) and, relatedly, was a central seaport in the transatlantic slave trade. Thus whilst Liverpool did not experience sizeable immigration from the Caribbean or Indian subcontinent in the aftermath of the Second World War, it possesses 'the longest standing and largest *indigenous* black population in the country', many of whom are of dual white British/black African ethnicities.[39] Almithak was formed after a merger between two clubs, Dingle Rail and Saana FC, the latter possessing Yemeni origins. Almithak has always been a club for Liverpool's greater black community though and has been an important cultural resource for this marginalized and alienated population.[40]

The 1980s was a period of stark contrasts in the city. Football was enjoying a golden age with Everton and Liverpool dominating both domestic and European competitions, whilst local communities were suffering the repercussions of deindustrialization, unemployment, poverty and the influx of heroin. On the pitch, whilst a middle-class Jamaican migrant by the name of John Barnes was on the way to becoming one of the all-time biggest black stars in English football, locally-born black players continued to be denied the opportunities to make it as professionals.[41] Barnes was only the second black player to represent Liverpool, after Toxteth-born Howard Gayle in the early 1980s, whilst it would not be until the signing of Nigerian international Daniel Amokachi in 1994 that Everton would field another black player, following Mike Trebilcock and Cliff Marshall in the 1960s and 1970s, respectively. Black supporters were also a rarity, with Goodison Park and Anfield (in the north end of the city) both notorious for terrace racism during this period.[42] Exclusion from the city's professional and amateur football cultures meant that clubs and community institutions, such as Almithak and Stanley House (for whom Gayle played before joining Liverpool), were left to try and fulfil the aspirations and ambitions of generations of talented young black players.[43] Almithak won the FA Sunday Cup – a national knock-out tournament for amateur clubs – in 1989, seven years after Dingle Rail were the competition's victors.

To borrow the motto of giants FC Barcelona, the likes of Highfield Rangers and Almithak can thus be seen as 'more than a club'. They are inherently political institutions in that they have sought to engage in forms of cultural resistance against a dominant, often oppressive, sporting culture. As Fleming and Tomlinson state with reference to Accra, a black team from Brixton, south London, such clubs are 'valuable social institution(s) which can help prepare young black men for the difficulties they are likely to encounter in a racist society'.[44] Similarly, Westwood describes a process of 'collective mobilization through football that calls up black masculinities as part of the resistances that black men generate against the racisms of British society and by which they validate each other'.[45]

The rise of British Asian clubs

The clubs listed at the beginning of this section appear to verify Johal's (2001) claim that the majority of British Asian teams in the immediate post-migration era were made up of Punjabi Sikhs. This is unsurprising given the fact that this group represented one of the first, and most substantive, sections of the Indian population to migrate to Britain and also possessed a rich history of playing football back in the subcontinent.[46] However, Johal's suggestion that this remains the case at the beginning of the twenty-first century is questionable, with teams based around Pakistani and Bangladeshi players, in particular, making significant strides in the amateur and semi-professional game.[47]

More recently-established British Asian teams have continued the playing successes of their pioneering counterparts, whilst also expanding the community functions and wider capacities of their clubs. With many former players now involved in management and other important, voluntary off-field responsibilities – as coaches, chairpersons, treasurers, fundraisers and as representatives on committees and federations – their enthusiasm and dynamism is being passed onto new generations of players. The aspirations of many clubs now extend beyond consolidating the presence of British Asians in amateur football and they are working assiduously towards the bigger project of getting more British Asians into the professional game. In 2009, the number of British Asian professional footballers could be counted on one hand with a complex configuration of exclusionary and discriminatory procedures continuing to prevent this figure from rising.[48]

Faced with a lack of meaningful action by professional clubs and governing bodies, together with widespread marginalization from the decision-making processes initiated by these and other agencies, the burden of responsibility for challenging this state of affairs has, in many ways, been left to British Asian clubs themselves. For instance, Guru Nanak of Gravesend have initiated links with Charlton Athletic, whilst the Khalsa Football Federation (which oversees Sikh football clubs in Britain) have forged connections with Millwall and Wycombe Wanderers. Whether this will lead to more British Asian players progressing into the ranks of professional clubs remains to be seen though, for the rhetoric of intent that emanates from the professional game often proves to be little more than lip-service to the anti-racist football movement and race equality bodies. Indeed, evidence suggests that some British Asian semi-professional players are taking matters further into their own hands, turning their backs on the English game and looking beyond the British Isles for opportunities to embark on a professional career. For example, following trials held by the Pakistan Football Federation at Rotherham United in 2007, a number of talented British Asians were recruited to go and train with teams in Pakistan.[49]

A counter-argument often raised by professional clubs is that whilst young players ideally need to be under the tutelage of their coaches before they reach their teens in order to stand a chance of making the grade, British Asian clubs have not paid enough attention to issues of youth development. Despite the blame-shifting nature of this claim, there has traditionally been a degree of veracity to it, although in most cases this is due to a lack of resources rather than ignorance of the importance of providing opportunities for young people. However, current evidence points towards great strides being made by British Asian clubs with regard to implementing sustainable structures in this area. One such club is Albion Sports of Bradford. Formed in 1974, they became the first British Asian club to win the FA Sunday Cup, 21 years after their foundation. Albion place a significant focus on young people and youth development, employing qualified youth coaches and running junior sides spanning a range of age groups. These structures provide the basis for a link with nearby professional club Leeds United, whereby Albion host an Inner City Football Development Centre in Bradford, which will potentially feed into United's youth academy. Equally importantly, the club are also making some encouraging inroads into women's football, with the introduction of teams for girls and young women. Other examples of good practice in relation to youth development are Luton United (formerly Luton Asians) and Leicester Nirvana. The latter, originally known simply as Nirvana, grew out of Red Star (see next section) in the 1980s. Frustrated with a lack of opportunities in local adult football, the club reformed in 1994 with an explicit youth focus.[50]

Two of the most progressive British Asian clubs are also those that have been the most successful – Sporting Bengal and London APSA, with whom this essay began. Sporting Bengal are the representative side of the Bangladesh Football Association (BFA). A registered charity, the BFA was founded in 1996 and oversees a variety of aspects related to British Asian football in Greater London. The Sporting Bengal squad is selected from the annual League Bangla, the football league run by the BFA (and, since 2007, affiliated to the London FA) and contested in Victoria Park, east London over the summer months. The league was originally established both to high-light the level of talent in the community and to overcome territorial divisions between different groups in the borough of Tower Hamlets. Not only do Sporting Bengal and the BFA aim to challenge the under-representation of British Asians in British profes-sional sport, especially football, but they also work towards assisting the structural development of the broader local football scene, by offering courses on coaching, refereeing and the treatment of injuries, and helping to establish girls' football teams. Their activities are by no means limited to football *per se*, however, for the wider issues of facilitating community cohesion, engaging and empowering young people, and developing citizenship skills are central to all their projects. The high regard in which the BFA is held for its community work is reflected in its annual awards ceremonies which have been attended by a number of distinguished guests, such as the Bangladeshi High Commissioner, Superintendent Dal Babu of the Metropolitan Police, and professional players Dan Shittu (Bolton Wanderers) and Anwar Uddin (Dagenham and Redbridge). In 2007, the event was also broadcast on the satellite tele-vision station Channel S and proceeds were donated to the victims of the Bangladesh cyclone.

London APSA was formed in east London in 1993 as Ahle Sunnah. The club competed in various local leagues before entering the first Asian Football League (see below). The club strives to form meaningful relationships with businesses and sport-ing organizations, and planned initiatives include a comprehensive scouting network, coaching and development programmes, fast track promotion of gifted sportspeople, and establishing channels of communication with professional clubs.[51] The club represents a key focus for the sporting aspirations of British Asian male youth in east London and their status is highlighted by the fact that they have played a series of matches against the Pakistan national team and been the subject of their own BBC television documentary.[52] The role of Sporting Bengal, London APSA and other clubs of similar ethno-religious background in supporting, empowering and representing young British Muslims is of great importance in the current political epoch. With the widespread demonization of young Muslim men and the climate of intolerance and oppression towards British Muslim communities that has been created since 7/7 by politicians, the media and security forces, these clubs have crucial roles to play in fighting stereotypes and creating a positive impression of Islam in Britain.

Ethnicity, identity and the politics of multiculturalism

As the above discussion has demonstrated, minority ethnic amateur football clubs have often represented specific ethnic, cultural or religious communities. This is frequently reflected in the dominant background of the playing personnel and/or in the choice of team name.[53] However, other clubs have historically adopted a broader secular or multiethnic identity. This has sometimes been underpinned by an overt political motive, as was the case during the late 1970s/early 1980s when the member-ship of some clubs began to embody the era's dominant anti-racist approach to community mobilization and fighting prejudice.

One of the distinctive features of British anti-racism during this period was the fact that the term 'black' began to be used in a symbolic, political sense to refer to *all* non-white groups (and sometimes also white minorities, such as Irish migrants). This shift was premised on the belief that forming pan-racial coalitions was less divisive than focusing on ethnic diversity and thus it was the commonalities between minority ethnic groups, rather than their differences, that should be emphasized. This new discourse acknowledged common experiences of racism and a shared history of colonialism, engendering a politics of resistance between diverse, oppressed minorities.[54] As Mercer states, this shift 'demonstrated a process in which the objects of racist ideology reconstituted themselves as subjects of social, cultural and political change, actively making history, albeit under circumstances not of their own choosing'.[55] This was widely reflected in practice where, in many areas, a sense of unity and solidarity developed between British Asian and black communities.[56]

Central to this position was the creation of grass roots political movements, sometimes with a generic focus, but often oriented towards women or young people, such as Southall Black Sisters, Organisation of Women of African and Asian Descent, Peoples Unite, Bradford Blacks, Hackney Black People's Defence Organisation and the Asian Youth Movements.[57] Whilst it has arguably not received the attention that it warrants, football also played a small part in this process, forming cross-cultural solidarities between young people. For example, whilst Highfield Rangers has always been perceived as a black club in an *ethnic* sense, this applies more accurately to its political stance, as a number of British Asian and some white players have turned out for them over the years. Latterly, this is reflected in the diverse backgrounds of its coaches and young players. Chairman and founder member Delroy King states that:

> One of the principles that we've always operated the club on is that it's a club that belongs to everybody. What we are about is people coming together and enjoying themselves. That's basically it really, that's the philosophy on which we operate.[58]

As Williams points out, the club represents the people of Highfields as a whole, and shared interests and neighbourhood experiences, as well as a common class location, have often been more important in gaining inclusion in the club than ethnic background.[59]

Fellow Leicester side Red Star embodied this position in a more overtly political manner. Formed in the early 1980s, and subsequently developing into a broader youth project, Red Star's membership was predominantly British Asian, but its public identity was black in a political sense, enabling a sense of solidarity and resistance to the racial discrimination they frequently experienced when playing white clubs outside of their immediate locality.[60]

The 1990s witnessed the demise of political blackness and the associated rise of identity politics, whereby groups began to identify increasingly in terms of specific ethnic or religious signifiers rather than in relation to a wider racial or class location. Increasing conflicts between minority ethnic groups – such as African-Caribbeans and Pakistanis in Birmingham, and Bangladeshis and Somalis in parts of London – have heightened this situation, leading many commentators to decry the end of multiethnic solidarities, sporting or otherwise. An additional element in this equation is contemporary opposition – from across the political spectrum – to municipal multiculturalism which, due to its overt celebration of difference and diversity, is (mistakenly) believed to have caused Britain's minority ethnic groups to isolate themselves from other groups and, subsequently, to have hindered their socio-economic achievement. This is mirrored in football where British Asian clubs, in particular, are often accused of practicing self-segregation. However, this claim represents one of the biggest common misunderstandings about minority ethnic football clubs. It fails to take into account the context in which clubs were formed, their importance in articulating community identity and the ongoing influence of racism, but also, and most importantly, it ignores the fact that it is empirically flawed. Many British Asian clubs have players, coaches and managers from a variety of ethnic backgrounds. This reflects a widespread acknowledgement amongst British Asian footballers of the importance of playing with and against players of other ethnicities, together with a desire for their clubs to balance retaining their identities with becoming more inclusive institutions.[61] Indeed, if any clubs are guilty of practising cultural separatism, it is the large number of all-white teams that participate in amateur football throughout England.

All-Asian leagues are likewise targets for criticism, regarded in the popular imagination as segregationist, and sustaining the exclusion of British Asians from mainstream football structures rather than challenging it. The fact that their existence runs somewhat counter to getting more British Asians into the professional game is difficult to dispute, given the reluctance of professional clubs to scout them. However, their establishment is highly rational, as they represent important socio-cultural spaces and environments where British Asians can play without fear of racial abuse or violence – a function that continues to remain necessary given the continuing presence of racism in amateur football.[62] Furthermore, their existence has historically been vital to the provision of organized football in British Asian communities, given the lack of support for British Asian teams within mainstream, FA-affiliated leagues.

Notwithstanding this, like the teams discussed above, membership of leagues administered by British Asian organizations and federations is rarely mono-ethnic. The Asian Football League in London – formed in 1993 and now sponsored by Mercedes-Benz Direct – restricts the number of British Asian players that can turn out for each team, as do the big tournaments held up and down the country during the summer months. The fact that the most successful professional player to come through the League Bangla system in east London, Dan Shittu of Bolton Wanderers, is of black African background is a case in point. Furthermore, the breakdown of registered players for the 2006 league (over 1,100 in total), shows that 51% were British Bangladeshi, 16% were British Asian Other, 12% were white, 11% were African-Caribbean, 4% were Somali, and 6% were of other backgrounds.[63]

Conclusion: minority ethnic football clubs in England – the next 50 years

As was signposted at the beginning of this essay, the focus of analysis has been directed towards those clubs that represent British Asian and black communities, due to the fact that in the period under examination – the post-war mass migrations up to the present day – they have been the largest minority ethnic populations in Britain and they have had the most notable involvement in organized amateur football. However, the maps of multiethnic Britain – both at national and municipal levels – have changed substantially over the last decade. At present, the majority of migrants entering and settling in Britain are no longer from Britain's former colonies, but from other parts of Asia, Africa and Eastern Europe, and so the amateur football sphere is likely to become even more diverse over forthcoming years.

These changes to the ethnic demographics of English amateur football are being reflected in the creation of new leagues and tournaments. One such competition is the Unity Cup Festival, a knock-out tournament involving migrant, refugee and other displaced communities from all over Britain. According to the anti-racist pressure group Kick It Out, which helps to organize it, the Unity Cup has three main aims. First, to break down negative perceptions of those seeking refuge; second, to empower displaced peoples to engage with mainstream sports bodies such as football clubs and local authorities; and third, to build solidarity and links amongst refugees in different parts of the UK.[64] The tournament reached its fifth anniversary in 2007 and, for the first time, the number of teams entering the competition meant that the national finals needed to be preceded by regional heats in different cities, rather than operate as a single-venue event as had previously been the case. Some teams are characterized by a dominant ethnicity, but many display a wide ethnic mix. The tournament has an important integrative role to play, given the widespread discrimination faced by refugees and asylum seekers in Britain, and reflects the need for anti-racist football organizations to modify their strategies and policies beyond simplistic black-white binaries and a focus on 'established' minority ethnic groups, to an awareness of the new discourses of contemporary racisms.[65]

A further significant aspect of contemporary migration is the shifting locations of settlement for migrant communities. Whilst many of the post-war migrants took up residence in Britain's major towns and cities – due to their employment in manufacturing, heavy industry and public sector services such as transport and health – changing demands for labour – with tourism and hospitality industries, and fruit and vegetable harvesting recruiting large numbers of seasonal migrant workers – as well as the government's controversial dispersal system for those seeking asylum or refuge, mean that new migrant communities are being established in small coastal towns and rural areas. This is already having significant implications for local football cultures. For example, at the beginning of the decade, one would probably not have predicted that the town of Ipswich, in the predominantly rural county of Suffolk, would hold its inaugural One Community Cup in 2007 with Bulgarian, Bangladeshi, Kurdish, Czech, Iraqi, Polish and Zimbabwean communities competing in a football tournament at Ipswich Town's Portman Road stadium. Initiating anti-racist practices in non-urban and semi-rural areas is an immediate priority for amateur football. Not only do these locations witness some of the worst contemporary manifestations of racism,[66] but evidence also suggests that the regional committees and associations – usually comprised largely, if not exclusively, of white men – that govern the game in these areas are often the most ignorant of the issues and problems facing minority ethnic football players and teams.[67]

This essay has demonstrated the importance of situating the experiences of minority ethnic men's amateur football clubs firmly within the prevailing social conditions and racial politics of the last half century. It has highlighted the diversity of minority ethnic experiences in the sphere of amateur football, but also the commonalities shared by players and clubs. Arguably, the most prominent of these is the ongoing experience of racism. Racism in football operates in increasingly complex, subtle and nuanced ways, existing not only on the pitch, but also in the structures and procedures that characterize the way that the game is governed. Whilst football's governing bodies are increasingly reproducing the rhetoric of inclusion and equity, there is a still a long way to go before we can say that minority ethnic football clubs are playing on a level field. There are certainly grounds for optimism, but we must remain cautious to claims that progress is being made towards achieving racial equality in amateur football. The story of the next 50 years may turn out to be very different in terms of the communities and clubs involved, but for the time being at least, many of the old issues and problems appear to be here to stay.

Notes

1. Two other British Asian clubs, Beaumont FC and London Tigers, plan to join London APSA and Sporting Bengal in entering the FA Cup for the 2008–09 season.
2. Burdsey, *British Asians*.
3. 'APSA Plan to Make Capital Gains in Cup'. *Hackney Gazette*, August 9, 2007.
4. Riordan, 'The Workers' Olympics', 98.
5. An important exception is Highfield Rangers Oral History Group/Sir Norman Chester Centre for Football Research's (1993) account of Highfield Rangers.
6. Burdsey, *British Asians*.
7. Vasili, 'Walter Daniel Tull'; *The First Black Footballer* and *Colouring Over the White Line*.
8. Hornby, *Fever Pitch*.
9. Bonilla-Silva, *Racism Without Racists*.
10. Fryer, *Staying Power*; Ramdin, *Reimagining Britain* and Visram, *Asians in Britain*.
11. See for example, Smith, *Asians in Britain; Coming to Coventry*; Dasgupta, *Salaam Stanley Matthews*; Bance, *The Sikhs in Britain*; Gilroy, *Black Britain*.
12. See, for example, the photo galleries/oral histories provided by GNG of Leicester (www.gngfc.com) and Guru Nanak of Gravesend (www.gurunanakfc.co.uk).
13. Hylton, '"Race", Sport and Leisure', 85.
14. Singer, 'Understanding Racism', 370.
15. Williams, '"Rangers is a Black Club"', 153.
16. Westwood, 'Racism, Black Masculinity'.
17. For a further discussion on this nomenclature, see Burdsey, *British Asians*.
18. According to the 2001 census, the total British population stood at just under 59 million people. Of these, 1,053,411 people are of Indian background, 747,285 are of Pakistani background, 283,063 are of Bangladeshi background, 565,876 identify as Black Caribbean and 485,277 identify as Black African.
19. Scraton, Caudwell and Holland, '"Bend it like Patel"'; Ratna, 'A "Fair Game"?'
20. Burdsey, 'No Ball Games Allowed?'
21. *Coming To Coventry*.
22. Bains and Johal, *Corner Flags*.
23. Johal, 'Playing their Own Game', 162.
24. Burdsey, *British Asians*.
25. Burdsey, 'No Ball Games Allowed?'
26. Hall *et al.*, *Policing the Crisis*.
27. Talbot and Böse, 'Racism, Criminalization'.
28. Lord Scarman was the chair of the public inquiry into the urban unrest in Brixton, south London in 1981.
29. Carrington, 'Sport, Masculinity'.
30. Hesse, 'White Governmentality'.
31. Sivanandan, *Communities of Resistance*.
32. Farrar, 'Migrant Spaces'.
33. Singh, 'A City of Surprises'.
34. Highfield Rangers Oral History Group/Sir Norman Chester Centre for Football Research, *Highfield Rangers*, 101.
35. Ibid.
36. Williams, '"Rangers is a Black Club"', 166.
37. Ibid.
38. Burdsey, '"One of the Lads"?'; King, *Offside Racism*.
39. Small, 'Racialised Relations in Liverpool', 514, emphasis added.
40. Hill, *Out of His Skin*.
41. Ibid.
42. Hill, 'From Barnes to Camara'.
43. Deborah Mulhearn, 'Forward Thinking in a Community'. *Guardian*, November 15, 2000.
44. Fleming and Tomlinson, 'Football, Racism', 93.
45. Westwood, 'Racism, Black Masculinity', 71.
46. Dimeo, 'Colonial Bodies'.
47. Predominantly Hindu football clubs are a rarity in English football. See, in this context, Johal, 'Playing their Own Game'.
48. Burdsey, *British Asians*.

49. In an associated move, the Pakistan Football Federation have also recruited four British-born players to represent the national side during its 2010 World Cup qualifying campaign: professional players Zesh Rehman of Queens Park Rangers and Adnan Ahmed of Tranmere Rovers, together with semi-professional players Adam Karim of Porthmadog (in the League of Wales) and Amjad Iqbal of Farsley Celtic (in the Blue Square Conference). 'Brit of a Chance', *Eastern Eye*, October 12, 2007; 'Five Live Sport', *BBC Radio*, BBC Radio Five Live, July 24, 2007.
50. 'Asians Can Play Football' *Asians in Football Forum,* 2005.
51. 'Searching for our Next Sporting Hero' *London APSA,* (no date).
52. 'They Think it's All Islam', *BBC Television*, BBC2, August 16, 2001.
53. Burdsey, 'No Ball Games Allowed?'
54. Hall, 'New Ethnicities'.
55. Mercer, *Welcome to the Jungle*, 271.
56. Campaign Against Racism and Fascism/Southall Rights, *Southall*; Sivanandan, 'From Resistance to Rebellion'.
57. Ramamurthy, 'The Politics of Britain's Asian Youth Movements'; 'Kala Tara'.
58. Cited in MacDonald and Benfield, *Football United*.
59. Williams, '"Rangers is a Black Club"'.
60. Westwood, 'Racism, Black Masculinity'; 'Red Star of Leicester'.
61. Burdsey, 'Obstacle Race?'
62. Ibid.
63. Bangladesh Football Association Awards Ceremony, September 20, 2007. See for details 'About BFA', at http://www.bfauk.com/red.2.content.php?template=template3.php&pageid=168&pagename=Aims%20&%0Objectives.
64. 'Unity Cup Festival 2006 P:rogramme', Kick It Out/Football Unites Racism Divides, Sheffield, July 14–16, 2006.
65. Kundnani, *The End of Tolerance*.
66. Burdsey, 'Obstacle Race?'
67. Long *et al.*, *Part of the Game?*; Lusted, 'Amateurism, Leisure and Equity Policy'.

References

Bains, J., and S. Johal. *Corner Flags and Corner Shops: The Asian Football Experience.* London: Gollancz, 1998.

Bance, P. *The Sikhs in Britain: 150 Years of Photographs.* Stroud: Sutton Publishing, 2007.

Bonilla-Silva, E. *Racism without Racists: Colour Blind Racism and the Persistence of Racial Inequality.* Boulder, CO: Lynne Rienner Publishers, 2003.

Burdsey, D. 'Obstacle Race? "Race", Racism and the Recruitment of British Asian Professional Footballers'. *Patterns of Prejudice* 38, no. 3 (2004): 279–99.

Burdsey, D. '"One of the Lads"?: Dual Ethnicity and Assimilated Ethnicities in the Careers of British Asian Professional Footballers', *Ethnic and Racial Studies* 27, no. 5 (2004): 757–79.

Burdsey, D. 'No Ball Games Allowed? A Socio-historical Examination of the Development and Social Roles of British Asian Football Clubs'. *Journal of Ethnic and Migration Studies* 32, no. 3 (2006): 477–96.

Burdsey, D. *British Asians and Football: Culture, Identity and Exclusion.* London: Routledge, 2007.

Campaign Against Racism and Fascism/Southall Rights. *Southall: Birth of a Black Community.* London: Institute of Race Relations/Southall Rights, 1981.

Carrington, B. 'Sport, Masculinity and Black Cultural Resistance'. *Journal of Sport and Social Issues* 22, 3 (1998): 275–98.

Coventry Teaching Primary Care Trust/The Herbert. *Coming To Coventry: Stories From the South Asian Pioneers.* Coventry: Coventry Teaching Primary Care Trust/The Herbert, 2006.

Dasgupta, S. *Salaam Stanley Matthews.* London: Granta Books, 2006.

Dimeo, P. 'Colonial Bodies, Colonial Sport: "Martial" Punjabis, "Effeminate" Bengalis and the Development of Indian Football'. *International Journal of the History of Sport* 19, no. 1 (2002): 72–90.

Farrar, M. 'Migrant Spaces and Settlers' Time: Forming and De-forming an Inner City'. In *Imagining Cities: Scripts, Signs, Memories,* ed. S. Westwood and J. Williams, 104–24. London: Routledge, 1997.

Fleming, S., and A. Tomlinson. 'Football, Racism and Xenophobia in England (1): Europe and the Old England'. In *Racism and Xenophobia in European Football,* ed. U. Merkel and W. Tokarski, 79–100. Aachen: Meyer & Meyer, 1996.

Fryer, P. *Staying Power: The History of Black People in Britain: Black People in Britain Since 1504.* London: Pluto Press, 1984.

Gilroy, P. *Black Britain: A Photographic History.* London: SAQI, 2007.

Hall, S. 'New Ethnicities'. In *Stuart Hall: Critical Dialogues in Cultural Studies,* ed. D. Morley and K.-H. Chen, 441–9. London: Routledge, 1996.

Hall, S., C. Critcher, T. Jefferson, J. Clarke, and B. Roberts. *Policing the Crisis: Mugging, the State, and Law and Order* London: Macmillan, 1978.

Hesse, B. 'White Governmentality: Urbanism, Nationalism, Racism'. In *Imagining Cities: Scripts, Signs, Memories,* ed. S. Westwood and J. Williams, 94–103. London: Routledge, 1997.

Highfield Rangers Oral History Group/Sir Norman Chester Centre for Football Research. *Highfield Rangers: An Oral History.* Leicester: Leicester City Council, 1993.

Hill, D. *Out of His Skin: The John Barnes Phenomenon.* London: When Saturday Comes Books, 2001.

Hill, D. 'From Barnes to Camara: Football, Identity and Racism in Liverpool'. In *Passing Rhythms: Liverpool FC and the Transformation of Football,* ed. J. Williams, S. Hopkins, and C. Long, 129–45. Oxford: Berg, 2001.

Hornby, N. *Fever Pitch.* London: Gollancz, 1992.

Hylton, K. '"Race", Sport and Leisure: Lessons from Critical Race Theory'. *Leisure Studies* 24, no. 1 (2005): 81–98.

Johal, S. 'Playing Their Own Game: a South Asian Football Experience'. In *'Race', Sport and British Society,* ed. B. Carrington and I. McDonald, 153–69. London: Routledge, 2001.

King, C. *Offside Racism: Playing the White Man.* Oxford: Berg, 2004.

Kundnani, A. *The End of Tolerance: Racism in 21st Century Britain.* London: Pluto Press, 2007.

Long, J., K. Hylton, M. Welch, and J. Dart. *Part of the Game? An Examination of Racism in Grassroots Football.* Leeds: Kick It Out/Centre for Leisure and Sport Research, School of Leisure and Sports Studies, Leeds Metropolitan University, 2000.

Lusted, J. 'Amateurism, Leisure and Equity Policy: Resisting Race Equality in English Local Football Governance'. Paper presented at Annual Leisure Studies Conference on 'Whatever Happened to the Leisure Society? Critical and Multidisciplinary [Retro]spectives', University of Brighton, July 2007.

MacDonald, G., and A. Benfield. *Football United: Volume 1 – Highfield Rangers.* Consequential Films, 2007.

Mercer, K. *Welcome to the Jungle: New Positions in Black Cultural Studies.* London: Routledge, 1994.

Ramamurthy, A. 'The Politics of Britain's Asian Youth Movements'. *Race and Class* 48, no. 2 (2006): 38–60.

Ramamurthy, A. *Kala Tara: A History of the Asian Youth Movements in Britain in the 1970s and 1980s.* Preston: Department of Humanities, University of Central Lancashire, 2007.

Ramdin, R. *Reimagining Britain: 500 Years of Black and Asian History.* London: Pluto Press, 1999.

Ratna, A. 'A "Fair Game"? British-Asian Females' Experiences of Racism in Women's Football'. In *Women, Football and Europe: Histories, Equity and Experiences,* ed. J. Magee, J. Caudwell, K. Liston, and S. Scraton, 69–88. Oxford: Meyer and Meyer Sport, 2007.

Riordan, J. 'The Workers' Olympics'. In *Five Ring Circus: Money, Power and Politics at the Olympic Games,* ed. A. Tomlinson and G. Whannel, 98–112. London: Pluto Press, 1984.

Scraton, S., J. Caudwell, and S. Holland. '"Bend it like Patel": Centring "Race", Ethnicity and Gender in Feminist Analysis of Women's Football in England'. *International Review for the Sociology of Sport* 40, no. 1 (2005): 71–88.

Singer, J. 'Understanding Racism Through the Eyes of African-American Male Student-Athletes'. *Race, Ethnicity and Education* 8, no. 4 (2005): 365–86.

Singh, G. 'A City of Surprises: Urban Multiculturalism and the "Leicester Model"'. In *A Postcolonial People: South Asians in Britain,* ed. N. Ali, V. Kalra, and S. Sayyid, 291–304. London: Hurst, 2006.

Small, S. 'Racialised Relations in Liverpool: A Contemporary Anomaly'. *New Community* 17, no. 4 (1991): 511–37.

Smith, T. *Asians in Britain.* Stockport: Dewi Lewis Publishing, 2004.

Talbot, D., and M. Böse. 'Racism, Criminalization and the Development of Night-time Economies: Two Case Studies in London and Manchester'. *Ethnic and Racial Studies* 30, no. 1 (2007): 95–118.

Vasili, P. 'Walter Daniel Tull, 1888–1918: Soldier, Footballer, Black'. *Race and Class* 38, no. 2 (1996): 51–69.

Vasili, P. *The First Black Footballer: Arthur Wharton 1865–1930.* London: Frank Cass, 1998.

Vasili, P. *Colouring Over the White Line: The History of Black Footballers in Britain.* Edinburgh: Mainstream Publishing, 2000.

Visram, R. *Asians in Britain: 400 Years of History.* London: Pluto Press, 2002.

Westwood, S. 'Racism, Black Masculinity and the Politics of Space'. In *Men, Masculinities and Social Theory,* ed. J. Hearn and D. Morgan, 55–71. London: Unwin Hyman, 1990.

Westwood, S. 'Red Star of Leicester: Racism, the Politics of Identity and Black Youth in Britain'. In *Black and Ethnic Leaderships: The Cultural Dimensions of Political Action,* ed. P. Werbner and M. Anwar, 146–9. London: Routledge, 1991.

Williams, J. '"Rangers is a Black Club": "Race", Identity and Local Football in England'. In *Game Without Frontiers: Football, Identity and Modernity,* ed. R. Giulianotti and J. Williams, 153–83. Aldershot: Arena, 1994.

Playing games with ' race': understanding resistance to ' race' equality initiatives in English local football governance

Jim Lusted

Division of Sport, Exercise & Life Sciences, University of Northampton, Northampton, UK

Introduction

Football continues to play a leading role in discussions around the politics of 'race' and social integration in European nation-states. Given its recent history of anti-racist activity, English football is often cited as a figurehead example of challenging racism through popular culture and encouraging ethnic minority participation.[1] Yet, despite the growing prominence of black players in the professional game in England, people from ethnic minority backgrounds are rarely represented in other parts of the football industry, particularly in coaching and managerial positions or in administrative roles with real power and authority.[2] Local football[3] – an area largely bereft of any sustained research attention – mirrors this trend, with growing numbers of ethnic minority participants failing to cross over into the governance of the local game. Little is currently known about the organization and governance of grass-roots football. This is surprising, given the popularity of the local game in England (12 million participants according to The Football Association[4]), often playing a central role in localized (especially male) identity construction and politics and – particularly for the purposes of this essay – on local interpretations of 'race' and racialized power relations. Previous research has uncovered entrenched, often violent, racism in the local game, while also identifying some *resistance* to the anti-racist sentiment that appears to have been broadly embraced by the professional game.[5]

Focusing on local football in a specifically English setting, this essay explores in detail the organization of the local game, examining the role played by the 43 semi-autonomous regional County Football Associations (hereafter County FAs) that govern local football across England. While these organizations have traditionally enjoyed a low profile, both in the media and academic research, it has previously been suggested that County FAs are often discriminatory in their interactions with British ethnic minorities in a number of ways. Long *et al.* pay particular attention to the handling of disciplinary cases that involve accusations of racist abuse on the pitch.[6] County FAs also fail properly to reflect their local football demographics, with County FA personnel being overwhelmingly white (99.7%) and male (97%).[7]

The relative autonomy from the parent body, the English Football Association (hereafter, The FA), has sheltered English local football governance from the heightened accountability, and enforced changes in structure, policy and tone that have occurred centrally at The FA in recent years.[8] This means that enduring *local* decision-making structures remain informed by longer-standing, and perhaps peculiarly British, traditional values of amateurism and voluntary commitment.

Since 2000, The FA has begun a process of professionalizing local football governance, challenging the traditionally amateur ideals of County FAs and their monopoly over the local game. This coincides with The FA's first tentative attempts to implement new anti-discriminatory principles across English football. The *Ethics and Sports Equity Strategy*, adopted by The FA Council in 2002, aims to 'ensure football is accessible to all communities across England',[9] focusing on women and girls, and people with disabilities, but with a particular emphasis on ethnic minorities. This attempt to introduce an equity strategy at the local level is, predictably, meeting with a number of challenges.

Using data collected by the author during PhD research – from interviews and observations at five case study County FAs – the essay investigates how ideas of 'race' are routinely employed in a variety of ways to justify the scepticism towards adopting race equality initiatives into the local game. In particular, emphasis is placed on particularly Victorian ideologies concerning British sport that appear persistent in local football discourse in England and inform the dealings between local governing bodies and their ethnic minority participants. Castells'[10] three types of identity formation – legitimizing, resistance and project – are applied in an attempt to account for some of the racialized power relations in the local game. From this, it is suggested that accounts of racism that utilize an individual prejudice thesis – an approach that informs much anti-racist sport policy – are insufficient to interpret fully the complex ways that ideas about 'race' are used to continue to exclude ethnic minorities from key decision-making roles in the governance of English local football.

'Race', racism and English local football

It is now a relatively well-rehearsed claim that British sport and leisure sociology has largely relied on common sense and individualized notions of 'race' and racism in its analysis.[11] This mirrors a popular interpretation of racism in both political and social discourse;[12] that racism was seen as 'package of irrational beliefs: a prejudice',[13] or simply an intellectual error.[14] Moreover, given the priority shown in most recent research on British football to both football hooliganism and also the *professional* game,[15] detailed studies of social divisions in local sport remain few and far between. This relative lack of research on the 'grass roots' is mirrored, more generally, in British sport and leisure sociology. An investigation into racism in local cricket, for example, points to an 'absence of … critical enquiry at the "grass roots" of the sport'.[16] Williams[17] provides an important introductory account of English local football in relation to local 'race'-based identities, while the sustained work led by Jonathan Long with collaborators from Leeds Metropolitan University[18] provides a useful entry point into understanding English grass-roots sport. Long's account of the 'denial of racism'[19] in local sport has particular relevance to this essay and frames many of the debates that follow.

Much of the literature on racism and sport in Britain has focused on the experiences of (largely black and Asian) ethnic minority participants and on the consequences that racism has for identity construction.[20] These largely ethnographic accounts are important, yet can overstate the level of social agency, neglecting the ways in which 'individual identities and experiences are produced through oppressive social structures'.[21] Analyses of racism in sports further afield, including colonial resistance in the Caribbean,[22] the Civil Rights struggle in the USA,[23] and apartheid in South Africa[24] have provided more structural accounts of the origins and politics of racialized discrimination in sport.

Perhaps in the light of recent focus of British research, Daniel Burdsey asks, pertinently, 'while we know there is racism in football, do we really know exactly where, how and by whom it is instigated?'[25] Accounts based on the structural and organizational origins of such discrimination are, unfortunately, few and far between. This essay attempts to redress some of the imbalances, following a path outlined by Kivel by focusing on 'the construction of dominant discourses around race (e.g. whiteness) … in order to understand leisure's role in constructing and maintaining dominant identities of privilege.'[26] In short, shifting attention from the excluded and onto the *excluders* in local sport appears to be a necessary and long-overdue project; one that might help further to broaden our apparently limited understanding of the origins and nature of racism in football.

Taking local football seriously

Local football across the world is a hugely popular 'voluntary' pastime. Football's world governing body, FIFA (Fédération Internationale de Football Association) suggests that over 250 million people worldwide actively play the game,[27] while The FA has estimated that around half the population of England are 'involved' in football in some way.[28] Local football is an important site for local voluntary collective participation, argued to be in sharp decline in most western industrial societies.[29] Moreover, pitches across the globe can provide for non-formal social encounters between (usually young male but increasingly female) players and officials from different social, cultural and ethnic backgrounds – people who might otherwise lead very separate lives. The local game therefore provides an opportunity to perform and negotiate, in real settings, local understandings of difference, including those drawn from ideas of 'race'.

It is a little surprising that, given the apparent centrality of the local game to many people's lives, that little sustained research has taken place in the grass roots game. I suspect one of the reasons for this void is the obsession – shared by both the media and academics – with professional sport, football being no exception. Yet there are also important connections that exist between local and professional sport that are often ignored, particularly in analyses of racism in football. The grass-roots often provide the 'raw material' for the professional game. In England, for example, recruitment of players into the professional game has traditionally relied on informal connections between professional club scouts and select local amateur clubs, as Williams identifies:

> Knowledge of local male networks and of the interface between local, non-league and professional football is a significant currency inside the male communities which manage, play and support the game at the local level. The 'scouts' of professional clubs have a special, near-mystical status in this culture as they trawl the top local leagues in search of young men who have the elusive and indefinable 'right stuff.[30]

Burdsey has shown how this 'trawling' process invariably misses many of the established local British South Asian clubs in England, contributing to the continued absence of British Asian players in today's British professional game.[31] To fully understand how racism operates and impacts across global sport, it seems we might need a much better understanding of the structures and cultures found at the national grass roots. For example, the apparent local ambivalences shown in Spain towards the Spanish national football coach Luis Aragones following his racist abuse aimed at Arsenal's Thierry Henry in 2004,[32] or the more recent allegations of Serbian crowd and player abuse towards England's black players in the 2004 Under-21 European Championships,[33] are likely to be better understood if located within peculiarly Spanish and Serbian interpretations and experiences of immigration and racialized difference in civil society, including in leisure and sport.

Previous research shows that racism in English sport is often more entrenched and is more likely at the local, rather than at the professional, level. Long *et al*.[34] found that 62% of local football club secretaries surveyed in West Yorkshire thought that racism was 'the same' or 'worse' at grass roots compared to the professional game. Research on local sport, including football,[35] rugby league,[36] and cricket[37] – all suggest that racism is more prevalent in the local setting in England than at the professional level. Carrington and McDonald claim that 'who "owns" cricket is the subtext to understanding racism in cricket'.[38] Following this approach, it is necessary to consider how, and by whom, local football in England is 'owned'. If we consider specifically the English case, *County Football Associations* have held a virtual monopoly of control over the local game in England since their inception in the late nineteenth century. The next section provides an introductory account of these influential organizations – so far largely ignored in previous studies of racism in English football.

The English County FA: yesterday and today

> I would no longer encourage any other person from any other ethnic minority background to join [a County FA] Council … Certainly, I wouldn't want to be blamed for flagging them into a cauldron which I think is basically racist.[39]

The above comment was made by one of the very few black County FA Council members in England; it introduces a commonly held impression about County FAs among many English ethnic minority local players and officials. Since the rise in post-war Commonwealth migration from the 1950s onwards, tensions have emerged in local football in England over the past 50 years. To begin to account for some of these tensions, it is important to firstly map the historic social and cultural conditions of English County FAs before discussing some more contemporary developments, including the introduction of equity principles into English local football governance within a wider framework of modernization and reform of the local game.

While the story of formation of The English Football Association – named simply *The* Football Association to no doubt signify its seminal role in the origins of the global game – is familiar to many, little appears to be known about the local FA organizations that are, nonetheless, just as central to understanding the development of the game in England. Regional County FAs were formed soon after The FA in 1863, with a remit to implement the rules and regulations of The FA by organizing 'court' style disciplinary hearings and by adjudicating locally on the application of fines and bans for infractions. These functions continue to be the main focus of County FAs in England some 150 years later. County FAs have traditionally relied on significant voluntary commitment, mirroring some of the values and cultural nuances of the Victorian 'gentleman amateur'[40] and his moral stance of 'sport for sports sake'. Indeed, most County FAs in England were set up by ex-public school graduates who had played their part in the 'sportization'[41] of modern British sport. These sporting ideals regarding amateurism, fair play and meritocracy in sport are firmly rooted in Victorian Britain. This essay suggests that such notions provide an important cultural legacy for the enactment of local sports governance in England today. Moreover, they will help us begin to account for many of the policies and practices that continue in the local game and impact upon the opportunities available for ethnic minorities to participate in any meaningful sense.

County FAs follow an organizational structure akin to traditional democratic political structures. They contain a number of elected Council members, including a president, life vice presidents and a chairman, all of whom sit on committees (each with a chairperson) that make decisions on a variety of football matters, including discipline, club affiliation, referees, grounds and facilities, and competitions. An increasing number of paid employees at the County FA (including the secretary or chief executive) are in place to carry out the duties indicated by the committees. Local FA councils are dominated by older volunteers, (usually) men who have the necessary spare time to commit to such duties. Longevity of service is also encouraged, with the allocation of life vice-presidencies after a period of service (around 10 consecutive years). These older Council members, often led by a small number of locally well-known personnel, tend to form 'club cultures',[42] wielding significant control and influence on all County FA activities.

Local County FAs provide one member to sit on The FA's own national Council, making up approximately half the national Council membership. Despite (or perhaps because of) this national representation, and because of The FA's wider responsibilities in the professional game – e.g. in running the FA Cup competition and the England national team – the local associations have historically been left by The FA to govern their own local football matters. This autonomy has no doubt been sustained as a result of the long-standing problematic relationship between County FAs and their parent body that have included temporary breakaways and bitter disputes.[43] County FAs have also enjoyed relative financial independence from The FA, generating the majority of their income from local membership fees and disciplinary fines, rather than relying on central funding.

In 2000, The FA approved a Football Development Strategy (FDS) aimed at developing 'grass roots' football in the light of declining participation in FA-organized football.[44] The FDS introduced a series of changes aimed at transforming the role and purpose of the County FA while also attempting to address some long-standing concerns about the perceived intransigence and poor practice of many local football associations. The FDS reflected a wider reform attempt by the governing body to professionalize, or bureaucratize[45] local practices, testing the previous autonomy enjoyed by the local bodies. A Football Development Officer was introduced into each English County FA, funded and managed directly by The FA, with somewhat uneven local input.[46] Given the different ethos of the governance and development roles, alongside the disparate funding streams, job specifications and work patterns, the relationship between the new development staff and the longer-standing governance team at County FAs has invariably been strained. The following quote illustrates a commonly held feeling among development staff of the difficulties they have faced in integrating into the long-standing structures and cultures of County FAs:

> County FAs have been here for 100 years, we've been here for nearly 8, 9 years, and it's very new to them still – and a lot of Council members who don't understand what we do are old chaps who have been here for god knows how many years.[47]

These tensions appear to reflect much wider differences between the local body and the national FA. There is little room here to explore these in any detail, but Figure 1 summarizes some of the key polarities involved.

Given that County FAs had been largely left to decide their own local policies, these new national directives are often interpreted as challenges to local power bases and to the power County FAs are able to wield locally. The FDS has encouraged County FAs to become more accountable and more accessible to its local membership (including the growing number of ethnic minority participants).

The FDS also commits The FA to an area of wider reform, including change drawn from principles of 'equity and social inclusion'.[48] The approval of the FDS was

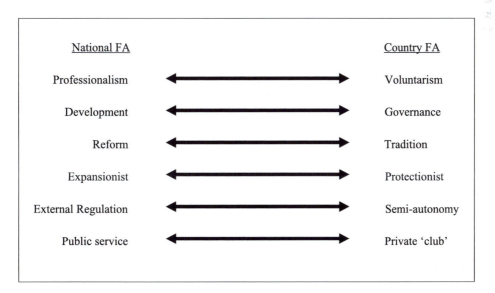

National FA		Country FA
Professionalism	⟷	Voluntarism
Development	⟷	Governance
Reform	⟷	Tradition
Expansionist	⟷	Protectionist
External Regulation	⟷	Semi-autonomy
Public service	⟷	Private 'club'

Figure 1. Local and national governance tensions in English football.

shortly followed by The FA's own Ethics and Sports Equity Strategy (E&SES),[49] approved by The FA Board in 2002. The concept of *equity* is relatively new to British sport policy, having been introduced by the Government's sport funding arm, Sport England, only in the early 1990s. Equity refers to tackling not only racism, but also gender and disability discrimination, social exclusion (predominantly poverty-based) and homophobia. Despite the broad range of groups targeted here, the relative maturity of anti-racism initiatives in football in England[50] means that 'race' equality continues to dominate the equity agenda.

Sports research in England in the early 1990s, led by Anita White,[51] utilized approaches developed overseas, particularly those in Australia and Canada that initially targeted sex discrimination. White defined the new approach thus:

> Equity in its simplest sense means 'fairness'. It goes a little bit further than equal opportunity as it acknowledges the need to eliminate inequities to achieve fairness. It implies the allocation or reallocation of resources and entitlements, including power, to achieve this end.[52]

Introducing 'equity' was an attempt to rejuvenate sports policy in Britain that aimed to tackle the unequal access to sporting provision. Here, equity was to build on the premises of equal opportunity policies: an approach that had focused on increasing and improving *individual* access to British sport. One of the outcomes of this policy direction was to inadvertently allow British sporting institutions to externalize sources of under-representation in local sport in Britain and to deflect any calls for change away from the internal structures and cultures of sport itself.

The FA's equity strategy identifies four underlying themes:

- Fairness and respect for all people
- Equality of access and opportunity
- Recognizing that inequalities exist and taking practical steps to address them
- Football needs to ensure it is equally accessible to all members of society[53]

The first two themes reflect the rhetoric of equal opportunity in sport, one that fits well with long-standing notions of fair play in British sport. An organizational commitment to equal opportunities has tended to be driven by an obligation to adhere to UK anti-discrimination legislation, such as the 1976 Race Relations Act.[54] Because of their autonomy, until the implementation of the FDS, County FAs had had little external compulsion to take any positive steps to challenge discrimination. Indeed, a recent survey[55] showed that only 62% of County FAs could say even that they had an equal opportunities policy in place.

As Long[56] has shown, 'recognizing that inequalities exist' seems particularly problematic in British sport. English County FA cultures often rely on the traditional ideals of being fair and 'unbiased'; values that were integral to the British Victorian amateur sportsman.[57] Relatively sheltered from constraining external influences, County FAs have, it is often said, represented all their members 'fairly' by making decisions for the 'good of the game' and not being influenced by external economic or political factors. As such, equity initiatives are often seen by long-serving local volunteers in England as merely pandering to excessive 'political correctness', or else as challenging the supposed view that sport 'is either naturally neutral in such considerations or a promoter of harmony'.[58]

Lincoln Allison notes that many British sports organizations were based on 'a cultural tradition which demands that "politics" is treated as dirty and peripheral in comparison to the interests of the club and the sport'.[59] This legacy clearly remains; changes implemented by The FA are often interpreted locally as a challenge to this perceived 'impartiality'. The E&SES asks for organizational responsibility for the exclusionary practice it claims exists in football. Failure to accept the existence of inequalities, let alone recognize the internal sources of exclusion, makes any commitment to pro-active strategies for change necessarily problematic. As I will show later, the inability to recognize inequalities within local football structures is also likely to lead to resistance to any policies aimed at tackling such disparities.

The social and cultural histories of English County FAs thus rely on embedded practices and ideologies, which mean that enforced external change is difficult to accommodate. In addition, I will suggest that these Victorian sporting ideologies harbour interpretations of 'race' that are more akin to initial encounters with the colonized 'other', than those better suited to contemporary multicultural Britain. As such, these ideologies exclude ethnic minorities within local football by both resisting change that is aimed at better accommodating the excluded, while also continuing to exclude others by calling upon traditional ideas of 'race'. These and other interpretations of 'race' are considered below, specifically with respect to the racialized power relations commonly experienced in local football governance in England.

Legitimizing power through 'race'

Castells'[60] theory of identity is particularly useful here. This approach identifies three key types of social identity: legitimizing, resistance and project identity.[61] Each has relevance to the contemporary power struggles of English local football. Firstly, *legitimizing* identities account for those who have an interest in maintaining the power status quo. They are central to this analysis as they connect the interests of the individual directly to the overarching structures and cultures found in English local football governance. As such, they remain personally loyal to the structural sources of exclusion related to ideas of 'race' central to the colonial politics of Victorian Britain. Secondly, *resistance*-based identities are common among the participants of local football who are placed *outside* the sources of power; people who may utilize 'race' strategically to challenge the exclusionary practice seen to be promoted by the local County FA. Finally, The FA Equity policy aims to impart a *project* identity, requiring everyone to 'seek the transformation of overall social structure',[62] as seen in The FA's slogan 'Football For All'.[63] This project identity appears to challenge the structures to which those already in power remain loyal, whilst encouraging a form of strategic essentialism[64] in the resistors.

While this legitimizing process is relatively easy to evidence, the forms of exclusion that it encourages are more complex. I identify three ways in which ideas of 'race' are utilized to legitimize power and continue to exclude ethnic minorities in English local football: 'race' denial, domination and derision. These interpretations of 'race' combine both older notions of European (colonial) racial science and hierarchy with more contemporary 'colour-blind' rhetoric, forming often contradictory processes of exclusion. This combination is particularly problematic as it is able to deflect any call for change, while simultaneously maintaining subtle, normalized forms of exclusionary practice.[65] Using illustrative quotes from interviews undertaken during case studies of two English County FAs, I explore below these various uses of 'race'.

The denial of 'race'

Long[66] has identified some of the forms that the denial of racism can take in British sport. These include arguments about 'merit': 'there have always been black players', 'if they're good enough they'll get in the team'; on character – 'everyone gets abused, you've got to learn to take it'; on transferring blame (i.e. ethnic minorities 'aren't interested'); and on social change – 'it was only a problem in the past'. Bourne[67] suggests the common institutional response to claims of racism in Britain is unequivocally to deny its existence, perhaps in fear of prosecution under UK equal opportunities legislation. This denial of internal racism is often accompanied by the denial of 'race' as a factor at all in local football.

Bonilla-Silva employs the concept of 'colour-blind racism'[68] to describe a shift, 'whereas white privilege was achieved through overt and usually explicitly racial practices, today it is accomplished through institutional, subtle and *non-racial means*'.[69] This practice relies on ideas of innate cultural difference, akin to Barker's 'new racism' thesis.[70] Thus, we should be wary when we see 'race' being claimed as irrelevant in local sport, as it often masks underlying processes of exclusion. The following example provides a typical account of colour blindness: ' I don't care if they're black or white, Asian or whatever. Get somebody on there who does a job, and helps run the league.'[71] This response alludes strongly to the meritocratic 'level playing field', a core historical feature of many sporting narratives across the globe.[72] It also connects to more contemporary anti-racist rhetoric that has become recently fashionable within English football, largely through high-profile campaigns such at *Kick It Out*.[73] Colour blindness is a key component of 'race' denial and it is often highlighted by the refusal to identify 'race' as an influencing factor on the playing field:

> It's just straight [sporting] rivalry, one trying to beat the other, irrespective of whether they're black, white, yellow, green or whatever.[74]

This approach interpolates with a commonly held view that when someone does claim racism in local sport – for example in a disciplinary case – it is more likely to be a 'heat of the moment' incident, a case of misidentified sporting banter. In the words of one local football club secretary in England, for example:

> The problem is, right, if you've got buck teeth and you're playing a game of football and you upset somebody, alright, somebody will say: 'You buck teeth bastard …' because that's the way of the world. And if you've got a black guy, you'll say: 'You black bastard!' Now, they're perhaps not being racist over there. It's just a comment because you are black and you are white. Or if you've got ginger hair, everybody calls you ginger.[75]

Such rivalry is seen here as purely 'sporting' and so quite unconnected to issues of 'race', and by implication, to racism. This approach to discrimination on the pitch has obvious implications for those charged with reporting incidents (referees), and those handling disciplinary cases involving racism (Council members). Moreover, as I explore later, the processes of denial make both local resistance on the basis of 'race' and racism, and the implementation of equity principles, very difficult to sustain, when those in control regularly avow apparently non-racialized, 'anti-racist' sentiments.

There are obvious parallels between notions of 'race' denial and white privilege. Long and Hylton[76] refer to the 'normalising' process of whiteness in local sport, whereby racialized privilege becomes so routine it is invisible to those who it empowers. For such people at least, it seems difficult to locate 'race' ideas in their own identity and immediate social relations; they are, in other words, 'raceless'.[77] Back, Crabbe and Solomos[78] show how such privilege can also be institutionalized, so that its structural location supersedes individual culpability or intention, again making it difficult to self-identify. Given Castells'[79] view that legitimizing identities are intertwined with the structural conditions they wish to perpetuate, we must consider racism in local sport not as a form of individual prejudice – as is so often the case in academia as it is in sports policy – but rather as part of a much wider system of social arrangements and ideologies.

Given that administrators and officials of English County FAs see themselves as part of an inherently anti-discriminatory, unbiased operation, 'new' equity principles are often viewed as being simply unnecessary. As such, any potential use of 'race' as a basis for change is seen as highly dubious, and is often interpreted as the sort of 'political correctness' which directly challenges cherished values and ideologies of meritocracy and apolitical amateurism. This helps explain why local responses to The FA's national equity strategy are invariably ones of suspicion. The denial of 'race' is thus one way in which those whose interests lie in maintaining the current system *rationally* reject the changes proposed by both the new equity strategies and by the local resistance of ethnic minority participants.

The domination of 'race'

We could take this colour-blind approach at face value and view it as a progressive development towards an all-inclusive English sporting utopia. Indeed, pointing to the success of black professional footballers in England in order to deny racism in the sport has some credence. While not without criticism in this respect,[80] professional sport does provide one of the few avenues for substantial black social mobility in western industrial societies. This colour-blind rhetoric thus requires problematizing in order to show how it can mask more subtle forms of exclusion that rely on ideas of 'race'.

Historical interpretations of 'race' that were bound to theories of racial science and European colonialism were integral aspects of the development of modern British sport at home and overseas.[81] These ideologies connect with the Victorian British sporting values upon which English County FAs were modelled and which continue to dominate in local associations. I explore below two ways in which these longer standing ideas of 'race' are used to rationalize the domination of local racialized participants.

- First, the problem of under-representation is often seen at the local level as the result of cultural *incompatibility* found among 'other' groups that are defined, among other things, by biological difference (such as skin colour), nationality and/or religion.
- Second, some ethnic minority participants are seen to lack the necessary knowledge and experience to be suited to governance work in local football. As such, they are often subjected to sustained processes of control and assimilation – processes of 'civilizing' – into this 'authentic' British footballing culture.

a)   Cultural incompatibility

As County FAs are invariably seen as 'open' and 'democratic' by their members, it follows that those outside must actively 'choose' not to become involved, or are simply unsuited to positions of power. This approach, one that 'transfers blame' of under-representation[82] onto ethnic minorities, is based on a premise of cultural and biological difference, which helps to legitimize the status quo. This essentializing of cultural difference here is a key component of hegemonic sporting cultures and discourses in Britain, as others have noted.[83] It is thus the *inherent* cultural tradition of non-participants that provides barriers to their involvement, along with their unwillingness to conform to hegemonic practice:

> The actual culture of certain minorities can hold them back to get involved. The Asian population, basically, are an insular population, certainly the older population, where you've still got the same old ways, their creed etc, etc. And they weren't into socialising outside of their situation.[84]

> If you've got a team of blokes playing hockey, 10 of them were Asian, because that's the game they played over there. Cos they've got no bloody grass over there! When they come over here ... why play soccer?[85]

It is interesting that both the comments above relate to British *South Asian* participants. This may be because of the relative willingness of black (African/Caribbean) British players to adopt dominant cultural practices; as King phrases it, by 'playing the white man'.[86] Indeed, the ability to concur with British football's peculiarly masculine cultural practices are said to constitute important aspects of black cultural resistance in British sport.[87]

The comments above also typically conceptualize British ethnic minorities as sports *players*, rather than in any other positions, particularly in those crucial 'behind the scenes' roles. This contingent acceptance is countered by the routine processes of discipline and sanction that the County FA in England uses to control its players. As this next section shows, the principle of control is a central component to the power relations of English local football, and it is a common reaction to the arrival of 'new' footballing communities in their particular locales.

b)   Continuing the 'civilizing mission'

D. Stanley Eitzen[88] outlines some of the many ways in which sport has been theorized as a form of social control. Victorian Britain is an era often quoted in this context. As the public schools of nineteenth century England began to embrace organized sport and leisure through ideas of 'muscular Christianity' and 'rational recreation',[89] so sport became merged with wider elite political projects of the time. Upon election in 1868 (just five years after the formation of The FA), British Prime Minister Gladstone pronounced his mission to 'pacify Ireland' using sport and leisure – including the offices of The FA – as central components.[90] Further afield, the rise of the nation-state in Europe and the associated Empire building through colonial expansion was also aided by sport and leisure. Colonial subjects faced civilizing missions that imparted the dominant cultural values of Britishness, often through the sporting contest.[91]

These long-standing connections between sport and the 'missionary spirit'[92] seem to linger today:

> We do get problems of misbehaviour. Some of them [ethnic minority players] seem to be on a very short fuse and some of them seem to have to learn how they can and can't behave on a football field. It could be that they are deprived anyway, the Eastern Europeans. It could just be the way they go on in their own environment, I don't know.[93]

As Holt[94] suggests, the Victorian culture of amateur sport in England was informed by the increasingly popular social-Darwinian theories of human evolution that posited the existence of discrete, unalterable 'races' of people, 'differentially endowed such that some were inherently superior to others'.[95] Thus, encounters with the racialized 'other' had the effect of reinforcing this hierarchy through both violent control and by imparting appropriate hegemonic ideologies. Not too much seems to have changed today:

> [This city] has a number of areas that are deprived ... immigrant population, asylum seeker population ... Whether it be sport or bible reading ... it can give them something to do. If they haven't got anything to do ... are they going to go out mugging or, you know, you just don't know what people do.[96]

I have shown that a key remit of the County FA is that of control; to implement rules and regulations, and to judge disciplinary cases and appeals. Cases here often resemble mini-court hearings and are often chaired by (early retiring) ex-police officers who provide a regular source for Council membership. Mention is made here of the importance of educating players into 'acceptable' English sporting cultural practice, as if following their Victorian school-master forefathers. This putative 'civilizing' mission in local sport gains particular resonance when directed at the racialized 'other'. Placed in the context of disciplinary cases involving players from the ethnic minorities, we can see how these particular ideas of 'race' can encourage uneven treatment in local football.

To summarize, ideas of cultural incompatibility and a desire to control the racialized 'other' provide two cautionary counters to the rhetoric of 'colour-blindness'. Here we begin to see how more subtle forms of exclusion operate to discourage the involvement of local minorities, particularly from positions involving powerful, decision-making duties. As King[97] and Burdsey[98] have shown, football networks regularly place the onus on the 'other' to confirm to the hegemonic codes of British football discourse. This process of 'othering' also provides another technique to legitimize power among those in current control of the local game. Constructions of the 'other' are, necessarily, connected to understandings of the self;[99] constructing a racialized 'other' who requires controlling and civilizing thus vindicates the self (in this case, FA Council members) as the most appropriate person(s) to control and educate the constructed 'other'.

Deriding 'race' as resistance

Rejecting the validity of 'race' as a credible source of resistance is another common technique used to legitimize power in English local football. Often called 'playing the race card', this derision of 'race'-based resistance is particularly common in disciplinary situations. Here, claims about the existence of racism are often seen as an illegitimate way to resist County FA decisions and policies. 'Race' is also claimed to be used by ethnic minorities to seek *unfair* privileges within English local football networks: 'There's loads of money going into ethnic football, and I tell you that does get the backs up of a lot of white clubs … You see, it's not an even basis.'[100]

These views also allow those in power to be cynical of policies aimed at encouraging ethnic minorities to have more of an active stake in the local game. Simply put, if 'race' and racism are denied as factors in English local football (for those in power at least), then any claims to make it an issue can be seen as political manipulation and an attack on the non-partisan 'amateur' ethos of the County FA. As one Council member states: 'They [ethnic minorities] feel that they are picked upon, singled out, judgement passed upon them because of that race card.'[101]

One prominent local Council member recalled a claim of racism from a referee at a disciplinary hearing. In so doing he highlights his own deep derision about 'race' that is worth recounting in full:

> I remember one – we used to call him Prince Monolulu – who were a ref[eree]. He was – I don't know – a Nigerian prince or something. Well I was chairman of a [disciplinary] meeting, and I kicked him out of the bloody meeting. And I have never come across a liar like him. Ooh, he were a killer! He says: 'The crowd got me', and all this, and: 'I was locked in a toilet because it kept me safe.' But when I found out, I [did] some research of me own. There were one man and a dog watching the match, you know what I mean?[102]

As already suggested, English County FAs rely on the basic premise that there is very little racism within the game. As such, when racism *is* claimed, Council members are prepared to go to some lengths to counteract such accounts. It is in their interests to deny existing racism in order to protect the very principles and values of meritocracy and fair play that historically underpin the County FA's mission. A legitimizing identity helps sustain these organizational values by embedding them into the significant voluntary commitment that those in power give, benevolently, to local football. Such claims about 'racism' are therefore also taken as personal attacks: 'I want them [ethnic minorities] to play football, but why people are emphasising the ethnic minority side of it – I think that, in my considered opinion, is causing a barrier.'[103]

The drive for change, such as that contained in The FA's equity strategy, is seen by some local FA officials as simply encouraging new problems and tensions. Those who attempt to resist racism locally, are seen, instead, to be using ideas of 'race' to undertake a more fundamental, and *illegitimate* political project. In other words, the use of 'race' here has an ulterior motive:

> If you're not careful, any [ethnic minorities] that do come forward are the more outspoken [ones] that don't want to go through the system, but want to break into having a platform for themselves.[104]

One explanation for this perceived illegitimacy of 'race'-based resistance is that for those in power, 'race' is likely to bear little relation to their own interpretations of privilege and status; a key feature of whiteness as a form of 'malevolent absence'.[105] When emphasized in this way, 'race' is therefore seen as a device used to claim unfair advantage and privilege, challenging not only the values of the County FA, but also the long standing power relations of local football governance.

Conclusions and implications

I suggested earlier that much social analysis, including studies on racism in sport, relies on a theory of racism as a form of individual prejudice.[106] It is tempting to locate contemporary racism – particularly in English local football – within a small number of aged individuals for whom multicultural Britain is a much less 'lived' experience than it has been for subsequent generations. But to do this neglects the structural sources of such discrimination. As Morgan reminds us:

> The organisation is not simply a passive recipient of racism; it actively reproduces it in many formal and informal ways. Organisational programmes to tackle racism should not, therefore, treat it simply as an expression of individuals' attitudes but as a set of institutionalised practices within the organisation and society as a whole.[107]

By shifting analysis onto the *structural* origins of such exclusionary practices, I have shown the important role that historical legacies of institutions perform in local sports governance. These organizations – in this case the English County FAs – harbour remarkably stable and uniform hegemonic ideologies of amateurism, fair play and meritocracy, derived from Victorian British values about sport. Moreover, these ideologies make important connections with residual ideas about 'race' which may help us better understand the exclusionary practice that exists in local football in England today. Castells' understanding of 'legitimizing identity'[108] helps to connect individual power, status and authority to the hegemonic structural ideologies from which such privilege derives. This approach highlights how theories of individual prejudice cannot, in themselves, account for the sustained processes of exclusion that continue to occur in English local football. It also suggests that such processes are likely to be maintained as long as they go unchallenged structurally.

The denial of 'race', through an overt colour-blind rhetoric, can clearly mask longer-standing interpretations of a racialized 'other'. These include ideas of 'race' associated with colonial domination,[109] alongside the 'new' racism characterized by notions of cultural incompatibility.[110] Deriding 'race' as a form of resistance in local football is a major barrier to implementing equity principles in this setting and connects with the previous uses of 'race' I have outlined. If 'race' is *denied* through colour-blind rhetoric, there is likely to be reinforced suspicion among the powerful when 'race' ideas are used to challenge them.

I have argued that a feeling of 'race-lessness'[111] is one process that makes the normalized privilege gained from racism invisible to those in power. 'Race' is thus interpreted as a political tool to gain unfair privilege. It is taken as a direct challenge to the dominant values of local sports bodies as 'apolitical' and 'neutral' organizations that demand legitimation. The FA in England should be commended for committing to a process of internal change that includes making the game more accessible to ethnic minorities. But to see this change occur at the local level, I would argue that we need a much more nuanced understanding of the multiple and contradictory uses of 'race' in the local context, alongside a better appreciation of the ways in which 'unrecognised, normalised, everyday racism can damage sport and its (potential) participants'.[112]

One of the biggest barriers for meaningful ethnic minority involvement in local football in England seems to be the inability of those in power locally to recognize the structural sources of 'race'-based inequalities. Until this occurs, local FA Council members are unlikely to embrace the change proposed by the FA's new equity strategy. Moreover, we cannot erase the complex historic, social and cultural conditions that have shaped local football governance in England. I would contend that it is the intense loyalties that such organizational structures both demand and receive from local power holders that must be both acknowledged and deconstructed before we can contemplate the sustainable and meaningful involvement of ethnic minorities in such English leisure settings.

Acknowledgments

This essay is based on research undertaken with the support of an ESRC CASE studentship in partnership with The (English) Football Association (number PTA-033-2004-00070). The author would like to thank John Williams at the University of Leicester for his assistance in constructing the essay.

Notes

1. Garland and Rowe, *Racism and Anti-racism*.
2. King, *Offside Racism*.
3. The term 'local' is used here to refer to non-professional, but generally organized local neighbourhood sport, often performed in open, public spaces.
4. Statistics taken from the FA website http://www.thefa.com/TheFA/TheOrganisation/.
5. Long, Hylton and Welch, *Part of the Game?*
6. Ibid. See also Welch, Spracklen and Pilcher, *Racial Equality in Football*.
7. The Football Association, *Ethics*.
8. Hamil *et al.*, *Football in the Digital Image*.
9. The Football Association, *Ethics*, 8.
10. Castells, *The Power of Identity*.
11. Birrell, 'Racial Relations'; Hylton, '"Race", Sport and Leisure'; Kivel, 'Leisure Experience'.
12. Bonilla-Silva, *White Supremacy*. Castells, *The Power of Identity*.
13. Barker, *The New Racism*, 12.
14. Bonnett, *Anti-Racism*.
15. For more on this, see Back, Crabbe and Solomos, 'Beyond the Racist/Hooligan Couplet'.
16. Carrington and McDonald, 'Whose Game Is It Anyway?', 50.
17. Williams, 'Rangers is a Black Club'.
18. Long and Hylton, 'Shades of White'; Long *et al.*, *Part of the Game?*; Long, Robinson and Spracklen, 'Promoting Racial Equality'.
19. Long, 'No Racism Here?'
20. See for example, Carrington and McDonald, '*Race*'; Jarvie, *Sport, Racism and Ethnicity*; MacClancy, *Sport, Identity and Ethnicity*.
21. Kivel, 'Leisure Experience and Identity', 81.
22. James, *Beyond a Boundary*.
23. Edwards, *Revolt of the Black Athlete*; Wiggins, 'The Year of Awakening'.
24. Booth, *The Race Game*.
25. Burdsey, 'One of the Lads?, 296.
26. Kivel, 'Leisure Experience and Identity'.
27. FIFA, *Activity Report*.
28. The Football Association, *Football Trends Report 2004*.
29. Putnam, *Bowling Alone*.
30. Williams, 'Rangers Is a Black Club', 160.
31. Burdsey, 'Obstacle Race?'
32. Bradbury and Williams, 'New Labour'.
33. See for details http://news.bbc.co.uk/sport1/hi/football/internationals/6753585.stm.
34. Long *et al.*, *Part of the Game?*
35. Burdsey, 'Obstacle Race?'.
36. Spracklen, ''Black Pearl'.
37. Carrington and McDonald, 'Whose Game Is It Anyway?'.
38. Ibid., 50.
39. Interview with Council Member, County FA 1, April 29, 2005.
40. Holt, *Sport and the British*, 98–117.
41. Dunning, *Sport Matters*, 54–61.
42. Handy, *Understanding Voluntary Organisations*, 85.
43. Young, *A History of British Football*.

44. Football participation is unlikely to have declined in real terms. The growth of private sector small-sided football centres and leagues that are beyond the control of The FA have accounted for much of the decline in local FA affiliated football.
45. Slack, 'The Bureaucratization of a Voluntary Sport Organisation'.
46. CFA Chief Executives are also charged with managing local development staff, although many initially chose (and some continue) a 'hands-off' approach to the staff, leaving them to follow National FA directives independently.
47. Interview with County FA Development Staff Member, September 2006.
48. The Football Association, *Football Development Strategy*.
49. The Football Association, *Ethics*.
50. See Garland and Rowe, *Racism and Anti-racism* for an overview of some of the key anti-racist campaigns in English football.
51. White, 'Sports Equity'; White, 'Campaigning for Equity'.
52. White, 'Sports Equity', 2.
53. The Football Association, *Football Development Strategy*, 3.
54. Bourne, 'The Life and Times'.
55. Welch, Spracklen and Pilcher, *Racial Equality in Football*.
56. Long, 'No Racism Here?'
57. McIntosh, *Fair Play*, 20–37.
58. Long, 'No Racism Here?', 122.
59. Allison, 'Sport and Civil Society', 715.
60. Castells, *The Power of Identity*.
61. Ibid., 8.
62. Ibid.
63. The Football Association, *Football for All*.
64. Spivak, *The Spivak Reader*.
65. See Bonilla-Silva, *White Supremacy*, 137–66.
66. Long, 'No Racism Here?'
67. Bourne, 'The Life and Times of Institutional Racism'.
68. Bonilla-Silva, 'Racial Attitudes'; Bonilla-Silva, *White Supremacy*.
69. Bonilla-Silva, *White Supremacy*, 12.
70. Barker, *The New Racism*.
71. Interview with Senior Administrator, County FA 1, April 20, 2005.
72. McIntosh, *Fair Play*.
73. Garland and Rowe, *Racism and Anti-racism*, 55–62.
74. Interview with Council Member, County FA 2, March 7, 2006.
75. Interview with a local club secretary, March 23, 2006.
76. Long and Hylton, 'Shades of White'.
77. Dyer, *White*.
78. Back, Crabbe and Solomos, *The Changing Face of Football*, 166–73.
79. Castells, *The Power of Identity*.
80. See, for example, Cashmore, *Black Sportsmen*; Hoberman, *Darwin's Athletes*.
81. See Beck, *Scoring for Britain*; Birley, *Sport and the Making of Britain*; James, *Beyond a Boundary*.
82. Long, 'No Racism Here?', 128.
83. See for example Back, Crabbe and Solomos, *The Changing Face of Football*; Bains and Patel, *Asians Can't Play Football*; Long, 'No Racism Here?'
84. Interview with Council member, County FA 1, April 18, 2005.
85. Interview with club secretary, March 23, 2006.
86. King, *Offside Racism*.
87. Carrington, 'Sport, Masculinity'.
88. Eitzen, 'Social Control and Sport', 370–81.
89. Holt, *Sport and the British*.
90. Birley, *Sport and the Making of Britain*, 263.
91. James, *Beyond a Boundary*.
92. Birley, *Sport and the Making of Britain*.
93. Interview with Council Member, County FA 1, April 19, 2005.
94. Holt, *Sport and the British*.
95. Solomos and Back, *Racism and Society*, 43.
96. Interview with Council Member, County FA 1, April 19, 2005.

 97. King, *Offside Racism*.
 98. Burdsey, 'One of the Lads?'
 99. Said, *Orientalism*'.
100. Interview with Council Member, County FA 2, March 7, 2006.
101. Ibid.
102. Ibid.
103. Interview with Council Member, County FA 1, April 20, 2005.
104. Interview with Council Member, County FA 2, March 7, 2006.
105. Garner, 'The Uses of Whiteness', 259–60.
106. Bonilla-Silva, *White Supremacy*, 21.
107. Morgan, *Organizations in Society*, 59.
108. Castells, *The Power of Identity*.
109. Miles and Brown, *Racism*.
110. Barker, *The New Racism*.
111. Dyer, *White*.
112. Long, 'No Racism Here?', 131.

References

Allison, L. 'Sport and Civil Society'. *Political Studies* XLVI (1998): 709–26.
Back, L., T. Crabbe, and J. Solomos. 'Beyond the Racist/Hooligan Couplet: Race, Social Theory and Football Culture'. *British Journal of Sociology* 50, no. 3 (1999): 419–42.
Back, L., T. Crabbe, and J. Solomos. *The Changing Face of Football*. Oxford: Berg, 2001.
Bains, J., and R. Patel. *Asians Can't Play Football*. Solihull: Midland Asian Sports Forum, 1996.
Barker, M. *The New Racism*. London: Junction Books, 1991.
Beck, P. *Scoring for Britain: International Football and International Politics 1900–1939*. London: Frank Cass, 1999.
Birley, D. *Sport and the Making of Britain*. Manchester: Manchester University Press, 1993.
Birrell, S. 'Racial Relations Theories and Sport: Suggestions for a More Critical Analysis'. *Sociology of Sport Journal* 6, no. 3 (1989): 212–27.
Bonilla-Silva, E. *White Supremacy and Racism in the Post Civil Rights Era*. London: Lynne Rienner, 2001.
Bonilla-Silva, E. 'Racial Attitudes or Racial Ideology? An Alternative Paradigm for Examining Actors' Racial Views'. *Journal of Political Ideologies* 8, no. 1 (2003): 63–82.
Bonnett, A. *Anti-Racism*. London: Routledge, 2000.
Booth, D. *The Race Game: Sport and Politics in South Africa*. London: Routledge, 1998.
Bourne, J. 'The Life and Times of Institutional Racism'. *Race and Class* 43, no. 2 (2001): 7–22.
Bradbury, S., and J. Williams. 'New Labour, Racism and "New" Football in England'. *Patterns of Prejudice* 40, no. 1 (2006): 61–82.
Burdsey, D. 'Obstacle Race? "Race", Racism and the Recruitment of British Asian Professional Footballers'. *Patterns of Prejudice* 38, no. 3 (2004): 279–99.
Burdsey, D. 'One of the Lads? Dual Ethnicity and Assimilated Ethnicities in the Careers of British Asian Professional Footballers'. *Ethnic and Racial Studies* 27, no. 5 (2004): 757–79.
Carrington, B. 'Sport, Masculinity and Black Cultural Resistance'. *Journal of Sport and Social Issues* 22, no. 3 (1998): 275–98.
Carrington, B., and I. McDonald, eds. *'Race', Sport and British Society*. London and New York: Routledge, 2002.
Carrington, B., and I. McDonald. 'Whose Game Is It Anyway? Racism in Local League Cricket'. In *'Race', Sport and British Society,* ed. B. Carrington and I. McDonald, 49–69. London: Routledge, 2001.
Cashmore, E. *Black Sportsmen*. London: Routledge & Kegan Paul, 1982.
Castells, M. *The Power of Identity*. 2nd ed. Oxford: Blackwell, 2004.
Dunning, E. *Sport Matters*. London: Routledge, 1999.
Dyer, R. *White*. London: Routledge, 1997.
Edwards, H. *Revolt of the Black Athlete*. New York: Free Press, 1970.
Eitzen, D. 'Social Control and Sport'. In *Handbook of Sports Studies,* ed. J. Coakley and E. Dunning, 370–81. London: Sage, 2000.
FIFA, *Activity Report: April 2002–March 2004*. Zurich: Fédération Internationale de Football Association, 2004.

Garland, J., and M. Rowe. *Racism and Anti-racism in Football.* Basingstoke: MacMillan, 2001.

Garner, S. 'The Uses of Whiteness: What Sociologists Working on Europe Can Draw from US Research on Whiteness'. *Sociology* 40, no. 2 (2006): 257–75.

Hamil, S., J. Michie, C. Oughton, and S. Warby. *Football in the Digital Image: Whose Game Is It Anyway?* Edinburgh: Mainstream Publishing, 2000.

Handy, C. *Understanding Voluntary Organisations.* London: Penguin, 1988.

Hoberman, John M. *Darwin's Athletes: How Sport Has Damaged Black America and Preserved the Myth of Race.* Boston, MA: Houghton Mifflin Co., 1997.

Holt, R. *Sport and the British.* Oxford: Oxford University Press, 1989.

Hylton, K. '"Race", Sport and Leisure: Lessons from Critical Race Theory'. *Leisure Studies* 24, no. 1 (2005): 81–98.

James, C.L.R. *Beyond a Boundary.* London: Serpent's Tail, 1967.

Jarvie, G., ed. *Sport, Racism and Ethnicity.* London: Falmer, 1991.

King, C. *Offside Racism: Playing the White Man.* Oxford: Berg, 2004.

Kivel, B. 'Leisure Experience and Identity: What Difference Does Difference Make?' *Journal of Leisure Research* 32, no. 1 (2000): 79–81.

Long, J. 'No Racism Here? A Preliminary Examination of Sporting Innocence'. *Managing Leisure* 5 (2000): 121–33.

Long, J., and K. Hylton. 'Shades of White: An Examination of Whiteness in Sport'. *Leisure Studies* 21, no. 1 (2002): 87–103.

Long, J., P. Robinson, and K. Spracklen. 'Promoting Racial Equality within Sports Organisations'. *Journal of Sport and Social Issues* 29, no. 1 (2005): 41–59.

Long, J., K. Hylton, and M. Welch. *Part of the Game? An Examination of Racism in Grass Roots Football.* London: Kick It Out, 2000.

MacClancy, J., ed. *Sport, Identity and Ethnicity.* Oxford: Berg, 1996.

McIntosh, P. *Fair Play: Ethics in Sport and Education.* London: Heinemann, 1979.

Miles, R., and M. Brown. *Racism.* 2nd ed. London: Routledge, 2003.

Morgan, G. *Organizations in Society.* Basingstoke: Palgrave MacMillan, 2001.

Putnam, R. *Bowling Alone: The Collapse and Revival of American Community.* New York: Simon & Schuster, 2000.

Said, E. *Orientalism: Western Conceptions of the Orient.* London: Penguin, 1995.

Slack, T. 'The Bureaucratization of a Voluntary Sport Organisation'. *International Review for the Sociology of Sport* 20, no. 2 (1985): 145–66.

Solomos, J., and L. Back. *Racism and Society.* Basingstoke: MacMillan, 1996.

Spivak, G. *The Spivak Reader.* London: Routledge, 1996.

Spracklen, K. 'Black Pearl, Black Diamonds: Exploring Racial Identities in Rugby League'. In *'Race', Sport and British Society,* ed. B. Carrington and I. McDonald, 70–82. London: Routledge, 2001.

The Football Association. *Football Development Strategy.* London: The Football Association, 2000.

The Football Association. *Ethics and Sports Equity Strategy.* London: The Football Association, 2004.

The Football Association. *Football for All.* London: The Football Association, 2004.

The Football Association. *Football Trends Report 2004.* London: The Football Association, 2004.

Welch, M., K. Spracklen, and A. Pilcher. *Racial Equality in Football: A Survey.* London: Commission for Racial Equality, 2004.

White, A. 'Sports Equity: A New Concept?' Paper presented at *Sport and Leisure Scotland Conference*, Scotland, 1991.

White, A. 'Campaigning for Equity'. Paper presented at *Institute of Leisure and Amenity Management (ILAM) Conference*, Blackpool, 1993.

Wiggins, D. 'The Year of Awakening: Black Athletes, Social Unrest and the Civil Rights Movement of 1968'. *The International Journal of the History of Sport* 9, no. 2 (1992): 199–208.

Williams, J., 'Rangers is a Black Club: "Race", Identity and Local Football in England'. In *Football, Identity and Modernity: Fans and Players in the World Game,* ed. R. Giulianotti and J. Williams, 153–83. Manchester: Manchester University Press, 1994.

Young, P. *A History of British Football.* London: Stanley Paul & Co, 1969.

North or South? Darron Gibson and the issue of player eligibility within Irish soccer

David Hassan, [a] Shane McCullough[a] and Elizabeth Moreland[b]

[a]School of Sports Studies, University of Ulster, Jordanstown, Northern Ireland; [b]University College Dublin, Ireland

Introduction

Soccer in Ireland has had a chequered history. This is a result of the complex way in which the sport has been organized on the island as well as tensions that emerged between the two rival governing bodies of the game, the Irish Football Association (IFA) and the Football Association of Ireland (FAI), following the partition of Ireland in 1922.[1] Reflecting upon aspects of this often fractious relationship, this essay will offer an analysis of the sporting and political tensions surrounding soccer in modern-day Northern Ireland. In particular, it will focus upon the issue of player selection and eligibility at international level, which has received considerable coverage in recent times following some high profile defections to the Republic of Ireland.[2] Indeed, it seems that talented young players from Northern Ireland are switching their allegiances to the Republic of Ireland in ever increasing numbers. It is apparent therefore that any analysis of soccer in Northern Ireland also requires an examination of the game in the Republic of Ireland. Players who have chosen to represent the latter rather than Northern Ireland in international soccer have exclusively emerged from the Catholic/nationalist community within Northern Ireland. In simple terms, they are choosing to play for the Republic of Ireland because they experience a greater degree of affinity with it than they do to the country of their birth.

A history of subjugation in Northern Ireland at the hands of the British state and sections of the majority Protestant community has left some Catholics wary of becoming overly acquiescent to life in this most westerly part of the United Kingdom.[3] Three decades of ethno-sectarian conflict during the latter part of the twentieth century has created a legacy of distrust and resentment between Catholics and Protestants, Nationalists and Unionists, which some sections of society in Northern Ireland have been reluctant to move away from. This is despite the signing of the Belfast/Good Friday peace accord in April 1998, which brought to an end a period of unprecedented change in the history of Northern Ireland. Thus whilst there has been a political settlement that has allowed the establishment of a devolved power-sharing executive and a return to some degree of 'normality' in the country, below the surface considerable tensions remain.[4] This manifests itself in a number of different ways. For example in the case of soccer a degree of rejectionism defines the attitude of some Catholic followers towards those governing the game in Northern Ireland.[5] Indeed whilst no single explanation can be offered as to why talented young soccer players from Northern Ireland's Catholic community are choosing to play for Republic of Ireland teams, there are clearly a number of interlocking issues motivating such a move. These include the nature of the communities in which players reside, family ties, political affiliations, personal and national identities (including social class), sporting pragmatism and, last but by no means least, the perception of the IFA held by some nationalists in Northern Ireland, which has rarely been favourable.[6]

Of course the ultimate arbitrator in this contentious matter is soccer's governing body Fédération Internationale de Football Association (FIFA). Article 15 of FIFA's Statutes outlines the principles under which players may be selected for association teams in international competition. It states that, 'Any person holding the nationality of a country is eligible to play for the representative teams of the Association of that country'.[7] In keeping with the terms of the Belfast/Good Friday Agreement, individuals born on the island of Ireland may, if they choose, declare themselves as being Irish, British or other. Hence young talented players from Northern Ireland may conceivably decide to adopt an Irish nationality and play for the Republic of Ireland. Reluctant to become embroiled in a sensitive, somewhat politically imbued issue, FIFA has always adopted a 'hands off' approach to the Irish situation. As a result the association has proved itself less than decisive when arbitrating on disputed cases between the two governing bodies in Ireland. However under pressure from the IFA, FIFA has recently provided some clarification on the issue of player eligibility in such cases. On 1 June 2008 FIFA ruled that any player wishing to play international football for the Republic of Ireland must have been born there, have a parent or grandparent born there, or have lived there continuously for two years. Whilst the IFA 'was glad that FIFA had clarified the issue' the FAI argued that nothing had changed on FIFA's stated position that any player from Northern Ireland is eligible to play for either Northern Ireland or the Republic of Ireland.[8] It appears agreement on this issue is some way off as a dispute that has served only to exacerbate an already troublesome relationship between soccer's governing bodies in Ireland gathers pace.

A history of soccer in Ireland

A codified version of soccer developed throughout Ireland in the late nineteenth century following its initial promotion by influential Anglo-Irish figures within the capital city, Dublin.[9] Sugden and Bairner argue that because soccer was regarded in many ways as the 'garrison' game by the indigenous community, an anathema for most Irish men and women, its significance lay more with those sympathetic to the Union with Britain including the large Protestant community in the north of Ireland.[10] As soccer became evermore popular, a governing body for the game, the IFA, was formed in Belfast in 1880. This was important because as a result of this decision the 'home' of Irish soccer had been established in Belfast rather than Dublin, where the majority of national governing bodies were located. From its inception, therefore, soccer sat apart from other sports in Ireland, which was to exercise a telling influence on the game's role as a medium of nationalist expression in the decades up to partition. Even on the field of play the principle contenders for the prestigious Irish Cup competition at this time were teams that relied heavily on serving British soldiers stationed in Ireland and/or sides from Belfast and its surrounding hinterlands.

Thus from the outset soccer was widely implicated in the promotion of a distinctive British sporting culture, which ran counter to the aims and objectives of rival, indigenous sporting entities.[11] Foremost amongst these was the Gaelic Athletic Association (GAA), a robust nationalist sporting body that advocated the playing of uniquely Irish sports and a rejection of activities that continued to promote a British presence in Ireland. The GAA placed a ban on its members participating in such 'foreign' sports, which essentially meant soccer, as interest in and the availability of other activities that might fall into this category was minimal. In the late nineteenth century the 'image of football that the rhetoric of the GAA helped to create', principally the view that soccer was a British game and therefore an affront to all right thinking Irish men, was the most explicit link between sport and politics in Ireland at that time.[12] Since then the GAA has had a significant role to play in perpetuating a more erstwhile, traditional form of Irish nationalism and even to this day is closely tied to what might be seen by some as a 'purer' form of Irish identity.[13] For this reason Gaelic Games remain a popular sporting choice for many Irish nationalists, particularly those in Northern Ireland. Here the formation of an Irish national identity has been the product of ongoing contestation and struggle with rival British political and cultural values.

As indicated earlier, the formation of the Irish Free State in 1922 also signalled an official break between the IFA and those involved with soccer in the south of the country. Indeed, Sugden and Bairner note that the impact of this division was to highlight the political and cultural divisions between the associations in the north and the south of Ireland.[14] These political implications were manifested primarily in the football relationships between the national teams of Northern Ireland and the Republic of Ireland, as well as relations between the two main communities living in Northern Ireland. Thus the establishment of two national teams on one island brought to the fore issues of identity and community affiliation, particularly for Catholics resident in Northern Ireland who were most affected by the decision to form two separate governing bodies for the sport.[15] That said, there is by no means a binary division between Catholics and Protestants in Northern Ireland when it comes to negotiating the role of soccer in the creation of national identity. As Guilianotti and Finn confirm, there is 'no simple, direct relationship between football culture and national identity' and this is no less true of the situation in Ireland.[16] Some Catholics in Northern Ireland are content to operate within the confines of the country and accept the right of the IFA to govern soccer there, whilst others hold the opposite view and resolutely oppose the association's attempts to exercise authority over the game. As if to highlight this point,

Guilianotti and Finn argue that 'while political and cultural elites try to employ the game to promote common senses of national identity, football will facilitate the repro-duction of social inequalities and the popular expression of conflict and difference'.[17] The expression of conflict and difference referred to here assumes a very real signifi-cance when one considers that the major international matches that have taken place between Northern Ireland and Republic of Ireland over the last three decades, espe-cially those played in 1978, 1979, 1988, 1989 and infamously in 1993, required considerable security measures and restrictions on travelling supporters.[18]

It appears that in general the international sporting arena is a ready vehicle through which to unpack contentious debates surrounding national identity and, more specifi-cally, citizenship.[19] Discussions concerning national identity highlight the civic and ethnic aspects of nationalism to which people relate as a means of ascertaining the extent of their citizenship of a particular country. To divide these concepts though is arguably to create a false imposition on the process of identity construction. Instead it is more accurate to consider the civic and ethnic approaches as part of a broader continuum of identity, recognizing the influences of both on an individual's personal make-up. Eligibility for either of the two international teams on the island of Ireland stretches the boundaries of civic nationhood. Arguably the Republic of Ireland soccer team, particularly over the last two decades, is the most salient example of how citi-zenship legislation has been exploited in order to select leading players who have not been claimed by the country of their birth.[20] That said for some considerable time following partition, indeed up until the mid-1950s, the 'two Irelands' continued to select players from the entire island and in so doing paid very little attention to the directives issued by FIFA on this matter. Indeed, as the latter part of this essay will make clear, the stance adopted by FIFA to the Irish 'situation' has offered little in the way of clarity regarding the issue of player eligibility. In contrast its attitude has been defined by one of benign engagement and gentle encouragement aimed at diffusing an ever growing sense of suspicion between the two national associations on the island. Its success in doing so has been negligible and has served only to provide confusion where clarity and leadership is required.

Therefore international soccer in Ireland offers something of a dilemma in terms of Irish identity, as the existence of two separate representative sides on the interna-tional stage challenges the legitimacy of a traditional definition of Irish nationalism. In its place a form of 'state based' identity is revealed, even if such divisions carry little currency in a divided society. This view is supported by Cronin who argues that the Republic of Ireland soccer team is an example of a statist version of nationalism in that it was formed around the boundaries of a political state, i.e. the Irish Free State and later the Republic of Ireland. He argues that the FAI 'built its identity around the nation state, and not, as with the GAA, a mythical ideal of the nation'.[21] This is an interesting point as although the creation of a national identity associated with soccer was based on the idea of the nation state, the players who came to embody this identity during the team's heyday, throughout the late 1980s and 1990s, emerged from a vari-ety of 'national' backgrounds. That it did so required the support of the game's governing body, the FAI, as it appeared willing to adopt a very flexible interpretation of eligibility, no doubt under the influence of its head coach at the time, Jack Charlton. Indeed it is precisely this view of the FAI as a governing body that is somewhat nonchalant about the issue of player eligibility, which arguably has created the most difficulty for its contemporaries in Northern Ireland. The latter appear uncertain as to whether the FAI is genuinely interested in achieving a satisfactory resolution to the dispute over this issue or are deliberately procrastinating in order to benefit from the talents of players who otherwise would have no option but to play for Northern Ireland or withhold their services altogether.

Soccer and northern nationalists

One of the key features to have emerged within Irish soccer over the last 20 years has been a new sense of sporting nationalism amongst certain sections of the Irish people. The Republic of Ireland soccer team draws its support base from members of the Irish Diaspora, large numbers of Catholics (nationalists) resident in Northern Ireland, as well as its traditional fan base in the Republic of Ireland.[22] The support from northern nationalists is particularly important when unpacking issues surrounding national identity, as well as matters of political and community affiliation. Although northern nationalists are not politically conjoined to the Republic of Ireland, resident as they are outside its state borders, by supporting the team the northern nationalist community is able to 'negotiate their (northern) Irish nationalist identities and, in the process, construct a sense of shared nationalist meaning amongst the broader Catholic community'.[23] In this sense it could be argued that the identity available through association with the Republic of Ireland soccer team is not concerned with boundaries established along territorial lines but exists instead in the minds of those who would attach themselves emotionally to its broader constituency. International soccer does not present many opportunities for this type of behaviour. Only in divided societies do citizens feel suitably compelled to publicly display their allegiances to a rival nation, in this case one that as recently as 1997 had held a territorial claim over their place of residency. Whilst all states contain within their boundaries those whose allegiances rest with other nations, the absence of a political dimension to such behaviour means that considerably less significance is afforded such activity. In contrast where the shifting of sporting allegiances appears to have, as their very basis, a political undertone, issues of national identity are rarely far from the surface.

The nuances apparent within the Irish situation have been discussed by Fulton who notes that 'paradoxically, their [northern nationalists] affinity with the Republic Ireland is both premised on the existence of the border, and is a means through which it can be deconstructed'.[24] The support for the Republic of Ireland team by northern nationalists lends recognition to the political border despite their opposition to the separation of Ireland. However, this affiliation with the Republic of Ireland team also demonstrates a rejection of Northern Ireland as their support 'introduces a sense of aspirational nationalism, an allegiance to a 32 county independent Republic … (and thereby) imposes a more complicated relationship between soccer and Irish sporting nationalism'.[25] However, the precise nature of this 'aspirational nationalism' is interesting as, in the minds of many Irish republicans living in Northern Ireland, a divided Ireland in which 26 counties form the Republic of Ireland and the remaining six constitute Northern Ireland, still falls short of their ultimate demand for a united and sovereign 32-county Irish state. This occasionally leads to the refrain '26 are as bad as 6' when explaining their unwillingness to support either of the two international teams on the island.[26] Instead the 'aspiration' to which Fulton refers may be more about a narrowly defined view of Irish identity, one that is free from the spectre of Unionism, is essentially Catholic and at ease with its own constitution.[27] There is a sense that support for the Republic of Ireland, indeed for those talented enough to be able to choose, opting to play for the 'south', is as much a rejection of the social and political make up of Northern Ireland as an independent political entity as it is a reflection of sporting expediency, designed to improve the careers of those who recognize an opportunity to improve their earning potential by courting the attention of Europe's leading club sides.

Thus, in its widest sense, support for the Republic of Ireland team by northern nationalists and the Irish Diaspora could also be regarded as diluting the idea of a state-based identity for the Republic of Ireland. However, Fulton argues that its international soccer team has in fact offered a 'vehicle for the expression of a specifically southern brand of nationalism' and suggests that the fan base outside of the nation state is subsumed as part of the Republic of Ireland and not necessarily acknowledged in its own right.[28] This may be because despite citizens of the Republic of Ireland having negotiated their own separate form of southern nationalism (which is represented by its soccer team), this does not mean that others cannot affiliate with this particular form of Irish identity, merely that they then attach their own interpretation to it. What is important is that soccer has 'helped to challenge the notion of a single Irish national identity' and provides the opportunity for Irish people to celebrate their national identity in an unrestrained fashion.[29] Evidently, there is not a single view of Irish nationalism or Irish national identity to which the people of Ireland can agree, but rather a number of co-existing ideas are present which at times overlap and contradict one another. Maguire's assertion that 'instead of viewing a person's identity as fixed and immovable, it is more appropriate to view identity as a plural process subject to change' can be readily applied to Irish sporting identity, not least when examining the case of soccer.[30]

Of late there have been a number of examples of players from Northern Ireland who have offered their allegiances to the Republic of Ireland soccer team. Even more remarkable is a situation in which certain players contracted to the same professional club, Derry City FC, have simultaneously declared for Northern Ireland and the Republic of Ireland when given a free choice of which team to play for. Although the affairs of Derry City FC offers a unique insight into the politics of sport in Northern Ireland, there is still something exceptional about the decision of players on the same team, emerging from very similar socio-economic and political backgrounds, to declare for different international teams.[31] A number of theories can be forwarded in an attempt to explain what appears to be quite a personal decision on the part of individual players. In the main these can be loosely broken down to reflect the influences of distinctive political, cultural and economic issues.

The first of these relates to an affiliation with the Republic of Ireland soccer team for reasons of personal and national identity. For many northern nationalists the Republic of Ireland team offers a more tangible link to the sort of Irish identity they wish to promote in comparison to that offered by the Northern Ireland team. Eddie Mahon, who has been central to the re-emergence of Derry City FC and its acceptance into the Eircom League of Ireland in 1985, argues that northern nationalist players sense the 'Northern Ireland team (has) more of a British ethos or Protestant ethos'.[32] This assertion that the Northern Ireland team is more representative of the Unionist community in the country has been a consistent theme of soccer in that part of Ireland since 1922. Indeed a view exists amongst some northern nationalists that the IFA has been complicit in the fostering of this image and this has led to some members of this community outwardly rejecting soccer's governing body in the 'north'.[33] The political climate in Northern Ireland has meant that in the past a number of Catholic players have received sectarian abuse whilst playing at Windsor Park, the venue for Northern Ireland's home international games. Mahon contends that this has been a cause for concern amongst young players. He notes

> Over the years Windsor Park hasn't been a very friendly place for Irish Catholics. Anybody who has ever played for (Glasgow) Celtic like Allen McKnight and Neil Lennon have had to pack it in because they have got booed out of Windsor Park. So obviously with a background like that, you don't even have to be political, you just don't want any aggravation and a lot of these young guys have a far greater chance to get capped for Northern Ireland than the south but they don't want the aggravation of going up there (from Derry to Belfast) and being booed off the pitch.[34]

Here Mahon confirms that the players are not basing their decisions to reject Northern Ireland soccer on political grounds *per se* but rather that issues imbued with political undertones effect their decision-making process. Thus, in the case of some young northern nationalists, declaring for Northern Ireland may constitute much more of an issue than for others from the same section of society. In practice such a decision is also likely be informed by the wishes of their families and friends as well as the immediate locality in which they reside.

The period from 1986 to 1998, commonly referred to in Irish soccer history as the 'Charlton Era' brought about a new found success for the Republic of Ireland team. The novel and inventive style of management offered by former England World Cup winner Jack Charlton resulted in the team qualifying for its first ever European Championships held in Germany in 1988 and subsequently for World Cup finals staged in Italy (1990) and the USA (1994). The legacy of Ireland's glorious failure continues to resonate with some northern nationalists for whom a contrast between the heroic achievements of Charlton's men and the continued underachievement of the Northern Ireland side exercise a powerful influence. With (relative) success brings a level of prestige and for many young footballers the opportunity to be included in a squad that they perceive as having a greater international standing (even if this is not actually the case according to FIFA's current rankings) than the team representing their place of birth is also an important consideration. Whereas a large number of those playing for the Republic of Ireland are currently contracted to Premier League clubs in England, the players selected to play for Northern Ireland emerge in the main from the comparatively less glamorous surroundings of lower league football.

Together these political, cultural and economic factors combined offer the basis of an explanation as to why a player from Northern Ireland may choose to play instead for the Republic of Ireland team. However, there are also those Catholics who decide to remain loyal to the Northern Ireland team and in doing so follow in the footsteps of players like Martin O'Neill, Pat Jennings and Gerry Armstrong, amongst the side's most decorated performers. The smaller pool of players in Northern Ireland means that the chances of getting selected for the team at international level are significantly higher than is the case with the Republic of Ireland. That said young northern nationalists are still prepared to declare for the Republic of Ireland, which continues to sit uneasily with IFA officials. Whilst there have been several defections over recent years it appears none has received as much publicity as that of the young Derry player, Darron Gibson, whose decision to declare for the Republic of Ireland provoked an unprecedented reaction from IFA officials.

**A bridge too far? player eligibility, the two Irelands and the case of
Darron Gibson**

Darron Gibson is a 21-year-old footballer contracted to the 2008 UEFA Champions
League winners, Manchester United FC. Given the depth of midfield talent at United,
the prospects of him establishing a place in the club's first team at present are slim.
As a consequence, the player has been loaned to Wolverhampton Wanderers FC, a
former force in the game but now languishing in the second tier of the English leagues.
However, despite his relative inexperience, Gibson has already gained the distinction
of representing the Republic of Ireland at senior international level, having played in
the qualifying campaign for the European Championships held in Austria and
Switzerland in June 2008, and was recently listed in *The Observer* newspaper as one
of the 'ten best players outside the English Premier League'.[35] Whilst this recognition
bears testament to his undoubted ability and potential, his selection by the Republic of
Ireland has caused considerable controversy, not least because he was born and raised
in Northern Ireland and had already represented that country at Under 16 and Under
17 levels.

Despite the strident protestations of the IFA, who also lays claim to the player,
Gibson's defection to the Republic of Ireland appeared to have the tacit approval of
FIFA. This happened despite Gibson's decision being in breach of FIFA's own statutes and indeed directly contravening the latter's apparent 'clarification' issued in
June 2008. That said, as has become implicit in this essay thus far, these regulations
vacillate to such an extent that they have become increasingly vague and open to interpretation and occasional abuse. Instead it appears Gibson has benefited from developments in the political domain, which have precious little to do with the effective
governance of the global game.

The Good Friday agreement has smoothed Gibson's chosen path and, while the
agreement has brought a decade of peace to Northern Ireland, it has left certain sporting bodies on the edge of civil war. The agreement's provision for the shared British/
Irish birthright and the 'parity of esteem' for both Irish and British cultures meant
Gibson was free to choose whether to represent Northern Ireland or the Republic and
leave the IFA and FAI to fight over the implications.[36]

Until relatively recently FIFA's statutes in respect of eligibility appeared straight-
forward. A player was deemed eligible to represent a country if:

(1) He (the player) was born on the territory of the relevant Association;
(2) His biological mother or biological father was born on the territory of the
    relevant Association;
(3) His grandmother or grandfather was born on the territory of the relevant
    Association;
(4) He has lived continuously for at least two years on the territory of the relevant
    Association.

The problem in this case however was that Gibson met none of these stipulations
when opting to play for the Republic of Ireland. FIFA's revised regulations, however,
are more convoluted and their ambiguity, seemingly designed to give it license to
arbitrate in disputed cases, have only created loopholes that players and national
governing bodies have been willing to exploit.

Prior to the Gibson controversy there have been surprisingly few cases that have
brought this matter into such sharp relief. This may be testament to the FAI's restraint

in the pursuit of Northern Irish players, although this stance was in part obligated by the IFA's persistent antagonism in the face of such a clear threat to its sovereignty. The FAI's selection of Manchester City's Alan Kernoghan in 1993 tested the patience of the IFA, although the fact that he was actually born in England muddied the waters sufficiently to obscure the specifics of the case. Having moved to Northern Ireland, the birthplace of his mother, at an early age, he worked his way into that country's U16 and U18 international squads before opting for the Republic of Ireland when approached by the aforementioned Jack Charlton. At the time FIFA's regulations governing eligibility were somewhat less contrived than they are at present. However, despite this and in common with the Darron Gibson case, Kernoghan again met none of the stipulated criteria required to declare for the Republic of Ireland team. This clearly was of little concern to Charlton and the FAI who had adopted an aggressive corporate strategy in the recruitment of players and in so doing had dispensed with any semblance of political sensitivity amid a pursuit of global sporting respectability.

It is arguable that FIFA has been further complicit in the dilution of nationhood by countenancing a policy of widening access to international football. This serves to benefit small countries whose populations and football infrastructures make it difficult for them to produce competitive teams. The redistribution of talent from those countries with an excess to the benefit of those with precious little does not appear problematical from a football perspective as it serves to raise standards and offers players an incentive to showcase their talent on the international stage. However, recent speculation linking Arsenal's Spanish-born goalkeeper Manuel Almunia with an England call-up is an illustration of how controversial FIFA's current statutes have become. The fact that this may compromise individual patriotism and national heritage appears of little consequence to those operating within the professional game. That said, as other codes, notably the sport of Rugby Union, adopt interpretations of eligibility that are even more unfettered than those employed by FIFA, it appears that the Gibson case may merely prove to be the first of many in the years ahead.

The IFA, however, has been slow to embrace FIFA's generosity, seemingly reluctant to sully a national identity that has been persistently debated, undermined and/or threatened. Rather than exploit what was euphemistically referred to as the 'grand-parent rule', the IFA chose for some time to ignore it, this form of selection to the national team clearly being too nebulous for the somewhat conservative administrators of the IFA. Arguably such idealism now has little place in international football and the current manager, Nigel Worthington, recognizes that every effort must be made to unearth talented players who possess even the most tenuous link to the Province.

Nigel Worthington is resisting renewed calls to select only players born in Northern Ireland. The international manager is under pressure in some quarters to stick with home-bred stars but insists: 'I'll continue to spread the net in search of eligible players. It doesn't matter to me where they were born, whether in England or elsewhere, just as long as they meet the criteria outlined by FIFA.'[37]

Political pressure on the IFA has led to an ongoing policy of protecting the British identity of Northern Ireland's Protestant majority, a move that has, as a result, alienated the Catholic minority. For many, the adoption of the Union Jack as the team's flag and 'God Save the Queen' as the national anthem of choice demonstrates a calculated disregard for northern nationalists.[38] The IFA's decision to enter into a 99-year lease agreement with Linfield FC for the staging of international matches, a club that for many years was the antithesis to Irish nationalism, was further evidence of a unionist agenda that served to promote the football team as a symbol of British sovereignty in Northern Ireland. The location of Windsor Park, in the staunchly loyalist 'Village' area of south Belfast, presented a further barrier to nationalist engagement and instead facilitated the colonization of the national team by a vocal minority of openly sectarian supporters who often diverted attention from football and focused it instead on anti-Catholic vitriol.

That said, the IFA deserves considerable praise for the pro-active stance it has adopted in tackling the issue of community relations in Northern Ireland football and transforming the atmosphere at international games. Indeed, the sea-change has been such that Northern Ireland supporters were recently voted the best in Europe by UEFA and tickets for international fixtures at an inadequate 'national stadium' are at a premium. Despite this positive progress, the political and cultural vagaries of Ireland are such that the antagonism and suspicion cultivated over centuries will not be readily dispersed. Indeed, it is ironic that having come through a particularly fractious era comparatively unscathed in terms of footballing defections, the IFA is now threatened by Darron Gibson's decision to de-camp to the Republic of Ireland. The FAI has demonstrated its willingness to fully exploit the loophole it perceived FIFA prevarication as having created, and further risked the ire of the IFA, by selecting Northerners Tony O'Kane, Marc Wilson and Michael O'Connor for a Republic of Ireland U21 squad. The inclusion of O'Connor is particularly pertinent given that he has already represented Northern Ireland six times at this level, including competitive internationals, and as such he should not have the option of transferring his allegiance under FIFA's own statutes.

Clearly FIFA's regulations have again been superseded by the politics central to a convoluted Irish peace process:

> On October 20th, FIFA's Heinz Tainler, Director of Legal Services, and Corina Luck, Head of General Legal, wrote a joint letter to the IFA, which was copied to the FAI … In it they informed the IFA that 'the existing situation in Northern Ireland allows players to choose whether they represent Northern Ireland or the Republic of Ireland'.[39]

Indeed, the threat of further players declaring for the Republic of Ireland may be even greater if the views expressed in a reader's letter published in the *Belfast Telegraph*, Northern Ireland's biggest selling daily newspaper, are to be countenanced.

> It is only a matter of time before other players from all backgrounds in the North (Northern Ireland) follow Darron's example and opt to play international football in a plush modern stadium in front of 50,000 plus multicultural, apolitical fan base, away from the decrepit environs of Windsor Park and the monoculturally supported IFA team.[40]

The IFA, naturally alarmed at the loss of its leading players, has mounted a vigorous campaign to force FIFA to abide by its own regulations and in so doing solicited a review of its current policy on player eligibility from the governing body. Merely holding a passport does not, it now appears, offer sufficient entitlement to merit selection.

> FIFA's Executive Committee overturned a proposal made by their top legal minds six weeks ago which would have allowed a player born anywhere in Ireland to chose whether to represent Northern Ireland or the Republic. At a meeting in Tokyo on Saturday world football's top brass elected to leave the rule unchanged and both the Irish FA and the FA of Ireland then claimed victory in the wrangle.[41]

This apparent lack of firm governance on the part of FIFA may be seen as indicative of policies so poorly defined and regulated that players can interpret and manipulate them to suit their own ends. Governing bodies could also be taken to task given their willingness to embrace those football exiles who wantonly defect to a country with which they have no actual affiliation. Qatar's policy of offering talented young Brazilian players domicile and passports appears to have alerted FIFA to the lengths some associations may go to exploit apparent flexibility in the current regulations. Significantly, the IFA has re-enlisted O'Connor and Kane, both players perhaps enticed by the promise of elevation to the senior international squad. There was speculation at the time that the IFA may attempt to coerce Gibson back into its fold, although this has proved to be unfounded.[42] On the other hand it may equally be content to 'sacrifice' Gibson and draw a line under the whole affair if the haemorrhaging of players can be abated. The IFA must, therefore, solicit from FIFA an unequivocal ruling that will halt this drain on its resources and also erase the political spectre dominating this case.

It is important not to lose sight of the individual in such debates and thereby retain a degree of sympathy for Gibson, whose motives differ radically from players like Englishmen Tony Cascarino (88 caps for Republic of Ireland) or Vinny Jones (ex-captain of Wales) who frantically researched their genealogy to unearth a national identity they didn't know existed. Where the Gibson scenario contrasts with these and other such examples is that the player himself is not a footballing free agent seeking repatriation, but rather an innocent victim of a tribal tug-of-war. As a Manchester United player, Gibson has a potential international pedigree that the respective governing bodies north and south of the Irish border will fight to retain. In his case though the IFA can perhaps claim the moral high ground in that not only was he born in Northern Ireland but he came through its development programmes and junior international squads. The IFA clearly contributed significantly to his football education and invested time and resources to provide him with opportunities to hone his talent. Indeed Gibson captained the Northern Ireland Under 15 and Under 16 international squads and was tipped as a potential future senior international captain. His elevation to the Under 17 squad whilst still eligible for the Under 16 side did, however, raise the prospect of him having to face a 'point of no return' by playing in an officially sanctioned competitive fixture and so, after featuring in a handful of U17 'friendly' internationals, he opted to return to the U16 squad. According to Shane McCullough, one of the co-authors of this essay and Gibson's international team manager at U16 level, the player appeared to lack full commitment to playing for Northern Ireland when asked to step up to a higher grade.

> To my mind Darron's demeanour and his level of commitment at this point was not what it had been and I believe that the IFAs decision to select him for U17 UEFA fixtures had forced a career decision upon him too soon. Given time to form an affinity with players his own age Darron may have chosen a different path but having been forced to make a career-defining choice at such a young age his instinct was to back away. The FAI was a willing recipient of his talents and is seemingly keen to capitalise further upon the license it perceives it has been granted by FIFA.[43]

Michael O'Connor, a rising star at Crewe Alexander FC, also played for and captained the same U16 side as Gibson and his apparent willingness to renounce his Northern Irish roots when called upon by the Republic of Ireland's U21 team clearly alerted the IFA to the scale of the threat it faced from Dublin. Raised in the staunchly nationalist Whiterock estate in west Belfast, O'Connor was ill at ease at having to stand to attention for the playing of 'God Save the Queen' as part of the preliminaries to the 'Victory Shield' home internationals televised 'live' on Sky television. Being placed in such a compromising position is likely to influence the thoughts of any young player and it is apparent, therefore, that the IFA needs to radically rethink how it manages the aspirations of all those coming through its ranks. According to Michael Boyd, Community Relations Officer with the IFA,

> I think the whole issue is a potential 'banana skin' for the IFA. We need to treat the problem like a mirror and ask the hard question as to why some players from Northern Ireland would rather play for the Republic of Ireland – then we need to remove as many of the barriers to inclusion as we can.[44]

Much has been made of FIFA's indecision in the Gibson case but the governing body's dalliance is a consequence of the disorientation experienced by most outsiders when confronted with the question of Irish identity. As with the recent political settlement in Northern Ireland, the answer to such a complex and contested issue lies not with an external body such as FIFA but with the two parties at the heart of the dispute. Arguably the FAI has been too willing to capitalize upon a disputed piece of legislation and may be accused of lacking ethical integrity and common courtesy towards their northern neighbours, particularly given the role played by the IFA in the development of players that the FAI have claimed to be rightly theirs.

The IFA, meantime, has done little to tackle the issues that have led to a flow of talent across the border into the welcoming arms of the FAI. This sporting 'Cold War' will not have the catastrophic consequences of the recent ethno-sectarian conflict in Northern Ireland that claimed over 3,000 lives, but football's two ruling bodies in Ireland need to recognize that they have a social responsibility that supersedes a desire to produce winning teams. As such they should strive to find common ground and a shared understanding of the issue of identity that will demonstrate a willingness to reflect the efforts of those in the political domain by moving forward to a settled future rather than embracing the tribalism of the past.

Conclusion

Sport offers a framework for people to build allegiances to their nation or nation-state and to each other. In this case the emergence of two separate governing bodies in Ireland clearly had implications for the use of soccer as a game around which players and spectators could cohere. This was especially true for those who wished to use it as a means of promoting their national identity. The idea of boundary marking, implicit within sport in a divided context, is particularly pertinent when discussing soccer in Ireland. Although both national teams are clearly established within political jurisdictions, support and identification with either team in the international setting and their respective national identities have much wider appeal.

The decision of young Catholics from Northern Ireland to turn their backs on the chance to represent the country of their birth at senior international level is a worrying trend for those governing the game there. Their decisions are essentially the product of socio-political issues where the views of significant others, including the player's perception of his role as a community representative, holds considerable sway. What appears, on the face of it, to be a domestic dispute assumes a wider significance when one considers the role of soccer's governing body, FIFA, in this issue of player eligibility. A failure to properly identify the conditions under which a player may declare for an Association other than the one that they may naturally be assigned through birth remains problematical. It is apparent that such prevarication will have further impact in other national settings throughout the world.

Whilst the IFA was understandably upset with the loss of some of its players to the Republic of Ireland during the 1990s and early part of the current decade, it was not until Darron Gibson, a player contracted to English team Manchester United FC, decided to defect that it became a major diplomatic incident. Relationships between the IFA and the FAI have, on the face of it, been relatively cordial but the Gibson case has soured this considerably. Yet Gibson may argue he is merely interested in pursuing his career within a context he feels more comfortable with and, in their current format, the FIFA statutes allow him to do exactly this. In all likelihood though, his decision simply confirms that some northern nationalists still have reservations about the IFA, the Northern Ireland football team and their place within society generally. Whilst the IFA has been lobbying FIFA to issue more stringent directives to the FAI about the recruitment of players they believe to be rightfully theirs, its arguable that a more effective use of the IFA's time would be to remove the barriers young Catholics like Gibson face when deciding whether or not to represent the country of their birth in the international domain.

Notes

1. Brodie, *100 Years of Irish Football*.
2. A recent example of this includes 'FIFA Rules on Player Eligibility', www.news.bbc.co.uk/sport.
3. Gallagher, 'After the War Comes Peace?', 633.
4. Ibid., 636–7.
5. Hassan, 'A People Apart', 66.
6. Ibid., 68.
7. *FIFA Statutes*, 60.
8. 'FIFA Rules on Player Eligibility'.
9. Brodie, *100 Years of Irish Football*.
10. Sugden and Bairner, *Sport, Sectarianism and Society*.
11. Ibid.
12. Fulton, 'Northern Catholic Fans', 142.
13. Fahy, *How the G.A.A. Survived*.
14. Sugden and Bairner, *Sport, Sectarianism and Society*.
15. Hassan, 'A People Apart', 66.
16. Giulianotti and Finn, 'Epilogue', 260.
17. Ibid., 260.
18. Sugden and Bairner, *Sport, Sectarianism and Society*.
19. Bairner, 'Sportive Nationalism', 315.
20. Cronin, *Sport and Nationalism*.
21. Ibid., 124.
22. Fulton, 'Northern Catholic Fans'.
23. Ibid., 152.
24. Ibid., 153.
25. Hassan, 'Sport and National Identity', 200.
26. Ibid., 201.
27. Fulton, 'Northern Catholic Fans'.
28. Ibid., 140.
29. Holmes, 'Symbols of National Identity', 83.
30. Maguire, 'Globalization, Sport', 295.
31. Platt, *A History of Derry City*.
32. Interview with Edward Mahon, 11 January 2008.

33. Hassan, 'A People Apart', 73.
34. Ibid.
35. 'Sport Monthly Magazine'. *The Observer*, February 3, 2008, 16.
36. 'Player Eligibility Row Rumbles On'. *The Sunday Times*, April 13, 2008, 5.
37. 'Gibson Case still Unsolved'. *The Sunday Life*, March 30, 2008, 104.
38. Hassan, 'A People Apart'.
39. BBC Sport Website, www.bbc.co.uk/ni/sport (accessed May 6, 2008).
40. *The Belfast Telegraph*, April 17, 2008.
41. *The Belfast Telegraph*, December 17, 2007.
42. 'Gibson to return to North', *The Sunday Times*, August 26, 2007, 13.
43. Interview with Shane McCullough, May 5, 2008.
44. Interview with Michael Boyd, May 6, 2008.

References

Bairner, Alan. 'Sportive Nationalism and Nationalist Politics: A Comparative Analysis of Scotland, the Republic of Ireland, and Sweden'. *Journal of Sport and Social Issues* 20, no. 3 (1996): 314–34.

Brodie, Malcolm. *100 Years of Irish Football.* Belfast: Blackstaff Press, 1980.

Cronin, Mike. *Sport and Nationalism in Ireland: Gaelic Games, Soccer and Irish Identity since 1884.* Dublin: Four Courts Press, 1999.

Fahy, Desmond. *How the G.A.A. Survived the Troubles.* Dublin: Merlin Publishers, 2001.

FIFA Statutes 2007. Zurich: FIFA, 2007.

Fulton, Gareth. 'Northern Catholic Fans of the Republic of Ireland Soccer Team'. In *Sport and the Irish. Histories, Identities, Issues,* ed. Alan Bairner. Dublin: UCD Press, 2005.

Gallagher, Tony. 'After the War Comes Peace? An Examination of the Impact of the Northern Ireland Conflict on Young People'. *Journal of Social Issues* 60, no. 3 (2004): 629–42.

Giulianotti, Richard, and Gerry Finn. 'Epilogue: Old visions, Old issues: New Horizons, New Openings? Change, Continuity and other Contradictions in World Football'. In *Football Culture: Local Contests, Global Visions,* ed. Gerry Finn and Richard Giulianotti, 256–82. London: Frank Cass, 2000.

Hassan, David. 'Sport and National Identity in Northern Ireland: The Case of Northern Nationalism'. PhD diss., University of Ulster, 2001.

Hassan, David. 'A People Apart: Soccer, Identity and Irish Nationalists in Northern Ireland'. *Soccer and Society* 3, no. 3 (2002): 65–83.

Holmes, Michael. 'Symbols of National Identity and Sport: The Case of the Irish Football Team'. *Irish Political Studies* 9 (1994): 91–8.

Maguire, Joseph. 'Globalization, Sport and National Identities: the Empires Strike Back?' *Society and Leisure* 16, no. 2 (1993): 293–323.

Platt, William. *A History of Derry City Football and Athletic Club 1929–1972.* Coleraine: Self-Published, 1986.

Sugden, John, and Alan Bairner. *Sport, Sectarianism and Society in a Divided Ireland.* Leicester: Leicester University Press, 1993.

Deutschland über Alles: discrimination in German football

Christos Kassimeris

Department of Social and Behavioural Sciences, European University, Cyprus

Introduction: the fascist legacy of German football

Football in Germany suffered the embarrassment of extreme nationalism ever since the game arrived there at the turn of the nineteenth century. Habitually condemning all things English, football was introduced to the German people as a ball game played in the wider area during the Middle Ages – not the British-invented game. As it happens,

> Historically, racism, xenophobia and the most vicious nationalisms have arisen in those societies least confident of themselves, or in those most divided. Nationalism is never so intense as among people whose national identity has been cast into doubt, has not been fully developed or is challenged by a group within. At the end of the last century the introduction of football instead of Rugby can be attributed to three causes, of which the following one is extremely relevant for an understanding of the roots of nationalism surrounding soccer in Germany. Of political importance was that soccer could be declared to be 'German football' while Rugby was considered to be 'English football'. Since Koch, the German equivalent of Thomas Arnold, was aware of the resentments the introduction of an English game would provoke, he tried to provide evidence that football also had a long tradition in Continental Europe and that it was already played in 'Germany' in the Middle Ages. He did this in order to gain approval from the members of the Gymnastics Movement (Turnbewegung). In the second half of the 19th century the entire concept of competitive (English) sport was disapproved by the Germans because it was labelled decadent, un-German, trivial and most important because it was essentially English.[1]

Critical anti-English discourse reached a crescendo in 1898 when Karl Planck went so far as to criticize the beautiful game for its English antecedents. Drawing from his experience as a physical education instructor, Planck's *Fusslümmelei* condemned the game because of its English origins and, most importantly, for the undignified style of play and the ape-like movement that characterized it.[2]

Before long, German nationalism, compounded with the rise of the Nazi party, manipulated the popular game for the sheer purpose of promoting a distinct sense of national identity. To this end, Bernhard Rust, the Minister of Education, announced on 2 June 1933 the banning of Jews from all activities related to the public domain including, of course, sports. Not surprisingly, perhaps, the German Football Association (Deutsche Fußball-Bund) had only just made a relevant announcement some two months earlier through the sports magazine *kicker*, founded by Walther Bensemann of Jewish origin, urging its member clubs to expel their Jewish staff. Eager to serve the new Nazi masters of the German football governing body, clubs such as Karlsruher Fussball Verein, 1. FC Nürnberg and Eintracht Frankfurt wasted no time in forcing out their Jewish members. By contrast, club officials at FC Bayern München maintained support for their former Jewish president Kurt Landauer, thus prompting the Nazi authorities to favour city rivals TSV München in retaliation to the defiance of the former.[3] In essence thus, recent evidence suggests that the role of football was of significance in Adolph Hitler's endeavours to consolidate power. The following relevant commentary is telling:

> Hoping to come to terms with their Nazi past before the World Cup starts, German football leaders have broadened their examination of their shameful history in the Third Reich and embraced their critics. The German football federation (DFB), now eager to come to terms with its enthusiastic support of the Nazis during the Hitler era after covering it up for six decades, has thrown open its soul, and archives, to try to purge that nightmare past. At the symposium held in a small town near Stuttgart, football leaders and historians spent two days debating issues such as whether the DFB collaborated with the Nazis more than the public at large. Another issue concerns the depth of DFB crimes against the Jews. The consensus was that German football helped stabilise the Hitler regime, failed to do anything for Jews and in some areas was overly eager to please the Nazis even if its overall level of support for the regime only mirrored that of the public. The self-critical examination in Bad Boll followed last year's publication of a book by the same title that cast light on how the DFB climbed into bed with the Nazis at an early date. The book, which the DFB commissioned, detailed how Jewish players, club owners, sponsors and journalists were all excluded from 1933 when Hitler came to power. Many German Jews, including former leading national team hero Julius Hirsch, later perished in Nazi death camps. Although few in the DFB were Nazi party members or especially vocal advocates of the regime's racist doctrines, the book found most were willing tools or opportunists who let themselves be used out of ignorance or professional ambition.[4]

Disturbingly, the club members that remained in their posts did not escape similar humiliating experiences as they were all asked to prove their Aryan origins, while the younger members were selected to join the Hitler Youth, thus bringing the game under the authority of the National Socialist Workers Party of Germany (NSDAP). The intervention of party officials was prompted by the need to merge certain football clubs to emphasize the new political realities of Nazi Germany. Further plans to transform the game into an efficient propaganda apparatus were thwarted when the Second World War broke out in 1939.[5]

Taking into account the politically motivated decision of Germany to withdraw from the League of Nations in 1933, football became the only vehicle capable of promoting the country's image abroad by means of participating in prominent international tournaments such as the 1934 and 1938 World Cup competitions.[6] Winning football matches elevated the national team to ambassadorial-like status. With the notable exception of a heavy defeat at the hands of the Swedish national football team, the German footballers had no problem defeating their opponents.[7] Nevertheless, one memorable football match that is definitely worthy of note concerns an encounter between the national football teams of Germany and England. During what was a friendly football match held on 14 May 1938, the players of the England squad raised their arms to salute the audience in the well-known fascist manner, an occasion that encouraged speculation regarding the apparent support of the English Football Association toward the Nazi regime.[8] Interestingly, no matter what ideological traits the Nazis had in common with the regime of Francisco Franco in Spain, their fascist allegiance was seriously questioned when the German national football team visited the Mediterranean country for a friendly game in 1936. On the occasion, the two 'sides argued over whether "Deutschland über Alles" would be played and whether the Germans would salute',[9] thus indicating that the Spaniards were clearly not as enthusiastic in accommodating the propagandistic objectives of their guests.

Yet football in Germany suffered almost as much during the Nazi party's stay in power as in the post-war period, when Germany was divided after the implementation of the Yalta Agreement. The admittedly slow development of football in West Germany meant that the *Bundesliga*, the German national football league, would not materialize until 1963, just as football's proper expansion in the German Democratic Republic was halted by the manipulative schemes of the local authorities.[10] West German football might have produced a number of talented football players like Franz Beckenbauer and Karl-Heinz Rummenigge, better known as *Der Kaiser* and *Der Blonde Bomber* respectively; however, their most significant contribution – as their nicknames suggest – concerns the strengthening of national identity.[11] Although East Germany claimed as many gifted players, including Matthias Sammer, Carsten Jancker and Alexander Zickler, to name a few, footballing success was rare for the German Democratic Republic at both national and club level, as only one club managed to claim a European Cup-Winners Cup while the national football team boasted nothing more than a single World Cup appearance. In any case, football in East Germany was instrumental in constructing a distinct sense of collective identity that would promote the cause of the communist regime.[12] On the whole, football was instrumental to the construction of a distinct collective identity that crystallized national sentiments in the case of both Nazi Germany and the two Germanys that emerged in the aftermath of the Second World War. Nevertheless, 'western' identity differed from 'eastern' as much as West German football was more successful than its counterpart across the border. The so-called 'Miracle of Bern', for example, commands our attention because the West German national football team defeated the fancied Hungarians to claim the nation's first World Cup trophy in 1954. It was the first occasion where Germans felt pride in feeling German ever since the end of the Second World War. On the other hand, their eastern neighbours were less privileged and had to await reunification in 1990 to achieve a sense of collective national consciousness.

Combating racism in German society

The footballing fate of Germany did not alter significantly following the country's reunification, given that the German national football team claimed only two successes, in the World Cup (1990) and the European Championship (1996), compared to two World Cups (1954 and 1974) and as many European Championships (1972 and 1980) during Germany's Cold War division, but her demographic profile changed drastically. Even though the collection of statistical information concerning the ethnic background of German citizens is limited to nationality alone, the majority of 'guest workers' originates from Turkey (30% of the foreign population), former Yugoslavia (9%), Italy (8%) and Greece (5%).[13] As far as racist incidents are concerned, a European Monitoring Centre on Racism and Xenophobia report indicates that their vast majority takes place in eastern Germany, though it stresses that while some incidents are not recorded as racist acts, other are not even reported.[14] More often than not, most victims are third country nationals and asylum seekers, usually, of African, Turkish and Vietnamese origins.[15] Taking into consideration the standardized identity of the perpetrators, German authorities are closely monitoring the activities of certain extreme right-wing groups and parties that are typically associated with xenophobia and anti-Semitism. Worthy of note is the fact that racist crime increased in the early 1990s.[16] More recently, the Federal Office for the Defence of the Constitution revealed that the number of violent racist acts is increasing, again in the eastern part of Germany, although the number of extreme right group members is declining since 1998.[17]

In an attempt to combat all forms of discrimination, the German Government endorsed the 'Forum against Racism' (1998) and 'Alliance for Democracy and Tolerance against Extremism and Violence' (2000) projects and ratified the Convention on the Elimination of all Forms of Racial Discrimination (1969), the European Charter for Regional or Minority Languages (1998) and the ILO Convention 111 (1961) barring Protocol No.12 to the Convention, which calls for the Protection of Human Rights and Fundamental Freedoms. The European Framework Convention for the Protection of Minorities came into force in 1998. Germany's Criminal Law includes the all-important Laws for the Protection of Youth, which prohibits the dissemination of materials inciting racial hatred; yet Civil Law makes no legal reference to anti-discrimination legislation pertaining to discrimination on the base of race and ethnic origin.[18] However, specialized equality bodies are conspicuous by their absence, though similar institutions exist in the form of the Commissioners for Foreigners, the Forum against Racism, Alliance for Tolerance and the German Institute for Human Rights.[19] Likewise, the Federal and Regional Centres for political education have recently introduced measures intended to eliminate prejudice and xenophobia, whereas the Federal Agency for Civic Education has focused almost exclusively on measures devoted to combating right-wing extremism.[20]

Still, the German state has signed, but not ratified, Protocol No.12 to the ECHR, the European Convention on the Legal Status of Migrant Workers (1977) and the European Convention on Nationality (February 2002). It has also signed the Additional Protocol to the Convention on Cyber-crime (January 2003), but not the International Convention on the Protection of the Rights of All Migrant Workers and Members of their Families and was about to sign the Revised European Social Charter and the European Convention for the Participation of Foreigners in Public Life at Local Level, but not the provisions of Chapter C that concern the granting of eligibility and voting rights to alien residents. Finally, Germany endorsed in 2001 the International Convention on the Elimination of All forms of Racial Discrimination declaration of Article 14.[21] Ultimately, Germany modified in January 2000 the Nationality Law to relax the process of obtaining German nationality. Interestingly, a considerable number of non-citizens, particularly of Turkish origin, have decided against it. While there has been a staggering increase of naturalizations every year (56%), the fact that applicants are asked to denounce their nationality before acquiring the German one (offspring of third country nationals must declare one single nationality prior to reaching 23 years of age, if born in Germany) has clearly persuaded some against the merits of this policy.[22]

Racism in German football

Racism appears to have become a major issue in German football following reunification in 1989, even though a number of foreign players were among those that kicked off the inaugural 1963 *Bundesliga*. Evidently,

> By the late 1980s, a hybrid of xenophobia, hyper-nationalism and anti-communism had begun to take shape among a section of the skinheads. Among their targets were foreign contract workers from countries such as Mozambique and Angola. Their antagonism towards foreigners also coincided with mounting popular antipathy towards the Vietnamese who were seen, especially in the industrial conurbation of the southern regions, as rivals for consumer goods in short supply.[23]

According to Giulianotti, 'terrace racism is associated with the rise of the far right particularly in the east where deep social and economic insecurities prevail'.[24] The following account, as chronicled on the official webpage of the German national football league, is certainly intriguing:

> In the beginning, when the Bundesliga started in 1963, there were just three 'legionnaires', as they were rather disrespectfully dubbed at the time.
>
> Austria's Willy Huberts (Eintracht Frankfurt), Dutchman Jacobus 'Co' Prins (1. FC Kaiserslautern) and Yugoslavia's Petar Radenkovic (TSV Munich 1860) were the only foreigners on the pitch on day 1 of the Bundesliga, but they were the first of the more than 1,000 foreign players who have graced the Bundesliga over the years. Many, like Kevin Keegan in Hamburg, proved to be hits, but many quickly faded away into obscurity.
>
> The first Asian player
>
> Germany did not have to wait long for its first Asian player. While holding a training course for Japanese players at the German sports academy in Cologne, Hennes Weisweiler promptly discovered Yasuhiko Okudera, who went on to play 234 Bundesliga matches for 1. FC Cologne and Werder Bremen between 1977 and 1986. South Korea's Bum Kun Cha enjoyed even more success after switching to Eintracht Frankfurt and then Bayer 04 Leverkusen after just one match for Darmstadt 98. Cha played 308 Bundesliga matches, scoring 98 goals and even winning the UEFA Cup. His son, Du Ri Cha, played for Arminia Bielefeld for a season before also moving to Eintracht Frankfurt in 2003.
>
> Scandinavians at Mönchengladbach
>
> Borussia Mönchengladbach was the first club to sign Danish players on a regular basis. Allan Simonsen scored 76 goals for them between 1973 and 1975, while a Dane with a French-sounding name, Ulrik Le Fevre, once scored the 'goal of the season' as voted for by viewers of terrestrial TV channel ARD. Le Fevre is now a player's agent. Belgian winger Roger van Gool became the Bundesliga's first million deutschmark player when he moved from FC Bruges to 1. FC Cologne in 1976.

First black player

Peru's Julio Baylon was the first black player in German professional football when he moved to Fortuna Cologne in 1973, but he was the first of many, including Anthony Yeboah and Augustine 'Jay-Jay' Okocha. As the number of foreigners in the Bundesliga increased, the league stepped up its efforts to combat racism. On the last matchday before the winter break in the 1992/93 season, all 18 Bundesliga teams wore shirts bearing the 'My friend is a foreigner' slogan.

Key role for Brazilians

Brazilians have obviously had a key role to play in the German league. They all play wonderful football, but not all have shown the same levels of discipline as Jorginho. Ailton is renowned for suddenly deciding to extend his holidays as well as for his rodeo escapades back home in Brazil, but compared to Zeze, Ailton's actions pale into insignificance. In 1964, Zeze walked out of 1. FC Cologne at the first sight of snow after just five matches and one goal.[25]

Interestingly, although Jorginho's discipline is commended, the same does not apply to fellow Brazilian football players Ailton and Zeze. The description of Ailton's apparent lack of professionalism and the reaction of Zeze to snow do not necessarily reflect prejudice. Nevertheless, the 1992–93 anti-racism campaign is indicative of an all-expansive phenomenon that would soon transform the otherwise festive atmosphere during football matches to a more hostile environment. In fact, the alarmingly growing significance of neo-Nazi groups in the early 1990s and their engagement in a number of violent football-related incidents matched the findings of a nationwide survey which revealed that:

> although Nazi symbols and Hitler salutes have been observed during international matches, researchers do not regard these as evidence of significant neo-Nazi involvement in football hooliganism. An analysis of the political attitudes of German fans indicates that these symbols do have political meaning for around 20% of supporters, who reported sympathy with the neo-Nazi movement, and explicit links have been noted between some fan-groups and extreme-Right organisations. The majority of fans, however, either support one of the mainstream democratic parties (35%) or have no politics at all (24%).[26]

Along similar lines, Giulianotti noted that:

> racism among supporters is often pinned on hooligan groups, particularly from the East, but their use of Nazi symbols and slogans reflects a deeper alienation towards wealthier Westerners rather than a political ideology. Punks during the 1970s were similarly interested in using swastikas to upset and shock rather than to signify fascist sentiments.[27]

The dominant presence of extreme right groups in the football stadiums of clubs like Hamburger Sport Verein and FC St Pauli inspired fans of the latter to establish the *Millerntor Roar!* anti-racism group. More precisely,

> from 1986 onwards a new group of supporters became obvious at St Pauli club who combined enthusiasm for the style of the team with left-wing politics, turning this into a symbol of the club. They initiated anti-racist campaigns and founded *Millerntor Roar! (MR!)*, the first anti-fascist and anti-corporate German fanzine. With their leaflets they called upon fans to take up the fight against racism in the stadiums and even convinced the team to support this. In autumn of 1991, *MR!* were largely responsible for St Pauli

becoming the first German club to adopt rules which banned supporters' racist chants or banners in the stadium. In 1992 anti-fascist demonstrations in Hamburg were organised to follow immediately after St Pauli home games.[28]

What is fascinating is that

> most of St Pauli older supporters did start off as supporters of HSV, but during the 1980s the atmosphere for fans became unpleasant at HSV's Volksparkstadion, as the club became notorious for its fascist hooligans. In 1982, the first skinheads appeared in the stands wearing badges 'No More Foreigners! Vote NPD' (the NPD was for a long period after 1945 Germany's principal neo-Nazi party). Members of the far-right HSV fan club Löwen (Lions) mainly working class, unemployed and with criminal convictions, were targeted by the neo-Nazi Aktionsfront Nationaler Sozialisten (ANS – since prohibited). In 1983, the magazine *Der Spiegel* wrote: 'Football violence and the far right are especially interconnected on the West terrace of Volksparkstadion'. At Volksparkstadion there are still plenty of connections between hooligans and regional right-wing extremists.[29]

A similar extreme right group that tormented Ballspiel Verein Borussia 1909 Dortmund concerned a section of supporters that maintained close links with neo-Nazi movements, including the National Democratic Party. That said, it is hardly surprising that the contract of Julio Cesar with the aforementioned club included an unusual opt-out clause that could have been put into effect by the Brazilian player in case he suffered racial abuse during home matches. Still, the first football players that experienced racial discrimination had Turkish origins, since footballers from other backgrounds were a rare sight, as already mentioned above. Today, racial discrimination probably accounts for the absence of football players from the Turkish community in Germany. Along the same lines, it appears that exclusive Turkish football clubs, financed by Turkish business houses, existed during the 1990s for the sole purpose of satisfying the appetite of Germany's largest, football deprived minority.[30] The same kind of segregation in football regarding the Turkish community is nowadays well documented. Halm stresses that German people view these all-Turkish amateur football clubs as a serious impediment to the successful integration of this particular community into the wider German society,[31] while some also consider the apparent cultural mismatch equally significant.

However, it remains a fact that those players typically victimized by extreme right elements are black footballers. For instance, FC Gelsenkirchen Schalke 04 commenced their 2003–04 football campaign with a number of poor performances, yet the club's fans concentrated their frustration on Victor Agali of Nigerian origins for failing to score enough goals for his team. Despite the commendable support the player received from the club's general manager, Rudi Assauer, and the Schalker Fan-Initiative anti-racism group, Agali seems to have had no options available other than quitting the club.[32] Another FC Gelsenkirchen Schalke 04 football player was racially abused during a German football cup tie against a minor club that played its football in the regional league of Hansa Rostock. On the occasion, Gerald Asamoah played throughout the entire match, even though his manager offered to replace him,[33] thus delivering a powerful message to those fans that continued to degrade him and even managed to cap his performance with one goal and three assists.[34]

Similar racist acts have marred games in Germany's lower football leagues. For example, supporters of FC Energie Cottbus displayed in December 2005 an anti-Semitic banner in their club's away game against SG Dynamo Dresden, whereas the more inventive fans of 1. FC Lokomotive Leipzig did not hesitate to form a human swastika during a match against FC Sachsen Leipzig. Surprisingly, neither incident attracted the attention of the German media, though the considerably less glamorous nature of clubs competing in the lower leagues may account for the lack of media coverage. Then again, the same media completely ignored the ill-treatment of Asamoah during an UEFA Cup tie against Bulgarian side FC Levski Sofia, even though the FC Gelsenkirchen Schalke 04 manager duly complained during the press conference that followed the match, while the match official too reported the incident to UEFA. Similarly, racist conduct of German fans was overlooked during international matches in France, Italy, Slovakia and Slovenia in 2005 and 2006. The German media, eventually, took notice of racism in the game when fans of VfL Halle 1896 racially abused Adebowale Ogungbure of FC Sachsen Leipzig in March 2006. Once the game ended the insulted African player confronted his abusers by giving them a Nazi salute, but was brought to justice – even though he was soon after released from custody – as any act or symbol that exposes the country's shameful Nazi past is prohibited in Germany. While the reasons for which the player behaved in such manner were never mentioned, the media focused upon what seemed like an issue of social exclusion, ultimately prompting the German Football Association to carry out an investigation.[35] Again, during a football match between FC St Pauli and Chemnitzer FC, fans of the latter displayed 'red banners with empty white circles – the allusion to far-right symbols was clear'.[36] Evidently, racism in German football reached new heights as referee Michael Weiner came close to bringing the game between TSV Alemannia Aachen and VfL Borussia Mönchengladbach to an abrupt end because a group of Aachen supporters degraded Mönchengladbach's Brazilian player Kahe, at the same time as Mönchengladbach fans racially abused Aachen's Moses Sichone.[37]

Merkel, Sombert and Tokarski's account of the German Football Association's early attempts to rid the game of racism records certain admittedly insufficient measures, more often than not, concerning legal issues and the general safety of football supporters in stadiums.[38] More recently, Germany's football governing body embraced the so-called Dortmund fan project, supported the 'Kick Racism Out' campaign, screened the official webpage of all top three divisions' football clubs for racist material, promoted a CD-ROM that provided guidelines to stewards for combating racism during football matches and commissioned Nils Havemann's *Fußball unterm Hakenkreuz* [Football under the swastika], a book that exposes the role of the German Football Association in the Nazi era. What's more, the game's authorities in Germany are now carefully scrutinizing the content of all banners displayed in stadiums during matches of the national football team. Any material alluding to racism is then submitted to the 'Central Information desk for Sport employment', *Zentrale Informationsstelle für Sporteinsätze*, for further investigation and action, if deemed necessary.[39]

As one might expect, hosting the 2006 World Cup must have overwhelmed the football governing body and all pertinent actors in Germany. Keeping neo-Nazi groups at bay, all the while stressing the safe environment that is Germany, was central to the proper organization of the world's most illustrious sports competition. When a black German was assaulted nearly a month before the competition kicked off, police authorities went into overdrive and suggested that no neo-Nazi demonstrations would take place in the vicinity of any one of the World Cup venues.[40] In what was a colourful football competition, taking into consideration the participation of

Angola, Ghana, the Ivory Coast, Togo and Tunisia, it was a heavy burden for the German authorities to maintain a racism-free environment for all to attend the matches. Unfortunately, the 2006 World Cup did not escape the embarrassment of racist incidents, as one neo-Nazi group published a 'World Cup guide' featuring a German football player in the number 25 shirt with a message reading 'White. It's not only the colour of the kit. For a real NATIONAL team!' What is certainly not a coincidence is that Patrick Owomoyela of Nigerian origins wore that shirt, prompting the German Football Association to demand the withdrawal of all such material.[41] Yet Owomoyela was not the first black player to suffer from such abuse. Actually, Ghanaian Asamoah became the first black footballer to represent Germany (2001), which inspired a neo-Nazi group to produce a photograph depicting him and a message stating 'No Gerald you are not Germany'.[42]

A number of World Cup matches were marked with similar incidents. During the match between the national football teams of Italy and Ghana, fans supporting the former performed the fascist salute when the Italian national anthem was played; an inflatable banana was constantly on display to ridicule the African players; and observers from the 'Football against Racism in Europe' network discovered an 'Ultras Italia' graffiti illustrating a swastika on their way to the stadium that hosted the game. Likewise, the much anticipated for-all-the-wrong-reasons match between Germany and Poland was preceded by violent clashes between rival fans that continued after the game's final whistle. Among the German perpetrators were some extreme right elements shouting 'Sieg Heil', just as Polish fans wore scarves displaying Celtic crosses and the infamous Waffen-SS skull. On another occasion, despite the fact that Turkey had not qualified for the World Cup finals in Germany, fans of Switzerland were given the opportunity to express their anti-Turkish feelings simply by purchasing relevant merchandise after their country's game against France had come to an end. The odd memorabilia included scarves that read 'Bye bye Turkey – Turkish man stays at home', possibly inspired by the violent events that occurred during Switzerland's visit to Turkey during the qualifying round. In another case, Serbian fans displayed a banner featuring a Celtic cross during the match against the Netherlands.[43] Finally, given that 'German law forbids the use of symbols specific to the Nationalist Socialist era (1933–45)',[44] an English fan was banned from attending football matches for 25 months for having had a swastika painted on his chest.[45]

It is noteworthy, nevertheless, that no race-related violence took place during the World Cup.[46] To this end, officials from 'Football against Racism in Europe', *Fédération Internationale de Football Association* and the World Cup Local Organizing Committee made good use of the World Cup finals by disseminating anti-racist information and relevant material. More precisely, the world football governing body utilized 'matches to send out an anti-racism message by declaring the quarter-final matches in Germany as anti-racism games. Before every quarter-final match, team captains read a personal pledge against racism and teams came together behind a banner.'[47] Impressive as it was, in all 64 football matches a banner reading 'Say Not to Racism' covered the entire centre circle of the pitch before kick off.[48]

Conclusion

Football is widely known for its popularity and, to a great extent, its unique nation-building capacity. For these reasons, football in Germany was clearly subjected to ill-conceived schemes, ever since its arrival, all aiming at the manipulation of the beautiful game for the purpose of promoting a distinct sense of national identity. Evidently, the Nazis exploited the otherwise positive qualities of the game to construct an admittedly forged collective identity that would allow the Nazi party officials to consolidate authority and prolong their stay in power. The policies of the Nazi party, in particular, regarding the 'proper' Germanization of the game, from an inherently Aryan perspective, damaged the integrity of the game and hindered its subsequent development. However, football managed to survive the agonizing embarrassment of pre-war racial discrimination and even helped crystallize the West German's identity in the post-war period. Yet prejudice had not left the game and lurked under the surface until the moment Germany was reunified.

As already mentioned, racism in German football became a rather serious issue in the early 1990s, soon after the country's reunification, when extreme right groups gained prominence. As neo-Nazi groups came to dominate the terraces, the festive atmosphere that usually characterizes football games was, unsurprisingly perhaps, transformed into a hostile environment that, in due course, succeeded in intimidating non-white football players. Given that the disturbing phenomenon never really subsided, despite anti-racism campaigns and relevant acts of legislation, it was imperative that all pertinent actors stepped up to combat racism in football. Hence, when Germany hosted the 2006 World Cup finals, the country attracted worldwide attention not just in terms of spectatorship, but also because of its anti-racist stance. It suffices to say that the contribution of both the 'Football against Racism in Europe' network and the *Fédération Internationale de Football Association* was instrumental in educating the spectators and raising awareness against racism, in turn helping to do away with the country's fascist past.

Notes

1. Merkel, Sombert and Tokarski, 'Football, Racism and Xenophobia', 154.
2. Murray, *The World's Game*, 26.
3. Hesse-Lichtenberger, *Tor!*, 63–4.
4. Erik Kirschbaum, 'German FA Tries to Purge NAZI Past before World Cup'. *Kick It Out*, April 11, 2006, http://www.kickitout.org.
5. Hesse-Lichtenberger, *Tor!*, 62.
6. Ibid., 73.
7. Ibid., 91–3.
8. Kuper, *Soccer against the Enemy*, 36–7.
9. Ibid., 38.
10. Hesse-Lichtenberger, *Tor!*, 101–15.
11. Wagg, *Giving the Game* Away, 119.
12. Hesse-Lichtenberger, *Tor!*, 222–7.
13. Chopin, Cormack and Niessen, *European Commission against Racism*, 36.
14. Jochen Blaschke and Guillermo Ruiz Torres, *European Commission against Racism and Intolerance*, 117.
15. Chopin, Cormack and Niessen, 'European Commission against Racism', 169.
16. *Racist Violence in the 15 EU Member States: A Comparative Overview of Findings from the RAXEN National Focal Points Reports 2001–2004.*, 78–9.
17. European Commission against Racism and Intolerance. *Third Report on Germany*, 28.
18. Chopin, Cormack and Niessen, 'European Commission against Racism', 36–7.
19. Ibid., 39–40.
20. European Commission against Racism and Intolerance. *Third Report on Germany*, 30.
21. Ibid., 7.
22. Ibid., 8.
23. Dennis, 'German Hooliganism', 61.
24. Giulianotti, *Football*, 160.

25. 'From Keegan to van der Vaart'. Bundesliga (DFB) website: http://www.dfb.de.
26. Carnibella *et al.*, *Football Violence in Europe*, 69.
27. Giulianotti, *Football*, 161.
28. Martens, 'Here to Stay', 179.
29. Ibid., 181.
30. Merkel, Sombert and Tokarski, 'Football, Racism and Xenophobia', 153–60.
31. Halm, 'Turkish Immigrants', 84–90.
32. 'Racism in a New Guise'. http://www.flutlicht.org, November 1, 2006.
33. 'Asamoah Targeted by Racist Taunts'. *Kick It Out*, September 12, 2006. http://www.kick-itout.org.
34. 'German DFB Fine Rostock for Racist Chants'. *Kick It Out*, September 15, 2006. http://www.kickitout.org.
35. Raphael Honigstein, 'Blot on German Landscape'. http://www.uefa.com.
36. 'Racism in a New Guise'.
37. 'DFB Launches Racism Inquiry'. http://www.uefa.com.
38. Merkel, Sombert and Tokarski, 'Football, Racism and Xenophobia', 161–4.
39. For Fair Play and Tolerance. Against Violence, Racism and Xenophobia in Football, Chronology of selected measures and projects taken by the DFB (German football association) since 2003.
40. 'German Police Urge NAZI March Ban'. *Kick It Out*, May 4, 2006. http://www.kick-itout.org.
41. Honigstein, 'Blot on German Landscape'.
42. 'Stop Racist neo-NAZIS at World Cup says Asamoah'. *Kick It Out*, May 30, 2006. http://www.kickitout.org.
43. 'Media Information'.
44. Merkel, Sombert and Tokarski, 'Football, Racism and Xenophobia', 159.
45. 'Swastika Fan given 25-Month Match Ban'. *Kick It Out*, June 14, 2006. http://www.kick-itout.org.
46. 'Anti-racism Success of World Cup 2006 Should Spur Action at EU Level'. *Kick It Out*, July 5, 2006. http://www.kickitout.org.
47. 'FARE at the World Cup'. http://www.uefa.com.
48. Football Against Racism in Europe, 'Joint Media Release of FIFA, LOC and FARE, Football against Racism at the 2006 FIFA World Cup – Alliance between FIFA, LOC and FARE', June 9, 2006. http://www.farenet.org.

References

Blaschke, Joohen, and Guillermo Ruiz Torres. *European Commission against Racism and Intolerance. 'Racism in Rural Areas'. Final Report.* Berliner Institute Für Vergleichende Sozialforschung Mitglied in Europäinschen Migrationszentrum (in cooperation with Eurofor), 2004.
Carnibella, Giovanni, Anne Fox, Kate Fox, Joe McCann, James Marsh, and Peter Marsh. *Football Violence in Europe: A Report to the Amsterdam Group.* The Social Issues Research Centre, July 1996.
Chopin, Isabelle, Janet Cormack, and Jan Niessen, eds. 'European Commission against Racism and Intolerance'. *The implementation of European anti-discrimination legislation: work in progress. The implementation of the Racial Equality Directive (2000/43/EC) and the Employment Equality Directive (2000/78/EC) as it relates to religion and belief in 15 EU Member States.* Migration Policy Group, 2004.
Dennis, Mike. 'German Hooliganism in the German Democratic Republic'. In *German Football: History, Culture, Society,* ed. Alan Tomlinson and Christopher Young, 52–72. London and New York: Routledge, 2005.
Giulianotti, Richard. *Football: A Sociology of the Global Game.* Cambridge: Polity Press, 1999.
Halm, Dirk. 'Turkish Immigrants in German Amateur Football'. In *German Football: History, Culture, Society,* ed. Alan Tomlinson and Christopher Young, 73–92. London and New York: Routledge, 2005.

Hesse-Lichtenberger, Ulrich. *Tor! The Story of German Football.* London: WSC Books, 2003.

Kuper, Simon. *Soccer Against the Enemy: How the World's Most Popular Sport Starts and Stops Wars, Fuels Revolution, and Keeps Dictators in Power.* New York: Nation Books, 2006.

Martens, Rene. 'Here to Stay with St. Pauli'. In *Hooligan Wars: Causes and Effects of Football Violence,* ed. Mark Perryman, 179–90. Edinburgh and London: Mainstream Publishing, 2002.

'Media Information, Cologne, Anti-racism Network Sees Positive Start to World Cup'. *Football Against Racism in Europe,* June 20, 2006. http://www.farenet.org.

Merkel, Udo, Kurt Sombert, and Walter Tokarski. 'Football, Racism and Xenophobia in Germany: 50 Years Later – Here We Go Again?' In *Racism and Xenophobia in European Football,* ed. Udo Merkel and Walter Tokarski, 143–68. Aachen: Meyer & Meyer, 1996.

Murray, Bill. *The World's Game: A History of Soccer.* Urbana and Chicago, IL: University of Illinois Press, 1998.

Racist Violence in the 15 EU Member States: A Comparative Overview of Findings from the RAXEN National Focal Points Reports 2001–2004. April 2005.

Third Report on Germany (Adopted on 5 December 2003). Strasbourg, June 2004.

Wagg, Stephen, ed. *Giving the Game Away: Football, Politics and Culture on Five Continents.* London and New York: Leicester University Press, 1995.

The dream of social mobility: ethnic minority players in Danish football clubs

Sine Agergaard [a] and Jan Kahr Sørensen[b]

[a]Department of Exercise and Sport Sciences, University of Copenhagen, Denmark;
[b]Department of Sport Science, University of Aarhus, Denmark

Introduction

Young working-class men have long regarded a career in professional sport as a step-ping stone to upward social mobility, and a chance to enhance their social status and economic wealth.[1] Football, in particular, tends to recruit participants predominantly from a working-class background.[2] The high salaries are one of the reasons these youngsters are attracted to a career in soccer, but the myths surrounding top level sport and the apparent potential for dream fulfilment play a role, too.[3]

It is common for young people at school and post-school levels to identify with sporting personalities. Moreover, ethnic minority youngsters seem to be particularly motivated to establish a career in sport. Primarily, this is likely to be because sport is one of the few spheres which has provided black people with a chance of upward mobility. Secondly, success in top level sport is seen as an alternative to stigmatization in society.[4] However, as Hoberman has pointed out, stereotypes of black physical superiority are enacted in sports.[5] Moreover, studies have shown that racial discrimination is an integrated part of sport, for instance through stacking: the discriminatory allocation of positions in football and other team sports.[6]

In the long run only a tiny proportion of the ethnic minority youths who dream of social mobility will make a decent living out of sports. A sports career is often without financial security or structure, injuries can result in retirement as well as loss of income and even disability, and the career is short. Also, for ethnic minority players, there are remarkably few opportunities to progress into management or coaching positions. Maguire points out that even if some ethnic minority players succeed, the stratification structure (and cultural categorization) in the sports system may not change.[7] Moreover, the players' social mobility may be transitory and last only while their talents are regarded as relevant to the specific clubs.

But, despite this cautionary note, there are plenty of studies that show that youths from households with low socio-economic conditions as well as those with minority status are highly motivated to follow a career in football. The literature points out, however, that it is not only the length of a football career that can dampen dreams of social mobility. According to Collins and Butler, children from socially deprived areas do not have sufficient support (social capital), to provide them with equal opportunities to perform in high-performance sport in England.[8] Moreover, Eitle and Eitle point out that lacking cultural capital (in this instance not participating in culturally recognized classes and activities) results in an increased motivation to participate in sport among Afro-Americans, but this then means that they start becoming dependent upon sport for finding a career.[9]

This essay focuses on young males from ethnic minority backgrounds who are attempting to establish careers in Danish football clubs, and considers their chances of becoming more socially mobile. Bourdieu's concepts will be used to analyze whether the players have their football skills acknowledged and converted into the fundamental forms of cultural, social and economic capital that altogether enhance their social recognition.

Sports participation and mobility of youngsters from a ghetto area

The background for our current study is a survey of participation of 10–16-year-old youngsters in sports in a suburb of a Danish provincial city – a suburb that politically has been identified as a ghetto area.[10] The inhabitants share low socio-economic living conditions and around half of the population have an ethnic background other than Danish.[11] The survey shows that immigrant and descendant boys in the area are very active in sports; 93.6% of immigrant boys and 89.5% of descendant boys, compared to 87.4% of the Danish boys from the same living area participate regularly in sports.[12] The most popular activity for these boys is football (75.2% of immigrant boys and 80.8% of descendant boys play football). The boys mainly play self-organized games around the streets and green areas of their neighbourhood, rather than going to a dedicated football pitch or attending clubs with scheduled training sessions and competition fixtures. Club leaders inside and outside of the ghetto area believe that there is a considerable pool of talent in the suburb and that it is a collective dream of the area, as well as for the boys individually, to become professional footballers.

The survey has also given us access to geographical information about the places where the youngsters participate in sports. We found, for instance, that only around 30% of the groups made up of descendants and immigrant boys and girls participate in sports outside the ghetto area. For various reasons, ethnic minority youngsters seem to be more restricted in their spatial movement compared to ethnically Danish youngsters of the same age and from the same living area. This has implications for those wishing to pursue a career in football as there are relatively few sports clubs in the ghetto area and none offer top level football. Moreover, the few football clubs that do exist tend to be ethnic minority clubs where the Arabs, Turks, Kurds etc. meet. So, it is a fundamental premise for boys who dream of becoming professional footballers that they must travel outside of the area (where they feel at home) and into football clubs, where ethnic Danes are the majority.

Thus the essay enumerates the challenges facing young male football players from ethnic minority backgrounds, living in both the ghetto area as well as other parts of the city, who would like to become professional footballers. The players' geographical mobility to Danish football clubs are considered as attempts to obtain social mobility.[13]

Method

Through the survey we have identified a number of clubs that ethnic minority boys often frequent when developing their football careers. These include two ethnic minority clubs in the ghetto area, three clubs that function as transit clubs and the city's premier league club. Initially, we contacted an experienced coach and club leader in the principal ethnic minority club in the ghetto area and the officer of talent development in the premier league club. These key informants were interviewed along with six experienced coaches from the aforementioned clubs, all of whom had worked with ethnic minority boys. The key informants also helped us to identify 10 talented players with ethnic minority backgrounds. In so identifying 'talent' we follow in the wake of Bourke. Bourke, who suggested the concept of pre-elite talent, recruited her informants by asking key personnel in the context of origin and destination to identify young talented football players by evaluating their playing potential.[14]

In our study, the players' ages range between 14 and 21 years. According to theories of career transitions in sport, the players are at key stages in their talent development, investing in the possibility of, and moving into, high achievement and adult sport.[15] In other words, the youngest players we have interviewed are moving into the world of elite sports and all that entails in terms of demanding practice, while the oldest players are making the transition from youth to senior sport.

All of the players have a Muslim background but their religious practice varies widely (as was illustrated during Ramadan). Moreover, their minority backgrounds are also varied with players having Bosnian, Turkish, Palestinian and Iranian descent. The young players can also be further divided into two groups since five of them live in the so-called ghetto area while the other five live in other parts of the city. This provides us with an opportunity to compare the challenges facing football talents who are based in an ethnic minority neighbourhood and have low socio-economic conditions with those who come from a more privileged background.

All 18 interviews lasted between 30 minutes and an hour and a half. In the interviews we used two semi-structured interview guides for coaches and players, respectively. The interviews were transcribed shortly after the meetings, which meant that information from earlier interviews could be used to inform the later discussions. The fact that the under-representation of ethnic minority players in Danish top-level football is criticized in the Danish media might have made the coaches and club leaders tight-lipped. Moreover, the ethnic minority players might have been reluctant to talk to us about the challenges they meet since in most cases they were interviewed in their present clubs after a session of training. A further factor to take into consideration is that both of the interviewers (the authors) are Danish academics and are therefore considerably different from the players. Still, our interest in the single informant and the challenges that they faced created a positive relationship with the players and coaches alike, and it is our general impression that the interviews gave us relevant and valid information.

Theory of social mobility

Theoreticians of social mobility distinguish between *intergeneration* mobility, that is when children move to higher or lower classes than their parents, and *intrageneration* or career mobility which describes the possibility for individuals within a generation to improve (or not) their social standing.[16] It is the latter that is relevant for us. A theory of social mobility for our purposes must be able to explain what constitutes social mobility in a sports career and the ways in which the chances of social mobility vary for specific athletes. We have, therefore, chosen to apply Bourdieu's classical social theory of concepts of field, habitus and capital.

From Bourdieu's perspective social mobility is a change of position within a stratification system. In other words, social mobility has to do with the chances that individuals with a specific habitus and capital have to improve their position in a specific social field. In this case, the athletes struggle to achieve a literal position on the field in a sports game but also to become acknowledged in a specific social context.

In his work Bourdieu has argued on several occasions for a sociology of sport and he has also compared social life with sports.[17] When interviewed by Wacquant, Bourdieu drew an analogy between a social field and a game. From his perspective, the two things differ only by the fact that unlike a sports game the social field is not created deliberately and the rules are often not explicit.[18] In both situations there is, however, strong competition between individuals or groups, and in both instances the ultimate aim is to win.

In Bourdieu's perspective gaining social mobility is concerned with an individual's advancement through accumulating capital and, equally importantly, having that capital acknowledged by peers in a specific social field. In other words, it is no good having capital if it is not acknowledged by others in a way that benefits one's social position. In this case, our informants are footballers, who have accumulated a physical capital that we will define below. What is interesting here is whether their physical capital is acknowledged in the field of football and converted to the fundamental forms of cultural, economic and social capital. From Bourdieu's perspective, it is both the composition and the sum total of the capital that determines an individual's chances of social mobility, which explains why not everyone has an equal chance of social mobility.[19]

The quest for capital

For this study, the most important form of capital is what has been called physical capital or bodily capital.[20] Bourdieu does not use these concepts; instead he talks about embodied capital as a sub-division of cultural capital.[21] This essay would argue that the ethnic minority players have embodied a physical capital that is not immediately linked to the cultural capital that is acknowledged in the field of football.

Our starting point for analyzing the ethnic minority players' chances of having their capital acknowledged and converted so it results in social mobility is Schilling's definition of physical capital:

> The *production* of physical capital refers to the *social formation* of bodies by individuals through sporting, leisure and other activities in ways which express a class location and which are accorded symbolic value.[22]

Physical capital is a form of capital that we must engage in physical activity to obtain. It is, for instance, power, speed and agility. As Schilling points out above, physical capital is affected by our particular social position and can be acknowledged in a way that enhances its value. In our analysis, we question whether the ethnic minority players have their physical capital acknowledged in the field of football and whether they are able to convert their capital into forms that enhance their chances of social mobility.

Bourdieu has defined three fundamental forms of capital; namely economic, social and cultural capital.[23] Economic capital is money and property rights while social capital in short is social network. The definition of cultural capital is a bit more complicated. Cultural capital can exist in three forms; embodied, as long-lasting dispositions of the mind and body; objectified, in the form of goods such as books, pictures etc.; and institutionalized, for instance as academic qualifications. Particularly interesting for us here is the embodied form of cultural capital that must be accumulated personally and over time can become what Bourdieu calls culture, cultivation, *Bildung*.

The possibility of obtaining social mobility through a football career is linked to the players' opportunities of converting their physical capital into the fundamental forms of capital. First of all, the question is whether the players' physical capital can be converted into cultural capital (in this context to learn to behave according to the more or less explicit rules of a Danish football club). Secondly, the question is whether the players' physical capital can be converted into social capital; that is the building of social relationships with fellow team members and a wider network that can support the development of their career. Thirdly, there is the question of whether it is possible to convert physical capital into economic capital (for instance by gaining financial funding for training and ultimately by winning a contract that gives access to a steady salary).

Taking into account Bourdieu's view that it is the sum total of the capital that determines an individual's chances of social mobility, it was essential for this study to consider not only the players' physical capital, but their opportunities to convert this into all three forms of fundamental capital. Previous studies have focused on young football players lacking development of cultural capital in the form of academic qualifications, and there have been numerous discussions about players focussing on their careers rather than following through with their education.[24] This essay considers all the forms of capital that are relevant for the social mobility of young ethnic minority players who hope to follow a career in professional football.

The field of football

The current organization of football as a particular sports discipline in Denmark can best be understood when it is defined as a sub-field of Danish sport in general.[25] A sub-field that is defined by its own logic, rules and regularities.[26] Football in Denmark is underpinned by the logic of competition, but it is also governed by ethical rules and regularities for the development of the field. Together this creates a stratification system that affects the evaluation of the capital of the ones who enter the field.[27]

The logic of competition is expressed in the fact that football players generally are divided into teams and levels with possible promotion or relegation. This has been reinforced in recent times following the professionalization, albeit rather late, of football in Denmark in 1978. Media coverage and commercialization also reinforces the logic of competition as fundamental for the football clubs and coaches, who must produce results to sustain the interest of the media and support from sponsors.

In fact, the logic of competition also underlies many of the strategies pertaining to elite level football since the aim is to optimise talent development, the education of coaches, facilities etc, so that the competitiveness of Danish football will be reinforced. Recently, the Danish Football Association (DBU) started a licence scheme for youth football under which clubs are awarded an A+, A or B licence; depending on their facilities, coaches' level of education and expertise, milieu to talent development, etc.[28] The teams are then delegated to play in a specific league so that the logic of promotion and relegation is suspended in order to promote talent development. It is our impression that the regulation of development is becoming increasingly important in Danish football and that it may have the potential to create more opportunities for clubs to invest in the development of talent from ethnic minority backgrounds. But, there is still some way to go since many of the coaches in youth elite football are volunteers and/or former players. DBU's coach training programme has a shortcut for former Division 1 and Premier League players, which doesn't include tuition on working with ethnic minority talents.[29] In addition, the coaches are influenced by the logic of competition since winning is the most obvious way for them to demonstrate their skills as a coach.

In addition to the logic of competition, football in Denmark is governed by rules that manifest themselves both in the football culture and in individual games. This 'ethical code' provides a culturally specific way of understanding the game. The DBU's code includes 10 ethical rules of the game along with guidance on more general sporting etiquette such as the acknowledgement that the success (and in more abstract terms, reputation) of the team is dependent on the effort and behaviour of the individual on and outside of the field. The code is an attempt to make a number of rules explicit that to some extent are already implicit norms in the field, and to make these rules count for all of the players, coaches, club leaders, referees etc.[30] The rules have to do with showing respect, avoiding provocation and doping, protecting the game from racism and corruption, following the rules, accepting defeat, performing well in terms of social behaviour, sharing your knowledge of the game, taking responsibility, knowing the consequences of your behaviour, and showing that football is about feelings, excellence and honesty. Many of these rules are directly opposed to the logic of competition or what Møller has characterized as the crucial code of winning and losing in sports.[31] So, what actually happens is that club leaders and coaches will emphasize the ethical code verbally, but on the pitch the rules seem to become more negotiable. Overall, the ethical rules can be seen as norms for the cultivation of the game which are emphasized by the persons in charge of the players' socialization.

Later in our analysis we will describe how the norms of team sports behaviour, in particular, function as a specific cultural capital in the field, and that the coaches from Danish football clubs often find that the talented young males with ethnic minority background lack this capital. The coaches and club leaders we interviewed can be seen as key representatives of the field of football. In the daily training of youngsters in various clubs the coaches are the administrators of the logic of competition, the overseers of development and the regulators of the ethical rules.

Physical and cultural capital

The starting point for our analysis is ethnic minority players' physical capital, which is challenging to describe since it is held in the form of embodied skills. In the interviews we have asked the players to describe what they are particularly good at on a football field, while the coaches were asked to describe what it is that makes the ethnic minority players that they know talented. The answers are remarkably consistent. Both the players and the coaches point out that ethnic minority players in general possess speed, (ball) technique, power and that they perform well individually. The convergence in this description might be due to fact that the coaches (and we as interviewers) contribute to a categorization of ethnic minority players as a uniform group, and the players themselves mis-recognize this cultural categorization and therefore reproduce it. In Bourdieu's words, a symbolic violence that is accepted because it is not recognized as violence.[32]

The coaches also noted that ethnic minority players often get to participate in talent training in football clubs at a later stage than ethnically Danish players.

> Generally the ethnic minority players are very technical, they are also very fast. However, they lack a good understanding of the tactics – also virtually none of them have had the opportunity to follow an elite training programme from a young age and so they tend to be lacking in coordination and tactical game play; this is definitely something that the players need to work on when they arrive in the junior and youth teams. (Peter)[33]

Besides pointing out speed and technique as skills of ethnic minority players, the coach above also mentions skills that he feels are lacking; that is tactical understanding of the game and coordination, which the players seemingly do not possess as part of their physical capital. To understand this observation we need to remember that for Bourdieu embodied capital is a form of cultural capital and it is a form of capital that takes time to accumulate. In other words the physical capital that young males with ethnic minority background possess from playing many self-organized football games cannot automatically be converted into the cultural capital that is considered as appropriate in club football. In particular, the players from the ghetto area often get to the football clubs relatively late – in their teenage years – compared to their ethnically Danish teammates, and this apparently has an impact on their physical training as noted above, but it also seems to affect their cultural understanding.

This is reinforced by the fact that the football skills of ethnic minority talents are described in a way that links their physical capital with common stereotypes about young males with immigrant background: ethnic minority players cannot control their temper, they are aggressive, etc. Below a coach describes what he sees as the difference between ethnic minority players and ethnically Danish players:

> If we have a bunch of [ethnically] Danish footballers and a group of second generation immigrants, the Danish kids find it easier to become team players, whereas the immigrants are more individualistic and more self focused; I can do it, I will do it, and that is a problem. (Esben)

Here the coach seems to think that being individualistic and self-centred is an internal cultural characteristic of immigrants. The coach's preference for team players can be interpreted as a consequence of the logic of competition: all players have to perform well to win the game. At the same time this can be understood as a product of the ethical code of behaviour according to which all players should be team players. The key point is that ethnic minority players' physical capital is not seen as complete. Even though some of their football skills are highlighted as extremely good, it is the skills that are associated with a process of cultivation in the clubs that are presented by the coaches as inadequate. Ethnic minority talents must learn not to focus on their individual competence, they must downplay their individual will and temper, they must take turns, both on and off the playing field, e.g. when collecting balls and water etc.

In particular, it is our interviewees from the ghetto area who identified as not having the informal education that would provide them with an understanding of the unwritten rules, or etiquette, of a Danish football club. For example, there is an expectation that in cases of absence from training, a player will send their apologies. Also, the coaches have their own expectations concerning appropriate behaviour. For instance a coach considered an ethnic minority player's apology for absence, because of a family birthday, as a lack of interest in the football team. Young males with an ethnic minority background living in other parts of the city are more successful at converting their physical capital into cultural capital. They seem to have a better basic understanding of the style of behaviour expected in the football clubs. This brings us to an analysis of the players' social capital.

Social capital

Here the question arises as to whether young males with an ethnic minority background can develop a supportive social network for their football career. Being able to convert physical capital into social relationships with teammates, coaches, club leaders, etc. could provide the players with a chance of enhancing their social status. Several of our informants living outside of the ghetto area such as Furkan, Nenad and Hakan were already acquainted with some of their teammates and have quickly become part of the social network surrounding their football team. Their relationships with teammates also provide them with precedents for the ways to relate to the coaches and club leaders. In some cases, the fathers of the players also contribute to the development of their son's social position. For instance, Ceyhun's father has become involved in voluntary work in the club and thereby has gained social respect that his son also benefits from.

For our informants living in the ghetto area the establishment of social relationships in the clubs is a bit more complicated. Maahir and Onur are examples of young males with ethnic minority background who feel alienated. Onur mentions that he has not mastered the language and therefore does not understand the instructions as fast as his Danish teammates. Meanwhile Maahir says:

> I have sometimes played with players from the national team, players who have a contract and so on. But I always felt like a foreigner when I was with these players. That is how I felt, anyway. (Maahir)

Maahir expresses the feeling of being different from the ethnically Danish majority in such a way that it remains unclear for us whether he is stigmatized by others or himself. Scambler and Hopkins distinguish between enacted and felt stigma and points out that felt stigma is complex because it refers to a fear of stigmatization.[34] Here, a fear of stigmatization seems to be a central part of the explanation why Maahir does not develop social relationships with his teammates.

Players like Maahir and Onur have moved between different transit clubs and premier league clubs (in and outside the city) without settling down and establishing a social network that can support the development of their football career. Also Osman, Gamal and Semih seem to have kept very close ties to their family, friends and minority group. Some of our oldest informants, Semih and Maahir, have returned to an ethnic minority club in the ghetto area. The feeling of belonging is a common motive for participating in ethnically separated clubs, where one shares manners, habits and language with his teammates and often also with the coach.[35]

A coach in the ethnic minority club describes their role in evaluating things when footballers, such as the informants described above, return 'home' after playing for one or more of the city clubs.

> Of course when we say to our players that they can move to a different club, we always leave the door open so that they can come back. When they do come back I always have a little chat with them and ask them why they have returned. When they tell us the reasons it is nearly always because they feel isolated. (Amin)

Our informants from the ghetto area often feel alienated and without social relationships in the majority clubs, whereas the players living in other parts of the city are more likely to develop social relationships in the clubs. A supportive social network seems important for the players' persistence in their football career.

Relevant here is Portes' idea that social capital can have both a positive and negative side,[36] and Putnam's distinction between bridging social capital– outward looking and crossing social cleavages, and bonding social capital – inward looking and reinforcing identities in homogenous groups.[37] In this case it is the bridging social capital that can contribute to the development of social relationships between minority and majority youngsters. The bonding social capital occurs both with a positive and negative side: positive in reinforcing the identity of ethnic minority youngsters once they return to ethnic minority clubs, and negative in the sense that it reinforces the isolation of ethnic minority talents.

Economic capital

The last part of our analysis has to do with whether the boys are able to convert their physical capital into economic capital. The challenge here is first of all whether young males with an ethnic minority background are able to raise the economic resources to develop their football career and in the longer run gain a contract with a regular salary.

First of all, economic capital is particularly needed for the players living in the suburb (the ghetto area) because many of them have low socio-economic resources. For instance:

> You can see because of my background – my father works in a factory and my mother is unemployed, and I have 3 or 4 brothers already, it is difficult anyway, this just is the way things are, regardless of whether I am the world's best footballer. (Onur)

As described above, Onur is resigned about his socio-economic situation and family support. In contrast, the family of another informant, Serdar, has moved from the countryside to a city apartment very near to the premier league club. Before the move the family used a lot of resources transporting their son to the daily training. As Kay points out, family support for children's' sporting talent can be both practical (providing finance, time and transport) and emotional.[38] Successful players such as Furkan and Serdar have a lot of support. Their families encourage them in difficult times and share the joy over their achievements.

Some of the subjects of our interviews were able to win economic funding as a result of their physical prowess. For instance, some clubs would arrange transport to training, or ignore the fact that they have not paid their membership fee. This kind of practical support is important for the young players' development, and ultimately their chance to improve their economic standing. So, for example, some of the players living in the ghetto area have been invited to attend test training for a short period in premier league clubs in other parts of the country. Given this opportunity, Osman, who is young and has a supportive family, was able to take advantage of the opportunity, whereas Onur only managed to arrange his transport the first couple of times. Moreover, due to the low socio-economic conditions of many young males of ethnic minority background, many are required to work for family businesses from a young age. For instance, Maahir was responsible for one of his family's shops while playing in a premier league club. Later he was offered the opportunity to move to Sweden and train with a Swedish club, with the prospect of receiving a contract, but he could not leave the family's firm. However, this may have been an excuse for a lack of willingness to move to another country where he might feel even more alienated from the majority society.

But, in turning down this invitation he also missed one of the crucial opportunities for ethnic minority talents to convert their physical capital to economic capital through obtaining a contract. One of the players living in the city, Serdar, holds a contract and another one, Furkan, thinks he ought to have a contract. Furkan and several other players suggest that there is a discriminatory practice taking place.

> When I think of the contract and such like, it's as if we Danes with different ethnic backgrounds need to be twice as good as the [ethnically Danish] Danes in order to get a contract. (Furkan)

Furkan's statement might be due to the fact that he feels deselected (or not fully acknowledged) as a football player or that he is simply not skilful enough. The interviewer asked Furkan's coach if he thought it was realistic for Furkan to expect to get a contract? The coach answered:

> Yes, I think so – well maybe. But he has to show that he is worth it – and I think he knows that. On the other hand I know of some coaches who say that if he doesn't play his part in defence, they won't use him at all. (Henning)

Interestingly, Furkan's possibility to convert his physical capital to economic capital (in the shape of a contract) is dependent on him proving that he can perform within the informal rules of team sports behaviour. Here it is helping out the defenders and in more general terms understanding the game's etiquette of taking turns, performing before enjoying, proving instead of telling your worth etc. that is pointed out as inadequate and seemingly will lead some coaches to deselect the player. This is paradoxical, since Furkan and other ethnic minority players are very dependent on their coaches' investment of time in developing their talent and crave acknowledgement from their coaches.

In spite of the fact that talent development is becoming more regulated in Danish football, our material indicates that club leaders and coaches are reluctant to allocate contracts to ethnic minority talents. Following the logic of competition, it is too risky and lengthy for them to invest in the development of ethnic minority players since it involves an investment of time to educate them into club culture, while they are under constant pressure to prove their success as coaches. Several of the coaches admit that they might tend to choose an ethnically Danish player rather than one with an ethnic minority background because then you know what you get. Moreover, most of the coaches have a background as volunteers or football players and seldom a professional education relevant for working with young males from ethnic minority backgrounds. As one of the club leaders says, it takes resources (both economic and professional) if the clubs are really to make progress in their work with ethnic minority talents.

Summing up

Seen from our perspective, young males with low socio-economic and ethnic minority background do not have a good chance of promoting their social mobility through a football career. First of all, their often self-acquired skills of speed, technique, individual performance, etc. are seen as inadequate, since these skills have not been accumulated together with an understanding of Danish football playing style and club etiquette, and several coaches think it would take too long to change this behaviour to make it worth their while. Secondly, several of the minority players find it difficult to develop social relationships with teammates, coaches and club leaders, who could equip them with a supportive social network and an enhanced social status in the field. In fact, the players from the ghetto area tend to feel like outsiders and instead return to their original social networks. Thirdly, young males with ethnic minority background often have few economic resources and the coaches are wary about allocating contracts to talents with an ethnic minority background.

As pointed out earlier, it is the composition and sum total of one's capital that underpins social mobility. In the case of the young footballers under discussion, the players' physical capital must be combined with the relevant cultural capital (the etiquette of the football club) and social capital (supportive social network), which altogether seem to enhance the players' persistence and chance of obtaining economic capital and thereby attaining social mobility.

To account for the fact that ethnic minority players' capital is composed in a way that does not seem to enhance their social mobility, it is relevant here to sum up the difficulties the concept of ethnic capital, which is defined as:

> the whole set of ethnic characteristics – including culture, attitudes, and economic opportunities – that the children in particular ethnic groups are exposed to. I want to argue the obvious: ethnic capital influences the socioeconomic development of children.[39]

What is interesting here is that George Borjas, the American researcher of migration and social mobility, points out that the capital young males of ethnic minority background possess is not always a benefit, but may in some circumstances have negative effects. Within a specific ethnic environment (ghetto or city, poor or more privileged, and more or less encompassing) they acquire a set of ethnic characteristics that influence their chances of obtaining social mobility. In Bourdieu's words, young males with ethnic minority background are equipped with a distinct habitus that is difficult to change.

Even if some of the ethnic minority talents are successful, it does not mean that the chances of social mobility for ethnic minority players as such are enhanced. The most successful player, Serdar, describes how his success developed after he, with support from a coach, went through a period of cultivation: learning how to contribute as a team player and downplay his individual performance. Other studies have also shown that the success of ethnic minority players might not create bigger variety in the field; but rather reinforce the cultural categorization or underemphasize differences in heritages.[40]

Moreover, the possible social mobility that ethnic minority talents can obtain as football players is transitory, since it is their physical capital that is the source of their acknowledgement. Some of the players might manage to convert their physical capital into an understanding of the team code, into influential social relations or economic wealth. Still, it is a fundamental problem for all football players that their careers are short. These problems are reinforced for ethnic minority players since they do not have precedents for taking over coaching or management positions in Danish football clubs.

Concluding perspectives

Even though we do not see good prospects for social mobility in our study we cannot dismiss the possible pattern breaker and the fact that some players might even develop their skills better under resistance. For example, the French football player Zinedine Zidane was brought up in an underprivileged area with working-class parents from Algeria. As France's highest-paid athlete he has become a symbol of the hopes of integration of ethnic minorities in France but he has also remained a contradictory figure in public discourse.[41] As Maguire has described, ethnic minority players (in his study on Afro/Caribbean black Britons) can and have become socially mobile as a result of either contest or sponsored mobility evident in professional soccer.[42] Maguire points out that black working-class athletes need sponsored help to a greater extent than their middle- and upper-class counterparts. It is also our impression that ethnic minority talents from low socio-economic conditions and ghetto areas would need substantially more help than ethnic minority youngsters from a more privileged background.

Even though Bourdieu with his set of concepts attempts to integrate our understanding of the ways in which social structures are present in, and developed through, practice, he has been criticized for giving too little attention to the agency of the individual.[43] An agency of the individual football player that our analysis has shown must be supported, for instance, by the coach's willingness to make a more long-term investment in the development of ethnic minority players. Moreover, Bourdieu developed his set of concepts in Algier within the frame of the French class system and there is therefore a tendency that analysis inspired by Bourdieu does not cover social change and thereby gives very negative prospects for social mobility. If the chance of social change is to be available for young ethnic minority males like those interviewed for this study, football clubs and other sponsoring institutions seem to be crucial agents of change that can contribute to the field by developing explicit policies for managing the training of ethnic minority players, setting up talent schools in ghetto areas, and employing personnel that are qualified to work with young males from ethnic minority backgrounds.

For the moment, however, we must conclude that the dream of social mobility that drives so many ethnic minority talents, particularly those from low socio-economic conditions, is not likely to be fulfilled in Danish football clubs. It is, as Maguire argues in a wider context, a myth that sport enhances social mobility.[44] A myth that is linked to the idea that sport is good and has the capacity to integrate ethnic minorities.[45]

Further research must be done to inquire into the (at the moment mainly implicit) strategies of integration in Danish sports clubs, reflecting the surrounding society ethnically. Danish club leaders and coaches tend to expect ethnic minority players to adapt to their clubs' cultures. However, with the growing number of football migrants and the presence of ethnic minority players, the clubs may yet be challenged to develop their management strategies to work in a multicultural context.

Acknowledgements

This essay is based on a second study in a two-year long research project on sports and integration focusing on problems stemming from a ghetto area in a Danish provincial. We would like to thank the Danish Cultural Ministry, Committee on Sports Research for funding the research project. Thanks also to Line Vindbæk Andersen for transcribing the interviews and for useful help through the research process. Last but not least a special acknowledgement to John Bale and Niels Kayser Nielsen for inspiring the research.

Notes

1. Carrington, 'Social Mobility', 3.
2. Eitle and Eitle, 'Race, Cultural Capital', 133; Collins and Buller, 'Social Exclusion', 425.
3. Bourke, 'The Dream', 406.
4. Carrington, 'Social Mobility', 11–12.
5. Hoberman, *Darwin's Athletes*, 5.
6. Various studies cited in Woodward, 'Professional Football Scouts', 358–61.
7. Maguire, 'Sport, Racism and British Society', 95.
8. Collins and Buller, 'Social Exclusion', 438.
9. Eitle and Eitle, 'Race, Cultural Capital', 141.
10. Programbestyrelsen, *Programbestyrelsens strategi mod ghettoisering*, 8.
11. Epinion, *Evaluering af Urbanprogrammet*, 39f.
12. Agergaard, 'Unges idrætsdeltagelse og integration ', 8.
13. Bell, *Middle Class Families*, 164.
14. Bourke, 'The Dream', 400.
15. Bloom, Coté and Stambulova, cited in Wylleman, Alfermann and Lavallee, 'Career Transitions in Sport', 10.
16. Bell, *Middle Class Families*, 21.
17. Bourdieu, 'Sport and Social Class', 819f; Bourdieu, *In Other Words*, 156f.
18. Bourdieu and Wacquant, *An Invitation*, 98.
19. Munk, *Social mobilitet*, 11f.
20. Schilling, 'Educating the Body', 653f; Wacquant, 'Pugs at Work', 65f.
21. Bourdieu, 'The Forms of Capital', 243.
22. Schilling, 'Educating the Body', 654.
23. Bourdieu, 'The Forms of Capital', 243; Bourdieu and Wacquant, *An Invitation*, 119.
24. Eitle and Eitle, 'Race, Cultural Capital', 123f; McGillivray and McIntosh, '"Football is My Life"', 371f; McGillivray, Fearn and McIntosh, 'Caught Up', 102f.
25. Agergaard, 'Dualities of Space', 261–2.
26. Bourdieu and Wacquant, *An Invitation*, 104.
27. Munk and Lind, *Idrættens kulturelle pol*, 24.
28. 'DBU Licenssystem – til gavn for spillernes udvikling'. http://www.dbu.dk/print/print_news.aspx.
29. According to a telephone conversation with Peter Rudbæk, manager of education in DBU.
30. 'Etisk Kodeks – for fodbold organiseret under Dansk Boldspil-Union', 1, edition December 21, 2006. http://www.dbu.dk/print/print_page.aspx..
31. Møller, 'What is Sport', 12–13.
32. Bourdieu, *In Other Words,* 84–5.

33. All names of informants have been changed and detailed information about the informants' club affliation, age etc. is not given due to the issue of anonymity.
34. Scambler and Hopkins, 'Being Epileptic', 33.
35. Elling, De Knop and Knoppers, 'The Social Integrative Meaning', 422.
36. Portes, 'Social Capital', 1f.
37. Putnam, *Bowling Alone*, 22.
38. Kay, 'Sporting Excellence', 156.
39. Borjas, *Heaven's Door*, 148.
40. Burdsey, '"One of the lads"?', 764.
41. Dauncey and Morrey, 'Quiet Contradictions of Celebrity', 303.
42. Maguire, 'Sport, Racism and British Society', 95–6.
43. Emirbayer and Mische, 'What is Agency', 964.
44. Maguire, 'Sport, Racism and British Society', 94.
45. Krouwel *et al.*, 'A Good Sport', 167.

References

Agergaard, Sine. 'Dualities of Space in Danish Sports History'. *Sport in History* 27 (2007): 260–75.

Agergaard, Sine. 'Unges idrætsdeltagelse og integration i idrætsforeninger i Århus Vest' [Youngsters' sports participation and integration in sports clubs in the western part of Aarhus]. København: Idrættens Analyseinstitut, 2008. http://www.idan.dk/vidensbank/forskningoganalyser/stamkort.aspx?publikationID=9883af93-ed74-464f-8085-9af000f1116e.

Bell, Colin. *Middle Class Families: Social and Geographical Mobility.* London: Routledge. e-book, 2000.

Borjas, George. *Heaven's Door. Immigration Policy and the American Economy.* Princeton, NJ and Oxford: Princeton University Press, 1999.

Bourdieu, Pierre. 'Sport and Social Class'. *Social Science Information* 17 (1978): 819–40.

Bourdieu, Pierre. 'The Forms of Capital'. In *Handbook of Theory and Research for the Sociology of Education,* ed. J.G. Richardson, 241–60. New York/Westport/Connecticut/London: Greenwood Press, 1986.

Bourdieu, Pierre. *In Other Words. Essays Towards a Reflexive Sociology.* Cambridge: Polity Press, 1990.

Bourdieu, Pierre, and Loïc J.D. Wacquant. *An Invitation Towards a Reflexive Sociology.* Cambridge: Polity Press, 1992.

Bourke, Ann. 'The Dream of Being a Professional Soccer Player: Insights on Career Development Options of Young Irish Players'. *Journal of Sport and Social Issues* 27 (2003): 399–419.

Burdsey, Daniel. '"One of the Lads"? Dual Ethnicity and Assimilated Ethnicities in the Careers of British Asian Professional Footballers'. *Ethnic and Racial Studies* 27 (2004): 757–79.

Carrington, Bruce. 'Social Mobility, Ethnicity and Sport'. *British Journal of Education* 7 (1986): 3–18.

Collins, Micheal F., and James R. Buller. 'Social Exclusion from High-Performance Sport. Are all Talented Young Sports People being given an Equal Opportunity of Reaching the Olympic Podium'. *Journal of Sport and Social Issues* 27 (2003): 420–42.

Dauncey, Hugh, and Douglas Morrey. 'Quiet Contradictions of Celebrity. Zinedine Zidane, Image, Sound, Silence and Fury'. *International Journal of Cultural Studies* 11 (2008): 301–20.

Eitle, Tamela McNulty, and David J. Eitle. 'Race, Cultural Capital, and the Educational Effects of Participation in Sports'. *Sociology of Education* 75 (2002): 123–46.

Elling, Agnes, Paul De Knop, and Annelies Knoppers. 'The Social Integrative Meaning of Sport: A Critical and Comparative Analysis of Policy and Practice in the Netherlands'. *Sociology of Sport Journal* 18 (2001): 414–34.

Emirbayer, Mustafa, and Ann Mische. 'What is Agency'. *The American Journal of Sociology* 103 (1998): 962–1023.

Epinion. 'Evaluering af Urbanprogrammet' [Evaluation of the urban programme]. Municipality of Aarhus: http://www.aarhuskommune.dk/ files/ aak/ aak/content/filer/urban/2005_-_Evaluering_af_Urbanprogrammet__ 20-10-05.pdf.

Hoberman, John. *Darwin's Athletes. How Sport has Damaged Black America and Preserved the Myth of Race.* Boston, MA: Houghton Mifflin, 1997.

Kay, Tess. 'Sporting Excellence: A Family Affair?' *European Physical Education Review* 6 (2000): 151–69.

Krouwel, André, Nanne Boonstra, Jan Willem Duyvendak, and Lex Veldboer. 'A Good Sport. Research into the Capacity of Recreational Sport to Integrate Dutch Minorities'. *International Review for the Sociology of Sport* 41 (2006): 165–80.

Maguire, Joe. 'Sport, Racism and British Society: A Sociological Study of England's Elite Male Afro/Caribbean Soccer and Rugby Union Players'. In *Sport, Racism and Ethnicity,* ed. Grant Jarvie, 94–123. London and New York: Routledgefalmer, 1991.

McGillivray, David, and Aaron McIntosh. '"Football is My Life": Theorizing Social Practice in the Scottish Professional Football Field'. *Sport in Society* 9 (2006): 371–87.

McGillivray, David, Richard Fearn, and Aaron McIntosh. 'Caught Up In and By the Beautiful Game. A Case Study of Scottish Professional Footballers'. *Journal of Sport and Social Issues* 19 (2005): 102–23.

Møller, Verner. 'What is Sport: Outline to a Redefinition'. In *The Essence of Sport,* ed. Verner Møller and John Nauright, 11–34. Odense: University of Southern Denmark, 2003.

Munk, Martin. *Social mobilitet. Social mobilitet i Danmark set i et internationalt perspektiv* [Social mobility. An international perspective on social mobility in Denmark]. København: Socialforskningsinstituttet, Arbejdspapir 9, 2003.

Munk, Martin, and Jakob Lind. *Idrættens kulturelle pol. En analyse af idrætsfeltets autonomi belyst ved Pierre Bourdieus metode* [The cultural pole of sports. An analysis of the tonomy of the field of sports using Pierre Bourdieu's method]. København: Museum Tusculanums Forlag, 2004.

Portes, Alejandro. 'Social Capital: Its Origins and Applications in Modern Sociology'. *Annual Review of Sociology* 24 (1998): 1–24.

Programbestyrelsen. *Programbestyrelsens strategi mod ghettoisering. Strategi 2005–2008* [Strategy by the committee of experts on the prevention of ghetto areas]. The Ministry of Refugee, Immigration and Integration Affairs. http://www.nyidanmark.dk/bibliotek/ publikationer /strategier_politikker/2005/programbestyrelse_strategi_ 0508/index.htm.

Putnam, Robert D. *Bowling Alone: The Collapse and Revival of American Community.* New York: Simon & Schuster, 2000.

Scambler, Graham, and Anthony Hopkins. 'Being Epileptic. Coming to Terms with Stigma'. *Sociology of Health & Illness* 8 (1986): 26–43.

Schilling, Chris. 'Educating the Body: Physical Capital and the Production of Social Inequalities'. *Sociology* 25 (1991): 653–72.

Wacquant, Loïc J.D. 'Pugs at Work: Bodily Capital and Bodily Labour Among Professional Boxers'. *Body & Society* 1 (1995): 65–93.

Woodward, J.R. 'Professional Football Scouts: An Investigation of Racial Stacking'. *Sociology of Sport Journal* 21 (2004): 356–75.

Wylleman, P., D. Alfermann, and D. Lavallee. 'Career Transitions in Sport: European Perspectives'. *Psychology of Sport and Exercise* 5 (2004): 7–20.

The promise of soccer in America: the open play of ethnic subcultures

Derek Van Rheenen

Graduate School of Education, University of California, Berkeley, USA

Introduction

The dominant narrative of American soccer has been a tale of promise unfulfilled. The story runs something like this: despite more children playing soccer than any other sport in many American youth leagues, professional soccer has not gained a stronghold as a major spectator sport in the United States. The relative lack of success of the men's national soccer team in international competition has also led to its limited public and media attention.[1] This narrative is part of a larger dialogue framed within a sporting hegemony specific to the United States in the late twentieth and early twenty-first centuries. This *common sense* understanding of an American sport ethic privileges men over women, power and performance over pleasure and participation, and national pastimes over imported sports.[2] Where the dominant sports of baseball, basketball and American football captivate the masses and comprise the majority of media attention, soccer remains in the popular culture margins. American soccer's marginalization, however, has allowed the sport to retain a certain richness of cultural and historical expression, particularly in soccer's juxtaposition with American dominant sports.[3] From a socially marginalized position, soccer as ethnic subculture[4] has demonstrated a potential to redefine the dominant notion of sport as an agent of social assimilation and mobility. Thus, rather than a tale of promise unfulfilled, American soccer has provided an open terrain for new ethnicities to mark space in an emerging nation.

The potential assimilation and integration of ethnic groups into dominant or core society through sports has been noted in the literature throughout the twentieth century.[5] The power of sport as an assimilatory agent depends not only on the sport and the participating ethnic group, but also on the historical and cultural context within which the game is played. As Jarvie reminds us, 'there may be a strong element of volunteerism and freedom of choice in sport, but it is only within a range of negotiated and socially produced limits and pressures'.[6] This subtle dialectic between agency and structure in sport selection is further confounded by the age of the participants and their relative freedom of choice. Children who are 'signed up' for Little League Baseball or Pop Warner Football will likely have qualitatively different cultural experiences than men and women volunteering to participate in an adult soccer league. In the United States and other countries, where soccer is subordinate to other national pastimes and often perceived as a foreign or ethnic game, the role of sport in cultural assimilation or fortification is nuanced and varied. In this regard, modern sport has been a powerful means for both ethnic restriction and release, disenfranchisement and enfranchisement.[7]

Regarding adult urban soccer leagues, Pooley found that ethnic soccer clubs in Milwaukee, Wisconsin inhibited the structural assimilation of its team members into core society.[8] McKay and Day found that heightened competition and player recruitment led to increased cultural assimilation within Canadian ethnic soccer leagues.[9] For many clubs, the allure of having a winning record through the recruitment of non-ethnic but skilful players may be more important than maintaining a singular ethnic identity. These conflicting findings are not unusual, but seem to depend largely on the historical context of a given sporting practice in a given time and place. While Lever found that Brazilian soccer helped to integrate disparate social communities,[10] Cheska argued that sport in the American southwest served to reaffirm ethnic boundaries among Native Americans.[11]

Thus, drawing on the research of ethnicity and sport in the United States and elsewhere, it appears that sport, so commonly seen as a functional means for assimilation and integration, may maintain rather than integrate ethnic boundaries. This more complex reading of sport and ethnicity further problematizes the process of immigration and assimilation, where national boundaries and identities are blurred while steadfastly protected.[12] As Hallinan and Krotee noted about non-Anglo Celtic soccer clubs in Wollongong, Australia, the sport has 'provided something of an agency to suppress the process of being culturally drowned by the hegemonic Anglo-Celtic discourse'.[13] This freedom to assert an oppositional ethnic identity to core or dominant society may have been part of the reason that Soccer Australia (formerly the Australian Soccer Federation) banned all A-League teams from ethnic team names, displaying ethnic insignia on uniforms and prohibited fans from bringing national flags into the stands in the early 1990s. Thus, Sydney Croatia became Sydney United, for example, in order to 'de-ethnicize' the sport and curb potential violence among opposing clubs and their respective fans.[14] This effort to make more Australian 'wogball' or the 'ethnic game'[15] is paralleled in the United States where soccer retains its rich ethnic traditions.

'Americanizing' the beautiful game

During its tumultuous tenure from 1968 to 1984, the North American Soccer League (NASL) likewise attempted to 'Americanize' the professional soccer league by altering the rules of the game and limiting its reliance on foreign players. The rules were changed in order to make soccer more exciting for American fans. A clock that counted down to zero rather than up to the standard 45-minute half was used. The traditional midfield line for off-sides was replaced with a 35-yard line, with the hopes of generating more scoring.[16] Finally, a shoot-out was implemented to ensure a winner by deciding matches that ended in a draw.

Seeking greater excitement and more goals for the American fan, a hybrid-game of indoor soccer was also created in the United States in the 1970s, culminating in the establishment of the Major Indoor Soccer League (MISL) in 1978. The field resembles a regulation-size hockey rink, commonly 200' by 85', with goals recessed into the walls of an indoor arena. Goals, and the corresponding penalty area, are smaller than in standard soccer. Indoor soccer is generally played with six active players per team, one of which is the goalkeeper. Players can use the walls during competition and there is no off-sides rule, which promotes a higher-scoring game. Despite the attempted Americanization of soccer with the development of this hybrid-indoor game, the MISL and indoor soccer has also actively recruited foreign players. The league recognizes two teams of All-Stars, the MISL USA team, comprised of US citizens, and the MISL International squad, made up of foreign citizens. In their annual All-Star Game, these two teams compete for league dominance.

As such, American professional soccer has often had to address its over-reliance on foreign nationals. Ironically, however, the heyday of the NASL came in the mid to late 1970s when players such as Pelé, Eusébio, Franz Beckenbauer and Johan Cruyff were recruited to play for teams such as the New York Cosmos, St Louis Stars, Chicago Sting and the San Jose Earthquakes. Crowds in excess of 70,000 came to watch the Cosmos play when Pelé and other international stars were on the roster. But this popularity for professional soccer in America was fleeting. Soon, the crowds diminished and the league struggled financially, especially after paying some of these star players exorbitant salaries to play in the United States.

Responding to the desire by fans to watch American rather than foreign stars, the league implemented a rule in the early 1980s which required that each team have at least five American players on the field at all times during competition. The NASL also created a new club, Team America in 1983, comprised entirely of US national team players and based in the US capital, Washington DC. Despite the league's attempt to further Americanize the game, several teams, most notably the New York Cosmos, refused to release their US national team players. Due to league infighting, competition with the Major Indoor Soccer League, declining attendance and the loss of their television contract with ABC, the NASL officially folded in 1985.[17]

The current professional soccer league in the United States, Major League Soccer (MLS), established in 1993,[18] has also tried to limit its reliance on foreign players. Originally comprised of ten teams, the league has expanded to 14 teams in 2008 and hopes to expand even further to 18 teams by 2010–11. With the expansion in 2008, the league's foreign player rule, limiting the number of foreign nationals on a roster, has been revised to include eight rather than seven foreign players.[19] While deputy commissioner Ivan Gazidis notes that 'the reality of MLS budgets is that teams don't have the money to go out and become Chelsea or Arsenal',[20] the purchase of celebrity international players such as David Beckham to play for the league's Los Angeles Galaxy seem to suggest the beginnings of an economic arms race. Beckham's contract with the Galaxy made him the highest paid MLS player in history and has upped the ante for buying soccer talent abroad. Thus, despite the game's rich history of ethnic and youth participation in the United States, American professional soccer continues to rely on foreign players.

Playing America the beautiful: the San Francisco Soccer Football League (SFSFL)

The historical efforts to 'Americanize' soccer in the United States appear to be connected to both reducing foreign influence on the game while espousing a commercialized sport ethic. While professional sport leagues in the United States, such as the National Football League (NFL) and the National Basketball Association (NBA), have been strikingly adept at expanding markets abroad and selling an American dream of commodified popular and material culture, soccer in America continues to be seen as an imported product. In the United States, importing the global game of soccer has been far less popular among American spectators than exporting so-called American sports and the dominant values associated with these sports. The fact that soccer was imported into the United States hundreds of years ago and played broadly by its new citizenship does not seem to lessen soccer's perceived foreign character. Thus, this public perception of soccer as non-American is striking given the sport's long history in the United States and its tremendous popularity among youth and adult amateur athletes today.

Prior to the proliferation of youth soccer leagues, adult amateur and semi-professional American soccer leagues have long relied on the ethnic participant and fan. Despite some form of the game being played in the early seventeenth century in the American colonies, the first written accounts of soccer matches involve intramural contests at major colleges and universities in the Northeast United States. The first intercollegiate game to adopt the London Football Association's rules took place in 1869 between Princeton and Rutgers, in which Rutgers won 6-4. These rules allowed 25 players, a 24 foot wide goal and the use of all parts of the body, including hands. The ball could be batted or held but not carried or thrown, and the first team to score six goals was deemed the victor. Ironically, this game is also recognized as the first American football game.[21]

As immigration increased during the nineteenth century, so too did local and regional leagues begin to proliferate. The San Francisco Soccer Football League (SFSFL),[22] established in 1902, provides a rich example of the complex ways in which sport and ethnicity intersect to give meaning to both over time. The SFSFL is one of the oldest and most cosmopolitan semi-professional and amateur leagues in the United States, predating the establishment of the Fédération of International Football Association (FIFA). Today, the SFSFL is the oldest American soccer league in continuous existence.

In a May 1948 local publication entitled *California Soccer Football*, J.N. Young describes the history of soccer in San Francisco. Noting that Association Football (soccer) had been played on the Pacific Coast since the late 1880s, the author describes the sport's foreign influence. Young writes,

> Wherever you find a colony of Britishers you will find a Soccer ball and men to play with it. The introduction of the game to San Francisco can be traced back to the time when 'windjammers' plied the seas from foreign ports ... Every ship had a football in its locker and when port was reached it was natural for the sailors to get out to a field and release some of the energy that had been pent up during the three or four months it took to make the trip here.[23]

Young describes how these seafaring men would meet at the Sailors Institute on Stuart Street, where 'boys met and challenged each other to a game of soccer, their national pastime'.[24] In addition to these sailors passing through, San Francisco was a city of immigrants. In 1852, more than half of all males in the city were foreign born.[25] Many of these men likewise elected to play at what they sought to create as their new American pastime of soccer. As such, the SFSFL had old world or ethnic affiliations from its inception. The first league champions were the American British Rifles, but other teams in the league included the San Francisco Scottish Thistle Club, French Athletic Club and the Occidentals.

San Francisco witnessed various waves of immigration throughout the twentieth century; generally, the influx of immigrants led to increased club representation in the San Francisco Soccer Football League. Following the First World War, the league added a second division to accommodate the growing interest in fielding soccer teams comprised of German, Russian and other European immigrants to the city. The Teutonia Football Club (originally AAC Teutonia) was established in 1923 'by eight boys who came here from Germany'.[26] Similarly, the Mercury Athletic Club was founded the same year, when, according to Boxer, three men met in church on Russian Easter: 'All were new to this country so started asking each other where a Russian soccer club was. It turned out that there were none here so they organized the Russian Athletic Club – Mercury.'[27] Other ethnic clubs established during this time included Hakoah or the Jewish Athletic Club (1926), Unione Sportiva Italiana Virtus (1926) and Union Española Club (1926), 'the pathfinder team for a growing Latin community in San Francisco'.[28] In fact, Club Peru (1926) and Mexico AC (1927) soon followed as members of the San Francisco Soccer Football League (SFSFL).

After the Second World War, San Francisco experienced another wave of immigration, which prompted the addition of more teams and the establishment of a third division in the league. Athletic Clubs such as the Greek-Americans (1949) and the Sons of Italy (1950) were established and joined by additional Latin American teams such as El Salvador (1950), Columbia AC (1954), and Guadalajara (1956). Today, over one half a century later, the San Francisco Soccer Football League is comprised of 70 teams, represented across six divisions (Premier, Major, First, Second, Third and Fourth). Club names continue to be ethnically marked, with relative newcomers, such as Jalisco (1989), the Haitian Express (1998) and Bosnajci (1998), competing in the same league with the more traditional SFSFL clubs of El Salvador, Club Peru, Sons of Italy and the San Francisco Scots, among others.

Reshaping ethnicity as open terrain on a soccer pitch in San Francisco: the Greek-American Athletic Club

Just as sports vary from one historical period to another and from one culture to the next, and the choice to participate within a given sport is negotiated within socio-cultural limits and pressures, so too is ethnicity a negotiated terrain. As Stuart Hall argued in his seminal article 'New Ethnicities', 'the term "ethnicity" acknowledges the place of history, language, and culture in the construction of subjectivity and identity, as well as the fact that all discourse is placed, positioned, situated, and all knowledge is contextual'.[29] Ethnicity, like identities of class, race, gender and sexuality, are not fixed but fluid. These fluid identities are at play in the social construction of games and sports. Depending on the game, the participants, the place and historical moment, the range of intersecting social meanings is vast. As MacClancy writes, 'The creative possibilities by which people, via sports, can play with their identity is only limited by the sports available to them at any one time within their lived space. In other words, sports are ways of fabricating in a potentially complex manner a space for oneself in their social world.'[30] In today's San Francisco Soccer Football League, soccer's polysemic possibilities – the potential for multiple signification – marks ethnicity as primary within this open terrain of social identities. Thus, when discussing a male soccer player representing a team with an ethnic moniker, such as the Greek-Americans or the San Francisco Scots, the symbolic representation of ethnicity takes primary signification in the politics of identity, traversing frontiers of race, class, gender and sexuality. The fluidity of self articulation on the soccer field is not unlike the motion of the game itself, at times conservative, at others creative and open.

The complex play of ethnic identification through sport acknowledges a range of cultural possibilities within the same game. As Cronin and Mayall assert, 'it is possible for immigrants to express their distinct ethnic identity by participating in or supporting a (native) sport or team, but otherwise and for the most part seeking, consciously and deliberately, to assimilate into the host society and to lose any signs of separateness in a multicultural whole.'[31] While some ethnic clubs or teams within the San Francisco Soccer Football League have made direct reference to their ethnically-based American citizenship, such as the British-American Rifles or the Greek-Americans, others identify solely with their native countries. *Being American*, whether hyphenated in name-sake or not, is perhaps assumed as part of league membership; however, *being ethnic* is distinctly marked in almost all club's athletic production. This production is complicated as more and more members of the team no longer share their team's ethnic affiliation. This team integration, as it turns out, may shed light on the actual process of becoming American. The Greek-Americans, for example, became the most dominant team in the history of the league, and perhaps the entire west coast of the United States, as evidenced by their league, state and national cup championships.[32] But this athletic dominance witnessed a shift in player personnel that mirrored a particular ethnic community's complex assimilation into a San Francisco sports league and American society overall. And yet, this shift from a team comprised solely of Greek players to a roster with not a single Greek-American player may have been more a reflection of wanting to win games than a strong desire to integrate fully into the dominant society.

The San Francisco Greek-American Athletic Club was organized by two Greek brothers 'as a diversion for young Greek immigrants who had settled in the Bay Area after the war'.[33] Established in 1949 as the Pan-Hellenes, the club was initially under the auspices of the Greek Orthodox Church of Annunciation in San Francisco, where many of the players were also members of the church choir. As the soccer team began to play on Sundays during season, an inherent conflict developed. An ethnic soccer team was established, but the team's participation came at the expense of missed church services and a depleted choir. After two years of these Sunday conflicts, the team name was changed to the Greek-Americans under the leadership of the Greek-American Youth Club. Whether as the Pan-Hellenes or Greek-American Athletic Club, the team recruited players from their own ethnic community throughout the 1950s.

In 1952, the team was promoted to the First Division of the SFSFL, largely as the result of the 43 goals scored that season by Cypriot Mike Nicholas. Every player on that team was of Greek descent. After one year in the top division of the league, the team was demoted back to the Second Division. The team climbed back into the first division a few years later, only to be demoted again after the 1958–59 season. According to the original founders and owners of the Greek-American Athletic Club,

GREEK AMERICANS - Left to right: Victor Gavalllos, George Anagnostou, John Rally , Harris Giannoulis, Mike Courtis, Ted Constantinou, Themis Kotronakis, Chris Anagnostou, Mike Davos, John Trellon, Peter Zarkades, Mike Nicolas, Jim Rally,
At Microphone: Supervisor George Christopher and League President Matt Boxer during presentation of 2nd Division Championship Trophy for 1952-53 season

Figure 1.   Greek American soccer team of SFSFL, 1952–53. Second division champions. All players were of Greek origin.

John and Jim Rally, these demotions proved to be a turning point as the club made the decision to recruit the best players for the club team, regardless of national heritage.[34] It was only after this conscious decision to recruit non-Greek players that the club began to dominate the SFSFL. The late 1950s and early 1960s were dominated by the San Francisco Scots and Teutonia, the German-American club. Between 1958 and 1966, the San Francisco Scots won five league titles while Teutonia took three. But over the next seven years, the Greek-Americans won five titles and began to assert their league dominance. Alongside forward and Greek-American Kirk Apostolides, the club recruited former English professional player, Scottish striker Tommy Dawkins, to help score goals and win games.[35]

Victories and league championships prompted continued recruitment of non-Greek players. The team won seven of ten league titles and eight of ten Northern California Open Cup championships during the 1980s. It was during this decade, in particular, that the Rally brothers built a soccer dynasty comprised of international and American-born players, many of whom had played in the local colleges and universities. At times, the team's roster read like a United Nations assembly, with members from Europe, Africa, Central and South America and the Middle East. When the Greek-Americans won the Open Cup National Championship in 1984, the team was comprised of mostly foreign-born players who had emigrated from Sweden, Scotland, Holland, Belgium, Honduras, Nigeria, Turkey and Iran. There were only four American-born players on the team.

The Greek-American Athletic Club was clearly not opposed to recruiting immigrants who could play soccer well; the historical trend merely shifted from the recruitment of Greek immigrants to those from other countries. Most of these international players had already been recruited to the San Francisco Bay Area to compete for local colleges and universities, particularly from the University of San Francisco, a Jesuit university and soccer powerhouse during this period. Professional coaches were likewise recruited and paid. During the San Francisco Greek-American's heyday in the late 1980s and mid 1990s, the club hired Lothar Osiander, one-time US National team coach. In fact, Osiander managed the San Francisco Greek-American Soccer Club while representing the United States as national team coach. The Club's strategy to recruit the best players and coach paid off in terms of wins and losses. During one period between 1986 and 1989, the San Francisco Greek-Americans were undefeated in 55 consecutive games.

The Club's dominance continued into the 1990s, but another shift took place away from recruiting foreign players to finding American-born players. In 1994, when the American Professional Soccer League (APSL) had folded in anticipation of the US-hosted World Cup and the formal launching of Major League Soccer (MLS), the Greek-Americans fielded a roster of former and current United States national team players, former professional players, with the former US National team coach at the helm. Once again, the club won the prestigious United States Open Cup National Championship, the last time that an 'amateur' team has won the cup. The Greek-American Athletic Club's roster for this national championship was comprised of 14 American-born citizens and four foreign-born immigrants. Only ten years earlier, when the club previously won the Open Cup, the ratio of foreign- to American-born players was reversed. By 1994, the American player had emerged in the SFSFL.

Figure 2.   Greek American soccer team of the SFSFL, 1994. U.S. National Open Cup Champions. No players were of Greek origin.

If the soccer players are the primary producers and representatives of the club in the SFSFL, the owners and managers of the teams are the direct link to ethnic pride and their community. They either established the club in the first place or are tied to its cultural history. They also finance the costs incurred as part of competition, which can be extremely expensive when paying players, paying league fees and the costs of travelling to regional, national and international tournaments. After winning the Open Cup National Championship in 1984 and 1994, the Greek-Americans represented the United States in the CONCACAF's (Confederation of North, Central American and Caribbean Association Football) annual Gold Cup, the main soccer competition of the 40 men's national soccer teams from North and Central America and the Caribbean. The team travelled in 1985 to Bermuda and to Mexico in 1995, financed entirely by the club. According to John Rally, President and founder of the Club, he spent approximately $75,000 a year for over 40 years of directing the team's soccer success.

In terms of the fluidity or stability of ethnic representation through team affiliation, the consumers or fans of their team in the SFSFL are steadfast and loyal. Their stable loyalty, win or lose, is first and foremost a result of ethnic pride. Members of the ethnic community might not attend games, but they would take pride in their successes through direct or indirect contact with the team. The community members might interact with players at a clubhouse or an affiliated business after games, where they would provide their support for the players, whether they shared their ethnic backgrounds or not. Sponsors of the team are most often ethnically affiliated, as well, perhaps a local business, such as a restaurant or bar with direct ethnic ties. Greek-American Athletic Club owners, John and Jim Rally, organized an annual Dinner Dance for over 40 years, drawing on the sponsorship of the Greek-American community. In the Greeting of the Dinner Dance Program dated Saturday 26 January 1985, Chairman Jim Rally writes: 'It is once again my great pleasure to welcome you all to our 35th Annual Dinner Dance, and to thank you for your continued moral and financial support. Our thanks are also extended to our advertisers in this yearbook, without whose generosity and understanding of our cause, the continuation of our work would be most difficult.' The programme or yearbook, 5″ × 8″ in size, was approximately 15 pages long. In addition to the Greeting, the programme included pictures of the current and former teams, several pages devoted to the History of the Greek-American Soccer Team, as well as a page devoted to the Club's Hall of Fame. The remainder of the programme was advertising from local proprietors such as Zeus Construction, Xenios Classic Greek Cuisine and Demetri's Deli and Catering, to name a few sponsors. Chairman Rally estimated that the Dinner Dance netted between $5,000 and $10,000 a year in support of the team.[36]

In his greeting, Rally continues:

> In thirty-five years of uninterrupted activity in soccer competition, our organization has accumulated a record that is unsurpassed in the annals of local athletics, having won a combined total of 28 league and cup championships. We are extremely proud of these achievements for it reflects well not only upon our organization, but upon our Bay Area Hellenic Communities and our glorious heritage.[37]

These words articulate the direct connection between ethnic pride and the athletic accomplishment of the club. That most of these championships have been won with players outside of the Greek-American community does not seem to dampen the spirit and celebration of the ethnic community itself.

This trend towards multiculturalism and ethnic heterogeneity among players in the SFSFL occurred with most teams in the league throughout the twentieth century. While some teams made greater efforts to recruit players from their ethnic communities and/or had a greater pool of talent from which to draw, no team in the SFSFL prohibits players from other nationalities, particularly if they can play. As the case of the Greek-American Athletic Club attests, some teams actively recruit players based primarily on competitive soccer skill rather than ethnic heritage. Thus, while the majority of the teams in the SFSFL retain an ethnic identity today, the selection process of players to teams is not unidirectional or top-down. There is an element of volunteerism at play as well. While the club's motivation may be to recruit players who share their ethnic background and/or are more competitive and skilful players, the players' motivations might be financial (pay for play), aesthetic (style of play) and/or cultural, such as playing for a team representing their ethnic heritage. For example, an ethnic affiliated team might be represented in a lower (or even in the same) division, but a more skilful player of that same ethnic heritage may opt to compete at a higher level for a different team with a different ethnic affiliation. The opposite might also be true. Despite the ability to compete at a higher level, and the active recruitment from another team, a player may opt to remain with a team comprised of fellow countrymen. Ethnic integration and assimilation through sport was often created, therefore, as a result of the club's active recruitment of players and the conscious decision of those players to compete for a more competitive team. Thus, there are often mixed allegiances by ethnicity, where a Scottish player might play for the Greek-Americans rather than the San Francisco Scots. The resultant heterogeneity of the players on these ethnic teams supports the possibilities of cultural integration and assimilation. The SFSFL therefore provides an American sporting experience in which national and ethnic identity is strengthened at the same time that a multicultural experience through sport is made possible.

The open play of ethnicity in the amateur or semi-professional adult SFSFL likewise confronts the dominant belief of sport as a vehicle for social mobility. Rags-to-riches stories through sport are rare even in major spectator sports, but achieving the American Dream through professional soccer is nearly impossible in the United States. In general, the San Francisco Soccer Football League is not a farm system for the professional ranks, although players have moved from the top division of the league onto professional and national team rosters. During the off season of the professional season and during periods when there was no American professional soccer league, the SFSFL, and other amateur urban leagues like it, provided the highest level of soccer in the United States. Over the years, therefore, there has been a blurring of the line between amateur and professional, whereby many of the recruited players were paid to play on Sundays. During the dominant reign of the Greek-Americans in the SFSFL, players received anywhere from $50 to $250 per game to play. In addition to seeking a more competitive level of play, this financial incentive may have trumped the desire to represent a club based upon ethnic affiliation. While playing for pay might be an incentive, none of these players perceived themselves as soccer professionals.

Many of the players in the SFSFL were college-educated and solidly middle class. Newly arrived immigrants were seeking their own economic security through work. Playing soccer was generally a diversion and not a primary means for financial gain.

As Martinez argues, 'soccer in the USA remains both a sport of middle-aged immigrant men and of middle class boys who don't need to succeed in sports in order to survive whatever adversity life has to throw at them'.[38] For the college-educated American soccer player, opting for a professional career in something other than soccer seems a rational decision. In 2007, the starting salary for a professional soccer player in Major League Soccer was $12,900, hardly a rags-to-riches story of upward social mobility.[39] This meagre salary in the US premier professional soccer league can be juxtaposed with the contracts of international players such as British midfielder David Beckham (earning $6.5 million dollars guaranteed), Mexican striker Cuauhtémoe Blanco (earning $2.5 million dollars guaranteed) and Columbia striker Juan Pablo Ángel (earning $1.6 million dollars guaranteed).

Conclusion

Thus, on the one hand, we see professional American soccer perceived as too 'foreign', as the premiere soccer league in the United States actively recruits international stars while simultaneously enacting rules which limit the number of foreign players. Today's David Beckham is yesterday's Pelé for professional soccer in the United States. However, soccer in America has enjoyed a tremendously rich history as an ethnic and amateur sport, simultaneously promoting cultural fortification and assimilation. From a socially marginalized position, soccer as ethnic subculture has demonstrated the potential to both reinforce and challenge the dominant notion of sport as an agent of social integration and assimilation. As the Greek-American Athletic Club illustrates, during the latter half of the twentieth century, amateur soccer has allowed space for immigrants and ethnic communities to play for and support their particular team. Within the SFSFL, increased competition and the blurring of amateurism and professionalism has significantly altered the process of player recruitment and volunteerism. This nuanced process has likewise altered the cultural composition of many ethnically-marked clubs, to the extent that some clubs like the San Francisco Greek-Americans now field a team with not a single player of Greek descent. The recruitment first of non-Greek immigrants, followed by the selection of American-born players for the roster, highlights a clear process of team and league assimilation. Whether this process for one team within the SFSFL represents a more general process of ethnic assimilation and integration in San Francisco, and the United States overall, is less clear. Nonetheless, San Francisco soccer fields have indeed afforded space for communities to assemble around a common goal. Thus, rather than a tale of promise unfulfilled, the San Francisco Football Soccer League, and American soccer in general, has provided an open terrain for new ethnicities to play and compete for cultural space in an emerging nation.

Notes

1. As of September 2009, the US Men's national soccer team is currently ranked eleventh in the world, based upon FIFA's revised ranking system. This statistic suggests that the US men have been extremely successful in international competition. And, in fact, the national team has fared well overall. But while the US men have qualified for the past five World Cup tournaments, the team has only won three games out of the eighteen games played during those five tournament appearances (the full results are three wins, twelve losses and three draws). Conversely, the US women's national team is currently ranked #1 in the world. The FIFA Women's World Cup has been contested five times,

with the US women winning the tournament twice (1991, 1999). Following the US women's first place finish in the 1999 World Cup, a professional women's league was established. It is possible that American women's success in soccer worldwide has negatively impacted the popularity of men's professional soccer in the United States. As Dolores Martinez notes (2008, 239), "the success of women could well be the final nail in the coffin of male soccer participation—if women can triumph in the sport, it really must not be tough enough to qualify as a true test of *American* masculinity" (author's italics).

2. See Sage (1998, 30) on hegemony in sport and the silent domination of subordinate groups through 'commonsense' and everyday practices. Thus, "modern sport, rather than being merely a diversionary entertainment, is considered to be an important popular culture practice upon which dominant ideologies are constructed, maintained, and reproduced." This works to the advantage of men over women or male hegemony, where "the traditions, symbols, and values of sport have therefore tended to preserve patriarchy and women's subordinate position in society" (64). See also Coakley (2011, 489-491) on the predominance of power and performance sports over pleasure and participation sports.

3. As Foer (2005, 237) points out, "soccer's appeal lay in its opposition to the other popular sports. For children of the sixties, there was something abhorrent about enrolling kids in American football, a game where violence wasn't just incidental but inherent. They didn't want to teach the acceptability of violence, let alone subject their precious children to the risk of physical maiming. Baseball, where each batter must stand center stage four or five times a game, entailed too many stressful, potentially ego-deflating encounters." This counter-cultural celebration of soccer and its positive socializing potential has led many parents, particularly fathers, to respond. Sport radio shock jock Jim Rome, who became popular in the mid-1990s, exemplifies this anti-soccer tirade, when he railed, "My son is not playing soccer. I will hand him ice skates and a shimmering sequined blouse before I hand him a soccer ball. Soccer is not a sport, does not need to be on my TV, and my son will not be playing it" (quoted in Foer, 242). Rome's resistance to soccer as an oppositional sport culture demonstrates an American masculinist sport ethic that is troubling, but all too common.

Soccer may not been seen by some fathers (or parents) as the best sport to instill conservative American values in their boys in particular, but other critics see the sport as anti-American from a geo-political perspective.

Jack Kemp, former Buffalo Bills quarterback and nine-term U.S. Republican Representative, was opposed to a 1986 resolution put before the Congress of the United States to support a bid to host the World Cup. He argues: "I think that it is important for all those young out there, who someday hop to play real football, where you throw it and kick and run with it and put it in your hands, a distinction should be made that football is democratic, capitalist, whereas soccer is a European socialist [sport] " (quoted in Foer, 241). Kemp was a leading Republican candidate for the Presidential election in 1988 and the Republican Vice Presidential candidate in 1996. He lost both of these bids for election, while the United States won the bid to host the 1994 World Cup despite his opposition.

4. Soccer has been described as the 'ethnic game' (Stoddart, *Saturday Afternoon Fever*; Hallinan and Krotee, 'Conceptions of Nationalism'), particularly when the players and/or fans are drawn primarily from ethnic populations. Given its marginalization vis-à-vis the dominant spectator sports of baseball, basketball and American football in the United States, soccer is likewise an American sport subculture. In his article, 'Subcultures in Sport: Resilience and Transformation', Donnelly writes: 'as cultural units that share in the dominant culture and maintain and produce a number of alternative cultural forms and ideologies, subcultures provide an ideal model with which to explore dominant, residual, and emergent aspects of culture' (121). As such, I use the term 'ethnic subculture' to describe American soccer.

5. Rader, *American Sports*; Eisen, *Ethnicity and Sport*; Franks, *Crossing Sidelines*.

6. Jarvie, 'Introduction', 2. See also Gruneau, *Class, Sports, and Social Development*.

7. Mangan and Ritchie, *Ethnicity, Sport, Identity*.

8. Pooley, 'Ethnic Soccer Clubs'.

9. McKay, 'Sport and Ethnicity' and Day, 'Ethnic Soccer Clubs'.

10. Lever, *Soccer Madness*.
11. Cheska, 'Sport as Ethnic Boundary Maintenance'.
12. As Cronin and Mayall assert, 'In its more "mature" form, a national identity can permit the blurring of differences and serve to unite a multi-ethnic people behind a single national ideal, as is encapsulated in the notion of the American Dream.' Cronin and Mayall, *Sporting Nationalisms*, 3.
13. Hallinan and Krotee, 'Conceptions of Nationalism', 131.
14. Hughson, 'The Boys are Back in Town'.
15. Stoddart, *Saturday Afternoon Fever*; Hallinan and Krotee, 'Conceptions of Nationalism'.
16. FIFA granted this rule change in the United States in 1973 but forced the NASL, and the American version of the game, to readopt the worldwide standard in 1983.
17. Litterer, 'An Overview of American Soccer'.
18. Major League Soccer (MLS) began play in 1996 but was formed on 17 December 1993, fulfilling a promise to FIFA from the US Soccer Federation to establish a 'Division One' professional soccer league in exchange for staging the 1994 FIFA World Cup.
19. Previously, the seven international players had to fall into two distinct groups of either senior (age 25 or older) or youth (age 24 or younger) players. Major League Soccer's revised foreign player rule now allows each club eight international players with no youth or senior designation.
20. Quoted in Davis, 'Desire to Maintain Quality'.
21. Allaway and Litterer, *The Encyclopedia*.
22. The San Francisco Soccer Football League (SFSFL) was originally known as the California Football League.
23. Young, 'Soccer in San Francisco', 1.
24. Ibid.
25. McGeever, 'San Francisco Soccer Football League'.
26. Kestler, 'A Brief Summary'.
27. Boxer, 'Highlights of the Mercury Athletic Club', 8.
28. McGeever, 'San Francisco Soccer Football League', 12.
29. Hall, 'New Ethnicities', 168.
30. MacClancy, *Sport, Identity, and Ethnicity*, 3–4.
31. Cronin and Mayall, *Sporting Nationalisms*, 9.
32. After their first SFSFL league championship in 1966–67, the Greek-Americans became the premier team in the league and one of the premier teams in both California and the nation. Between 1966 and 2006, the Greek-Americans amassed 55 trophies: SFSFL (16), Northern California National Open Cup (15), Northern California State Cup (15), California State Cup (4), National Open Cup (2), National Over-30 Open Cup (2) and National Over-40 Open Cup (1).
33. McGeever, 'San Francisco Soccer Football League', 15.
34. Much of the history of the Greek-American Athletic Club was obtained by interviews with the Club founders, John and Jim Rally, as well as the brief article, 'The History of the Greek-Americans Soccer Team', included in the 35th Annual Dinner Dance Program for the Greek-American Athletic Club.
35. McGeever, 'San Francisco Soccer Football League'.
36. 35th Annual Dinner Dance Program for the Greek-American Athletic Club, dated Saturday 26 January 1985. Event held at Holy Cross Church Hall, Belmont, California.
37. Ibid.
38. Martinez, 'Soccer in the USA', 239.
39. Of the 359 players listed by the MLS Player's Union in 2007, 55 earn $12,900 and an additional 35 earn $17,700. Nearly all who earn these paltry salaries are journeymen or developmental American players. In 2009, the minimum salary was raised to $20, 100.

References

Allaway, R., C. Jose, and D. Litterer, eds. *The Encyclopedia of American Soccer History*. Lanham, MD: Scarecrow Press, 2001.
Boxer, M. 'Highlights of the Mercury Athletic Club'. *California Soccer Football* 1 (1948): 7.

Cheska, A.T. 'Sport as Ethnic Boundary Maintenance: a Case of the American Indian'. *International Review for the Sociology of Sport* 19 (1984): 241–57.

Coakley, J.J. *Sport in Society: Issues and Controversies.* 7th ed. Boston, MA: McGraw-Hill, 2001.

Cronin, M., and D. Mayall, eds. *Sporting Nationalisms: Identity, Ethnicity, Immigration and Assimilation.* London and Portland, OR: Frank Cass, 1998.

Davis, S. 'Desire to Maintain Quality Drives Foreign Player Rule'. ESPNsoccernet, December 26, 2007. soccernet.espn.go.com/columns/ story?id=493683&root=mls& - 93k.

Day, R.D. 'Ethnic Soccer Clubs in London, Ontario: A Study in Assimilation'. *International Review for the Sociology of Sport* 16 (1977): 37–50.

Donnelly, P. 'Subcultures in Sport: Resilience and Transformation'. In *Sport in Social Development: Traditions, Transitions, and Transformations,* ed. A.G. Ingham and J.W. Loy, 119–45. Champaign, IL: Human Kinetics Publishers, 1993.

Eisen, G., and D.K. Wiggins, eds. *Ethnicity and Sport in North American History and Culture.* Westport, CT: Greenwood Press, 1994.

Foer, F. *How Football Explains the World: An Unlikely Theory of Globalization.* London: Arrow, 2005.

Franks, J.S. *Crossing Sidelines, Crossing Cultures: Sport and Asian Pacific American Cultural Citizenship.* Lanham, MD: University Press of America, 2000.

Gruneau, R.S. *Class, Sports, and Social Development.* Amherst, MA: University of Massachusetts Press, 1983.

Hall, S. 'New Ethnicities'. In *Black British Cultural Studies. A Reader,* ed. H.A. Baker, M. Diawara, and R.H. Lindeberg, 163–72. Chicago, IL: The University of Chicago Press, 1996.

Hallinan, C.J., and M.L. Krotee. 'Conceptions of Nationalism and Citizenship Among Non-Anglo-Celtic Soccer Clubs in an Australian City'. *Journal of Sport and Social Issues* 17 (1993): 125–33.

Hughson, J. 'The Boys are Back in Town: Soccer Support and the Social Reproduction of Masculinity'. *Journal of Sport and Social Issues* 24 (2000): 8–23.

Jarvie, G. 'Introduction'. In *Sport, Racism and Ethnicity,* ed. G. Jarvie. London: Falmar Press, 1991.

Kestler, G. 'A Brief Summary of the Origin of Teutonia A.A.C.'. *California Soccer Football* 1 (1948): 4.

Lever, J. *Soccer Madness.* Chicago, IL: University of Chicago Press, 1983.

Litterer, D. 'An Overview of American Soccer'. The USA Soccer History Archives. http://www.sover.net/~spectrum/overview.html.

MacClancy, J., ed. *Sport, Identity and Ethnicity.* Oxford and Herndon, VA: Berg, 1996.

McGeever, S. 'San Francisco Soccer Football League – The Centenary Celebration'. Unpublished Commemorative Journal honoring the 100th Anniversary San Francisco Soccer Football League, 1902–2002.

McKay, J. 'Sport and Ethnicity: Acculturation, Structural Assimilation, and Voluntary Association Involvement among Italian Immigrants in Metropolitan Toronto'. MS diss., University of Waterloo, 1975.

Mangan, J.A., and A. Ritchie, eds. *Ethnicity, Sport, Identity: Struggles for Status.* London and Portland, OR: Frank Cass, 2004.

Martinez, D. 'Soccer in the USA: "Holding out for a Hero"?' *Soccer & Society* 9, no. 2 (2008): 231–43.

Pooley, J.C. 'Ethnic Soccer Clubs in Milwaukee: A Study in Assimilation'. In *Sport in the Socio-cultural Process,* ed. M. Hart. 2nd Edn, 475–92. Dubuque, IA: W.C. Brown, 1976.

Rader, B.G. *American Sports: From the Age of Folk Games to the Age of Televised Sports.* 5th edn. Upper Saddle River, NJ: Prentice Hall, 2004.

Sage, G.H., *Power and Ideology in American Sport: A Critical Perspective.* Champaign, IL: Human Kinetics, 1998

Stoddart, B. *Saturday Afternoon Fever.* Sydney: Angus & Robertson, 1986.

Young, J.N. 'Soccer in San Francisco'. *California Soccer Football* 1 (1948): 1–3.

Association football to fútbol: ethnic succession and the history of Chicago-area soccer since 1920

David Trouille

Department of Sociology, University of California, Los Angeles, USA

Introduction

At the turn of the nineteenth century, soccer in Chicago area had developed from a minor pastime into a major component of the city's burgeoning sports landscape. By 1921, the game had also recovered from the interruption of World War I to usher in a period of unprecedented growth. As the game expanded into new areas in the 1920s, welcomed new groups, and competed favourably with baseball and football for local support, soccer's visibility and exposure would reach its highest peak. However, less than twenty years after this high point in the game's popularity, soccer would recede as a mainstream Chicago sport and enter a new chapter in its history.

In an earlier study, I examined the early history of Chicago soccer at the end of the nineteenth century and discussed soccer's period of rapid growth in the area at the beginning of the twentieth century.[1] In addition, it demonstrated the sociological relevance of a study of sport. In continuation of that attempt, the present essay critically examines the development of Chicago-area soccer from its popular peak in the 1920s to the present, thereby exploring the interconnections between the development of professional and amateur men's soccer in Chicago and theoretical understandings of race, ethnicity, immigration, integration and urban relations. Thus the essay makes an attempt to retrieve the rich yet neglected history of soccer in the Chicago area over the past 118 years.

Soccer's popular rise and decline, 1921–37

By the mid-1920s, sports had become more firmly implanted in the national culture, and soccer had emerged as a premier sport in the Chicago area.[2] The decade began with the much anticipated establishment of the Chicago Soccer League in 1921, which incorporated the leading teams from the Chicago and District Soccer League and resurrected the 1916 attempt to create an elite soccer league. According to the *Chicago Daily Tribune*, the Chicago Soccer League was 'one of the best leagues in the history of the game'.[3] The fanfare and optimism surrounding the new league's creation reflected the game's growing mass appeal.

The creation of the Chicago Soccer League ushered in the continued expansion of soccer teams and leagues playing in the area. By 1924, over 60 teams were competing in four Chicago leagues, in addition to the multitude of youth, church and recreational leagues also operating in the city. By the middle of the decade, many clubs were fielding up to four teams, including youth divisions. Soccer reached such a high pitch at the Western Electric Company that three new teams were added within 18 months. At this time, the German Football Club was fielding a total of five teams spread across three leagues. With players increasingly moving from club to club, wages most likely rose during this period as well, especially for the star players.[4] In addition, more teams acquired enclosed stadiums during this period, which allowed them to charge higher admission fees and acquire better players.[5] With so many teams competing, the soccer schedule was jam-packed and received substantial coverage in mainstream newspapers like the *Chicago Daily Tribune*. A typical newspaper during this period announced 30 to 40 local games on any given weekend and it was not uncommon for soccer to be the lead sports-page story – an amount of activity and exposure unheard of in previous decades.[6]

The growth of the game was celebrated by the *Chicago Daily Tribune*. In 1921, as attendance for local games broke all previous records, the paper declared that 'Soccer Shows Big Following'.[7] In 1922, soccer 'made great advances and the games were watched by larger crowds than ever witnessed them before'.[8] At the game's peak of popularity in 1925, the *Chicago Daily Tribune* asserted that 'soccer in the States is fast approaching the point it will be recognized as the premier fall and winter sport'.[9] According to the mainstream media of this period, soccer was surpassed only by baseball as the city's most popular sport, and therefore more 'premier' than college football, the other main sporting attraction at this time.

Soccer's growth during this period is best illustrated by its expansion beyond local league competitions. On any given weekend, soccer fans and community supporters had a variety of opportunities to watch the game. For example, on 16 November 1924, the *Chicago Daily Tribune* announced not only matches in the Major, District and International Leagues but local contests in the National Challenge Cup and Peel Cup as well (see Figure 1). The most popular matches were those where elite foreign teams came to compete against Chicago's finest teams. For example, a 1926 game between Hakoah, the celebrated Jewish team on tour from Vienna, and Chicago's Sparta drew 15,000 fans at Comiskey Park.[10] Later that year, a then record crowd of 30,000 spectators packed Soldier Field to watch the Midwest League All-Stars lose 1-0 to a visiting team from Prague.

Exhibition games with foreign teams were important events for the city and often entailed an official meeting with the mayor and a variety of special events with the visiting team's ethnic base in the city (see Figure 2 for a picture of the Czech team

Figure 1. *Chicago Daily Tribune*, 16 November 1924.

meeting with local politicians). For example, when the Hakoah soccer team visited Chicago, they were entertained by various local Jewish organizations, who enthusiastically hailed the team as a Zionist symbol of Jewish strength and rebuttal of anti-Semitism.[11]

As in the previous decade, national, state and local inter-league competitions continued to draw heavy fan interest in the 1920s. Games in the later stages of the National Challenge Cup and the National Amateur Cup, which began in 1924, always attracted large crowds. Several times in the 1920s, the Peel Cup finals were played at Soldier Field. In 1928, 15,000 fans watched the Bricklayers play the New York Nationals in the finals of the National Challenge Cup. There were also many other local cup competitions sponsored by local businesses and fraternal organizations. During this period indoor soccer and seven-aside outdoor competitions became increasingly popular as well.

Besides official competitions, the games that drew the most interest in the city were the exhibition matches. These games often kicked off the season or were played

[TRIBUNE Photo.]
FAMOUS CZECHO-SLOVAKIAN SOCCER TEAM ARRIVES IN CHICAGO. Sparta
Athletic club team of Prague at the La Salle street station. In the front row are: Ald. John
Toman, County Treasurer P. J. Carr, Lieut. Col. Joseph Maley, and Anton J. Cermak, presi-
dent of county board, who welcomed the players.

Figure 2.   *Chicago Daliy Tribune*, 29 September 1926.

as benefit matches for a variety of causes. All-Star games among the leagues were regularly played and were well attended, but games pitting nationalities against each other were by far the most popular form of exhibition matches. 'International' games – a tradition dating back to the early 1900s – became so popular during this period that in 1922 they were organized into an annual tournament honouring the city's mayor. In 1925, for example, 5,000 fans came out to watch the opening games of the Dever Cup[12] among British, Scandinavian, Jewish, Bohemian and German teams. In 1932, the five teams battling for the mayor's trophy were the Swedes, Norwegians, Danes, Germans and Polish-Italians.[13] By the 1930s, the event had become so popular that teams were chosen by a poll of fans. Besides the Mayor's Cup, it was not uncommon for a national or ethnic-based team to play a leading local soccer club. For example, a club of Jewish players chosen by the fans took on the mighty Sparta soccer team in 1932. While more research is needed, the heightened significance attached to these matches and the enthusiasm they generated can be read as examples of what Clifford Geertz refers to as 'deep play' in which the 'international' contests emerged as a 'metasocial commentary' on ethnic relations in the city.[14] These matches became, in a sense, Chicago's coliseum of ethnicity in which victory or defeat reflected a group's local standing, with the 'non-ethnic' authorities controlling the proceedings. Although only cursory, such analysis of the Mayor's Cup begins to address the important 'myth-making' qualities of sports, as detailed in a range of sport studies from the Olympic Games to cock-fighting.[15] I am convinced that a full-scale history of this annual competition would reveal the ways in which the Mayor's Cup – and soccer in general – emerged as both model and metaphor for urban relations and integration in Chicago.

The growing sociological relevance of the game was not lost on area sports promoters. In the summer of 1924, four of the premier teams in the region threatened to resign from the Major League to create a local super-league (Chicago National Soccer League), which would also play monthly matches against rival teams from St Louis. As the *Chicago Daily Tribune* remarked, 'This new arrangement will create a lot of regulars among the fans, as they are sure of seeing high class games every Sunday'.[16] Like the Chicago Soccer League (CSL) in 1921, the Chicago National Soccer League was another attempt to create a superior and profitable Chicago soccer league.[17] However, threatened with the loss of its premier status in the city, the CSL lobbied to block the new league's admittance into the Illinois State Football Association under the grounds that it was 'freezing out' the smaller clubs.[18] A week later, the CSL officially refused to accept the resignation of the 'Big Four'.[19] The Illinois State Football Association backed the endangered league by rejecting the application of the new league into the governing organization, which meant that it would not be able to compete in state and national competitions. Unwilling to give up the cup matches, Sparta decided to rejoin the CSL, and the new league folded as a result. Sparta recognized that, despite the new league's potential, it did not represent a superior space to the CSL unless it could offer sufficient allies and institutional support. The failure of succession in this case serves as a counter-example to the many previous and future instances of ethnic succession in Chicago-area soccer leagues.

In 1926, another attempt was made to create a premier soccer league and to capitalize on the game's growing appeal. Four leading teams from Chicago and St Louis formed the Midwest League, which hoped to create a regional super-league. However, after a month of competition, the league dropped the intercity games because they were a financial failure. The Midwest League continued as a Chicago-based association until 1929.

The rise and failure of these two highly-publicized attempts at premier soccer leagues in Chicago paralleled national developments. The American Soccer League (ASL) was established in 1921 as the first league with enough prestige to compete effectively for European players and even draw as many spectators as the early National Football League.[20] Backed by large companies like Bethlehem Steel, Robbins Shipyards and J&P Coats, the league had the financial clout to compete successfully for the best domestic and foreign players. It was not uncommon for games to draw over 10,000 fans, which compared favourably with attendance at professional football games.[21] With soccer competing on par with professional football at this juncture, the claim made by the authors of *Offside* that soccer came 'too late' appears incorrect. Contrary to their assertion, soccer was not crowded out by football and baseball in a saturated sports' field. I will argue that other factors led to the decline of the highly successful ASL, most notably a bitter dispute among rival soccer organizations, the Great Depression and the resulting decline in immigration to the United States.[22]

By the late 1920s, soccer was a key feature of the burgeoning US sports landscape. However, by the mid-1930s, soccer had lost its position as a commercial and professional American sport. The game's coverage, attendance and visibility experienced a marked decline. While the best games still attracted several thousand fans, by the end of the 1930s, average crowds were no more than a few hundred. Moreover, the *Chicago Daily Tribune*'s coverage of soccer markedly decreased; most reports simply listed scores, in contrast to the full-length accounts of the previous decades.

In the hope of revitalizing local soccer, three major leagues consolidated in 1935 to form the Chicago Soccer League. However, the new league collapsed when Sparta, its most successful team, joined the Inter-City League, another short-lived attempt to create a regional professional league. By 1938, the only local league to survive the game's mainstream demise was the International Soccer League (ISL). Soccer had entered a very different phase in its history, one which can be best referred to as a more complete 'ethnic period', which in many respects continues up to the present. There are several possible explanations for this change.

Developments in the soccer leagues offer a partial explanation. However, two significant historical factors contributed to the game's decline. First, the Stock Market crash in 1929 and ensuing Great Depression had a serious effect, especially on the larger clubs, which relied heavily on financial patronage from leading industrialists to secure the best players, maintain quality fields and pay for travel expenses. Despite efforts in 1935 to curtail the teams' financial difficulties by merging the leagues, many teams were unable to survive the Depression.[23]

The restriction of immigration in the mid-1920s had an equally detrimental effect on local soccer. This was especially harmful because many of the best players were recruited from Europe. As the players aged, there were fewer skilful young players to take their place, and the quality of play declined. Writing in the *Chicago Daily Tribune* in 1938, a sports reporter remarked: 'Perhaps the chief factor in soccer's decline is the fact that the class of play does not compare with that in America twenty years ago.'[24] This assertion effectively rescinded the paper's enthusiastic declaration in 1925 that soccer was surpassed only by baseball in popularity.[25]

The third factor that contributed to the decline of soccer was the wave of increased isolationism and xenophobia that swept over the United States in the 1930s. The game was undoubtedly harmed by its association with foreigners during this xenophobic period – in stark contrast to the cachet brought to the sport by talented immigrant players and visiting foreign teams in earlier decades. Moreover, it was at this juncture that baseball and football had been cleansed of any 'foreign taint'. In the opinion of Richard Crepeau, between the two world wars, baseball established itself as 'the undisputed National Pastime'.[26] Indeed, despite soccer's popularity with mainstream audiences in the 1920s, the repeated failure of the major professional teams and leagues in Chicago demonstrates soccer's inability to fully win over mainstream audiences and to establish itself as a wholly 'American' sport like baseball and football. The fact that the announcement of an important match or of a new team was often accompanied by an explanation of the rules of the game illustrates the continuing foreignness of soccer despite its widespread popularity in the mid-1920s. (See Figure 3 for an article from the *Chicago Daily Tribune* on 15 April 1928 previewing the Bricklayer's upcoming championship match against a visiting team from New York.)

By contrast, the ISL continued to attract new teams and to grow as other leagues faltered. Started in 1920 with little fanfare, the ISL never drew huge crowds or contested for major local or national championships but managed to hold its own even in the darkest days of the Depression. Most of the new teams in the ISL drew from

Figure 3.   *Chicago Daily Tribune*, 15 April 1928.

ethnic and immigrant communities particularly as soccer became less popular among native-born and more 'assimilated' immigrant athletes. In this respect, I agree with Markovits and Hellerman's claim that the game's mainstream accession proved short-lived.[27] However, I disagree with their contention that it was 'crowded out'. Quite the contrary, among immigrant and ethnic groups, soccer continued to thrive and serve as a vital source of identity and pride for these communities. However, because the game was so far removed from the mainstream sporting scene, soccer's existence during the middle of the twentieth century has largely been forgotten or ignored by historians.

It was at this juncture in the mid-1930s that Chicago soccer fully entered its 'ethnic period'. Although the game had always been enthusiastically embraced by immigrant and ethnic groups, they were by no means alone on the Chicago soccer scene. In the 1920s and 1930s, the game attracted a considerable number of American-born players and was beginning to make inroads as a mainstream American sport. However, these trends experienced a sharp decline by the end of the 1930s as soccer entered its fully 'ethnic period'.

The 'ethnic period', 1938–71[28]

The demise of the American Soccer League (ASL) in 1933 was the most visible sign of soccer's waning status among mainstream sports. By the end of the decade, soccer continued primarily at the semi-pro and amateur level in the United States, with most of the teams tied to ethnic or immigrant communities. During the following decades, the game remained within these confines and was increasingly viewed as an 'immigrant' pastime. This national trend was especially applicable to the situation in Chicago from the end of the 1930s through the 1970s, which may be described as its 'ethnic period'.[29]

Only the International Soccer League (ISL) survived the game's decline as a mainstream sport in the 1930s. Renamed the National Soccer League in 1943, the league emerged as the heart and soul of Chicago-area soccer, which it single-handedly organized over the next three decades.[30] Although the number of fans and spectators fell sharply and the game's mainstream media coverage diminished, the NSL steadily grew during these years. And, while immigration from Europe would never approach pre-Depression numbers (a key factor in the game's decline in Chicago and nationwide), the smaller influx of European immigrants displaced by the Second World War, especially from Germany and Poland, helped rejuvenate the league. By 1947, the NSL was probably the largest amateur soccer league in the country.[31] That year, the league boasted 43 senior, 12 junior and five youth teams within its nine divisions and covered a radius over 50 miles with teams in Illinois, Indiana and Wisconsin. During these years, the league became renowned for its success in national competitions and its popular indoor season. While only the most anticipated outdoor matches drew over a thousand fans, a series of Sunday indoor games at the Chicago Avenue Armory regularly drew 3,000 to 4,000. Indoor soccer became such a spectacle that WGN-TV began televising the games in 1950 and a feature article about the games appeared in the fashionable *Chicago* magazine in 1956.[32] In general, however, soccer steadily receded as a dominant sport in terms of participation, coverage and public perceptions, despite its continued popularity and support among immigrant and ethnic communities.

By the mid-1940s, teams were no longer organized by industry or neighbourhoods such as Pullman and Hyde Park, but almost exclusively by ethnic affiliation, which most often corresponded to European nationalities. For example, at one point during the 1940s, 1950s and 1960s, the German community was represented by Hansa, Schwaben, Fortuna, and Green and White; the Poles by Wisla and the Eagles; the Greeks by Hercules, Olympics and Apollo; the Scandinavians by the Vikings, Linneas and South Side Swedes; the Czechs by Sparta and the Slovaks; the Italians by Maroons and Giutsi; the Croatians by Adria and Croatans; the Ukrainians by the Lions and Wings; the Lithuanians by the Liths; and the Jewish community by Hakoah Center. (See Figure 4 for a picture of Hakoah Center competing against Hansa in the National Open soccer cup in the *Chicago Daily Tribune* on 5 March 1945.)

While there continued to be a few teams tied to residence (often remote teams like St Joseph, Michigan), the vast majority of teams were explicitly tied to immigrant and ethnic communities.[33] Although soccer teams had always been important to ethnic communities, the relationship became even more pronounced and prevalent in the 1940s, 1950s and 1960s. Moreover, soccer emerged as a significant vehicle for the construction and maintenance of collective identities and provided important functions and services for ethnic communities.[34]

While more research certainly needs to be done to better understand these relationships, this section provides a preliminary outline of the complex connections among soccer, ethnicity, immigration, integration and community in the Chicago area during the period 1938–71. In examining the ways in which groups created a sense of community through soccer while facing the challenges of new surroundings and pressures to assimilate, the following sections address a crucial and enduring sociological question. By examining the relationship between soccer and the construction of collective identities, this study illustrates how ethnicity is continually renegotiated, revised and revitalized, in addition to showing how the game *itself* has played an important role in the history and structure of immigration and ethnicity in Chicago. Moreover, because sports are rarely used to explore the meaning and construction of ethnicity and community, my study may help expand our understandings of these central sociological concepts.

Since the nation's founding, immigrants have always tended to develop subcommunities to replicate the Old World as much as possible in order to sustain their language, customs, religion and general sense of communal identity.[35] These ethnic subcommunities helped immigrants alleviate feelings of alienation and facilitate their adjustment to strange and hostile urban environments.[36] The soccer clubs became one of the focal points for the formation of ethnic communities in the Chicago area in several ways. For example, playing on soccer teams and attending matches was a way

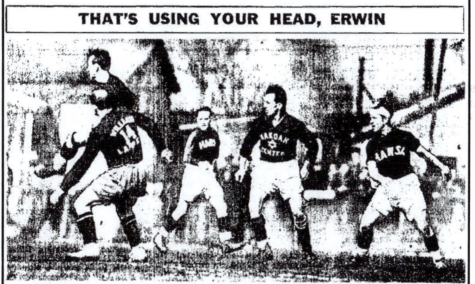

THAT'S USING YOUR HEAD, ERWIN
Chicago Daily Tribune (1872-1963); Mar 5, 1945; ProQuest Historical Newspapers Chicago Tribune (1849 - 1985)
pg. 20

THAT'S USING YOUR HEAD, ERWIN

In fast action in yesterday's National Open soccer cup match in Sparta stadium Erwin Pahalke of the Hansas jumps to head the ball after brushing Maxie Pearlman, Hakoahs, out of the play. Those in action, left to right, are Pahalke, Pearlman, Max Bruckmann, Hansa, Edward Lehman, Hakoahs, and Herbert, Sack, Hansa. The Hakoahs won, 4 to 1.

Figure 4.   *Chicago Daily Tribune*, 5 March 1945.

to feel pride in, and kinship with, one's ethnic group. Success on the soccer field served to reinforce the collective and bounded identity of players and spectators alike.[37] Soccer games and practices became important rallying points for the community to gather around on a weekly basis.

The importance of soccer teams for ethnic communities is clearly reflected in the pages of the ethnic newspapers as far back as the turn of the century. For example, in 1908, commenting on the Norwegian soccer team, *Skandinaven* proclaimed that the 'Norwegian sportsmen have won the respect and admiration of all sport-interested Americans to a higher degree then ever before'.[38] Similarly, when Sparta captured the league title, the Czech newspaper *Denni Hlasatel* proudly declared: 'There is no doubt that this recognition has great significance both as regards Bohemian sport events and the Bohemian people generally.'[39] Recognizing the importance of success on the soccer field, many of the ethnic newspapers pushed their teams to succeed. The German newspaper *Abdenpost* admonished the German Club 'to do it best always so that the German color will be well represented in the future games. Simultaneously, the clarion admonishes all German sportsmen to visit the contests, and thereby support the Club in its endeavors.'[40] Success on the soccer field was also seen as an opportunity to combat negative stereotypes in the minds of native-born Americans. For example, when a Jewish soccer team from Vienna visited Chicago in 1926, *The Jewish Daily* urged people to attend the game because the team 'demonstrates to the world that Jews possess in addition to spiritual power, also physical, and that they do not take a back seat in the sport world'.[41] The ethnic newspapers also stressed the impact of negative impressions and stereotypes. For example, a 1922 article in *Denni Hlasatel* deplored the behaviour of the Czech players in a recent match. Recognizing that the team was 'representing the Czechoslovaks before the football world', the paper demanded that the players improve their behaviour.[42] *Skandinaven* offered similar advice to the Fram soccer team: 'It is necessary that the boys stop scolding each other during the play. Avoid the bad impression.'[43]

The excitement and pride generated by games involving visiting foreign teams or matches between local 'national teams' is further evidence of the importance of soccer for ethnic communities. For instance, at the end of Vienna's Hakoah's defeat of Chicago's Sparta in 1926, thousands of Jewish fans swarmed Comiskey Park and raised the Jewish players to their shoulders. In discussing a later match with a visiting team from Prague, the *Chicago Daily Tribune* hypothesized heavy attendance because it would be 'induced by racial pride on the part of Czecho-Slovakians in this city'.[44] As Figure 5 illustrates, the prominent display of the Star of David on Hakoah's jersey publicly denotes identification and pride in the Jewish character of the club.

From these examples, we see how the soccer clubs encouraged and expressed ethnic pride. They also became an important locus for the community's cultural and social life. Second only to the church as an ethnic gathering place, the soccer clubs offered a frequent meeting place for ethnic communities. This was not limited to the soccer matches, since many of the teams had clubhouses, which often housed a restaurant, bar and meeting/party room. After games, players and supporters regularly socialized at their clubhouses.[45] An article in the *Chicago Tribune*[46] from 1977 documents this phenomenon: 'After the games, players and their families went to the team clubhouses and ate dumplings, or Polish sausage and sauerkraut, or German sausage, and many danced to accordion music.'[47] The clubs used the profits from their clubhouse bar and restaurant to help pay their teams' expenses. With many other activities at the clubhouses like dances, banquets and charity events, the social function of the soccer clubs extended well beyond the Sunday matches.

Soccer clubs played a crucial role in helping to alleviate the alienation many immigrants felt by providing a release from the often grim experiences at work and in the neighbourhood. This was especially true for new immigrants: 'I hated Chicago when I first came over. I was terribly homesick', recalled Ed Murphy, a local soccer star during this period. 'I was only seventeen when I left Scotland, and at that age you really miss your friends. Getting into soccer here was the best thing that ever happened to me.'[48] A soccer veteran quoted in *Soccerhead* captures the all-encompassing social function of the soccer clubs: 'The club was where they held your christening and your wedding reception – and where they laid you out for your wake.'[49] For many, soccer became the glue that held everything together.

Beyond their social function, many teams also provided important community services, such as helping players acquire jobs, housing and loans. The example of Julius Roth is typical. Born in Germany, Roth came to Chicago to work as a displaced jewel-cutter after the Second World War. Roth had been recruited to work for a jeweller with ties to Schwaben, a prominent German club and, unbeknownst to Roth, had been 'promised' to the team. His employer was incensed when Roth chose instead, by happenstance, to play for Hansa, a rival German team and stayed with them throughout his distinguished career.[50] In addition, it was not unusual for teams to financially support many of the players. Salaries were lucrative enough that many of the local stars played for whichever team paid them the most, regardless of their ethnic background. For example, Willie Roy, a national star of German descent, played not only for Hansa, but also for several non-German teams (including the Wanderers, Slovaks, Lions and the Maroons).

Although the teams were important symbols for ethnic communities, their players did not all necessarily share the same ethnic background. A columnist in the *Chicago Daily Tribune* questioned the team name of the South Side Swedes after pointing out that only two members of the teams were of Swedish extraction. Sparta, a team of great importance to the Czech community, rarely fielded an all-Bohemian team; indeed, the 1950 squad started five Scots. The sociological significance of this change in regards to the meaning of ethnicity and assimilation will be examined in a subsequent section detailing a later time when this practice became much more prevalent.

Within this setting, soccer emerged as a conflicted space that simultaneously heightened integration and segregation. On the one hand, competition and participation led to closer contact among immigrant groups and, to a lesser degree, with native-born Americans. Moreover, by using park spaces and successfully navigating the city's recreational bureaucracy, the teams raised their profile in the city. Soccer also became a space in which to demonstrate patriotism, especially during the Second World War. During the war, Chicago soccer clubs contributed to local patriotism by playing a series of exhibition matches at military camps and training centres in the area.[51] A number of teams held ceremonies honouring the many players who had joined the military. Chicago soccer promoters also responded to the war by having local rather than national teams compete for the Mayor's Cup and by changing the name of the Chicago soccer league from the International to the National Soccer League.

However, soccer continued to serve as a space for players to assert their ethnic identity and to engage in inter-ethnic rivalries. As soccer increasingly was viewed as an expression of cultural Otherness, many immigrant groups enthusiastically embraced the game as a form of resistance to the homogenizing pressures of American society. Some parents consciously pushed their American-born children to play soccer as a way of resisting assimilation and recreating an idealized vision of their home-land.[52] While giving players and their families a means to affirm their ethnic identity, soccer also gave them a space in which to act out traditional ethnic rivalries and hostilities. Indoor games between Serbian and Croatian teams became so hostile that, for many years, they had to be played in empty arenas. Tension also existed within national groups and competition was fierce to become the top team within a given ethnic group.[53] Following the formation of the Hercules in 1972, a columnist for the *Chicago Tribune* speculated that the new team would threaten the Olympics' stature as the only Greek team in the city. Rivalry between the two teams reached a peak during an indoor game in the mid-1970s when Olympics supporters charged the field and nearly started a riot.[54] Reports in the mainstream press indicate that matches between immigrant groups regularly ended in violence, which often became the focus of their articles. Headlines like 'Battling Fans, Players Break up Soccer Game' and 'Fists Fly as Hakoah Wins Soccer match' were typical of this period and perpetuated the image of soccer as a violent and foreign sport.

Despite the assimilative aspects of soccer, the game was increasingly viewed as ethnic and foreign. By the late 1950s, even though more and more suburban high schools were fielding teams, soccer was widely perceived as an alien sport played primarily by immigrants – part of the old cultural baggage from Europe that was a barrier to full assimilation. As Haner explains in *Soccerhead*, mainstream American sports fans saw soccer as a 'relic of a by-gone time, willed forward by a dwindling generation of players, managers, and coaches'.[55] By this period, soccer increasingly was viewed more as a 'foreign' activity than as an 'immigrant' pastime. The few feature articles on soccer in mainstream newspapers tended to reinforce these stereotypes by underscoring the foreignness of the game even though many of the players were US citizens. For example, in a 1979 article, the *Chicago Tribune* referred to soccer as the 'multi-national pastime of the Midway'.[56] Similarly, *Chicago Magazine* described the indoor soccer league as a 'version of the United Nations' with its 'babble of voices in the grandstands'.[57] In general, however, the game was increasingly ignored by 'Americanized' sports fans and the mainstream press.[58] This attitude was humorously expressed in a 1967 *Chicago Tribune* article that scoffed at Chicago's latest attempt to establish a professional team:[59] 'Many Chicagoans (and most Americans, for that matter) have been content in the past with the knowledge that the game of soccer takes up a whole page in the *Encyclopedia of Sports*, and have been perfectly willing to leave it there.'[60]

The ethnic fixation of Chicago-area soccer was further revealed by the frustration it caused officials from the handful of professional soccer teams that emerged during this period. For example, the director of public relations for the Sting, a Chicago-area professional team, found it distressing that 'ethnic groups will go out of their way to see members of their same group play other ethnic groups on an amateur level, but they won't come and see the professionals – many of whom are Europeans and South Americans'.[61] Many others were surprised and disturbed that the enthusiastic support for local soccer had not translated into a comparable level of support for the professional teams, especially given their much higher standard of play. What the promoters of the professional teams failed to recognize was the sociological importance of the amateur teams for ethnic and immigrant groups.

By the 1970s, there was grave concern within the soccer community that the perceptions of soccer as foreign and its increasing isolation from mainstream American sports were seriously impeding its development. The *Chicago Tribune* captured these anxieties with its 1972 headline 'Ethnic "Kick" Hurts Soccer'.[62] In this article, Murphy, himself a Scottish immigrant of Irish heritage, remarked that 'the game's ethnic structure just has to go because it has been choking the game to death'. For Murphy and many others, so long as soccer was seen primarily as an expression of ethnic rivalries – the Slovaks grumbling about the Greeks, the Lithuanians fighting the Ukrainians, and the Germans battling the Poles – the second generation (i.e., the grandchildren of immigrants), like the vast majority of Americans, would remain indifferent to the sport. This became even more problematic as fewer soccer players emigrated to Chicago and the children of immigrants gravitated to more 'American' sports like baseball and football.[63]

With a vast majority of the players foreign-born, there was growing concern that American soccer would eventually die out. However, in the 1970s and 1980s, two major trends emerged that would revitalize and fundamentally transform the soccer landscape both in Chicago and nationwide: the latinization and suburbanization of the game.

The latinization of the game: 1971 to the present

Soccer's development in the Chicago area has been heavily affected by shifts in immigration trends and continues to reveal patterns of ethnic succession. Through a process that dates back to the earliest days of soccer in Chicago and continues to the present day, the emergence of new teams and leagues has been tied to the arrival of new immigrant communities. Often the game's greatest source of vitality, these new teams and players have resulted in the continual reconfiguration of local leagues. By the 1970s, Chicago-area soccer had entered a new chapter. Just as previous waves of immigrants from the British Isles had shaped Chicago soccer's early years only to be displaced in their importance by immigrants from southern and eastern Europe, so too the massive influx of Latin Americans beginning in the 1970s reshaped soccer's local landscape once again, affecting the game in paradigmatic ways. Moreover, the newly formed soccer clubs filled much the same function for Latino immigrants as they had for other immigrant groups in decades past.

Although Latin American immigration to Chicago is often viewed as a recent phenomenon, Mexicans have emigrated to the city in large numbers since the 1920s. Like the European immigrants, they brought with them soccer traditions from their country of origins, which resulted in the quick formation of clubs in their adopted city. For example, Necaxa, a Mexican soccer team, was founded in 1927 and joined the NSL in 1937. Necaxa, which emerged as a premier team by the 1950s, was soon joined by other clubs from South and Central America, such as the Argentinean club Pampas, the Uruguayan squad Arauco, the Brazilian side Flyers, and Club Honduras. However, Mexican-American players were by far the largest contingent among Latin Americans in the league after teams including the Azteca, Atlas, Nacional, Leon and Ayulta joined Necaxa in the NSL in the 1950s and 1960s.

With the steady increases in immigration from Mexico, the number of Mexican-American teams in the NSL continued to grow – a development that created similar opportunities and tensions as in the earlier phases of demographic change in the local soccer leagues. Entry into the NSL gave Latino teams the opportunity to compete as equals with white Europeans and hence a way to gain respect from their opponents and to refute anti-Mexican stereotypes. The teams became a symbol of local autonomy and a source of collective pride for the Mexican community to rally around.[64]

At the same time, the NSL also became a locus for discrimination against Mexicans, much as newer European teams had been discriminated against by the older clubs in the past. Many players involved in the NSL at the time complained that Mexicans were treated unfairly both on and off the field. They were unjustly fined, received adverse decisions from referees, and most importantly, were unrepresented on the league's board of directors. As one official with a leading Latino league put it, 'we were not getting a fair shake because we were Mexican'.[65]

In the hope of improving their situation within the NSL, eight of the leading Mexican teams and two Ecuadorian clubs formed the Chicago Latin American Soccer Association (CLASA) in 1967. However, when the new association failed to improve conditions, most of the Mexican teams seceded from the NSL and launched CLASA as an independent league in 1973. Just as the Czech community was able to form its own league in the 1930s, the Latino community had grown large enough by the 1970s to support its own association. This is one more example of how shifts in relative bargaining power due to changing resources, like numbers, presented opportunities for minority groups to mobilize and protest for better conditions. Or, as Claude Fischer puts it, Latino players had reached the 'critical mass' needed to sustain a 'subculture' and to resist discrimination from the older clubs.[66] Commenting on the formation of the Mexican league, an official for the German club reflected this notion of critical mass in relation to the Mexican situation: 'They needed their own league. They had too many teams. I was in favor of them creating their own league.'[67]

The formation of CLASA is another striking example of ethnic succession. In this instance, the established league resisted 'invasion' by a group considered undesirable by the majority. Through defensive and often discriminatory tactics, the Mexican teams were forced out[68] and chose to form their own league – a scenario very similar to the circumstances that led to the formation of the International Soccer League decades earlier. Although CLASA was created out of frustration with the treatment of Latino players by the older clubs, its success has been a positive development, not only for the Latino community, but for Chicago soccer as a whole.

The formation of CLASA in 1973 precipitated the 'latinization' of Chicago soccer. While players of European descent continue to participate in local clubs, as do more recent immigrants from other parts of the world, the Chicago-area soccer landscape has since been dominated, at least numerically, by Latino – and especially Mexican – teams. This process has been rapid and continually changing as new waves of Mexican and other Latin American immigrants arrive in the city. Moreover, in 1975, only two years after its creation, CLASA experienced internal divisions that resulted in the formation of a rival Mexican league: the Hispano-American Soccer League (referred to today simply as Hispano).

The formation of Hispano is yet another instance of ethnic succession in Chicago-area soccer leagues. While officials at CLASA claim that the split resulted from an arbitrary dispute over preferred game days, the explanation provided by officials from Hispano is quite different and more convincing. They maintain that the new league was established by 'disgruntled' teams in CLASA who felt they were not accorded the respect or power due them because of their prominence in the league (in terms of quality of play, size of fan base and seniority). Their standing in the league was threatened by the league's democratic order – feelings that were exacerbated by the rapid entry of many new teams in the first two years after CLASA's creation. In 1975, following a common pattern in the history of Chicago soccer, they formed what they considered to be a superior league.

As immigration from Mexico and increasingly from Central America continued to replenish local soccer ranks, CLASA and Hispano grew rapidly. In 1977, for example, 200 of the 350 men's teams operating in the city were Latino. These numbers have continued to increase over the last quarter century. Today, with over 400 teams, CLASA is the nation's largest Latino league, while Hispano fields approximately 100 teams. Compared to the 50 teams currently in the NSL, these numbers are enormous and clearly reflect the ascendancy of Latino teams in Chicago. Moreover, in response to continually growing numbers, several other Latino leagues have since emerged in the city (including Inter-Americano, Internacional and Centro Americano), as well as several large leagues in the Chicago suburbs. These leagues account for the hundreds and hundreds of Latino soccer teams, most of which of Mexican descent, which are now operating in the region. This proliferation of Latino teams over the past 30 years is a sign not only of the game's 'latinization', but also of its continuing appeal to immigrant groups, although the primary language spoken now is Spanish, rather than German or Czech.

My preliminary research suggests that Latino teams and leagues have served important functions similar to those of the European clubs discussed in the previous sections. Pescador's extensive study of Mexican-American soccer clubs in Chicago and Milwaukee over the past three decades supports this view. According to Pescador, these soccer clubs and the matches they organize have provided an important social space in which to carve out a cultural space for themselves and 'celebrate a notion of Mexicanness based on the Mexican experience in the United States'.[69] He maintains that the soccer teams became especially important as a means of disproving ethnic stereotypes and portraying Mexican-Americans as successful, vibrant and dynamic. The clubs also give Latinos an opportunity to assert their rights as area residents to public services and public spaces. As Pescador observes, 'By playing soccer every Sunday, Mexicanos are reshaping the American recreational landscape, asserting their rights to public spaces, and taking the first steps in the complex processes of community organization and identity formation.'[70] The fact that CLASA and Hispano both operate outside the governance of the Illinois State Soccer Association (ISSA) (which they chose not to join) demonstrates their independence and vitality.

Soccer matches have become permanent gathering spaces for Mexican families and central events around which to organize weekly activities. The soccer fields themselves have emerged as multidimensional border spaces, where cross-cultural and transnational social relationships are forged. Typically, teams are named for the home communities of the majority of players or after popular professional teams from their home country – names that evoke both loyalty and rivalry. For example, Hispano's Major Division is currently made up of such teams as San Pedro, Guerrero, Taxco and Real Aguilas. According to Pescador, 'the game constitutes a source of pride, cultural tradition, popular folklore, and psychic and social connection to distant homelands'.[71] As with European clubs, to play and love soccer, then, is to take part in what it means to be – or not to be – culturally Latino in the United States. 'Kicking the ball holds our people together', observed the secretary of CLASA in a 1979 interview. 'Regardless of the poverty of the neighborhood, the problems of immigration, the troubles at work and in the home, there's always soccer. It's the way we get away from it all.'[72] Marie Price and Courtney Whitworth demonstrate the ways in which Latino soccer leagues satisfy the desire for status within their communities. According to the authors, the soccer leagues emerge as 'communities of meaning in which status claims are interpreted via shared histories and understandings of practices, rituals, goods, and other social markers'.[73] My preliminary research suggests that the success of the soccer clubs also serves as a source of status for the clubs' directors. According to an administrator of a local Latino league, the passion for the game was 'really about the directors'. Although he admired their enthusiasm, he criticized their at times excessive competitiveness: 'Sometimes people go too far with it and it takes over their life; they want to have a winning team so they can brag about it.'[74]

Fuelled by continuing immigration from Latin America, the latinization of the men's game is no doubt the most significant development in soccer both in the Chicago area and nationwide. Today, with a large portion of men's soccer in the city organized by the Latin-American leagues, the sight of Latinos playing in Chicago's parks has become commonplace.

Following the creation of the Champions League in 2006,[75] the top Chicago teams all hoped to compete in this premier tournament. However, because it was organized by the ISSA, only teams affiliated with the state governing body were eligible to compete. Due to long-standing disputes, neither CLASA nor Hispano are associated with the ISSA, which meant that their teams could not compete. To become eligible for the tournament, four of the top veteran Mexican clubs formed a new ISSA-affiliated organization, the Latin Premier United Soccer League. While the league is only temporary and the teams remained in CLASA, it is one more example of the same process described earlier, in which elite teams begin to outgrow the confines of their league. The probability of secession from a league generally increases in relation to the number of years a team has existed and its success on the field. It is therefore very likely that the clubs in the Latin Premier United Soccer League will eventually secede from CLASA to create a smaller, more elite league. Moreover, as teams grow more elite, they tend to become increasingly heterogeneous – a trend that has already begun with the top Latino teams in Chicago. For example, the majority of the teams in CLASA and Hispano are strongly based on shared ethnic identities, some of which are tied to cities or towns in Mexico. Yet several of the larger Latino clubs have begun to draw players from all over Latin America and even several non-Latino additions. In this way, the Latino leagues are demonstrating the same patterns that have characterized Chicago-area soccer for over a century.

The suburbanization of Chicago soccer: 1981 to the present

The growth of the suburbs has also significantly transformed the character of Chicago-area soccer. After the Second World War, the Chicago area underwent a massive population shift as more and more people settled in the suburbs. While people have always resided on the periphery of central cities, the 1950s witnessed an unprecedented growth in suburban populations, which would transform Chicago and the United States as a whole economically, politically and socially.[76] The rapid expansion of Chicago's suburbs had an equally profound impact on the development of soccer in the region. As increasing numbers migrated to the suburbs, there was a dramatic shift in the game's focus and direction. Just as immigration from Latin American was reshaping soccer's urban landscape in Chicago, so too suburbanization was reshaping the face of soccer in the city's periphery.

Even though many soccer players remained in the city, by the end of the 1970s there was a growing consensus that the future of the game lay in the suburbs. And although there was a resurgence of immigration from Europe after the war, soccer officials realized that if they did not capture the interest of American-born youth, the future of the sport was in danger. 'It was a matter of self-preservation', remarked George Fishwick, former president of the ISSA. 'Players had gotten used to just calling to the old country when they needed more players. It took them a while to face up to the fact that they had to teach the kids here if they wanted soccer to continue to exist.'[77] While there had always been minor youth divisions in the National Soccer League, there had never been an effort to actively recruit players from outside ethnic communities. Developing soccer in the new suburban spaces and 'Americanizing' the clubs was seen as necessary for the sport's survival.

The suburbs offered a solution to one of the game's perennial problems: the lack of space in the city for quality fields and clubhouses. Away from the congested, often under-funded and contentious city, the suburbs offered ample space and resources for the soccer clubs. Moreover, by moving the game to more appealing and harmonious suburban spaces, the clubs were better able to attract young players and their families (see Figure 5). This move was motivated by forces similar to those that compelled millions of people to migrate to the suburbs. In contrast to the city – increasingly viewed as hostile, impoverished and alien – the suburbs were considered safe, prosperous and familiar. For soccer players of European descent, the urban soccer landscape seemed increasingly foreign, even inhospitable, following the influx of Latin American, African and Caribbean teams. 'The city game was out of control and completely overrun by people who knew nothing about running a soccer league', according to one player during this period. 'And it was getting dangerous and violent because none of the teams got along, especially the newer ones.'[78] The suburbanization of the game offered an escape from the problems of the city and a boost to the social status of the club and their players. The formation of suburban soccer clubs helped signal their transition from immigrants to ethnic Americans. Moreover, as participants often explained this move in highly racialized ways, the relocation to the suburbs serves as an another example by which European immigrants have attempted to distance themselves from non-whites in the hope of being considered as white. As one old-timer put it, 'The new teams in the city weren't like us and we no longer felt comfortable in the same league so it was time to move.'[79]

Despite the foreignness of the game, playing soccer in white suburban spaces away from the non-white city teams was a significant step in the process of 'becoming white'. As such scholars as Mathew Faye Jacobson and David Roediger have suggested in their studies of assimilation patterns since the nineteenth century, being viewed by others as white was a central objective of immigrants.[80] However, as I argue in the concluding sections of this essay, the meaning and function of these Chicago-area soccer clubs reflects more complex notions of ethnic identity among European whites at the end of the twentieth century than the sometimes linear and uniform understandings of assimilation that have been proposed in past studies of immigrant groups.

The suburbanization of soccer was also an astute business decision. In order to finance the team and recruit the best players, clubs were always looking for ways to raise money. From a purely financial perspective, the suburbs appeared to offer far better opportunities than the city. By the late 1970s, the suburbs were home to a new soccer boom spurred on in large part by the formation of the American Youth Soccer

Tribune Photo by William Kelly

A kicking good time

Pupils from the Wheaton Christian Grammar School are totally enthusiastic in playing soccer during their gym class on the lawn in the west suburb.

Figure 5.   *Chicago Tribune*, 19 September 1974.

Organization (AYSO) in 1964 and to a lesser extent, the rapid expansion and popularity of the Pelé-inspired North American Soccer League (NASL). In a 1979 article, a sportswriter for the *Chicago Tribune* declared that the game was 'skyrocketing at the youth level'.[81] Soccer would continue to grow as a popular youth sport, especially in the suburbs, where it was quickly becoming the game of choice for many children of both sexes. The establishment in 1968 of the Young Sportsmen Soccer League (YSSL), a governing body for suburban youth soccer, and the formation of the Illinois Women's Soccer League in 1974 signalled that the sport had firmly taken root in suburban Chicago. Its growing mainstream popularity was also clearly reflected in the rapid expansion of suburban high school programs. Whereas only 32 teams participated in the Illinois High School Association soccer tournament in 1972, over 140 teams competed in 1979. The *Chicago Tribune* heralded this change in 1984 when it proclaimed that soccer 'is no longer just a game for immigrants and first-generation youngsters. In recent years it has caught the fancy of thoroughly American kids who play it in competition all year long.'[82]

A number of the urban soccer clubs hoped to capitalize on the rise of suburban soccer by relocating to the suburbs and launching ambitious youth programmes. For example, in 1970 Schwaben moved out of the city to suburban Buffalo Grove, where it developed an 18-acre soccer complex with a clubhouse and manicured fields that were the envy of rival clubs for years to come.[83] The move resulted in a change in membership from German-American to largely American-born players. Green and White, another German club, made a similar move when it leased a large plot of land from the town of Mount Prospect, also in Chicago's northwest suburbs. According to a former head of the NSL's youth division, these moves were a commercial proposition and a chance for the clubs 'to reinvent themselves and make more money'. Moreover, relocating to the suburbs represented a change in philosophy as many of the teams 'ceased to be soccer clubs and became instead profit-motive enterprises'.[84]

Developments in the NSL demonstrate the impact of these changes. Whereas in previous decades, the league had been dominated by German and Polish clubs like Schwaben and the Eagles, by the 1970s it experienced an influx of teams with players from areas of the world seldom before seen on Chicago soccer fields: the Baltic, the Middle East, the Caribbean, Africa and Latin America. Most of these new teams were primarily foreign-born and homogeneous (i.e., of a single ethnic group) and chose to remain in Chicago. By contrast, many of the older, more established clubs chose to move their operations to the suburbs, where they became much more heterogeneous. Not surprisingly, the two groups of clubs had increasingly divergent views of how best to foster the development of soccer. By the late 1970s, tensions within the NSL led to yet another reconfiguration of the Chicago-area soccer leagues.

In 1981, 14 of the more established central European clubs seceded from the NSL to form the Metropolitan Soccer League (MSL). This marked the end of the NSL's decades-long reign as the unchallenged leader of European soccer.[85] According to individuals involved in the MSL's creation, it was the disorganization and corruption plaguing the NSL that led to this decision to leave a league that many of these clubs had helped build. As a member of a German club put it, 'The NSL got too arrogant, and money was disappearing. They thought they could do whatever they wanted because they were the only league.'[86] Another official put it more bluntly, remarking that the NSL had 'completely lost control'.[87] As new teams entered the league, the frustration of the older teams only increased because they felt these teams, most often in the lower divisions, had disproportionate influence over league affairs. Even the official history of the NSL from 1984 speaks of this period as one in which a 'black cloud hovered over the league'. By the end of the 1970s, league affairs had worsened to the point that the United States Soccer Federation had to send representatives twice in three years to step in to help resolve the problems.

In addition, many clubs felt that the NSL failed to recognize the game's expansion in the suburbs and was too bogged down in old ethnic concerns. Many believed that the NSL was no longer capable of keeping up with the changing times. According to an official of one team that left the NSL, the league had 'gotten too big to be efficient. The leadership has failed the last three times and it's simply not part of the mainstream of what's happening in the sport.'[88] Many also felt that the league was shortchanging the youth teams; there were few senior soccer opportunities for the growing number of suburban soccer players with the NSL. The new league's first president explained why the MSL offered a better alternative: 'We feel the Metropolitan League will offer a viable alternative. At the present, there really isn't one. There are thousands of kids in the first wave close to moving into senior levels of competition. Where do they go?'[89]

Officials involved with the MSL viewed its formation as part of a natural evolutionary process resulting from the game's suburbanization. It was hardly a coincidence that the older, more established, clubs of similar national backgrounds led the separatist movement. According to one official, 'The older clubs were being met with new ethnic clubs and were not happy with this'.[90] The formation of the MSL thus represents a further example of ethnic succession in the history of Chicago-area soccer in which an influx of ethnic groups viewed as undesirable led the older and more established clubs to secede from the league and to move to what they considered a more desirable space.

The MSL was purposefully kept small, exclusive and suburban in the hope that it would become an elite league, especially in relation to the NSL. In 1982, the MSL opened with only 15 teams, whereas there were 43 teams in the NSL.[91] The following season, the MSL created two divisions with only eight teams in the top flight. While many teams have sought entry into the MSL, league membership has been deliberately limited. Moreover, over the years, the teams have continued to be dominated by players of central European background. For example, the Assyrian team Winged Bull has repeatedly been denied entry into the league. Indeed, the MSL has yet to admit a team that was not of European background.

Despite their new suburban location, the teams in the MSL still maintained an 'ethnic' identity. Although there were a few short-lived teams with non-ethnic identities, the majority of teams maintained explicit ethnic affiliations – a trend that continues to the present.[92] However, my preliminary research into this period suggests that these ethnic associations in suburban spaces differ significantly from those in previous decades in Chicago-area soccer.

Evolving notions of ethnic identity among Chicago-area clubs

Despite soccer's suburbanization and the ever-increasing number of American-born soccer players, the ethnic character of the game has persisted up to the present. As the author of a 1982 *Chicago Tribune* article remarked, Chicago-area soccer is still 'bonded with Old Country cement'.[93] The soccer clubs were never exclusively ethnic, however. Since the 1980s, soccer teams in both the urban and suburban leagues have become much more heterogeneous. This trend is especially true of the older clubs in the MSL and NSL since they are no longer benefiting from a steady influx of their countrymen to the Chicago area. The *Chicago Tribune* recognized the discrepancy between team names and players' names as far back as 1979: 'When you look closely at some of the rosters, you can see that some of the clubs that used to be just Italian or German or some other nationality are not that way anymore.'[94] The president of the Maroons, an Italian team, made a similar observation that year: 'Our team is named the Maroons because our colour are the same as Rome's – the centre of Italian civilization. But, today at best only 5 of our 11 starters are Italians. Our goalkeeper is German and the rest are Africans and South Americans.'[95] Today, there are few if any players of Italian descent on the Maroons. This example is typical of most of the older and well-established clubs still in operation. Indeed, clubs that failed to incorporate 'outsiders' generally folded.

Despite the ethnic diversity evident on their team rosters, the vast majority of teams in the NSL and MSL are still identified with a particular ethnicity and most often with a country in Europe.[96] For example, although few individuals of German descent play for Schwaben today, the club is still commonly viewed as German. Thus, the corporate bodies (the soccer clubs) have an ethnic identity even when their individual members do not.[97] One local soccer player captured the peculiarity of the situation when discussing the NSL team Winged Bull: 'There hasn't been an Assyrian on that team since they started, but everyone sees them as Assyrians.'[98] With the passage of time and a decrease in immigration from the original home country, a team's ethnic identity often becomes increasingly symbolic.[99] As one individual explained it, 'the club counts, not the individual'.[100] Most veterans of the game agree that this has become a much more common phenomenon in Chicago-area soccer than in previous decades. How then are these teams still ethnically identifiable when it is generally understood that their players no longer share the same ethnic background?

My initial findings suggest that the teams retain their ethnic identity because of the feelings of ethnic pride and kinship they inspire in the clubs' supporters and sponsors. Schwaben remains German because of the 'old-timers' who attend the games, social-ize at the clubhouse and provide financial support: As one veteran of the club put it, '[Schwaben] still feels German because the community still sees it as German'.[101] One finds a similar situation in many of the older clubs. For these individuals, who are often scattered throughout the Chicago area, soccer provides an important opportunity to come together and socialize through an ethnically marked activity. Yet few of the players participate in the club's social functions or feel particularly tied to its ethnic identity. For example, the president of a well-known 'Polish' club remarked that, 'it's only the old guys who come to the clubhouse to drink beer and sing songs; the players go home to their families'.[102]

The importance of the teams is furthered revealed by the amount of time and money many team organizers are willing to spend to recruit the area's best players, regardless of their ethnicity. Many of the top teams are paying up to a dozen players $100 to $200 a game, which translates to a rather hefty sum over a course of a 25-game season. The fact that people are willing to shell out thousands of dollars for local men's soccer clearly shows the clubs' importance.[103] 'It's the American Way, so why shouldn't I buy players?'[104] Not only does a team's achievement generate ethnic pride, but sponsoring a team or club provides individuals and companies with valuable social clout. The introduction of more local and national competitions has provided even more opportunities for ethnic communities to symbolically and substantively acquire social prestige through athletic achievement. For example, in spring 2006, the ISSA launched the Champions League to crown the Chicago area's top amateur men's team. Offering a $5,000 prize thanks to sponsorship from Nike, Ford and Westinghouse, the tournament represents the most significant showcase of area soccer in years and signals the game's growing commercialization. Supporters of soccer clubs are willing to spend large amounts of money to win such a tournament because they view it as a way to acquire prestige and honour for their community. As the game becomes increasingly commercialized, an ethnic group's ability to obtain the best players has become further proof of its success in the United States.[105] As one club sponsor put it, 'A win for the Eagles is a win for the Polish community because it shows people that we've made it'.[106] With increased financial investment by club patrons, Latino teams are demonstrating a similar pattern by which a club's triumphs are seen to reflect economic advancement, which for many immigrants best symbol-izes community success and assimilation in the United States. That a soccer team's success has become one of the most visible signs of a community's standing is reflected in a comment by a team benefactor who also described his investment in paid players as 'the American Way'.[107]

In general, the teams that have experienced the most diversification and professionalization of their rosters tend to be the older and more established clubs. They also tend to represent nationalities that have experienced a drop in immigration to Chicago. The importance of these clubs as a locus of ethnic identity reveals a great deal about the meaning of ethnicity for descendants of immigrants in the Chicago area, especially as 'traditional' bonds like language and shared customs weaken over time. For these groups, purchasing soccer success has become one of the surest means of fostering ethnic pride and a sense of belonging.

In contrast to the older clubs in the urban and suburban leagues, many of the newer teams continue to recruit players from a single ethnic group. This is still true of the NSL, which has benefited from the most recent waves of immigration to the Chicago area. Consequently, there are still a number of soccer clubs in the NSL that have remained ethnically more homogeneous (notably those from eastern Europe, the Caribbean and Africa). The continued immigration of Poles has resulted in the creation of more and more Polish teams. While the top Polish teams continue to play in the MSL and NSL, Poles are represented in such high numbers that there are now two exclusively Polish leagues in operation (Polish Soccer League and Polish Highlanders).[108] Similarly, the growth of Chicago's African and Caribbean populations has resulted in the creation of the World Soccer League, which organizes teams from these regions. While not nearly as popular as the 1920s version in honour of the city's mayor, the NSL's resumption of a local Cup of Nations in the winter of 2007 reflects the persisting importance of 'international' soccer competitions for immigrant groups. Moreover, with teams now representing Albania, Assyria, Bosnia, Croatia, Honduras, Mexico, Poland and Serbia, local soccer tournaments continue to reveal and celebrate Chicago's changing immigrant and ethnic make-up. For these teams, leagues and competitions, the ethnic period of soccer continues.

Conclusion

Soccer continues to be an integral part of the Chicago-area sporting scene. Although the city's professional soccer team now dominates media coverage, the heart and soul of the game remains within the local youth and adult teams and leagues, which have expanded to new spaces and unprecedented levels. For example, alongside the many non-affiliated leagues, the Illinois State Soccer Association now oversees 27 adult leagues in the state. Ranging from the ethnically homogeneous Mexican and Polish teams competing in the city to the diverse clubs based in the suburbs, Chicago-area soccer encompasses many different styles and traditions. Moreover, the ethnic make-up of clubs and leagues continues to reflect changing waves of immigration to the city, to reveal the processes of integration, and exhibit patterns of ethnic succession. There is much evidence to support the hypothesis that these patterns will continue to characterize the game's development in the Chicago area, especially given the continual arrival of new immigrant groups.

This essay was primarily intended to document and analyse the largely unknown history of soccer in the Chicago area. Employing the theory of ethnic succession as an analytical tool, it also points to the sociological importance of the soccer teams and leagues over time – an imprint and legacy that generally has been ignored. Specifically, it examines the ways in which soccer teams and leagues have repeatedly exhibited patterns of ethnic succession and filled important symbolic and substantive functions. Chief among their functions was – and is – the fostering and maintenance of ethnic identities and communities. Not only have they helped delineate more sharply defined boundaries, but they have also assisted in the creation of new social identities for immigrant and ethnic communities, whose status was continually open to negotiation and subject to conflict.

Due to the preliminary nature of my research, a number of topics remain undeveloped in my study. For example, I have only begun to explore the meaning and nature of immigrant and ethnic identity and the processes of transition from one to the other through the history of Chicago-area soccer. Similarly, the ways in which soccer teams and leagues foster the construction and maintenance of ethnic identities and communities deserve much more qualitative evidence. Moreover, since I focused on the general framework of soccer's history in the Chicago area, many potential sources beyond newspapers were left unexamined. This study is therefore an important first step. It is my hope that by introducing the sociologically significant history of Chicago-area soccer, my study will inspire further research.

For example, it is quite possible that the ever-increasing numbers of American-born players in area youth programmes, will fundamentally change the game's development. Today, there are several teams that already exhibit new patterns in relation to the game's evolving standing in the Chicago area. For example, jaHbat FC, the team I played with, is neither dominated by one ethnic heritage, nor is it merely a random collection of paid players. Based in Evanston, a suburb known for its diversity, jaHbat FC is a unique soccer club in the Chicago area. Formed in 1996 through long-standing friendships among Caribbean soccer players raised in Evanston, the club has since incorporated a broader assortment of players reflecting the town's diverse ethnic and racial makeup.[109] Moreover, unlike most competitive clubs, which include paid players from throughout the Chicago area, jaHbat FC is compromised largely of unpaid players originally from, or residing in, Evanston. Furthermore, many of the players are deeply connected to and integrated into the community, especially as soccer coaches and teachers. A fund-raising letter from 25 March 2000 speaks to this claim: 'What distinguishes our club from others is our involvement in the Evanston community. jaHbat FC has been working with Evanston's youth soccer players for many years. Between its players, jaHbat coaches 19 different youth teams in Evanston.' This involvement has created an exceptional degree of goodwill[110] and continuity, as younger players from Evanston replenish the ranks – a trend unusual for a team of this character[111] and skill-level.[112] As one player put it, 'I always know that whenever I come back the guys will be playing'.[113] jaHbat FC is also one of the few men's soccer clubs to have an affiliated women's team (Lady jaHbat) in the Illinois Women's Soccer League. Due to the players' history and involvement in Evanston, jaHbat FC appears from my research to be one of the few clubs that is significantly integrated into the larger residential community.

On the other hand, for many of the older Caribbean players growing up in the later 1970s and early 1980s, soccer was a foreign game symbolic of their heritage and hence a way to resist integration and to feel pride in their ethnic background. As one player put it, 'soccer was a necessity for us because it allowed us to never be embarrassed of being Haitian. Soccer gave us an identity, and we didn't have to blend in and assimilate.'[114] In this respect, for these players as children, soccer filled the important functions seen with the 'ethnic clubs'. However, as they moved into adulthood, the meaning of soccer changed. 'As soccer became more popular and we became a part of the community, it got watered down because it was no longer where you are from but where you're at.'[115] While the club has grown beyond its Caribbean heritage, it still serves to help foster and maintain a sense of community. The comparison of the early and more recent experiences of jaHbat players suggests that the club's evolution is not only a reflection of the game's past in the Chicago area, but may be a harbinger of its future.

Notes

1. Trouille, 'Association Football to Fútbol'. While his impressive findings are not incorporated into this article, see also Gabriel Logan's detailed dissertation on the early history of Chicago-area soccer, 'Lace up the Boots, full Tilt Ahead: Recreation, Immigration, and Labor on Chicago's Soccer Fields, 1890–1939', Northern Illinois University, 2007.
2. With people flocking to stadiums throughout the country, games increasingly covered by the media, and athletes like Babe Ruth and Jack Dempsey viewed as veritable heroes, sports became an integral part of American society during this period.
3. *Chicago Daily Tribune,* 'Soccer Elevens Start Play Today for League Honors, 18 September, 1921, A4.
4. While it is clear that the players were being paid, my research did not reveal the exact amounts. A few of the teams were fully professional but most of them provided only a supplement to the players' regular income, in addition to material benefits like meals, housing, loans and employment.
5. While my initial findings do not fully answer the question of gate receipts, it appears as if the larger clubs with enclosed stadiums charged admission while the smaller clubs that played in city parks did not.
6. For example, on 5 October 1924, the *Chicago Daily Tribune* announced 33 local soccer games in six different competitions.
7. *Chicago Daily Tribune*, October 25, 1921.
8. *Chicago Daily Tribune*, 1 January 1923.
9. *Chicago Daily Tribune*, 'Soccer Growing in Popularity', 25 October 1925, A1.
10. Comiskey Park was the home of the White Sox major league baseball team.
11. See the chapter 'How Soccer Explains the Jewish Question', in Franklin Foer's book, *How Soccer Explains the World* for a discussion of the Austrian club, especially in regards to notions of Zionism and anti-Semitism.
12. William Emmett Dever was the mayor of Chicago from 1923 to 1927.
13. The Poles and Italians probably joined forces due to an insufficient amount of quality players to field separate teams for the prestigious and highly competitive tournament.
14. Geertz, 'Deep Play'.
15. Hartmann, *Race, Culture*; MacAloon, 'Double Visions'; Geertz, 'Deep Play'.
16. *Chicago Daily Tribune*, 'Soccer Teams Adopt Different Style of Play Schedule, 20 July, 1924, A3.
17. All the teams in the Chicago National Soccer League played in enclosed stadiums and charged entrance fees.
18. *Chicago Daily Tribune*, July 28, 1924.
19. *Chicago Daily Tribune*, August 5, 1924.
20. Jose, *The American Soccer League.*
21. Waldstein and Wagg, 'Unamerican Activity?', 76.
22. See Colin Jose's excellent and thorough work on the ASL, *The American Soccer League.*
23. The majority of teams that collapsed were the industrial and residential teams like Hyde Park.
24. *Chicago Daily Tribune*, 30 January 1938.
25. *Chicago Daily Tribune*, 'Soccer Growing in Popularity', 25 October 1925, A1.
26. Crepeau, *Baseball*, ix.
27. Markovits and Hellerman, *Offside*.
28. In many respects, the 'ethnic period', continues to the present. However, with new developments reshaping soccer in the Chicago area over the past several decades, marked by a major moment in 1971, my examination of the 'ethnic period' is focused on these years.
29. For example, the list of winners for the US Open Cup and National Amateur Cup during this period reveals an overwhelming ethnic flavour to the national soccer scene (See Allaway, Jose and Litterer, *The Encyclopedia*, for a complete list).

30. The change in name was due perhaps to Second World War patriotism and growing desire to 'Americanize' the perception of the league.
31. Litterer, 'Chicago's Soccer History'.
32. Gleason, 'Football with Feet'.
33. For example, every team in the top division in 1970 was tied to an ethnic community.
34. See the following works for a discussion of the role baseball played in the construction of ethnic or minority communities during a similar period: Regalado, 'Sport and Community'; Alamillo, 'Mexican American Baseball'; and Ruck's *Sandlot Seasons*.
35. See Basch, 'The Vincentians and Grenadians' for a good discussion of how voluntary associations operate as adaptive mechanisms in situations of rapid change.
36. Although cultural events were important to ethnic subcommunities, they never exerted the influence of sporting activities as exemplified by the popular German Turners, Bohemian Sokols and Polish Falcons.
37. See Anthony Cohen's work, *Symbolic Construction of Community*, explaining how the community is 'imagined' as a group of people who perceive distinct boundaries and traditions that distinguish them from 'the Other' and Fredrik Barth's research, *Ethnic Groups*, on the importance of boundaries between ethnic groups in determining who is a member and who is not.
38. Henrik Braaten, *Skandinaven*, January 3, 1908, 5.
39. Radek Kolar, *Denni Hlasatel*, August 26, 1922, 8.
40. *Abdenpost*, August 22, 1924, 11.
41. *The Jewish Daily*, May 5, 1926, 4.
42. Magnus Odegaard, *Denni Hlasatel*, September 20, 1922, 9.
43. Cerek Krejci, *Skandinaven*, August 20, 1917, 11.
44. *Chicago Daily Tribune*, October 1, 1926, 27.
45. Socializing at the clubhouse was a practice carried over from Europe.
46. In 1942, the *Chicago Daily Tribune* changed its name to the *Chicago Tribune*.
47. *Chicago Tribune*, October 14, 1977, D1.
48. Gleason, 'Football with Feet', 56.
49. Haner, *Soccerhead,* 137.
50. Personal interview with Julius Roth, March 16, 2006.
51. This was probably especially important for German and Italian teams.
52. This was certainly true of my French father, but not for all immigrant groups by any means. Many pushed their children to play more 'American' sports like baseball or football instead.
53. Many of the most anticipated games of the season involved games within ethnic or national groups, which were often referred to as the 'local derby'. For example, according to the *Chicago Tribune*, the most important soccer match in 1968 was the annual rivalry between Hansa and Schwaben. With 40 years of rivalry behind them, it was regarded by fans of German descent as the 'local soccer derby' (December 8, 1968).
54. *Chicago Tribune*, May 14, 1972.
55. Haner, *Soccerhead*, 160.
56. Neil Milbert and Mike Conklin, *Chicago Tribune*, The City with a Kick, 6 July, 1979, E1.
57. Gleason, 'Football with Feet', 56.
58. The press's disregard of the game was also seen on the national level. For example, the US National Team's historic upset over England in the 1950 World Cup received little coverage in the national newspapers.
59. The Chicago Spurs in the National Professional Soccer League.
60. Jim Brosnan *Chicago Tribune*, 'Watch Willie Roy-Not Just for Kicks, 3 September 1967, F12.
61. Neil Milbert and Mike Conklin, Chicago Tribune, 'The City with a Kick', 6 July, 1979, E1.
62. *Chicago Tribune*, November 18, 1972.
63. Many of the older individuals I interviewed spoke despairingly of this period in which their children abandoned soccer to play more 'American' sports.
64. Shinn, 'Futbol Nation'; Pescador, '¡Vamos Taximaroa!'.
65. Personal interview with Carlos Gomez, vice-president of a local league, March 12, 2006.
66. Fischer, 'Toward a Subcultural Theory of Urbanism'.
67. Personal interview on April 3, 2006 with Jans Podolski, a player on a German team at the time of CLASA's formation in 1973.

68. Interestingly, all the South American teams remained in the NSL. It is possible that the South American teams identified more with the European clubs than with the Mexican-American ones. A few Mexican teams remained in the NSL, particularly those in the top division, but most of them eventually joined CLASA or other Latino leagues.
69. Pescador, '¡Vamos Taximaroa!', 361.
70. Ibid., 368.
71. Ibid., 370.
72. Neil Milbert and Mike Conklin, *Chicago Tribune*, 'The City with a Kick', 6 July, 1979, E1.
73. Price and Whitworth. 'Soccer and Latino Cultural Space', 186.
74. Personal interview with Gustavo Sanchez, April 16, 2006.
75. The creation of the Champions League tournament is discussed in the following section.
76. Jackson, *Crabgrass Frontier*; Sugrue, *The Origins of the Urban Crisis*; Hirsch, *Making the Second Ghetto*.
77. Mike Conklin, *Chicago Tribune*, 'Amateur Soccer may Kick Old Look, 27 December, 1981, C3.
78. Personal interview with Rafal Milkowski, May 3, 2006.
79. Personal interview with Petr Nowak, March 19, 2006.
80. Jacobson, *Whiteness of a Different Color*; Roediger, *Wages of Whiteness*.
81. Mike Conklin, *Chicago Tribune*, 'Soccer Grows as Fast as Children, 16 May, 1979, F1.
82. Bill Boyce, *Chicago Tribune*, 'Both Generations get a Kick out of own Brand of "Football"', A1.
83. The initial purchase was of eight acres, but in 1972, Schwaben bought an adjacent 10 acres.
84. Personal interview with Gerald Cook, April 19, 2006.
85. The Trevians, a team from the northern suburbs that had not been part of the NSL, also joined the MSL.
86. Personal interview with Heinz Muller, February 3, 2006.
87. Personal interview with Lars Hellerman, March 8, 2006.
88. Mike Conklin, *Chicago Tribune*, 'Amateur Soccer may Kick Old Look, 27 December, 1981, C3.
89. Ibid.
90. Personal interview with Gerald Cook, April 19, 2006.
91. The NSL has remained much larger and more urban. For example, in 2006, the NSL fielded 45 teams in four divisions, 28 of which were based in Chicago. The MSL currently has 22 teams in two divisions, the large majority of which are based in the suburbs.
92. The maintenance of ethnic affiliations by the clubs in the MSL contrasts with teams in less competitive leagues like the Northern Illinois Soccer League and Armitage Football Association, the majority of which are not based on ethnicity.
93. Richard Phillips, *Chicago Tribune*, 'I'm okay, you stink: the pride and passion of ethnic soccer', 1 October, 1982, C1.
94. Mike Conklin, *Chicago Tribune*, 'National Soccer League Changes with "the times"', 16 February, 1974, C6.
95. Steve Bogira, *Chicago Tribune*, 'Resolving an Identity Crisis in Chicago', 1 June, 1977 D1.
96. See Hughson, 'The Bad Blue Boys a', and Tuastad, 'The Political Role of Football' for similar discussions on the role soccer plays in the construction and maintenance of ethnic communities in Australia and Jordan.
97. This situation parallels the development of 'ethnic' neighbourhoods, which are no longer exclusively of any one ethnicity, yet still retain an 'ethnic' identity such as 'Little Italy' in Manhattan.
98. Personal interview with Yonas Pavicevic, April 22, 2006.
99. According to Herbert Gans, symbolic ethnicity is 'voluntary, diverse, or individualistic ethnicity' and 'takes an expressive rather than instrumental function in people's lives, becoming more of a leisure-time activity and losing its relevancy, say, to earning a living or regulating family life'. Gans, 'Symbolic Ethnicity', 9. Much more research would be required to demonstrate soccer's role in the construction of symbolic ethnicity.
100. Personal interview with Len Illic, March 27, 2006.

101. Personal interview with Hank Ziehm, April 4, 2006.
102. Personal interview with Julius Gross, March 3, 2006.
103. Most teams survive primarily through donations. In the case of jaHbat FC, one individual paid for all the team's expenses. This included substantial league fees, equipment costs and miscellaneous expenses.
104. Personal interview with Len Illic, March 27, 2006.
105. While most people I interviewed accepted the importance of paying players, not everyone approved of these changes. For example, one veteran of a Polish club remarked that 'you don't have the same closeness anymore and there's less pride about being Polish because they'll leave for the money'. (Personal interview with Rudy Tomecek, March 8, 2006.)
106. Personal interview with Hank Ziehm, April 4, 2006.
107. Personal interview with Francisco Ruiz, March 18, 2006.
108. The Polish teams are prominently covered by Chicago's two main Polish daily newspapers, *Dziennik Chicagoski* and *Dziennik Zwiazkowy*.
109. The name 'jaHbat' is an acronym that represents the respective nations and continents of its players: J-Jamaica; A-Americas; H-Haiti; B-Belize; A-Asia; T-Trinidad.
110. Due to many team members involvement with the local youth club (Team Evanston), jaHbat plays their home games at a local soccer field for free.
111. Most teams resembling jaHbat last only a few years.
112. jaHbat FC won the National Soccer League Major Division championship in 2005.
113. Personal interview with Claude Beauvais, May 2, 2006.
114. Personal interview with Francois Petite, May 8, 2006.
115. Personal interview with Jean Gaetjens, May 6, 2006.

References

Alamillo, Jose. 'Mexican American Baseball: Masculinity, Racial Struggle, and Labor Politics in Southern California, 1930–1950'. *Sports Matters: Race, Recreation, and Culture,* ed. J. Bloom, and M. Willard, 86–116. New York: New York University Press, 2002.

Allaway, R., C. Jose, and D. Litterer. *The Encyclopedia of American Soccer History.* Lanham, MD: The Scarecrow Press, Inc., 2001.

Barth, Fredrik. *Ethnic Groups and Boundaries: The Social Organization of Culture Difference.* Boston, MA: Little, Brown, 1969.

Basch, Linda. 'The Vincentians and Grenadians: The Role of Voluntary Associations in Immigrant Adaptation to New York City'. In *New Immigrants in New York,* ed. N. Foner, 159–93. New York: Columbia University Press, 1987.

Cohen, Anthony. *The Symbolic Construction of Community.* London: Tavistock, 1985.

Crepeau, Richard. *Baseball: America's Diamond Mind 1919–1941.* Orlando, FL: University Presses of Central Florida, 1980.

Fischer, Claude. 'Toward a Subcultural Theory of Urbanism'. *The American Journal of Sociology* 80, no. 6 (1975): 1319–41.

Fischer, Claude. *To Dwell Among Friends: Personal Networks in Town and City.* Chicago, IL: University of Chicago Press, 1982.

Foer, Franklin. *How Soccer Explains the World: An Unlikely Theory of Globalization.* New York: Harper Collin Publishers, 2004.

Gans, Herbert. 'Symbolic Ethnicity: The Future of Ethnic Groups and Cultures in America'. *Ethnic and Racial Studies* 2 (1979): 1–20.

Geertz, Clifford, ed. 'Deep Play: Notes on the Balinese Cockfight'. In *The Interpretation of Cultures,* 412–54. New York: Basic Books, 1973.

Gleason, William. 'Football with Feet'. *Chicago* (March 1956): 55–6.

Haner, Jim. *Soccerhead: An Accidental Journey into the Heart of the American Game.* New York: Rarrar, Straus and Giroux, 2006.

Hartmann, Douglas. *Race, Culture, and the Revolt of the Black Athlete.* Chicago, IL: The University of Chicago Press, 2003.

Hirsch, Arnold. *Making the Second Ghetto: Race and Housing in Chicago 1940–1960.* Chicago, IL: The University of Chicago Press, 1998.

Hughson, John. 'The Bad Blue Boys and the "Magical Recovery" of John Clarke'. In *Entering the Field: New Perspectives on World Football,* ed. G. Armstrong, and R. Giulianotti, 239–60. Oxford: Berg, 1997.

Jackson, Kenneth. *Crabgrass Frontier: The Suburbanization of the United States.* New York: Oxford University Press, 1985.

Jacobson, Matthew. *Whiteness of a Different Color: European Immigrants and the Alchemy of Race.* Cambridge, MA: Harvard University Press, 1998.

Jose, Colin. *The American Soccer League: The Golden Years of American Soccer 1921–1931.* Lanham, MD: Scarecrow Press, Inc., 1998.

Litterer, David. 'Chicago's Soccer History'. *The American Soccer History Archives,* http://www.sover.net/~spectrum/ (2005).

MacAloon, John. 'Double Visions: Olympic Games and American Culture'. In *The Olympic Games in Transition,* ed. J. Segrave, and D. Chu, 279–94. Champaign, IL: Human Kinetics Books, 1988.

Markovits, A., and S. Hellerman. *Offside: Soccer and American Exceptionalism.* Princeton, NJ: Princeton University Press, 2001.

Pescador, Juan Javier. '¡Vamos Taximaroa! Mexican/Chicano Soccer Associations and Transnational/Translocal Communities, 1967–2002'. *Latino Studies* 2, no. 3 (December 2004): 352–76.

Price, Marie, and Courtney Whitworth. 'Soccer and Latino Cultural Space: Metropolitan Washington *Fútbol* Leagues'. In *Hispanic Spaces, Latino Places: Community and Cultural Diversity in Contemporary America,* ed. D. Arreola. Austin, TX: University of Texas Press, 2004.

Regalado, Samuel. 'Sport and Community in California's Japanese American "Yamato Colony", 1930–1945.' In *Sport in America: From Wicked Amusement to National Obsession,* ed. D. Wiggins, 239–50. Champaign, IL: Human Kinetics, 1995.

Roediger, David. *Wages of Whiteness: Race and the Making of the American Working Class.* New York: Verso, 1991.

Ruck, Rob. *Sandlot Seasons: Sport in Black Pittsburgh.* Urbana, IL: University of Illinois Press, 1987.

Shinn, Christopher. 'Futbol Nation: U.S. Latinos and the Goal of a Homeland'. *Latino/a Popular Culture,* ed. M. Habell-Pallan and M. Romero, 240–51. New York: New York University Press, 2002.

Sugrue, Thomas. *The Origins of the Urban Crisis: Race and Inequality in Postwar Detroit.* Princeton, NJ: Princeton University Press, 1996.

Troullie, David. 'Association Football to Fútbol: Ethnic Succession and the History of Chicago-area Soccer, 1890–1920'. *Soccer and Society* 9, no. 4 (2008): 455–76.

Tuastad, Dag. 'The Political Role of Football for Palestinians in Jordan'. In *Entering the Field: New Perspectives on World Football,* ed. G. Armstrong and R. Giulianotti, 105–22. Oxford: Berg, 1997.

Waldstein, David, and Stephen Wagg. 'Unamerican activity? Football in US and Canadian Society'. In *Giving the Game Away: Football, Politics and Culture on Five Continents,* ed. S. Wagg. London: Leicester University Press, 1995.

No single pattern: Australian migrant minorities and the round ball code in Victoria

Roy Hay[a] and Nick Guoth[b]

[a]Deakin University, Victoria, and Sports and Editorial Services Australia, Australia;
[b]Australian National University, Canberra, Australia

Introduction

There is no better place to confound any generalization about the relationships between minority groups and sport in society than the experience of such groups in Australian society in relation to the round ball code of football.[1] Some migrant minorities have embraced the game as an important element of cultural identification and distinction, others have used it as one of a number of means of finding a way into some areas of Australian society and yet others have shunned the game as being un-Australian.[2] Moreover the relationships between the various minorities and Association football have never been unchanging for long, so that some groups who became heavily involved in the game were succeeded by migrants from the same area, but from a different social class who explicitly rejected any contact with the game. In some cases migrants were quite happy to play the game, but had no further involvement, while others used the game as a means of entry into 'mainstream' Australian society. A few used the code for political purposes, though far fewer and far less centrally, than many of the domestic commentators on migrants and football believed.[3] So football in Australia served a multiplicity of changing purposes and disentangling the reasons for the conflicting stories is far from easy. It would be hard to think of any sport which had, and still has, as much cultural baggage attached to it.

Within migrant communities it must be appreciated that only a minority were involved in sport as players, administrators or spectators and in most cases in lower proportions than the domestic population in Australia.[4] Even in the most sports-mad minority migrant groups it was relatively rare to find individuals whose lives were more influenced by football than by their employment, families, education, religion or

the other aspects of their social existence.[5] Immigrants were not the only minorities
involved in the game. Women have always been a minority of those participating as
players, though they have often been highly influential behind the scenes in many
football clubs. Until recently only a minority of Australians of long standing became
directly interested in soccer, and even today it would be hard to prove that a majority
of such Australians had anything other than a specific and passing interest in the game
when the national team qualified for, and subsequently played in, the World Cup in
Germany in 2006.[6]

Most of the debate and research about migrant groups in Australia has focused
on the national level. But within most migrant groups there are regional divisions.
This is very evident among Greeks and Italians in Australia. There is nearly always
tension between the levels. Sometimes the community comes together in a form of
national identification. At other times regional or local loyalties prove stronger.
This can give rise to differences between groups and sport. For example, in
Geelong the bulk of migrants came from the Greek islands where soccer was not
so strongly woven into social life, and largely as a consequence there were only
two relatively brief periods of club formation. In Melbourne where the number of
Greek migrants was much larger there have been huge variations over time.[7]
Recently the supporters of the Oakleigh and South Melbourne clubs have diverged
in their views of which club should represent Greek identity in Victoria. Some of
this can be attributed to differences between generations. Some younger elements
have been trying to maintain a Greek national idea, while others have argued that
such an approach would hold back the South Melbourne club and prevent any rein-
volvement in the new domestic national competition, the A-League.[8] Similar
debates have occurred or are still current among Serbians and Croatians in Australia as is demonstrated by the work of John Hughson and Chris Hallinan.[9] In
Canberra, the older generation of Croatian migrants was associated with the Deakin
club, while younger groups have now become involved with the emerging
O'Connor club.[10]

In the beginning[11]

Soccer clubs or teams preceded formal community organizations for at least some
migrant groups.[12] In some cases soccer clubs provided integrating facilities when
political concerns threatened to divide immigrant communities. Though often
portrayed as hotbeds of political activity, most clubs saw themselves as oases where
the various contending groups could meet without conflict. Even among the Croatians,
most often accused of political activism, the soccer club could be *neutralno tlo*,
neutral territory.[13] Bell Park was set up as an explicitly non-political and multiracial
club in Geelong. In the Macedonian, German, Hungarian, Ukrainian and Spanish
communities in Geelong the soccer clubs tried extraordinarily hard to attract and
retain members by eschewing political involvement. This was not always possible,
and the Dutch in Geelong had two separate soccer organizations – Olympia and the
Dutch Society of Geelong – reflecting existing differences, probably religious, which
could not be reconciled through soccer.[14]

Within migrant communities there were and are many different identities
involved – regional, local and familial as well as the ethnic nationalism on which
most research has focussed in recent years.[15] Analysis which stops at the level of
national ethnic groups in Australia is seriously deficient, as it probably is in England

too, as is made clear in the work of Tony Mason, which unpicks some of the sub-regional identities existing in the North of England.[16] When the Macedonian community in Geelong holds its annual picnics, at which soccer matches are played, the teams are drawn from the villages from which the migrants came in the former Yugoslav Republic.

In Australia the Italian, Greek, Croatian and Dutch have become divided in their sporting activities along regional, cultural, religious or familial lines, rather than political ones. Hence it has proved impossible to establish a long-lasting senior soccer club to represent the whole Italian community in Melbourne since the demise of Juventus in the 1980s. Juventus had been one of the most successful immigrant clubs of all in its early days in the 1950s, winning the top division in Victoria every year from 1952 to 1956 and again in 1958 and 1960. Juventus had been founded in 1948 with a policy of 'admitting all players and officials of the old teams and any other person without distinctions'.[17] At one of the first meetings it was clearly established that the club 'would not involve itself in politics, local or Italian', and the name Juventus was chosen 'because it was apolitical and as far as possible not adaptable to ideas and situations not connected with soccer'.[18] An incidental advantage in Victoria was that the black and white vertical stripes of Juventus were the colours of the Collingwood Australian Rules Football Club in Melbourne, thus providing a ready source of supply for shirts. The Italian Olympic cyclist Nino Borsari, by this time a successful Australian businessman, and his wife, the opera singer Fanny Cester, had a huge influence on both the on-field and off-field success.[19] But when Juventus eventually declined, after becoming national league champion in 1985, regional loyalties asserted themselves as the Italian communities were now so much larger and no single club could re-establish that central unifying role thereafter.[20] In 2008 there are two Italian clubs in the Victorian Premier League and several at lower levels.

Among the Greek community in Victoria, it was only in the second half of the 1990s that the National Soccer League club South Melbourne Hellas became the dominant Greek club in Melbourne, following the decline of Heidelberg Alexander, which represented the Greek Macedonians.[21] Even so there were four Greek clubs in the 12-team Victorian Premier League in 2008. Their supporter bases are not coterminous.[22] But it is far too simple to label the differences that exist as political; rather they tend to be regional or even familial. Political organizations sometimes claim a key role in the foundation and early history of Australian migrant soccer clubs, but this often results from trying to read history backwards.[23]

Religious organizations often worked symbiotically with soccer clubs. Three members of the Roman Catholic Church were present at the inaugural meeting of Juventus and its foundation was announced from the pulpits during masses in churches in West Melbourne.[24] Either the church was linked with the foundation of the soccer team or the religious leaders went to the clubs because that is where the young migrants were to be found.[25] Religion could be divisive, as with the Dutch community in Geelong, and Bill Murray remembers furious debates within the Maltese club for which he played in Adelaide in the 1950s.[26]

Soccer clubs performed vital socializing roles, even ran language classes, but their place in the sporting and wider society was often controversial.[27] They were accused of fomenting ethnic nationalism and violence, of being un-Australian, of continuing old loyalties which ought to have been abandoned on arrival and of encouraging the formation of ethnic ghettoes rather than seeking assimilation or integration.[28] These charges were not new when levelled against post-Second World War migrants from Europe, and many, if not all, had been uttered against Scottish and English arrivals many years before, even as far back as the 1880s.[29]

In many practical ways the soccer clubs helped minority migrants access the institutions of the host society and appreciate the nuances of this strange and subtle society in which they found themselves. Registering a club and its players, obtaining permits for building, conforming to local regulations, all required interactions with local organizations and bureaucracies. Frank Lowy, the current president of the Football Federation of Australia, purportedly the second richest man in Australia and the head of the multinational Westfield Group, learned some, though perhaps not all, of his lessons with the Hakoah Soccer Club in Sydney in the 1950s.[30] Earlier generations of migrants could help, often with what appear to be simple transactions. The father of one of the authors, a Hungarian like Lowy, and new to Sydney in 1961, needed transport. He was advised to go to a St George Budapest match to seek help to buy a car. There he met an earlier migrant who negotiated the purchase on his behalf. A week later the car was available and at the right price.[31]

Attributing to heritage or ethnic background that which may be family or personal preference is always problematic. The Alagich family produced male and female Australian representatives, state and national league players and one of the country's leading coaches and educators, but was that the result of their origins and background in the former Yugoslavia or years of involvement in the sport in Australia? Joseph Alagich arrived in Australia in 1924 from Dalmatia. He had three sons, Marin, Rudolph and Slavko. The Alagich family formed Yugoslav teams in Broken Hill in the 1930s but later some moved to Sydney, where Joe Alagich, the son of Marin, was a star of the Yugal Ryde team in the 1960s and early 1970s.[32] He represented both New South Wales and Australia. Colin Alagich, the son of Slavko, played in Port Adelaide, was a long time official of the Port Adelaide club and wrote the history of the game in that area.[33] Colin's son, Richie Alagich, played more than 250 games in total for West Adelaide and Brisbane Strikers in the National Soccer League and Adelaide United in the A-League. He represented Australia at Youth and Olympic level. Colin's daughter Dianne was a star with the Matildas, playing for more than a decade at the top level of the women's game.[34] Richard Alagich, the son of Rudolph, is one of Australia's leading coach educators, completing a degree in sports science in Zagreb. He is the author of several coaching books and a critic of the physical type of play which dominated Australian football over many years.[35] Always controversial, he resigned as coach of Manly in the New South Wales State League in 1978 after sensational press reports about his showing a film of Nazi atrocities at Auschwitz to his team shortly before they took the field against Melita Eagles.[36]

The Radojevic family in Geelong similarly was involved in the game at local, state, national and international level from the time the brothers Joe and Vinko arrived from Europe in the 1950s to the present day. Joe became secretary of the Croatia club in Melbourne in 1957 and transferred it to Geelong that year.[37] It reached the State League in two years, and moved back to Melbourne. Later he formed the North Geelong club in 1967. His elder son became an Australian Rules footballer, while his younger son played club soccer for North Geelong. His daughter Mary married Luke Didulica and her two sons played national league football for Melbourne Knights. John, the elder, was the CEO of the Australian Professional

Figure 1.   Scottish-born former Celtic and Scotland keeper Frank Haffey of St George-Budapest saves from Joe Alagich of Yugal Ryde in the New South Wales State League. Source: *Soccer World*, September 18, 1970.

Footballers' Association and is now the legal counsel for the Football Federation of Australia.[38] The younger son, Joe's grandson, Joey, has represented Croatia, but only after being overlooked by the then national coach, Frank Farina, for the Australian team which he was desperate to represent.[39] In Farina's defence it should be said that he had two or three top quality keepers at his disposal. Farina's predecessor, Eddie Thompson, made a practice of capping young talent to ensure it was tied to Australia, including the precocious Harry Kewell. At the time, Thompson's reputation was being challenged in a report on corruption in football, and it may be that Farina also wanted to be clear of any allegation that he capped players to increase their value on the transfer market.[40]

A similar story can be told at local level in Geelong where the Dorris and Muir families, originally from Scotland, and the Nelson family from Northern Ireland, have at least three generations of involvement in the game as players, coaches and administrators.[41] The Love family at Diamond Valley in Melbourne mirror that. In each case the senior member of the family emigrated or was brought to Australia by his parents, and his sons, and sometimes daughters and their children, grew up in this country.

The next sections examine the experience of three groups of migrants from countries which have a strong tradition in football and the different ways the game played out for the migrants in Australia. The first is one of the earliest groups of migrants, the second the most extreme case of the persistence of a species of ethnic nationalism and the third is a brief account of a migrant group which assimilated very rapidly indeed.[42]

Figure 2.   Programme of the Scottish Festival that kept England's first cricket team off the Melbourne Cricket Ground in 1861. Source: Chisholm, 1950, facing 8.

Scots

Scots have been a significant minority of Australia's population since the earliest days of European settlement. Convicts, radicals and the victims of the Highland Clearances found their way to the antipodes voluntarily or involuntarily, and they were soon accompanied by numbers of free settlers from both urban and rural areas.[43] Pockets of Scottish settlement occurred in the western district of Victoria and the Latrobe Valley, in the Hunter Valley in New South Wales, as well as in all the emerging major cities.[44] Caledonian societies were established in the early to mid-nineteenth century and highland games quickly became part of the sporting calendar of virtually every area where the Scots settled.[45] Football games were often part of the event. In 1861 the Caledonian society's games on 26–28 December kept the first English touring cricket team under H.H. Stephenson from practising on the Melbourne Cricket Ground, while 20,000 attended the Scottish festival. A football match was scheduled as part of the event, and the Caledonian Cup became an early Australian Rules football trophy.[46]

When what was to become Australian Rules football got under way in the 1850s and 1860s, the Caledonian Society put up the first trophy for competition by the Melbourne and Geelong clubs.[47] In those decades football was a much more fluid and inchoate game than it later became and it is often difficult to determine which form of the game was taking place.[48] An advertisement in a western district newspaper, the *Warrnambool Examiner* of 28 May 1861, announced:

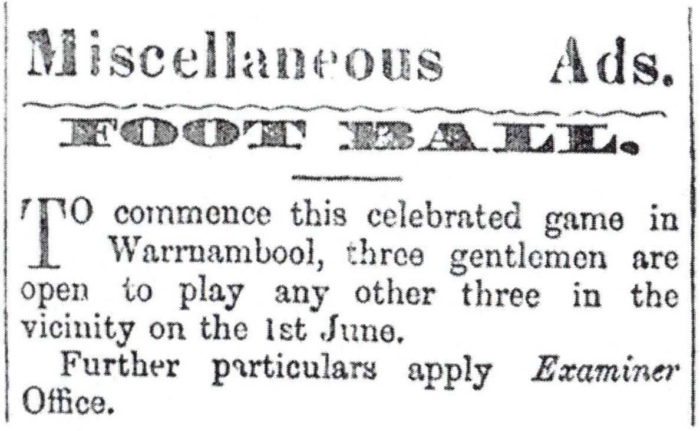

Miscellaneous Ads.

FOOT BALL.

TO commence this celebrated game in Warrnambool, three gentlemen are open to play any other three in the vicinity on the 1st June.

Further particulars apply *Examiner* Office.

Figure 3. Foot Ball advertisement. *The Warrnambool Examiner and Western Districts Advertiser*, Tuesday, May 28, 1861, 2.

A week later the paper reported that about 20 players turned up and two goals had been scored before the ball burst and the match was terminated. The paper went on, 'There is every prospect of the good old English game of football becoming quite a popular institution in this District during the winter time'.[49] A club was formed at the conclusion of the game and three more matches and a ready supply of balls was assured. The second president of the Warrnambool club was W.H. McKiernin, whose name suggests Scottish or Irish extraction. Eventually the club adopted Victorian Rules and an oval ball replaced the round one during the latter half of the 1860s.[50] By then the club was attuned to Victorian Rules.

A similar pattern of undifferentiated football followed by the adoption of one or other of the emerging codes can be found in the other colonies and it is not till the 1880s that unambiguous soccer matches can be clearly identified. They are usually referred to as being played under British Association rules.[51] For the most part it is clear that these are participant games, with few spectators involved. Scots are quickly prominent as players and administrators.[52] Club names indicate the backgrounds involved as Caledonians, Fifers and Scottish or Scots appear sometimes tied to a district to correspond with practice in the other codes of football.[53] Between 1884 and 1886, Minmi Rangers, Caledonians, Pyrmont Rangers, Granville and Hamilton Athletic were formed in New South Wales. All were Scottish clubs.[54] There is an upsurge of numbers of players and clubs with each successive wave of inward migration in the 1880s, 1910s, 1920s and 1950s–1970s. Clubs acted as meeting points and social contacts for groups of migrants and places where they could meet fellow countrymen of the previous generation and learn from their experience. In the interwar years, new Scottish clubs in Victoria included Melbourne Thistle and Fifers and Colac Thistle.[55] The Burns Club sparked the emergence of football after the First World War in Canberra. Local workers building the national capital took part. The soccer club died with the sport in the mid-1930s, although in the 1920s there were teams called Thistles, Rangers and Rovers and, in the country, the Wagga Caledonians.[56] Spectator attendance did not keep pace with the growth in clubs. Few identifiably Scottish clubs became major drawcards. Partly as a consequence the funds to pay players were hard to find and the growing numbers of Scottish players who arrived tended to gravitate to clubs with a bigger supporter base and consequently greater resources.[57]

It is often said in jest that every one knows that a good team needs 4–5 Scottish players; the problem for the national team is that it has to play 11.[58] In Australia the

Scots became the nucleus of successful Greek, Italian, Jewish and Croatian teams, lending their grit, determination to win and toughness to teams in which the application of skill alone was not achieving the results sought by supporters or patrons of the non-Anglo migrant clubs. Juventus in its heyday had Jimmy Millar, John Malloy, Eric Norman, David Closs, Alex Crombie, Sandy Irvine and Jimmy Bell. George Kinnell and Tommy McColl also starred in the black and white.[59] When Croatia won the Victorian State League and the Dockerty Cup in 1968 its complement of Croatian stars was built around the drive of several Scots including former Glasgow Celtic player Duncan MacKay, soon to be Socceroo Jim Mackay, Hammy McMeechan, Hugh Gunn, Bill McIntyre and Bill McArthur (see Figure 4). Most of these players had been recruited by the club as a result of an open cheque-book journey to Scotland by the club secretary Frank Burin in 1965.[60]

As late as 1985 the national team, the Socceroos, under Frank Arok, had two Scots-born players, Kenny Murphy and Joe Watson, in key midfield roles. Both played against Scotland in the World Cup qualifying matches that year.

In the post-Second World War years the recognizably Scottish clubs in Victoria included Moreland, Park Rangers (who amalgamated with Moreland), Footscray Thistle, which was succeeded by the Italian influenced Footscray Capri, which in turn was taken over by the Serbian Footscray JUST and the short-lived Fifers and Geelong Celtic. The last of these consisted of members of the State College of Victoria who had arrived from overseas as trainee teachers in 1950 and the next season they were scattered across Victoria. Their successors were Australian and not interested in the

Figure 4.   Croatia squad at Olympic Park in 1968. Back row, left to right: Frank Burin (Secretary), Horst Rau (captain), Mirko Kovacek, Billy McArthur, Frank Bot, Hugh Gunn, Mijo Kiss (coach), Jimmy Mackay, Duncan MacKay, Peter Davies, Zlatko Balic (Reserve goalkeeper), Ivan Mustapic (Property Steward). Front row: Billy Vojtek, Brian Adlam, Alfred Glaser, Hammy McMeechan, Billy McIntyre. Photo: Courtesy of Frank Burin.

game and the team folded.[61] Also in Geelong, Geelong Scottish was founded in 1955. It became Hamlyn Rangers and is now Geelong Rangers, though the Scottish influence is attenuated today.

What was true of Scots was generally true of British migrants as a whole. They did not take to the game in large numbers in Australia. While they might turn out to watch and support a visiting team from the UK, they would not attend local matches regularly.[62] One Melbourne club noted plaintively, 'Box Hill area has, I believe, a bigger percentage of British migrants than any other area of Melbourne, but do we of Box Hill Soccer Club get support; we most certainly do not.' Bill Murray, writing as an historian and a participant from the late 1950s in South Australia, noted: 'Attempts to form teams based on British migrants all failed, and this despite the fact that there were more British migrants after 1945 than all others combined.'[63]

Arguably, British migrants with no language barriers to overcome, more aware of Australian culture and norms and with a clear appreciation of the difference in standard between the game in Australia and that in the United Kingdom, made a rational choice not be involved in the code in this country. Especially when it was portrayed in the media as an immigrants game besmirched by violence and politics, even if that was a wild and often self-serving exaggeration. The Scots in Australia never considered themselves to be 'ethnics' but some of them used soccer clubs as part of their adjustment to Australian society from the 1880s through to the post-Second World War period in a variety of ways. They did not bring their domestic politics or religious divisions to their sporting activities as far as can be ascertained. Supporters clubs of the two Glasgow teams, Rangers and Celtic, exist throughout the major centres in Australia, and while it would be unwise to broadcast allegiance to one in the club of the other, there has been next to none of the visceral sectarian hatred which besmirched the West of Scotland scene over the last century.[64]

For the next generation the question of identity was neatly captured by Angus Drennen, one of the Australia's earliest post-war internationals who died on Easter Sunday 2008 at the age of 84. 'I had to go back to Scotland to discover that I was an Australian, not a Scot living in Australia.' Angus Drennen won three full caps for Australia on the tour of New Zealand in 1948 and 20 caps in all and represented Victoria many times in a career which lasted more than 30 years. Born in Sunshine in 1924, Angus Drennen was the son of a Scottish immigrant who worked as a piecework grinder at the Sunshine Harvester Company.[65]

Croatians

Croatians have been migrating to Australia since the early nineteenth century. For most of the period down to the 1920s they had little discernable contact with football.[66] In that decade socialist refugees from Yugoslavia arrived including the Alagich family, who were to have a major influence on the game in South Australia and New South Wales. In Western Australia, a study of timber workers does not have any sport or soccer references.[67] After the Second World War, a flood of migrants from the Dalmatian coastal strip arrived. Many of them were Catholic, anti-socialist and Croatian nationalist and they were to have an even greater influence than their predecessors. Large numbers of young players of Croatian heritage reached national league and representative levels. Some of them chose to represent Croatia rather than Australia. During the homeland war of the late 1980s much of the emphasis of activities associated with football was related to the conflict in Yugoslavia with some members of clubs returning to fight or to assist their counterparts. Since then middle-class migrants in the west have eschewed all contact with football.[68] The wheel has come full circle.

The first explicitly Croatian club in Victoria was formed in Melbourne in 1953.[69] Since its inception the club has been an important means by which young Croatian migrants have come to terms with Australian society. At a time when there were very few institutions catering for migrants to Australia and when the Catholic Church was much more attuned to the needs of Irish migrants, the Croatian soccer club became a vital resource for young people, many of whom had few, if any, family connections in this strange land. Later the club also acted as a neutral territory when political divisions occurred within the community. The drive for Croatian independence from Yugoslavia impinged on the club drawing on its resources. Now with independence achieved and a sharp fall in inward migration to Australia, the Croatian community is dominated numerically by people born in Australia, who are quite at home there, even though they have very strong feelings for the country from which their parents came. They are Australian-Croatians and do not need the club in same way that the older generation did. Hence while they turned out in thousands for the final game in the National Soccer League in 2004, they do not see their existence bound up in the club and as a consequence its survival in its present form is quite problematic.[70]

For much of the story of Croatia we have to rely to a great extent on oral sources and memory. Trying to tell the story of the club and its members and supporters on that basis is very worrying to the historian, for memory is fragile, variable and unreliable. Also it is capable of manipulation for the best of reasons, as well as for the worst. Yet people live by what they believe and what they remember, not by what 'actually' happened. This is true of all societies, probably at all times; it is not something which is unique to Victoria and its immigrant community, or the Croatian section thereof. But it has been suggested that there are reasons why there is less written evidence about the early days of Croatia, in particular, than about other similar clubs in Victoria and Australia. A former club secretary, Joe Vucica, has made a thorough search of the records of the club and can find nothing relating to the earlier years of its existence.[71]

Croatians who came to Australia in the 1950s and 1960s were, for the most part, formally citizens of the state of Yugoslavia. Some were political refugees and their opposition to the government in power was well known. Others were not in any overt sense political, but even to identify themselves as Croatian rather than Yugoslav was to make a political statement and one which carried potentially serious consequences. Croatians were more reluctant than most to have written evidence connecting them to anything which would bring them to the notice of the Yugoslav authorities. So basic documents like club membership lists or subscription lists tended not to be kept and, as was common enough in the Balkans and elsewhere, the majority of transactions were by word of mouth, face to face and, where finance was involved, in cash.

So much of the written evidence then is *about* Croatians rather than *by* Croatians in the early days, though by the 1960s several Croatian language newspapers were circulating and carrying reports on the soccer clubs and their activities. To make judgments about what the soccer club meant to Croatians on this evidence then is not an entirely satisfactory procedure and what is presented here must be regarded as tentative and in need of further research.

There is a fundamental dispute about the role of politics in the Croatian soccer clubs in Melbourne and Geelong. Croatian political groups seem to claim credit for the foundation, development and success of the soccer club, primarily as a contributor to the movement for Croatian identity and independence. This interpetation is supported by scholars like Phil Mosely, who stress links with the Ustashe and the Pavelic and his successors in Croatian fascism particularly in the 1970s.[72] Groups with overtly political purposes did play a part in the organization of soccer, and clubs and club officials seemed to defer to them on occasion. Political differences are also seen as underlying the violence associated with soccer from the 1950s to the 1970s. The chain of causation runs from the political groups to the behaviour and role of the soccer club.

> Actually I went to protect the referee when the trouble started last week. People get the wrong idea about these so-called national teams. We're not a bunch of revolutionaries of one kind or another running around looking for trouble. We're just soccer players who like the game and make a dollar out of it. Less than half the boys in our training squad would be Croats and as far as we are concerned it's got nothing to do with politics at all.[73]

Many of the people within the club argue strenuously that soccer was kept clear of politics and that the soccer club was neutral ground where all sections of the Croatian community could meet. They talk of successful avoidance of a political take-over of the club, whether it be in Geelong or in Melbourne. Yet these same people are often the most fervent supporters of the idea of Croatian identity and independence. Joe Vucica talks of his sense of personal responsibility that he has not done more to promote Croatia and its struggle for independence in Australia. He has also connected the move of the Croatia soccer club from Geelong to Melbourne with the setting up of the Croatian Liberation Movement's headquarters in Footscray which took place before the start of the 1962 season.[74] Joe Vucica argued the setting up of the Movement's headquarters necessitated the translation of the soccer club from Geelong.[75] Frank Burin, on the other hand, argues that by this time the largest concentration of Croatians was in Melbourne and hence it made sense to move the headquarters of the club back to the capital. As a member of the Victorian Soccer Federation by then he was aware that the Federation did not want regional clubs in the top league at that stage. This would appear to be confirmed by the actions of the VSF at the end of 1963 when it sent all the Geelong clubs back to play in the Ballarat and Geelong Districts Soccer Association.

The politicians claim credit for the foundation of the club, but the sources for this are the memories of people who were not necessarily around at the time and the book by Mato Tkalcevic which relies heavily on oral testimony.[76] If they did found the club, then the politicians did little to help it in the early days, when it struggled even to put 11 players on to the pitch on a regular basis. Moreover numbers of non-Croatians and even a few Serbians played with the club until the late 1960s. The same was true of JUST (Jugoslav United Soccer Team) which had a number of Croatian players in its ranks in 1960–61.[77] The claims of the politicians have been uncritically accepted by some subsequent writers. There is no doubt that later in its development the Croatian club did become a major political asset. At a time when the mainstream media was virtually closed to Croatian nationalist propaganda, a soccer club, at the highest level, kept the Croatian name before the public. Prior to reaching the State League in Victoria or later the national league, there was little value in a Croatian soccer club in terms of media coverage. Apart from the Croatian papers, games involving Croatia were not reported until the team was playing at State League level. At best a score might be recorded, or a violent incident, but there was no regular coverage or reports, and very few news stories.

In an attempt to reconcile these differing views it is arguable that in the early days there was relatively little political involvement in the soccer club and that it was only after it rose to prominence in the State League that its value as a political asset was appreciated and attempts were made to exploit it, sometimes successfully, sometimes, more often, not. Since there is such heavy reliance on oral memory, it is tempting to read the early activities of the club back through the lens of later political involvement and hence attribute a greater role to the political groups in the 1950s than was the case. This interpretation remains to be tested. Investigators from outside have tended to accept the claims of the politicians at face value.

The argument against this would point to the formation of Hajduk Melbourne in 1955, when there was a significant loss of players from Croatia Melbourne. Hajduk Split was associated with the partisans and played with a red star on their shirts. Hajduk Split had toured Australia in 1949. The suggestion is that the political division was there from the start, with Croatia associated with the anti-communist and anti-Tito forces, while Hajduk was if not pro-communist, at least not intensely anti.

Croatian migrants who arrived in Australia in the immediate post-war period faced major challenges in coming to terms with the new society in which they found themselves. Many were refugees from Yugoslavia, others came later under officially sponsored migration schemes. All faced the problem of establishing a form of identity in Australia. Croatian soccer clubs were among the first and the most wide-ranging institutions set up by migrants, and they played a significant role in the creation and shaping of self-conceptions and the attitudes of non-Croatian Australians from 1950 to 2000.[78]

The research which underpins this interpretation derives in part from many interviews with Croatians and non-Croatians involved in soccer in Australia and a life-time's involvement in the game in Britain and Australia. It is based on what several of that generation of migrants have revealed by their words and their actions and the interpretations which have been placed on them, by outsiders and by the migrants themselves. Many had not wanted to come to Australia in the first instance, but found it was either that or a return to a potentially hostile environment in Yugoslavia. Australia was accessible and it was cheap. Hence the Croatians were, on the whole, perhaps not quite as antipathetic about the prospect of Australia as some other migrants.[79]

The involvement of politics in sport is now established as fairly commonplace. Reiss writes about Irish nationalist associations involved with sport in the USA from the 1870s. Gaelic football was first played in New York in 1858. The German Turners used sport to promote ethnic identity and for political purposes. While Turners were generally very conservative and nationalist, nevertheless some socialist Turners were active in left wing politics.[80]

The use of soccer clubs for political purposes is quite commonplace in Europe, in the Basque country and Catalonia in Spain, to take only two well known examples.[81] Atletico Bilbao and Barcelona were and are the flagships of Basque and Catalan nationalism. The same was true in many parts of the Soviet Union, where Dinamo Kiev performed a similar role for Ukrainians. But in these cases the football club had to carry the nationalist flag only, it did not have to perform the socializing and integrating roles of the Australian Croatian clubs. It did not have to teach the language, as some migrant soccer clubs did in Australia.

The founders of Croatia Melbourne seem to have been a group of youngsters who wanted to play football. When they entered a team in the Victorian 'World Cup', a competition for ethnic teams, including those from the four home countries started in the early 1950s, they came up against political opposition. The appearance of a team labelled Croatia was opposed by JUST (Jugoslav United Soccer Team) and its Yugoslav backers. On the other hand, according to Ivica Marin, the entry of Croatia was supported by Hakoah, the Jewish club, and Kurt Defris, its secretary. Croatia Melbourne had many difficulties in its early days. Sometimes it had to use people off the street to make up teams, including non-Croatians and, according to two reliable sources, even Serbians on occasion. Only after the club began to move up through the leagues did political support kick-in. There is also a strong denial of political involvement from within the club. Joe Radojevic said of the Geelong Croatian club, 'I started it so my son could play' – family, not politics, was at the centre of things. In this he was to be disappointed as his elder son became one of the finest full forwards in Australian Rules with the VFA club Geelong West.[82] In the case of the other Croatian club in Melbourne there is a more political story to tell. Hajduk was formed after a tour of Hajduk Split in 1949 as a name likely to be known and understood by the Australian people. But Tito's claim that Hajduk players had enlisted en masse in the partisans gave rise to problems. The club did not last long. The Australian pronunciation of the name made it sound like a Walt Disney character. Little support was given. The club struggled to field players and folded in 1958.

An example of another kind of politics emerged when one of the authors was invited to help choose its team of the (half) century by Melbourne Knights in 2003. It was a daunting task to draw up a list of the 11 best players to represent Croatia during its 50 years. His co-selectors included Frank Burin, long time club secretary, Duje Zemunik, player and then coach of the club over several years, and Peter Desira, a leading journalist. Had he still been alive, journalist Laurie Schwab, that 'western suburbs nationalist' and supporter of Croatia, would have been the dominant figure on the selection panel, for no-one knew more about the club and its players in his generation.

Former Socceroo and star player with the Knights from 1987 to 1993, Alan Davidson was a unanimous choice of the selection panel but was removed from the list by the club committee and replaced by Josip Simunic who played for the Knights in 1995–97.[83] Simunic then left to play in Europe and chose to represent Croatia rather than Australia at international level, despite being a recipient of an Australian Institute of Sport scholarship designed to produce players to represent Australia. The decision emphasized Croatian links and may have been designed to assist the club to sell its next hot prospects to Croatian clubs.

At least three Australian born players have been selected to play for Croatia at senior level in recent years – Josip Simunic, Ante Seric and Joey Didulica. In 2008 controversy revived when Sydney United set up a talent identification scheme which was claimed to be designed in part to find players who could be sent to Croatia for further development, thus exposing them to greater risk of being selected for the Croatian national team.[84]

Dutch

A contrast to the Croatians can be found in the Dutch community in Australia. Once again the major phase of migration occurred after the Second World War, though it was on a smaller scale than that of the Scots or the Croatians. The migrants came from the Netherlands and the Dutch East Indies. In some cases the migration can be linked directly to the entrance of Dutch or Anglo-Dutch companies into the Australian market. For example the Shell company arrived in Geelong between the wars but

Figure 5.   Brothers in arms: Mark Viduka, who could have played for Croatia, hugs Josip Simunic, who could have played for Australia, during the World Cup in Stuttgart, Germany in 2006.
Source: Photo: Vince Caligiuri, *Sydney Morning Herald*, July 11, 2008. © Fairfaxphotos.com

engaged in a large-scale expansion of its petro-chemical operations in the post-war years.[85] A team called Shell based in Geelong took part in the Victorian league in 1953.[86] Two other Geelong-based clubs, Olympia and the Dutch Society of Geelong, played in both local and state competitions. In Melbourne the Wilhelmina club was the flag-bearer of Dutch involvement under the dynamic leadership of John van Hoboken.[87] It attracted a number of high quality Dutch players including Sjel (Mike) de Bruyckere, who went on to captain and coach Victoria. The Dutch players, along with Maltese and Austrians, were claimed by their Australian clubs as migrants, but the clubs with which they had played in Europe demanded compensation fees. This episode led to the suspension of Australia's membership of FIFA from 1958 to 1963.[88]

Wilhelmina prospered in the late 1950s and early 1960s, winning the Dockerty Cup in 1958, the Victorian State League in 1959 and the Ampol Cup in 1962. It built a new stadium in Ringwood in the far eastern suburb of Melbourne, but in 1973 it dropped out of the State League never to return. Olympia and the DSG had folded much earlier and only in Brisbane where the Hollandia club survived to become the nucleus of Brisbane Lions in the National Soccer League was a Dutch presence visible at senior level thereafter. Even that was attenuated.

The decline of the Dutch clubs can be largely explained by the fall off in Dutch migration to Australia, but also by the speed with which the Dutch integrated themselves into Australian society. Though they maintained their social clubs and many of their traditions, the Dutch adopted Australian mores more quickly than virtually any other group of migrants. They had no serious overseas political or religious issues to keep wounds open. The Dutch virtually disappeared into Australian life within a generation and their football clubs followed suit.

The story continues

More recently, South-East Asian migrants have come to Australia in increasing numbers from Vietnam, Malaysia, Singapore and China. Many of them bring a soccer awareness and have repeated the pattern of team and club formation. For some of these recent migrants physical differences have made participation in the still very robust local Australian leagues problematic. Partly as a result they have set up informal arrangements outside the governing bodies of the game in Victoria and Australia. This has given rise to disputes and bans on participation. On the other hand, Asian clubs have been welcomed into the Victorian Amateur League and have gone on through that to become members of the Victorian Soccer Federation and its successor the Football Federation of Victoria.

In the first decade of the twenty-first century, African and Afghani migrants have arrived in small numbers.[89] A television report in 2001 had a segment on a group of Afghan youths who had been smuggled to Australia by their parents.[90] A woman who was teaching them English took them down to a park one afternoon for relaxation and to overcome their loneliness. A ball was produced and they quickly started playing soccer. Seeing their commitment to the game, she looked around for a saviour and found it in a local fellow, who had never met any immigrants, saw them only in his newspapers and on television, but who took to the youngsters and the scales began to fall from his eyes. In the video clip, the kids were playing against a Brisbane Under-19 team whom they managed to beat one-nil. Once again, soccer helped some immigrants to come to terms with Australian society.

Notes

1. A good place to start is Mosely *et al. Sporting Immigrants*. The present essay draws most of its evidence from Victoria, though there are references to migrant minority experience in other states. The issues are discussed at greater length in Murray and Hay, *Social History of Australian Football*. Bill Murray made a substantial contribution to this essay.
2. Unikoski, *Communal Endeavours* is a pioneering treatment of migrant communities in Victoria which gives due weight to the role of football clubs in the migrant experience and draws heavily on interviews with migrants in its research.
3. In 2008, the Sydenham Park football (soccer) club, backed by the Macedonian community, was drawn into branch stacking allegations involving local politicians, but it seems clear that this was a case of migrant communities being used by others. David Rood, 'MP "Used Ethnic Groups to Stack Branches"'. *Age*, July 19, 2008, 9.
4. Australian Bureau of Statistics, 'Participation in Sport and Physical Activities'; Australian Bureau of Statistics, *Participation in Sport and Physical Activities*. Unfortu-

nately comparative statistics are not available for the critical periods of the 1950s to the 1970s when attendance at soccer matches was probably at its highest in Australian history until the setting up of the A-League in 2005. State league matches in Victoria regularly attracted attendances of between 5,000 and 10,000 people. Hay, 'Marmaras's Oyster', 14–16, has crowd data from 1961–62.

5. Hay, 'Soccer and Social Control'.
6. Hay and Joel, 'Football's World Cup'.
7. Between 1960 and 1963 a dozen Greek clubs were established in Melbourne. Georgakis, *Sport*, 196.
8. Some of this debate has been carried on in websites and blogs, in club meetings and on the terraces of both clubs. There is further discussion of the underlying issues in Hay and Pocklington, with Warren, *First Report*, especially Appendix G, Observational Report on South Melbourne versus Melbourne Victory, 20 June 2007. We are indebted to Ian Syson of Victoria University for information and assistance.
9. Hughson, 'Football, Folk Dancing', and Hughson, 'A Tale of Two Tribes'; Hallinan, Hughson and Burke, 'Supporting the World Game'.
10. Lustica, *From Hope to Glory*, and information from Nick Guoth, who also detects a division in Canberra between Croatians from the Dalmatian coast around Split and those from the inland around the capital Zagreb.
11. The following section draws on material published in Hay, 'Oral History' by kind permission of the editors.
12. There were only 60–70 Macedonian families in Geelong when the second Macedonian club, West Geelong, was set up in 1965 and no other community organizations existed, according to Rade Trajanovski. Notes on a conversation at Geelong Soccer Club (January 6, 1994). An earlier Macedonian club was founded in 1956.
13. We owe this reference to Tonic Prusac of the *Croatian Herald*.
14. At least according to Joe Radojevic and Billy Dorris – Hay, 'Soccer in Geelong Since the War'.
15. Hay, 'Problems of Biography and Identity'.
16. Mason, 'Football'. See also Collins, 'Myth and Reality', and Collins, 'Northerness and the Northern Union'.
17. Martin, *Juve! Juve!*. Martin's work, published in English and Italian under one cover, relies heavily on interviews with people involved in the club.
18. Ibid., 8.
19. Ibid., 7–29, 54–5; Hay, notes of interview with Nino Borsari, junior, Melbourne, January 6, 2002.
20. Even in 1958 there had been problems when it appeared that there might be three Italian teams in the new State League, Juventus, Footscray Capri and Geelong, then playing as IAMA (Italian-Australian Migrants Association). Hay, 'Marmaras's Oyster'.
21. Georgakis, *Sport*, 122–3, mentions the foundation of a short-lived club Apollon in 1934 which attempted to unite all Greek youth in Melbourne. It folded after less than a year. The same was true of interwar Greek clubs in Adelaide, ibid., 126. Post-war South Melbourne Hellas and Pan Hellenic in Sydney sought to become unifying clubs but neither really succeeded in sustaining the vision.
22. Information from research in progress by Ian Syson, John Kallinikios and Roy Hay.
23. Hay, 'Croatia', 58–61.
24. Martin, *Juve! Juve!*, 7–8.
25. Archbishop Matthew Beovich and Branko Filipi were involved in the sponsorship of young refugee Croatians in South Australia in 1954. Drapac, 'Croatian Australians Today', 249; Hay, 'Croatia', 55.
26. Bill Murray to Roy Hay, email, July 24, 2008.
27. Hay, '"Making Aussies"', citing *Sun-Herald*, March 30, 1958, 76.
28. Mosely, 'European Immigrants', 14–26.
29. Hay, 'British Football', 46–57; Hay, 'A New Look', 41–62 and references cited there.
30. Margo, *Frank Lowy*, 104–17.
31. Nick Guoth's recollection.
32. Murphy, *The Other Australia*, 186–91. Les Murray presented a collective biography of the Alagich family on SBS television on March 16, 2008.
33. Alagich, *100 Years*.

34. Dianne Alagich played 86 times for Australia and her last game was on July 12, 2009. Adam Mark, FFA media release, July 12, 2008.
35. Alagich, *Soccer*.
36. 'Nazi atrocities shown to motivate Manly', *Soccer Action*, July 19, 1978, 3.
37. Hay, 'A Short History of Croatian Soccer in Victoria, 1954–1994'. www.sesasport.com.au. Look under Archives, 8 Talks and other material, 'Short history of Croatian soccer'.
38. Roy Hay, 'Soccer's Legal Guru'. *Geelong Advertiser*, April 17, 2008, 39.
39. Roy Hay, 'National Coach Faces Tough Decisions'. *Geelong Advertiser*, January 22, 2004, 54.
40. Stewart. *Report to the Australian Soccer Federation*.
41. Roy Hay, 'Dorris Given Soccer Honour'. *Geelong Advertiser*, February 5, 2007, 31.
42. A more extensive discussion of these issues will be found in Murray and Hay, *A Social History*.
43. Richards, *A History of the Highland Clearances*.
44. Cage, *The Scots Abroad*; Prentis, *The Scots in Australia*.
45. Hay and Haig-Muir, '"Huntin, Shootin and Fishin"', 85–99.
46. Chisholm, *Scots Wha Hae*, 8–10; Hay, 'The Caledonian Challenge Cup', 28–37.
47. Blainey, *A Game of Our Own*, 55.
48. The *Port Phillip Herald* has advertisements for, or reports on, undifferentiated football games on March 30, 1850; August 14, 1851; December 25, 1851; December 30, 1854; December 17, 1855; and February 26, 1856. We owe these references to Dr Tony Ward.
49. *The Warrnambool Examiner and Western Districts Advertiser*, June 4, 1861, 2.
50. Cole *et al.*, *The Birth of the Blues*, 3–6.
51. *Age*, February 17, 1883; *Argus*, August 17 and 20, 1883.
52. 'The Scotchmen are evidently determined that their game shall not die a natural death for want of a bit of pushing, and their energy and enthusiasm appear to have kindled a flame of Anglo-Association fire, which has enveloped, and is enveloping, the town and suburbs, as a considerable number of clubs have enrolled themselves under the British Association banner'. Peter Pinder, 'Football Gossip', *Australasian*, April 19, 1884.
53. Murray and Hay, *The World Game Downunder*, 85.
54. Mosely, 'The Game', 138.
55. *Soccer News*, July 5, 1924; Hay, 'Soccer in Geelong Between the Wars', 47–60.
56. Howie-Willis, *Canberra and the Scots*, 163, and information from Nick Guoth, 22 July 2008 from his forthcoming book *Migration and Sport*. The Burns Club returned to playing football after the Second World War and still does so in 2008.
57. Payment of players was more common in New South Wales in the interwar years. For example, Jock Simpson, the father of Bobby Simpson, the Australian cricket captain, came to Granville around 1926 on a contract paying £50 ($100) per season. Doug Aiton, 'Settling the score'. *Sunday Age*, December 8, 1996, Conversations, Agenda: 5.
58. Philip Mosely uses a photograph from the *Sydney Mail* of 28 May 1913 showing a team in which six of the 13 men had Scottish antecedents: Mosely *et al.*, *Sporting Immigrants*, 157.
59. Martin, *Juve! Juve!*, 44–5.
60. Hay, 'Croatia'.
61. Hay, 'Soccer in Geelong Since the War', 87.
62. 'His First and Last Game!' *Soccer News*, September 17, 1960, 1; 'Box Hill Query This One Too!' *Soccer News*, October 1, 1960, 7.
63. Murray and Hay, *The World Game Downunder*, 91.
64. This observation is partly based on personal experience and the views of some Australian supporters of both teams. It may have been different earlier in the last century.
65. Roy Hay, 'Passing of Another Local Legend'. *Goal Weekly*, April 7, 2008, 11.
66. Sutalo, *Croatians in Australia*.
67. Gillgren, 'Boundaries of Exclusion', 71–82.
68. Colic-Peisker, 'Two Waves of Croatians', 353–70; Colic-Peisker, 'Croatian and Bosnian Migration', 117–36.
69. Roy Hay, 'Early Days of Croatia in Victoria'. *Goal Weekly*, March 10, 2008, 11.
70. Roy Hay, 'End of the Road for the Knights'. *Australian and British Soccer Weekly*, March 9, 2004, 14.
71. Joe Vucica was a major source for the research on *The Croatia Story*, Roy Hay's as yet unpublished history of the club.

72. Mosely, 'A Social History'; Mosely and Murray, 'Soccer', 213–30; Mosely, *Ethnic Involvement*; Mosely, 'European Immigrants', 14–26.
73. Jimmy McKay interviewed by Lou Richards, 'Stars on the Loose'. *Sun*, August 8, 1972, 50; *Soccer Action*, September 26, 1984, 10.
74. 'Croatia Means Big Business'. *Soccer Weekly*, April 19, 1962, 2.
75. In conversation at the Croatian Sports Centre, October 3, 1993. Committee members of Croatia in 1962 included Branko Troskot, T. Jakobovic, I. Matkovic, V. Simek, S. Silver, J. Jakovijevic, N. Matijevic, P. Mazdar and N. Drk.
76. Tkalcevic, *Croats in Australia*.
77. 'J.U.S.T. is not Serbs' club, but a soccer club with equal rights for all sport-minded people. Out of 11 players who played against George Cross only Radibratovic is Serb, 4 are Croats, 1 Slovenian; 1 German, 1 Scotsman and 2 Hungarians born in Yugoslavia. President, vice-president, founder and patron of J.U.S.T., Mr. Ivan Kuketz are Croats and most followers are Slovenian and Croats.' Zika Nikolic, 'Why Not Stick to Soccer Sir?'. *Soccer News*, July 15, 1961, 3.
78. Hay, 'British Football'; Hay, '"Making Aussies"'.
79. Youngsters in Europe saw Australia as a land of snakes, venomous spiders and kangaroos, America as the land of fast cars and consumer goods; Martin Groher, interview August 13, 1992, tape recording in the possession of Roy Hay. Among less voluntary migrants, one internee jumped over the side of the *Dunera* when it was announced after ten days at sea that the destination was to be Australia not Canada. When they arrived in Hay, one camp specialized in handball, the other in soccer. Loewald, 'A *Dunera* Internee', 513, 518.
80. Reiss, *Sport in Industrial America*, 88–9, 94–7.
81. Maestro, 'Football and Identity'.
82. VFA is the Victorian Football Association which at the time ran the second level Australian Rules football competition in Victoria.
83. Davidson also played with South Melbourne Hellas, the main rival of the Croatian club and was named in the equivalent team when Hellas celebrated its anniversary. That may also have weighed against him in the minds of the Knights' committee. Information from Frank Burin.
84. Sebastian Hassett, 'Sydney club helps to poach talent for Croatia', *Sydney Morning Herald*, 11 July 2008, available at http://www.smh.com.au/news/football/sydney-club-helps-to-poach-talent-for-croatia/2008/07/10/1215658037280.html?page=1-2
85. Hay and McLean, *Business and Industry*.
86. Hay, 'Soccer in Geelong Since the War', 90.
87. Interviews with John van Hoboken (June 10, 1993) and Fred Hutchinson (June 23, 1992), an English referee who became secretary of the Wilhelmina club for several years. Tape recordings in the possession of the Roy Hay.
88. Hay, 'Marmaras's Oyster'.
89. Roy Hay, 'Soccer Eased Migrants into Aussie Life'. *Geelong Advertiser*, March 6, 2004, 31.
90. 7.30 Report, ABC television, October 2, 2001. See also Millar, 'The Universal Language', which tells the story of two Sudanese refugees and their arrival at Geelong Rangers soccer club.

References

Alagich, Colin. *100 Years of the World Game in Port Adelaide*. Adelaide: Port Adelaide Lion Soccer Club, 2007.
Alagich, Richard. *Soccer: Winning through Technique and Tactics*. Sydney: McGraw- Hill, 1995.
Australian Bureau of Statistics. 'Participation in Sport and Physical Activities'. *Year Book Australia*, 1998 (ABS Catalogue No. 1301.0). http://www.abs.gov.au/websitedbs/D3110124.NSF/14e59eeb4d4c9c94ca25670400073e4f.
Australian Bureau of Statistics. *Participation in Sport and Physical Activities*. Australia, 1999–2000, Cat No 4177.0.
Blainey, Geoffrey. *A Game of Our Own: The Origins of Australian Football*. Melbourne: Black Inc., 2003.
Cage, R.A., ed. *The Scots Abroad: Labour, Capital, Enterprise, 1750–1914*. London: Croom Helm, 1985.

Chisholm, Alec H. *Scots Wha Hae: History of the Royal Caledonian Society of Melbourne.* Sydney: Angus and Robertson, 1950.

Cole, Ron, Harry Keilar, Ron McCorkell, and Ian Wright. *The Birth of the Blues: Warrnambool Football Netball Club, 1861–2007.* Warrnambool: Warrnambool Football Netball Club, 2008.

Colic-Peisker, Val. 'Two Waves of Croatians in Western Australia: Class and National Identity'. *Australian Journal of Social Issues* 34, no. 4 (November 1999): 353–70.

Colic-Peisker, Val. 'Croatian and Bosnian Migration to Australia in the 1990s'. *Studies in West Australian History* 21 (2000): 117–36.

Collins, Tony. 'Myth and Reality in the 1895 Rugby Split'. *Sports Historian* 16 (May 1996): 33–41.

Collins, Tony. 'Northerness and the Northern Union: Regional Identity and Ideology in Rugby League'. Paper presented at the annual conference of the British Society of Sports History, Keele, 12–13 April, 1997.

Drapac, Vesna. 'Croatian Australians Today'. In *The Australian People,* ed. James Jupp, 246–9. 2nd ed. Melbourne: Cambridge University Press, 2001.

Georgakis, Steve. *Sport and the Australian Greek: An Historical Study of Ethnicity, Gender and Youth.* Rozelle, NSW: Standard Publishing Company, 2000.

Gillgren, Christina. 'Boundaries of Exclusion: A Study of Italian and Croatian Immigrants in the Western Australian Timber Industry, 1920–1940'. *Limina* 3 (1997): 71–82.

Guoth, Nick. *Migration and Sport: The History of Soccer in the Federal Capital Territory, 1910–1937* (forthcoming)

Hallinan, Christopher J., John E, Hughson, and Michael Burke. 'Supporting the World Game in Australia: A Case Study of Fandom at National and Club Level'. *Soccer and Society* 8, nos. 2–3 (April–July 2007): 283–97.

Hay, Roy. 'Soccer and Social Control in Scotland, 1873–1973'. In *Sport: Money, Morality and the Media,* ed. R. Cashman and M. McKernan, 223–47. Kensington: New South Wales University Press, 1981.

Hay, Roy. '"Making Aussies" or "What Soccer is all about": Soccer and European Migrants to Australia, 1945–93'. Paper presented at Bradman, Balmain, Barellan and Bocce, Australian Culture and Sport Conference. Australian Sports Commission/Australian Defence Forces Academy conference at the Australian Institute of Sport, Canberra, October 8–9, 1993.

Hay, Roy. 'British Football, Wogball or the World Game? Towards a Social History of Victorian Soccer'. In *Ethnicity and Soccer in Australia,* ed. John O'Hara, 44–79. *Studies in Sports History,* no. 10. Campbelltown: Australian Society for Sports History, 1994.

Hay, Roy. 'Marmaras's Oyster or Seamonds' Baby? The Formation of the Victorian Soccer Federation, 1956–1964'. *Sporting Traditions* 10, no. 2 (1994): 3–24.

Hay, Roy. 'Soccer in Geelong Between the Wars'. *Investigator* 29, no. 2 (June 1994): 47–60.

Hay, Roy. 'Soccer in Geelong Since the War'. *Investigator* 29, no. 3 (August 1994): 87–108.

Hay, Roy. 'Problems of Biography and Identity: Australian Soccer Players 1945–95'. Paper presented at the Football and Identities Conference, University of Queensland, March 1997.

Hay, Roy. 'Croatia: Community, Conflict and Culture: The Role of Soccer Clubs in Migrant Identity'. In *Sporting Nationalisms: Identity, Ethnicity, Immigration and Assimilation,* ed. David Mayall, and Michael Cronin, 49–66. London: Frank Cass, 1998.

Hay, Roy. 'A New Look at Soccer Violence'. In *All Part of the Game: Violence and Australian Sport,* ed. Denis Hemphill, 41–62. Sydney: Walla Walla Press, 1998.

Hay, Roy. 'Oral History, Migration and Soccer in Australia, 1880–2000'. In *Speaking to Immigrants: Oral Testimony and the History of Australian Migration,* ed. A. James Hammerton, and Eric Richards, 39–61. Visible Immigrants 6, History Program and Centre for Immigration and Multicultural Studies, Research School of Social Sciences. Canberra: Australian National University, 2002.

Hay, Roy. 'The Caledonian Challenge Cup'. *Investigator* 44, no. 1 (May 2009): 28–37.

Hay, Roy, and Marnie Haig-Muir. '"Huntin, Shootin and Fishin" and the Rest: Sports in Geelong in the Mid-nineteenth Century and Afterwards'. In *The View from Station Peak: Writings on Geelong – History and Literature,* ed. Tom Spurling, and Geoff Peel, 85–99. Geelong, 2007.

Hay, Roy, and Tony Joel. 'Football's World Cup and its Fans – Reflections on National Styles: A Photo Essay on Germany 2006'. *Soccer and Society* 8, no. 1 (January 2007): 1–32.

Hay, Roy, and G.A. McLean. *Business and Industry, Geelong: A History of the Geelong Chamber of Commerce, 1853–2005.* Teesdale, Victoria: Sports and Editorial Services Australia in association with the Geelong Chamber of Commerce, 2006.

Hay, Roy, and Michael Pocklington, with Ian Warren. *First Report on a Public Order Strategy for the City of Melbourne,* unpublished research report to the City of Melbourne, July 2007.

Howie-Willis, I. *Canberra and the Scots: The Canberra Highland Society and Burns Club: Its First 71 Years.* Canberra: The Society, 1996.

Hughson, John. 'A Tale of Two Tribes: Expressive Fandom in Australian Soccer's A-League', *Culture, Sport and Society,* 2, no. 3 (Autumn 1999): 10–30.

Hughson, John. 'Football, Folk Dancing and Fascism: Diversity and Difference in Multicultural Australia'. *Australia and New Zealand Journal of Sociology* 33 (1997): 167–86.

Loewald, K.G. 'A *Dunera* Internee at Hay, 1940–41'. *Historical Studies* 17 (1969): 510–18.

Lustica, Bernard. *From Hope to Glory: 40 Years of Croatia Deakin Soccer Club.* Canberra: Canberra Deakin Soccer Club, 1999.

Maestro, Jesus. 'Football and Identity in Spain'. Paper presented to the Football in Europe Conference, Leicester, June 1996.

Margo, Jill. *Frank Lowy: Pushing the Limits.* Sydney: Harper Collins, 2001.

Martin, Egilberto, *Juve! Juve!* Melbourne: Elabor Helena, 1990.

Mason, Tony. 'Football, Sport of the North'. In *Sport and Identity in the North of England,* ed. Jeff Hill, and John Williams, 41–52. Keele: Keele University Press, 1996.

Millar, Paul. 'The Universal Language of Soccer'. October 12, 2004. www.soccervictoria.org.au.

Mosely, Philip. 'A Social History of Soccer in New South Wales, 1880–1956'. PhD diss., University of Sydney, 1987.

Mosely, Philip. 'The Game: Early Soccer Scenery in New South Wales'. *Sporting Traditions* 8, no. 2 (May 1992): 135–51.

Mosely, Philip. 'European Immigrants and Soccer Violence in New South Wales, 1949–1959'. *Journal of Australian Studies* 40 (March 1994): 14–26.

Mosely, Philip. *Ethnic Involvement in Australian Soccer, 1950–1990.* Canberra: Australian Sports Commission, 1995.

Mosely, Philip, and Bill Murray. 'Soccer'. In *Sport in Australia: A Social History,* ed. Wray Vamplew, and Brian Stoddart, 213–30. Cambridge: Cambridge University Press, 1994.

Mosely, Philip, Richard Cashman, John O'Hara, and Hilary Weatherburn, eds. *Sporting Immigrants.* Sydney: Walla Walla Press, 1997.

Murphy, Brian. *The Other Australia: Experiences of Migration.* Melbourne: Cambridge University Press, 1993.

Murray, Bill, and Roy Hay, eds. *The World Game Downunder.* Melbourne: Australian Society for Sports History, 2006.

Murray, Bill, and Roy Hay. *The Social History of Australian football* (forthcoming).

Prentis, Malcolm D. *The Scots in Australia : a study of New South Wales, Victoria and Queensland, 1788-1900.* Sydney: Sydney University Press, 1983.

Reiss, Steven A. *Sport in Industrial America, 1850–1920.* Wheeling, IL: Harlan Davidson, 1995.

Richards, Eric. *A History of the Highland Clearances: Vol. II, Emigration, Protest, Reasons.* London: Croom Helm, 1985.

Stewart. D.G. *Report to the Australian Soccer Federation on the Transfer of Australian Soccer Players.* Sydney: Australian Soccer Federation, December 1994.

Sutalo, Ilija. *Croatians in Australia: Pioneers, Settlers and their Descendants.* Kent Town, South Australia: Wakefield Press, 2004.

Tkalcevic, Mato. *Croats in Australia: An Information and Resource Guide.* Burwood, Victoria: Victoria College Press, 1988.

Unikoski, Rachel. *Communal Endeavours: Migrant Organisations in Melbourne.* Canberra: Australian National University Press, 1978.

In search of an identity: the Muslims and football in colonial India

Kausik Bandyopadhyay

Department of History, West Bengal State University, Barasat, India

Introduction

That modern sports can be divisive despite their apparent integrative impact, that they can exacerbate conflict and jeopardize social structures, is beyond doubt. A new trend in Indian football of the 1930s was soccer's burgeoning communal encounter, which began to erode football's overwhelming status as an instrument of cultural nationalism. This trend can be meaningfully explained only in terms of the socio-political and economic life of Bengal in the 1930s. In the changed socio-political atmosphere of Bengal, the binary of Indian versus British in football came to acquire a new dimension: Hindus representing the *majority* versus Muslims representing the *minority*. The unhealthy clash between the Hindu *bhadrolok* dominated the Indian Football Association and the Mohammedan Sporting Club, representative of the Indian Muslim community, who began to suffer from a minority syndrome under the influence of representative political parties and personalities, often played a critical role in creating possibilities of communalization of sport in the 1930s and 1940s. This essay explores the key factors precipitating such communal conflict in Indian football. It shows how this communal tag overshadowed Mohammedan Sporting Club's five straight Calcutta Football League titles between 1934 and 1938, with the result that Mohun Bagan Club's victory against East Yorkshire Regiment in the IFA Shield final in 1911 is still perceived as a greater nationalistic triumph than Mohammedan's feat.

Representing minority community in football: early history of the Mohammedan Sporting Club

Muslim representation in Calcutta football began in the last decade of the nineteenth century when Mohammedan Sporting Club gained in prominence thanks to the efforts of some Muslim individuals. Mohammedan Sporting, established in 1891, was an institution of the progressive Muslims and was gradually carving out a niche in Calcutta's football scene. The initiative of some Muslim youths, both from Calcutta and its suburbs, who felt the need for the Muslim youth to have its own sporting club, founded the Crescent Club in 1889.[1] It is, however, said that the club had its predecessor in the Jubilee Club founded in 1887 in Calcutta thanks to the efforts of Khan Bahadur Aminul Islam, Maulavi Abdul Ghani of Malda and Maulavi Muhammad Yasin of Burdwan.[2] In 1890, the club's name was changed again into Hamidia Club. In 1891, finally, the club came to be transformed into the Mohammedan Sporting Club. Nawab Syed Amir Hossain, then Presidency Magistrate and Nawab Nasirul Momaleque Mirza Sujat Ali Beg were elected President and Vice-President of the club respectively, while Abdul Ghani and Nur Muhammad Ismail became Secretary and Assistant Secretary.[3] Nawab Sujat Ali Beg gave the club a donation of Rs.300 on behalf of Her Highness Samsuzzoha Begum of Murshidabad to start the 'Nawab Begum Football Cup' in her honour.[4]

The first annual meeting of the club was held in 1894 under the presidentship of Justice Sir Syed Amir Ali at the Calcutta Madrasa premises. Abdus Salam, a retired civil servant delivered a lecture on the physical culture of Mohammedan youths. This speech was later published in book form and was dedicated to Sir John Woodburn, the then Lt Governor of Bengal.[5] Shortly afterwards, a monthly journal called *Calcutta Monthly* was started under the auspices of the members of the club as a club magazine. Leading Muslim gentlemen of Calcutta were regular contributors to the magazine. The magazine, however, continued for only three years. The management of the club also started a reading room for Mohammedan students in Calcutta, which came to be known as the 'Diamond Jubilee Reading Room'.[6]

The Mohammedan Sporting Club had no grounds of their own when the club was founded. However, at the instance of its President Amir Hossain, the club obtained permission to play on the grounds of Calcutta Boys' School on each alternate day.[7] Subsequently, when the members of the club increased in number and other games were introduced into the club, three days in a week proved insufficient and the need for a regular ground was felt. Mr Lambert, the Police Commissioner, gave permission for them to use the grounds for the whole week while the Calcutta Boys' School was provided with another plot of land as their playground.[8] In its early days, Mohammedan's greatest triumph was the winning of the Coochbehar Cup in 1909.

The Annual Report of the Club in 1928 mentioned that when S.A. Rashid and I.G.H. Arif took over charge of the club in 1924, they found the affairs of the club in a poor state.[9] There was only Rs.9 to the credit of the club as a balance, while the outstanding bills of the different sports firms were not less than Rs.3,600. There were

208 members on the roll but the majority of them did not pay membership and the monthly collections under the head of membership were never more than Rs.25 or 30. The arrears of the servants' pay alone amounted to Rs.460. Not to speak of other games, even football did not remain of interest to most of the members. The club was not even represented on the major sports councils of Bengal including the IFA.[10]

In two years, however, working in excellent partnership, the Joint Secretaries succeeded in putting the state of things in good order. Most importantly, they put the club on a sound financial basis and effected a noticeable improvement in the club's interest and performance in all games. In 1927, the club came into prominence as it was promoted into the second division of the Calcutta football league. Moreover, it came to be represented through S.A. Rashid on all sports bodies.[11] As for the attempt to redress the financial bankruptcy of the club, an annexure to the Annual Report of 1928 mentions that the Joint Secretaries of the club made an appeal to all concerned 'to support a scheme of the club, *extending its activities in the social sphere for Muslims*'.[12] They also requested 'for donations amounting to Rs.3,500 to Rs.4,000'.[13] Although the response to this appeal was not enough to give effect to the scheme, the financial assistance that ultimately came through helped the club revive itself from its sinking financial position.[14]

It would be a mistake to argue that the club reflected communal overtones from its inception. But that it was anti-Congress even in the mid-1890s is a documented reality. The object of *Calcutta Monthly*, started in 1896 under the auspices of the club, was 'to discuss and ventilate literary, scientific, educational, social, moral, sporting and other cognate subjects of interest'.[15] Reacting to a criticism by a Muslim Congress leader of the hostile Muslim attitude towards the Congress,[16] the *Calcutta Monthly* in its editorial of December 1896 wrote:

> We wish we could induce Mr. Sayani to live for sometime in Bengal and see with his own eyes how Mohammedans fare at the hands of their Hindu friends in every matter ... and when he shall have done that, we have no doubt in our mind that he will pause thrice before committing himself to the espousal of a cause, the success of which will mean the gradual, but inevitable, extinction of his co-religionists as a political unit in India.[17]

Even with this generally anti-Congress tilt, the club showed, despite its apparent failure as a good football outfit, its sporting spirit in the truest appreciation of the game since its inception. In the aftermath of Mohun Bagan's Shield victory, the members of the Club, wrote *The Mussalman*, 'were almost mad and rolling on the ground with joyous excitement on the victory of their Hindu brethren'.[18] Another Muslim journal, *The Comrade*, of which Maulana Mohammed Ali was the founder editor at that time, said: 'We hereby join the chorus of praise and jubilation over the splendid victory of Mohun Bagan. The team did remarkably well throughout the tournament and won the Shield by sheer merit.'[19] Such reports were in tune with the general trend of the Muslim journals till the late 1920s, which speak more of amity than of conflict amongst the two communities. Recounting Mohun Bagan's status as a team beloved by both the communities, Achintya Kumar Sengupta wrote:

> Till then communalism had not entered the sports-field. Mohun Bagan then belonged to both the Hindus and the Muslims. The green galleries that burnt in the football stadium of the Calcutta that day carried the mark of both Hindu and Muslim hands. One brought the petrol and the other the matches.[20]

Revival and success of the Mohammedan Sporting Club

Until 1934, the year that marked the beginning of Mohammedan Sporting Club's glorious League victories – five in a row – Calcutta football remained more or less free from any communal overtones. It was, however, quite unfortunate that Bengali-cum-India's anti-British footballing identity came to be fractured from mid-1930s on communal lines.

It was only natural, however, for the Muslim community to find in Mohammedan Sporting a club that they could really call their own when it emerged as a powerful team in Calcutta football in the early 1930s. Although the achievements of Mohammedan Sporting Club were Indian success stories, the Hindu football-lovers felt only a mixture of respect and fear and no sensation of joy at all.[21] The Muslim League, by then a force hostile to the Congress, was also the ruling party in Bengal and had the support of the British. Even the Muslim nationalists held the Congress flag in one hand and the black-and-white banner of Mohammedan Sporting in the other, while the Muslim League itself used the club as an obvious example of Muslim superiority in Bengal. This was certainly a definitive indication of the club's growing popularity. Actually from the second half of 1930s, rivalry in Bengal football was no longer confined to the British versus the Indians, but had extended to include the Hindus versus the Muslims, adding definite communal overtones to sport. This new trend in Bengal football, however, needs to be understood in the changed socio-political scene in Bengal from the middle of 1930s.[22]

It was in the year 1932 that 'a group of young, energetic, patriotic and progressive men' in Calcutta formed the New Muslim Majlis.[23] The man spearheading this drive was Khwaja Nooruddin, cousin and brother-in-law of Khwaja Nazimuddin, who later played a heroic part in making the Mohammedan Sporting Club the premier football club. One of the main and immediate aims of the Majlis was to take over the Mohammedan Sporting Club and to develop it into the nation's premier club. The socio-political successes of the Majlis went hand in hand with the success on the football field achieved by the Mohammedan Sporting Club for which Khwaja Nooruddin deserves much credit. As Secretary General of the club, he brought to life a dying organization and made football history not only in Bengal but in the rest of India. A.K. Aziz, Secretary of the club in 1932–33 recorded:

> The season was the most successful in every sense. For the first time in the history of our club we could fulfil our long cherished desire to earn the right of playing in the first division of the Calcutta Football League. Though we started the season rather tamely we finished it brilliantly, winning the last eight matches consecutively.[24]

When the club went on to win the first division league on its first appearance, the repercussions were overwhelming. The club souvenir published in 1935 noted:

> In the 44th year of its existence we find the club not only makes its own history but history in Indian Football by winning the championship of the Calcutta Football League. When the Calcutta League, 1934, opened, the Mohammedan Sporting team were styled as the babes of the League owing to their promotion from the second division. From babes through the evolution of victory after victory and holding the top place on the League table they became the giants of the League and earned the coveted and unique distinction of being the first Indian team to win the League.[25]

It also pointed to enormous enthusiasm that the victory brought in its wake:

With their progress in the League there was unbounded enthusiasm among the Muslim public of Calcutta and the team were responsible for increasing the gates at whichever match they played fourfold. But not only in Calcutta was this enthusiasm manifested. In the mofussil, thousands followed each game with the greatest of interest, so much so that many used to walk miles to the railway station to meet incoming trains with Calcutta newspapers in order to get the results as soon as possible.

After their victory, the team was lionized in the city of Calcutta and it was not for some weeks after that they could call an evening their own without having to attend some function in their honour. They were given a civic reception at the Town Hall when an address was presented to them by the Mayor of Calcutta.[26]

Though the year 1934 was a great success for the club, the financial position of the club had not been satisfactory since the start of the decade despite contributions and advances made by a few people including Qazi Ashraf Ali, the Financial Secretary of the club. As the records of 1934 declared:

> As there had been signs of dissatisfaction shown by the public at the past management of the club and as rumours were in circulation owing to party feeling in the club the present Executive Committee decided to do their best themselves and not to go to the public for donations unless they could prove to the public that with all their difficulties they could set their house in order. Thanks are due to Mr. Zakaria, Mr. N. Anis, Mr. Qazi Ashraf Ali, Khan Sahib Rashid, Maulavi Gafur, members of the Committee who advanced large sums of money and saved an awkward situation.[27]

S.A. Rashid took upon himself to enlist prominent Muslims as life members and in such ways obtained the support of many to relieve the club of its financial difficulties. These first life members included Sir Nazimuddin, KCIE; Khan Bahadur Azizul Haque, Minister for Education; I.G.H. Arif, Bar-at-Law; and K. Sudderuddin. His Excellency John Anderson, Governor of Bengal, became the patron of the club.[28] The club also built an iron fencing around the club pavilion with the permission of A.D. Gordon, Commissioner of Police, and the financial assistance of Muslim merchants of Chandni Chowk, Calcutta's pre-eminent business district.[29]

Another step towards stability for the club was the establishment of a Board of Trustees to find ways and means of raising funds for the club. Many eminent Muslims agreed to serve on the Board. This was in accordance with the declaration made by the club souvenir in 1935:

> While the club is today on a very business-like footing, it is by no means clear of financial anxiety and it is surely up to the Muslims, who are today so proud of the achievement of the club team in football, to come forward and support their club in a greater measure. Funds are the mainstay of any club and brilliant and excellent performances on the field of play are prone to have a serious setback if the club is unable to maintain itself and is hampered with financial difficulties.[30]

In 1935 when Mohammedan Sporting won the League for the second consecutive time, it was deemed to be a great achievement by the Calcutta Muslims. The club souvenir thus recorded the immediate reaction to the victory:

> Tumultuous scenes were witnessed on the Calcutta ground after the match. The joy of the crowd was unbounded and each of the players were carried shoulder high while their bus was escorted in triumphant procession by thousands of Mohammedans wild with joy.[31]

One major factor precipitating Mohammedan Sporting Club's revival and success was the socially and financially influential base of its patronage in terms of members and players in the 1930s. The most important names in this regard were: Khwaja Sir Nazimuddin, ex-Minister of Education of Bengal; Sir Syed Sadullah, an ex-Finance member of the Assam Government; Subid Ali, a leading Calcutta merchant; Khan Sahib Syed Ahmed Rashid, the first Mohammedan appraiser; Syed Ahmed Afzal, a public accountant and auditor; Ishanul Huq, a zamindar and a merchant; K. Habibullah Chowdhury, a celebrated Muslim journalist; S.M. Yakub, Deputy Mayor of Calcutta; and K. Nooruddin, a councillor of the Calcutta Corporation and the Secretary of the Majlis.[32]

There were other sporting reasons for Mohammedan Sporting's success in overpowering all other Indian as well as British teams in the Calcutta league and other worthy tournaments outside Calcutta.[33] Of singular importance was the formation of a strong team by collecting top Muslim players from around the country. This gave them a definite edge over their Bengali Hindu counterparts to fight against the mighty British teams and to win the Calcutta football league five times in a row. Other Bengali clubs like Mohun Bagan or East Bengal hadn't thought of such an effective player recruitment policy. However, more significant was the club's decision to play wearing boots, especially on the rain-affected ground. The club took this pragmatic decision even before promotion to the first division league in 1933. The club authorities studied the reasons of failure of Indian teams 'despite their being rather superior to the European players in India in basic football skill'.[34] S.A. Aziz, the person in charge of building the club's football team, therefore decided to recruit booted players for the side in 1933. The result was instantaneous: six booted players in the team enabled Mohammedan Sporting to trounce the barefooted Nebubagan side 16-0 on a rainy ground in the second division league.[35]

The initial success encouraged Aziz to try experimenting with a fully booted side. Yet 'he was practical enough not to fully lose the advantage of barefooted play by the terribly fast players with uncanny footwork he had in the ranks of the club'.[36] So he conceived and experimented with the Fort William Cobblers to devise a form of light and soft boot, 'without, however, the knowledge of anybody else, lest a storm of objection upset his plans'.[37] Aziz's plan was fulfilled, as he was able to persuade the Mohammedan's new recruits to wear the desirable type of boots on wet ground. Thus he pioneered the new two-in-one system in Bengal football, i.e. playing barefooted on dry ground, but quickly donning boots, kept ready just beyond the sidelines, as soon as rain came. It was proved, noted one sports journalist, that the same player, who excelled in his own style of play when the weather was fair, could be equally effective with boots on a rainy turf without losing much of his basic efficiency.[38]

Impact of Mohammedan Sporting's successive league victories

The unprecedented success of Mohammedan Sporting in winning the Calcutta football league a record five times in a row had a visibly mixed impact on Bengal's footballing society. For many irrespective of their caste, creed or community, it was a worthy victory for the Bengalis as well as Indians on the sporting field. As the *Star of India* wrote:

> The incentive for a team to win the Second Division of the Calcutta Football League is that they will be promoted to the First Division, even though they have to bear for the

first year the label of 'Babes'. But in the first year of promotion to win the championship in the First Division is to hope for the impossible.

The 'Babes' came; they saw; they conquered. And their victory is doubly creditable inasmuch as they have the distinction of being the first *Indian* team to win the League. Mohammedan Sporting has thus written history in Calcutta football.[39]

The Statesman noted the enthusiasm in the wake of the victory:

There were unprecedented scenes of enthusiasm when, with a final flourish that dazzled Kalighat, one of the season's poor relations, Mohammedan Sporting became the first *Indian* team to win the League since its inception in 1898. The rejoicing was transferred from the Maidan to the city, where noisy but good tempered demonstration were the order.[40]

The supremacy the club began to show over British sides came to be hailed as an Indian victory in many quarters. It was expected to encourage the other Bengali clubs to follow in the footsteps of Mohammedan Sporting Club. The newly elected nationalist mayor of Calcutta, Nalini Ranjan Sarkar, called the occasion 'a great unifier … a matter of pleasure and gratification to all citizens'.[41] Such was his enthusiasm that he spent Rs.1,000 on a lavish civic reception organized to greet the players and the team management. By contrast, a mass rally the previous week in Calcutta for Mahatma Gandhi only warranted Rs.10 from the Mayor's purse.[42] For the Muslims in particular, Mohammedan's wins were seen in terms of the community's success to prove its mettle on the field of sport and were expected to inject confidence amongst them to gain similar victories in *other spheres of life*.[43] For some, a section of Hindus to be particular, however, the development was of concern as it represented a victory of Muslim confidence and superiority. An overview of the responses and tributes the club received on the occasion of its second straight league triumph in 1935, as gathered from the club's souvenir, reveals this mixed lot of reactions in the aftermath of the club's successes.

The secretary of East Bengal Club, one of Mohammedan Sporting's biggest rivals in Calcutta League, wrote: 'This is indeed a glorious achievement of your club and for all the *Indian* clubs to take a legitimate pride in.'[44] The tribute from the Aligarh University was on similar lines: 'The Mohammedan Sporting Club has done great service to India in general and Mussalmans of Calcutta in particular.'[45] The report of a particular newspaper is more revealing on this count:

The Mohammedans have created a new history in Indian football, being the first *Indian team* to achieve the league honours. Their success is no doubt a glory to *Indian football* which is but another name for speed and nippiness. The rapid advancement which the game of soccer has made among the Indians presents another problem to the foreign oppositions who will find it none too easy to solve.[46]

The Nawab of Murshidabab, Wasif Ali Meerza, also regarded the club's victory as an 'Indian' one and urged 'all lovers of sport' to acknowledge their splendid performance.[47] The Maharaja of Santosh, then President of the Indian Football Association, also struck a similar chord:

I fervently hope that you (Mohammedan Sporting) will keep your flag flying. Like Mohan Bagan and East Bengal you, too, have enhanced the reputation of *Indian footballers*. You naturally occupy a very warm corner of Bengal's heart and I am sure you will continue to do so as long as your efficiency is not impaired and your methods remain clean.[48]

Some even expected that Mohammedan Sporting's success would have a greater impact on social relations and augur social amity. As the Sheriff, Abdul Halim Ghuznavi maintained: 'In conclusion, I wish the club, its organizers and its players every success, and hope and expect that they will do everything to raise the standard of sports all round and increase a brotherly feeling amongst all classes and communities interested in outdoor games.'[49] Hassan Suhrawardy hailed the club for its great success and wished for greater success in 'a wider sphere of activities'. He, too, did not fail to take note of the potential for social amity on the occasion: 'In the healthy atmosphere of sports and manly games you will make friendships and understandings, irrespective of class, creed and colour, which will last through out your life time.'[50] Finally, R. Ahmed, the principal of Calcutta Dental College and Hospital, commented admirably of the far-reaching consequences of a recreational victory:

> There are reasons for believing that the pioneer Muslim sporting club of Bengal will keep up the lead and thus encourage the growth of healthful recreation amongst the masses. For after all, the greatest object lesson a sporting club can offer is the raising of a physique and health of the people in general. I hope the Mohammedan Sporting Club may continue to do so and thus help the country in a most tangible way.[51]

However, there were tributes and messages which clearly hailed Mohammedan's victory in terms of the success of a particular community. The Mayor of Calcutta, A.K. Fazlul Haque, commented on the occasion: 'The marvellous achievements of the Mohammedan Sporting Club on the football field have earned a name and fame for *Muslims* in the sporting world, of which *the community* may justly be proud.'[52] Syed Abdul Hafeez, a member of the Council of State, wrote in his message: '*The Muslims* of the sporting world take pride in the initiation taken by the Mohammedan Sporting Club of Calcutta. The club came into existence to fulfil a long felt want of the sporting spirit of *the community*.'[53] Another Muslim gentleman, M. Rafique, spoke of the importance of the club's success in terms of a great community service:

> Games and sports play a vital part in moulding and shaping the character and ultimately the destinies of individuals, no less than that of communities. The success of the Mohammedan Sporting Club will be a harbinger of greater successes in the *self-realisation of our great community in other branches of human endeavour*.[54]

That even only after the second year of its league success, the Mohammedan Sporting Club had already become a symbol of Muslim identity and confidence all over India was clear from the congratulatory messages it received from different corners of Bengal and the whole of India.[55] As K. Nooruddin, one of the revivers of the club in the 1930s, remarked, 'Their spectacular performance, in recent years, is the turning point for the Mussalmans of Bengal in the field of sports.'[56] More importantly, the club souvenir recorded the following about how the Muslim fans supported the club's cause throughout the years:

> Ever since their (the club's) chances were rosy (in clinching the League) in the League last year and throughout this year, they have had the solid backing of thousands of supporters who – rain, cloud or sunshine – have mustered to a man to see them play and encourage them.

Club football fans would be amazed to see who some of these supporters are. Business-men who leave their firms and shops to witness the games, old men who have lost inter-est in football for years, but who have had it resuscitated with the enthusiasm for Mohammedans.[57]

Recording the Mohammedan Sporting Club's huge fan following those days, Mohammad Nasiruddin, editor of *Saogat*, wrote:

Calcutta *maidan* used to witness large gathering on the days of Mohammedan Sporting's match. The crowd comprised educated and uneducated youth and old men along with maulavis and maulanas. When space on the sidelines of the ground proved insufficient, diehard fans climbed upon trees and sat on the branches to witness the matches of their favourite club. Kaji Nazrul Islam, the famous Muslim bard, called these over-enthusiastic fans 'branch-monkeys'.[58]

As a follow up on the success of the Mohammedan Sporting Club, a number of Muslim sporting clubs were established in the districts and sub-divisional towns. As *The Statesman* noted: 'The Mohammedan Sporting is as popular in the mofussil as in Calcutta and stories are current of crowds in Bengal towns collecting of an afternoon round wireless loudspeakers and echoing the cheers of its supporters from the Calcutta maidan.'[59] Thus the Muslims of Dhaka were inspired to form Dhaka Mohammedan Sporting Club in 1936.[60] This was, however, preceded by two more Muslim clubs: Muslim Sporting Club (1927) founded at the initiative of some of the members of Dhaka's Nawab Family at Dilkhusha House, and Kumilla Mohammedan (1928). While the first club was disbanded only after two years, the latter still exists.[61] The first President and General Secretary of the Dhaka Mohammedan club were Khwaja Md. Azmal and Khwaja Md. Adel respectively.[62]

When Mohammedan Sporting won the League title in 1938 to make it five times in a row, the jubilation went beyond description:

There was spontaneous demonstration after the match and also on the Mohammedan Sporting ground and finally around the Subid Ali Mansions. Thousands of Muslim supporters marched in procession with band and rent the skies with tremendous shouts of jubilation ... Till late in the evening it was impossible to enter the Mohammedan Sporting tent, there were thousands around it. A spontaneous Kabuli dancing recital was held under the skies of their ground. Led by buglers, the players returned to the club tent from the CFC ground and as they reached the club the flag was hoisted on the pole. The players were profusely congratulated from all round for bringing respect to the club and the Indian football.[63]

Muslim poets also felt the need to greet the club's success by writing poems in the club's honour. The poems of Nazrul Islam and Golam Mostafa on this theme became popular among Bengali Muslims. The poems and songs composed by Mostafa on the occasion were popularized by the Gramophone Record Company when they placed on sale records of those songs sung by famous singer Abbasuddin.[64]

The huge impact of Mohammedan Sporting's victories on Muslim society needs to be analysed in the larger socio-political context of Hindu-Muslim relations of the 1930s. However, the impact of the consecutive victories of the club in Hindu-Muslim circles, as has already been shown, was mixed. While the success of the club was regarded as a *Muslim* victory against the Hindus by many among both communities, many others considered it as an *Indian* victory to end British supremacy on the football field. But, in the long run, it must be added that the actual impact of the club's popularity played a key role in generating confidence among the Muslim masses and lending strength to the political cause of the Muslim League in Bengal.

Conflict between IFA and Mohammedan Sporting: context, growth and aftermath[65]

On the sidelines of the changes in the political equation in Bengal in the mid and late 1930s, Mohammedan Sporting had a continuous tussle with the IFA. Despite their gallant performances against leading European teams, they were not given recognition anywhere near that accorded to Mohun Bagan after their victory in the IFA Shield in 1911. The Muslim community always found the IFA to be discriminatory against Mohammedan Sporting. This so-called discrimination, as the most recent study on the subject suggests, was a response to the Muslim political ascendancy in Bengal in the 1930s.[66] According to this study, the Bengali *bhadroloks* began to feel threatened by the Muslim political ascendancy in Bengal in the middle of the 1930s.[67] It was also accompanied by Bengal's marginalization in national/Congress politics as the central Congress leadership had started displaying a growing apathy towards the *bhadrolok* who dominated the Bengal Congress.[68] Along with this, there also occurred a minimization of the *bhadrolok*'s regional hegemony, an outcome of what Joya Chatterji has called 'the emergence of the mufassil in Bengal politics'.[69] Chatterji shows how the metropolis, which had dominated Bengal politics till the end of the 1920s, increasingly became less significant from the early 1930s, as political fortunes began to be determined by the Muslim vote concentrated in rural and small town Bengal.[70] This transformation, an outcome of the Communal Award of 1932 and Government of India Act of 1935, which enlarged Muslim representation in the provincial assemblies at the expense of the Hindu vote, culminated in the accession of the Krishak Praja Party[71] – Muslim League ministry led by Fazlul Haq in 1937.

The new ministry soon set in motion a series of reforms that affected the interests of the Hindu *bhadrolok*. As Chatterji enumerates:

> In 1938, the Fazlul Haq ministry changed the rules about police recruitment so that 'while enlisting Bengali constables the Superintendent of Police must see that not less than 50% of the recruits are Muslims'. In the same year, the ministry passed legislation that stipulated that 60 per cent of all Government appointments be reserved for Muslims. In 1939, the Government instructed local bodies 'not to propose for appointment to local bodies persons who were known to be actively opposed to the policy of the Ministry', and slapped administrative controls on nominations to the Union Boards, which accounted for one-third of their total membership.[72]

Thus in almost every domain of the public sphere from higher education to administrative and political appointments, the Hindu *bhadrolok* preserves were under threat. It was in such a situation that leading patrons of sport started to look favourably upon British rule. In football they were opposed to the dominance of Mohammedan Sporting and tried their best to thwart it.[73]

The growing tension between the club and the IFA reached a climax in 1937 over a controversial incident during a league match between Mohammedan Sporting and East Bengal. In this match on 11 June 1937, it was reported, one influential member and player of the Mohammedan Sporting Club kicked at the face of one East Bengal official, who had run to the assistance of Rahamat, an injured player of the Mohammedan Sporting Club.[74] It was known to all concerned that the IFA would take appropriate action against him. The match was followed by disgraceful scenes. Immediately after the game, there were several cases of stabbing outside the ground, the most unfortunate victim being a boy of 13.[75] As one newspaper correspondent noted:

> Tempers ran riot and the gentleman who previously used to stroll about the Maidan under the name of 'sporting spirit' was shot dead outright and buried. Bitter partisan feelings of a none-too-specific type strode about menacingly like a moody child bent on mischief. Quiet lovers of the game had no other alternative but to seek the first available vantage-point of safety. The C.F.C. members had to extend hospitality to the distressed. There were assaults here and there and in a few cases dangerous weapons were used.[76]

A section of Muslims were blamed for the post-match violence:

> We have not the least doubt that none regrets more the disgraceful conduct of some of the Muslims among the spectators than the Mohammedan team. We trust the Muslim press will forget its communalism and condemn the conduct of those who had come to witness a first class sport, but exhibited a mentality that was as remote from sportsmanship as hell is from heaven. What can be more horrible than that people should come with daggers concealed in their person to use them against innocent spectators? These people no doubt belong to the class of goondas [goons] ... who flourish in this city despite the Goonda Act [the Criminal Act]. We wish it had been possible to dismiss the incidents as the hard work of a few desperados who really belong to the lawless class. But it is common knowledge that communal partisanship often finds very disgraceful expression in language whenever a Muslim player comes to the grief at the hands of his Hindu opponent ... Calcutta football maidan is no longer the respectable place that it once was. The invasion of communalism of sports has invested it with bad odour to decent people.[77]

The controversy arose over the identity of the Mohammedan Sporting Club player who committed the wrong. The club as well as newspapers representing Muslim sentiments such as the *Star of India* claimed that it was Sattar who actually hit at the face of Girin Ghosh, an East Bengal official.[78] The IFA, however, instead of taking stern action against Sattar, suspended Habib, one of the best players of the Mohammedan Sporting side.[79] The IFA, in its Governing Body meeting held on 14 June, took the following resolutions:

(1) Habib, the Mohammedan Sporting player, was unanimously found guilty of having assaulted Girin Ghosh, an official of East Bengal Club, during the match between East Bengal and Mohammedan Sporting on the C.F.C. Ground last Friday. He was suspended for three years.

(2) A committee consisting of Messrs. Nagle, Pepper, S.N. Banerjee, Sushil Sen, H.M. Hafeez, and both the joint honorary secretaries, was appointed to enquire whether Mohammedan Sporting was responsible for the Habib-Ghosh incident and whether the Club tried to shield Habib, and whether any action should be taken.

(3) A committee consisting of Messrs. G.C. Fletcher, A.K. Basu, K. Nooruddin, G.H. McIntyre, G.M. Habib and Inspector Ford, with the two joint honorary secretaries was appointed to devise ways and means to prevent, if possible, a recurrence of the incidents that followed last Friday's match.[80]

The Maharaja of Santosh, President of IFA, was however against placing the blame on 'the Mohammedan Club for the lawlessness of the vast crowd of their supporters'.[81] While he admitted that 'every club should do its best to check its

supporters from behaving badly', he also strongly argued that 'it would be stretch-
ing their (IFA's) rules to tell Mohammedan Sporting that they would be suspended
if there was a recurrence of lawless incidents among the bad characters on the
slopes of the Fort outside the ground'.[82] The Maharaja suggested that the club
'should form a set sort of volunteer corps from among their members to sit among
the spectators on the green stands and use their influence, with the help of the
police, in keeping order'.[83] It was also suggested elsewhere that 'Mohammedan
Sporting could print leaflets in Urdu appealing to the members of the Mohammedan
community to refrain from acting in such a way as would bring their *national* club
into disrepute'.[84]

After deliberating on these suggestions, the Executive Committee of the
Mohammedan Sporting Club notified the IFA that the suggestions were totally
unacceptable. According to it, 'one of the resolutions passed at the meeting of the
I.F.A. was humiliating for Mohammedan Sporting, and the club regret they will not
be able to play any more league matches until the resolution is rescinded and erased
from the books of the I.F.A.'.[85] The meeting also considered the Habib incident,
found after enquiry that Sattar, and not Habib, was responsible for the assault upon
Girin Ghosh, and forthrightly suspended Sattar indefinitely.[86] Commenting on the
humiliating suggestions of the IFA, the club authorities declared: 'A serious crisis
appeared inevitable and the Governing Body of the IFA created a situation that caused
great resentment not only amongst the members of the club but among the entire
Muslim public of Bengal.'[87] When the club's secretary, K. Nooruddin, protested
against this arbitrary decision-making, the apex body decided to ban him from
attending its Governing Body meetings for the next three years. As a mark of protest,
Mohammedan Sporting Club withdrew from the league on 16 June 1937.[88] The
Executive Committee of the club also condemned 'the malicious and one-sided
propaganda of a section of a press, and particularly of the "Statesman" against the
Mohammedan Sporting Club' and urged the Muslims,

> to boycott the 'Statesman' which has clearly deviated from its policy of impartiality and
> assumed the role of a propagandist in favour of anti-Islam Zionism in Palestine and of
> the champion of the anti-Mohammedan forces in the I.F.A., Calcutta, which have made
> an unholy alliance against the Mohammedans on purely communal grounds.[89]

These actions generated considerable ill feeling among the Muslims, evident from the
following editorial published in the *Star of India*:

> The inevitable has happened. The irresponsible and vindictive manner in which the
> Governing Body of the IFA had dealt with the situation created by false and malicious
> propaganda against Mohammedan Sporting has resulted in a deadlock, which may ruin
> Calcutta football forever. In our leading article yesterday, we pointed out the uncalled
> for insult which the IFA Governing body had offered the Mohammedan Sporting Club
> by the spiteful and shameful resolution appointing a committee to enquire into the
> conduct of the club itself in order to find out whether it had shielded Habib, the player
> wrongly punished by the IFA in the same meeting. We knew that the only answer, which
> the Mohammedan Sporting Club could give the IFA, consistent with self respect, was to
> decline to play any more games conducted by that Association. But yesterday we delib-
> erately wrote with restraint because we had faint hopes that a good night's sleep might
> help the Maharaja of Santosh and his colleagues on that governing body to realize the
> lengths to which they had been led on the evening previous. We had hoped that at least
> the Maharaja of Santosh would soon realize the mistake made and would use his
> influence to bring his erring colleagues to their senses and scrap the offensive, entirely

uncalled for, petty minded and absurd resolution ... entirely unworthy of grown up men who are expected to be reasonable and unbiased.

But wisdom has not yet dawned, and the infamous decision to hold an inquest on the conduct of a club managed and controlled by men, many of whom are held in higher esteem by the public than the more boisterous gentleman on the IFA Governing Body still stands. The Mohammedan Sporting Club has refused to stand this act of cold-blooded insult and deliberate injustice. If the men who voted for this monstrous resolution in the IFA meeting on Monday, despite protests from several other members, had any idea how men with any sense of self respect react to such insults as they were offering the Mohammedans, they would have hesitated a hundred times before mooting so unmannerly, so revengeful and so unprecedented a proposal before the meeting. But it is clear that the majority present on the occasion had gone there determined to punish the Mohammedans. The Mohammedans had in their eyes merited punishment not because of what happened or did not happen on Friday last; that was but the excuse of the Tiger to the Lamb.[90]

It went on to assert that,

the Mohammedans merited the severest punishment in their eyes for other reasons. They had driven out of the picture the 'Premier' Indian team and all teams, in fact, which had held supremacy before the advent of the all-conquering Mohammedans. They had taken the glory out of Hindu football, and had fought their way to a glory never before achieved by Indians. In this year of grace, the Mohammedans seemed to be once more on the high road to the same achievement – and if for the fourth year in succession the league honours went to them, would not this fair land of Indians be overcast with the clouds of ignominy? The very idea of so much glory to the Mohammedans seemed to have destroyed appetites and stolen sleep from the eyes of the thousands of the only loving children of Mother India.[91]

The Editorial concluded thus:

The tricks that were played to trip up the victorious Mohammedans on their onward march to victory, the accidents that robbed them of advantages on the field of play and the confused judgements of referees at the most crucial moments in the movement of the leather – all these and many things are too well known to tens of thousands of Muslims ... who have regularly watched the contests on the Calcutta *maidan*.

But we ourselves never took notice of these little ways or little men; we had confidence that as long as the Mohammedans played the splendidly efficient and commendably clean football which they alone can play at present, laurels would come to them despite all intrigue, impediment and controversy.

And now some of the men whom both chance and design have placed in a position wherefrom the strangler's rope can be fastened round the neck of the unloved Moham-medans, have created an opportunity to 'feed fat the ancient grudge.' It may be further noted that the Mohammedans are to have from next year a better field and an enclosure of their own in a part of the *maidan* which would make their club territorially the second best to Calcutta FC. Could there be a more bitter gall and wormwood for the unhappy nationalist who has invaded the field of sport? But the nationalist is a clever stage manager and plotter. He realized that if the Mohammedans could be driven to an intol-erable position, if on some pretext or other, they could be subjected to an insult, which they could not and would not brook, if a situation could be created in which the only alternative for the Mohammedan Sporting Club would be to cut themselves adrift from the IFA, then the unwanted Club and its unconquerable eleven could be effectively prevented from acquiring such permanent importance in the world of Indian football. That intolerable position has been created, that pretext has been invented, that situation has been engineered. And now is the exit of the Mohammedans awaited with hope and joy.

> The indecent haste with which the Governing Body of the IFA arrived at their decisions on Monday, was further proved when it was found that they had punished the wrong man. The Mohammedan Club executive after the enquiry have ascertained that it was their reserve player Sattar and not Habib who had assaulted Girin Ghose, and they have promptly suspended the guilty person, and naturally demanded that the IFA's wrong and slanderous act against Habib, the innocent, must be rescinded.[92]

Noting that public opinion had been mobilized against the IFA, the Maharaja of Santosh, President, hastened to find a peaceful solution to the controversy.[93] As a result, the IFA and the Mohammedan Sporting Club arrived at a temporary truce after K. Nooruddin, Secretary of the Club, met the Maharaja of Santosh at his residence.[94] At this meeting an agreement was signed between the two bodies:

(a) That time be given to the Mohammedan Sporting Club to reconsider the situation.

(b) That the Mohammedan Sporting Club shall lodge an appeal with the Indian Football Association in accordance with its rules and the Governing Body (of the IFA) will do all that is just and reasonable to redress the grievance of Mohammedan Sporting Club, if any.

(c) That in view of the understanding and in order to keep the doors of negotiation open, Mohammedan Sporting's matches were to be postponed as requested by the club.[95]

As per the terms of the understanding, Mohammedan Sporting Club appealed to the IFA on 19 June 1937, urging the Governing Body to reconsider decisions against the club.[96] Rather than softening their stand in view of the club's appeal, the IFA imposed a fresh series of conditions upon the club declaring that only if the conditions were met would their appeal be considered.[97] The primary condition given by the IFA was that the club would have to unconditionally withdraw all the resolutions and letters sent to the apex body. After its meeting of 6 July, the IFA asserted that the Maharaja of Santosh, President, had already notified the Mohammedan Sporting Club that if their letter of 16 June was not withdrawn their appeal would not be considered.[98] At this meeting, the IFA also decided that no more time would be given to the club and rejected the appeal by Mohammedan Sporting. This decision came only four days after the club registered its record fourth triumph in the Calcutta League on 2 July 1937. In doing so, the IFA also ignored the wishes of some of the European members of its Governing Body. G.C. Fletcher, a key member of the Governing Body, had moved a resolution whereby the Mohammedan Sporting Club was to be given a further 48 hours to withdraw their letter.[99] But the Indian members, mostly Hindus representing other clubs, were determined not to give the club any further time and wanted their appeal to be rejected immediately, as was eventually done:

> there was a feeling in many quarters in Calcutta that the IFA have been surrendering its legitimate right to control football in Calcutta and it looked as if there would be one body left to rule football that is either the IFA or the Mohammedan Sporting Club.[100]

Accordingly, Lt. Henson of the Army Sports Control Board strongly urged that the matter should be dealt with then and there and no further adjournment should be given, and if the Mohammedan Sporting Club be given any further opportunity to re-consider this point, Mr. K Nooruddin on behalf of the club should straightaway withdraw the letter and revoke the resolution adopted at the meeting.[101]

As against this, the Mohammedan Sporting Club authorities asserted, 'We submit that the Governing Body cannot reasonably take exceptions to our opinion expressed with regard to suggestions, which affects not only our club but also the good name of our community.'[102] Even when the club pleaded for a reconsideration of their appeal, the plea was rejected. Finally the IFA decided to forward to the club the following letter drafted by the President, the Maharaja of Santosh: 'I am directed to regret that under the rules of the Association they are unable to go out of their way to reopen the issue.'[103] Criticizing the IFA's stand, the *Star of India* stated:

> We tell the Maharaja of Santosh that the terms of an agreement to which he put his solemn signature have been violated and that he has himself been a party to that violation. Mr. Nooruddin did not give any 'assurance' over and above what was put down in writing and signed by him jointly with the Maharaja. When later there was a vague talk of 'assurances given by Mr. Nooruddin', the Mohammedans Secretary, we understand, several times protested against the suggestion that he had given any other assurances and asked for permission to contradict the reports. That permission was refused by the President of the IFA although Mr. Nooruddin was never told what the assurances he was supposed to have given were. And even if there were assurances, which there were not, the Maharaja of Santosh and the 'able lawyers' who are on the IFA should know very well that after two parties in dispute put down their agreement in writing and specify certain terms and conditions thereof, any subsequent understanding has no validity in law.[104]

Despite such criticisms, the IFA refused to alter its stance. Habib was under suspen-sion for three years and the censure against Secretary Nooruddin, who it was alleged, 'did not behave in a candid manner before the general body at its meeting held on 14 June and attempted to shield Habib'[105] stood unaltered.[106] Thus even after much deliberation, the conflict between the IFA and the Mohammedan Sporting Club did not abate and the situation remained unchanged.

Interestingly, in the midst of this atmosphere of continuing hostility, the club went on to register their fifth straight league triumph on 13 July 1938. 'The club had the proud distinction of winning this match and yet another record was set by winning the league for the fifth year in succession.'[107] Despite this performance, tensions esca-lated between the IFA Governing Body and the club, and in 1938 the Club again came to a serious tussle with the IFA authorities. The climax was reached when the question of the Australian tour came up. The suggestion of the club to postpone the tour until the end of the IFA Shield was ignored. However, the players rose to the occasion and showed their great love for the club and refused to join the Australian touring team till the end of the IFA Shield. By this time the members were exasperated, and a general demand was made that time had now come when the club, once and for all, should decide its line of action and withdraw from the Shield as a mark of protest. However, the Executive committee eventually decided to continue to play in spite of all opposition.[108]

According to the club souvenir published in 1939, central grievances of the club were 'maximum punishment for minimum offences, repeated bad referring, arbitrary decision with regard to the venue of matches and generally the tyranny of the major-ity of the council of the IFA against our club'.[109] Even though Mohammedan

Sporting competed in the 1938 IFA Shield under extreme duress, its continuous rift with the IFA had finally taken its toll and forced the Mohammedans to withdraw from the Calcutta Football League in 1939. On the eve of its second leg league match against Mohun Bagan on 24 June 1939, the club, already much aggrieved over poor supervision in most of their matches that season, decided to lodge a protest to the IFA against 'the manner in which the game has been supervised this season especially the matches in which the Mohammedan Sporting Club has played'.[110] Then, on 5 July 1939, Mohammedan Sporting, along with East Bengal, Aryan and Kalighat made it public that they would refrain from participating in any of the remaining games except East Bengal's charity fixture against Mohun Bagan on 8 July 'unless their grievances as set forth in their letter to the President of the I.F.A. are redressed forthwith'.[111] The Aryan, however, revised its decision overnight and rejoined the scheduled fixture. The IFA, on its part, considered the action of other three clubs to be a violation of its decision, 'tantamounting to flouting the authority of the Association' and, in an emergent meeting of the Governing Body, took an unprecedented decision to suspend the three clubs till 31 December 1939.[112] In response, the Executive Committees of the three 'rebel' clubs decided at a joint conference on 9 July to work towards an honourable settlement of their grievances with the IFA.[113] However, the meeting also resolved 'to take steps for the initiation of a separate football league, in the event of an honourable settlement arrived at'.[114] It was also decided to term the league as the 'Brabourne League'. The clubs played a number of exhibition matches between them at different venues throughout Bengal in July and August, which attracted large crowds on every occasion. Finally, a rival Bengal Football Association was born on 11 August 1939 with Nailini Ranjan Sarkar, Finance Minister of the Bengal Government, as the President.[115] The Association organized a knock-out tournament called the 'Brabourne Cup' in September. Though a temporary truce was once again arrived at in 1940, resulting in the re-entry of these clubs into the Calcutta Football League, 'the temporary parting of ways', particularly between the IFA and the Mohammedan Sporting, 'did have a lasting effect'.[116] The ill-treatment meted out to Mohammedan Sporting and the resultant rift between the IFA and the club, as has already been shown, had its roots in the changes in the balance of socio-political power in Bengal.

From *community* to *communal*: football and communalism in India

Thus a potential situation of extreme social tension was created in Indian football in course of the 1930s, when peaceful coexistence of two communities in challenging British supremacy on the soccer field gave way to a serious rift between the Hindus and the Muslims. This transition from *community* to *communal* in Indian football had several delicate moments, subtle shifts and also points of convergence.

There are ample examples available in contemporary periodicals to show that Mohammedan Sporting Club started representing purely community interests from the late 1930s. In 1934, a letter to the editor of a newspaper pointed out:

> Any lover of sports or any Indian who has the good of his or her country at heart cannot but be shocked to see how Calcutta football matches are spreading communalism among the masses. A match between Mohammedan Sporting Club and any other team draws tens of thousands of Mussalmans who want only the success of the said team, which they think glorifies the name of their community only and not of the whole Indian nation.[117]

The way football came to be interlinked with communalism also drew criticism from the press:

> What is football coming to in Calcutta? From sports it is definitely veering round to communalism and politics from which it should be thoroughly divorced ...

> The Mohammedan Sporting Club ... has earned all the praises bestowed on them from all parts of India. But to earn plaudits is one thing and to retain mentioning this fact had they not succumbed to the temptation of winning cheap clapstraps from their communal coreligionists. And in doing so they have ruined and are fairly in the way of still ruining their enviable record of non-stop victories.[118]

In the aftermath of the controversial Mohammedan-East Bengal match of 11 June 1937, a *Statesman* editorial argued:

> In India one community hate another virulently for the love of the game. If a side and its supporters cannot take a beating without showing the savagery seen on Friday it were better that inter community games be forbidden by some Criminal Law Amendment Act: A Communal Award could hardly rouse worse passions ...

> Calcutta football seems to be not a pale, but a highly coloured reflection of Bengal politics.[119]

The attempt of the Muslim press to exonerate the Mohammedan Sporting Club was criticized in the leading newspapers of Calcutta:

> What blood is to leopard, the football incident has been to the Muslim communalists, one shudders as one reads the onthrusts in a section of Calcutta's Moslem Press on the action taken by the IFA ... It (IFA) has by that decision become one of the 'tube of Paramanan-das' and its members have become 'Hindu Mahasabites'. It is 'revengeful' and 'spiteful' and its whole purpose is to deprive 'all conquering Mohammedans' of the glory that it knew was awaiting them even after their defeat at the hands of East Bengal ...

> Do we not know that continued indulgence from certain quarters has resulted in produc-ing the mentality that a Moslem, in the right or in the wrong, must be defended? This mentality has been created for political reasons ... How to cure this mentality?[120]

In 1938, for example, *Bharatbarsha* appreciated the club's decision not to play against the incoming Burmese national team at the Calcutta ground to protest the discrimination with regard to seat allotment for spectators. But it condemned Mohammedan Sporting's action to stop all its supporters from going to the ground on the match day:

> Special efforts were made to ensure that no Muslim fans visit the ground to watch the Burma team play. Muslims were stopped from going to the ground either by distributing handbills or by issuing orders to that effect. While Mohammedan's decision not to play can be defended for the sake of its opinion, the club's effort to withdraw its supporters from the match is by no means supported.[121]

In the same year, the club management also felt aggrieved over the issue of distri-bution of charity funds realized from Mohammedan's matches. It argued that while the realized fund from charity matches in 1936–37 amounted to Rs.70,000, only Rs.4,300 was donated to Muslim voluntary organizations.[122] Consequently, a meeting of the

Muslims was organized at the *maidan* on 31 July 1938. The meeting urged for more representation of Muslim members in the IFA Governing Body and requested the IFA to look after the basic amenities of the Muslim players in Calcutta.[123] However, as it seemed to the reporter of *Bharatbarsha*, these grievances and demands discussed in the meeting had no direct link with the Mohammedan Sporting Club as the Muslim leaders of the meeting threatened to boycott not only Calcutta football but also the Club if their demands were not properly considered by the authorities concerned.[124]

Victory of the Muslims against strong European and also Hindu teams on the football field instilled a spirit of self-confidence and pride in the Muslims of Bengal in particular, a vast majority of whom, through years of persecution and humiliation, had lost confidence in themselves and in their future.[125] It may therefore be argued that the contribution of the Mohammedan Sporting Club in making the Muslim League popular in Bengal was not insignificant.[126] The series of victories achieved by this club, even in the all-India competitions, considerably increased the prestige of the party. Its effect on Muslim fans 'was electrifying',[127] and a number of Muslim sporting clubs were established in the districts and sub-divisional towns.

On the other hand, the fact that the Muslim League was in power helped the club in getting government patronage.[128] Nazimuddin allotted plot no.41 at Calcutta *maidan* solely to the club in violation of the existing rules prescribed for it, and also stood surety on the club's behalf to the extent of Rs.12,000.[129] Such a policy, though on the pattern of the normal 'spoils system' of all democratic governments, had the effect of consolidating the Muslim League's hold over the administration and also of creating the image that the League was alive to the interests of the Muslims. As these measures were meant for the exclusive benefit of Muslims, Hindus raised the cry of 'communal overtone' against the Ministry.[130]

Suranjan Das's hint at Muslim 'self-mobilization'[131] around Mohammedan Sporting Club in the context of 1946 Calcutta-riots was not only confined to the Muslims. Such self-mobilization efforts were also noticeable among the Hindus under the aegis of Hindu Mahasabha. In fact, one strand of nationalist activities from the 1920s, as Tanika Sarkar[132] points out, which reinforced a sense of insecurity among Muslims, was the crop of physical culture associations or *akhras* for Hindu youths in Calcutta and mofussil towns. The presence of Hindu centres of *lathi* and dagger-play made the Muslims nervous and stimulated similar preparations among them. In the early 1940s when Hindu volunteer groups proliferated in Calcutta, smaller *para* ('neighbourhood') groups such as the 'Yuva Sampradaya' of Behala started by Nirmal Kumar Chatterjee in 1943 included in their functions 'football section' apart from usual *bratachari* and dagger-play, drama section and organizing Durga Puja and Saraswati Pujas.[133] On the other hand, the Muslims, who were 'rolling on the ground with joy' in 1911 at the victory of their Hindu brothers on the football field, had all disappeared, and been replaced by a new breed who came to watch the game carrying knives and bottles of soda water. While the knives were used to stab opponent supporters, the soda water bottles – mostly half-filled or empty – were thrown to the ground to hurt players or halt matches. Indians had never displayed such aggressive spirits on the Calcutta sports-field before. Das remarks of this communal situation on the *maidan* aptly: 'reverses suffered by the Mohammedan Sporting Club in football matches enraged Muslim feelings which were expressed in sporadic violence against the Hindus'.[134] Or, as another writer comments, 'with each victory, a communal wedge was driven deeper into Calcutta football if not into Calcutta society'.[135] Thus the decade between 1937 and 1947 saw a fundamental change of vision of football in nationalist discourse of both Hindus and Muslims.

The Quite India movement of 1942, the economic insecurity generated by the Second World War, the panic evacuation of Calcutta caused by the fear of Japanese bombs, the famine, restlessness among the youth, and the communal riots that broke out on the day of the call for 'direct action' by the Muslim League – the stress of all these events gradually wiped out any enthusiasm for football in Calcutta.[136] Because of the riots, there was no competition for the Shield in 1946 and the League was not played in 1947.

Unfortunately, the advantages of building a successful club entirely on the patronage of rich businessmen and political leaders from a particular community were offset with associated problems. As Moti Nandy writes: 'Who knows then their selfish needs would be over, when their largesse would come to an end? Immediately after the partition of August 1947, having finally achieved their heart's desire, the patrons of Mohammedan Sporting Club left for either East or West Pakistan.'[137] The club's fame of success was thus extinguished, never to be revived again.[138] Since independence it has been League champions on only three occasions.

Conclusion

The meteoric rise of the Mohammedan Sporting Club in the Bengal alias Indian sporting scenario in the early 1930s and its continuous clash with the IFA in the late 1930s and 1940s shows how football's role as a unitary nationalist force gave way to a divided sense of loyalties in Bengal. It also explains why a rich history of football in India around the club has been overshadowed by the politics that grew around the game. A study of contemporary socio-political realities of the late 1930s and the resultant communal strife in the 1940s demonstrates why, despite winning five straight Calcutta Football League titles defeating leading European sides, Mohammedan Sporting did not usher a new wave of sporting nationalism in colonial India. As a result, Mohun Bagan's solitary IFA Shield triumph in colonial India[139] continues to be regarded as a greater success of Indian nationalism on the sporting field. The factors influencing the gradual marginalization of the club from the Indian sporting scenario in the 1940s also throws light on the association between minority politics, religious communalism and sport in the Indian context. However, it was not simply 'the Bengali *bhadrolok*'s failure to come to terms with the spectacular success of Mohammedan Sporting that led to the erasure of a rich chapter of Bengal's sporting history'.[140] Rather, it was the oppositional perception of identity of two communities – majority and minority – in a tense socio-political context of Bengal, which led to the fracture of footballing nationalism from the 1930s. This chapter has attempted to consider football as an integral component of Indian political and social life, thereby drawing attention to the relationship between sport and identity in the colonial context. It thus tries to widen the conventional historical understanding of minority politics, communalism and identity in colonial India, using soccer in India of the 1930s–40s as a lens.

Notes

1. 'History of the Club', 27, 35–9.
2. Ritan, *Football*, 17. Also see Narayan Dasgupta, 'Kibhabe tinbar naam badle holo aajker Mohammedan' (How today's Mohammedan came into being changing its name thrice). *Khela*, September 18, 1998; Ajay Basu, 'Tumko lakho selam' (Salute you million times). *Desh*, December 22, 1990.

3. 'History of the Club', 27.
4. Ibid.
5. Ibid.
6. Ibid.
7. Ibid.
8. Ibid.
9. *Annual Report*, Mohammedan Sporting Club, 1928.
10. Ibid.
11. Ibid.
12. Ibid. Emphasis added.
13. Ibid.
14. Ibid. Also see, Dasgupta, 'Kibhabe tinbar naam badle holo aajker Mohammedan', 26.
15. *Calcutta Monthly*, July 1896.
16. Even years after the establishment of Indian National Congress, the majority of the Muslim community had not changed their attitude toward the national movement. In 1896 Rahmatullah Sayani of Bombay presided over the Congress session held at Calcutta. Sayani was a leading Muslim from Bombay, Honorary Magistrate, President of the Municipal Corporation, and member of the Legislative Council of Bombay. In his presidential speech, he criticized the hostile attitude of the Muslim community towards the Congress and urged that 'the Mussalmans, however, instead of raising puerile and imaginary objections from a distance, should attend Congress meetings and see for themselves what is going on in such meetings'. His speech provoked protests from the Bengali Muslims. For Sayani's speech, see *Report of the Indian National Congress*, 1896, 1–39, especially 24. Also see Ahmad, *Muslim Community*, 191–2.
17. *Calcutta Monthly*, December 1896, cited in Ahmad, *Muslim Community in Bengal*, 192.
18. Quoted in *Mohun Bagan Club Platinum Jubilee Souvenir*, 25.
19. Ibid.
20. Sengupta, *Kallol Yug*, 66, translation mine.
21. Comments of Muhammad Nasiruddin, the editor of *Saugat*, a periodical published from Dacca, quoted in Ritan, *Football*, 21.
22. For details on this, see Sen, *Muslim Politics*.
23. Ispahani, *Qaid-E-Azam Jinnah*, 4; McPherson, *The Muslim Microcosm*, 121.
24. *Annual Report, 1932–33*, Mohammedan Sporting Club.
25. 'History of the Club', 36.
26. Ibid.
27. Ibid.
28. Ibid.
29. Ibid., 39.
30. Ibid.
31. Ibid.
32. For details on these personalities, see *Mohammedan Sporting Club*, 29–30.
33. These included the Rovers Cup and the Durand Cup, both of which Mohammedan won as the first Bengal club.
34. RB, 'Indian Football and Boots'.
35. Ibid.
36. Ibid.
37. Ibid.
38. Ibid.
39. *Star of India*, July 6, 1934; emphasis added.
40. *The Statesman*, July 6, 1934; emphasis added.
41. *Amrita Bazar Patrika*, August 1, 1934.
42. *Forward*, July 12, 1934.
43. These *other spheres* included, amongst others, mainly education, government service and different professions.
44. *Mohammedan Sporting Club Souvenir*, 28; emphasis added.
45. Secretary of the University, F. Noor Muhammad, sent this congratulatory message to the club. Quoted in ibid.
46. *Amrita Bazar Patrika*, n.d., quoted in *Mohammedan Sporting Club*, 11; emphasis added.
47. *Mohammedan Sporting Club*, 16.
48. Ibid.; emphasis added.

49. Ibid., 18.
50. Ibid., 19.
51. Ibid.
52. Ibid., 12; emphasis added.
53. Ibid., 25; emphasis added.
54. Ibid., 26; emphasis added.
55. Hundreds of messages came from Muslim clubs and organizations of different parts of India including Shillong, Sylhet, Dacca, Rangpur, Tippera, Dinajpur, Jalpaiguri, Darjeeling, Purnea, Cuttock, Benares, Bombay, Bangalore and Calcutta. For details, see *Mohammedan Sporting Club*, 28.
56. Ibid.
57. 'Tribute from the Green Stands', in *Mohammedan Sporting Club*, 34.
58. Comments of Mohammad Nasiruddin, quoted in Ritan, *Football*, 20–1; translation mine. The terms 'maulavis' and 'maulanas', in the Indian context, commonly refer to Muslim religious leaders and scholars respectively.
59. *The Statesman*, July 6, 1937.
60. *Dhaka Mohammedan Sporting Club er Sankhipta Itihas*, 2.
61. Ibid., 2–3.
62. Ibid.
63. *Amrita Bazar Patrika*, July 14, 1938.
64. Ritan, *Football*, 24–5.
65. This section resonates some of the arguments and media extracts which I shared with my co-author Boria Majumdar in *Goalless!*, Chapter 5.
66. Majumdar and Bandyopadhyay, *Goalless!*, Chapter 5.
67. Ibid.
68. Bengal's marginalization in Congress-led nationalist politics was well-discussed in Gallagher, 'Congress in Decline'. For details on the Bengal Congress' growing rift with the central leadership, see Chatterji, *Bengal Divided*, 18–54, 103–49. In his two-volume autobiographical work published at the beginning of the 1930s, the famous scientist, Prafulla Chandra Ray, noted, 'The Bengali is now awakening to the fact that his leaders are very old men, that no one is taking their place, and that whether in Delhi or inside the Congress his representatives have little influence. The political centre of gravity is shifting northwards and westwards.' Ray, *Life and Experiences*, 471.
69. Chatterji, *Bengal Divided*, 55–102.
70. Ibid.
71. Led by Abdul Kasem Fazlul Haq, the Krishak Praja Party drew its strength from the mass following it enjoyed among Bengal's Muslim peasantry and intermediate share-holders.
72. Chatterji, *Bengal Divided*, 107–8.
73. Majumdar and Bandyopadhyay, *Goalless!*, 94.
74. *Amrita Bazar Patrika*, June 15, 1937, 11.
75. *Amrita Bazar Patrika*, June 12, 1937, 9.
76. Ibid., 11.
77. *Amrita Bazar Patrika*, June 13, 1937, 8.
78. *The Statesman*, June 16, 1937.
79. *Star of India*, June 16, 1937.
80. *The Statesman*, June 15, 1937.
81. Ibid.
82. Ibid.
83. Ibid.
84. Ibid.; emphasis added.
85. *The Statesman*, June 16, 1937.
86. Ibid.
87. *Mohammedan Sporting Club Souvenir*, 62.
88. *The Statesman*, June 17, 1937.
89. *Amrita Bazar Patrika*, June 17, 1937, 11.
90. *Star of India*, June 20, 1937.
91. Ibid.
92. Ibid.
93. *Amrita Bazar Patrika*, June 17, 1937.

94. *Amrita Bazar Patrika*, June 18, 1937.
95. Ibid.
96. *Amrita Bazar Patrika*, June 20, 1937.
97. *Amrita Bazar Patrika*, July 1, 1937.
98. *Amrita Bazar Patrika*, July 7, 1937.
99. Ibid.
100. Ibid.
101. Ibid.
102. Ibid.
103. Ibid.
104. *Star of India*, July 7, 1937.
105. Ibid.
106. Commenting on this injustice the *Star of India* wrote, 'At a stormy meeting of the Governing Body held last night, with the Maharaja of Santosh in the chair, at which the representative of the Mohammedan Sporting Club who is not a lawyer, had a rough time having repeatedly to seek the protection of the chair, which too was not always readily forthcoming. The Mohammedan Sporting Club was hanged, drawn and quartered for what? –for having, as luck would have it, created another piece of history in British Empire soccer, that of annexing the league championship for four years in succession.' *Star of India*, July 7, 1937.
107. *Mohammedan Sporting Club Souvenir*, 66.
108. Ibid.
109. Ibid.
110. *Amrita Bazar Patrika*, June 23, 1939, 14.
111. *Amrita Bazar Patrika*, July 6, 1939, 14.
112. *Amrita Bazar Patrika*, July 7, 1939, 14.
113. *Amrita Bazar Patrika*, July 10, 1939, 12.
114. Ibid.
115. *Amrita Bazar Patrika*, August 12, 1939, 14.
116. Majumdar and Bandyopadhyay, *Goalless!*, 101.
117. Beni Madhab Choudhury, Letter to the Editor, *Amrita Bazar Patrika*, July 4, 1934.
118. *Amrita Bazar Patrika*, June 6, 1938.
119. *The Statesman*, June 13, 1937.
120. *Amrita Bazar Patrika*, June 18, 1937.
121. *Bharatbarsha*, Asadha 1345 B.S. (1938), 150; translation mine.
122. *Bharatbarsha*, Bhadro 1345 B.S. (1938), 487–88; translation mine.
123. Ibid.
124. Ibid.
125. Ispahani, *Qaid-E-Azam Jinnah*, 12.
126. Shamsuddin, *Atit Diner Smriti*, 154–8.
127. Momen, *Muslim Politics*, 72.
128. Sen, *Muslim Politics*, 110–11.
129. A number of applications for allotment of the football ground were lying with the Government when the Muslim League came to power. Immediately, the Secretary of the Mohammedan Sporting Club wrote a letter for allotment emphasizing that this 'will remove the long-standing grievances of the Muslim community'. The sanctioning officer proposed to give plot no. 41 to the Mohammedan Sporting Club and the Kalighat Club as according to the existing rules a ground had to be shared by two clubs. However, Nazimuddin interfered and ordered the allotment of enclosure 41 exclusively to the Mohammedan Sporting Club and guaranteed ability to pay Rs.12,000 required for the development of the plot. At that time all the European and the Indian football clubs like the Dalhousie, Rangers, Mohun Bagan and East Bengal were sharing grounds in the Calcutta *maidan*. See *Government of Bengal, Home-Police Proceedings*, File 7-M of 1936, and File 7-M (1-3) of 1937, West Bengal State Archives, Kolkata.
130. With the advent of Mohammedan Sporting Club, the sporting situation in Calcutta *maidan* underwent change. In the mid-1930s just as the Congress was branded by the Muslim League as the Hindu organization, Mohun Bagan came to be called by the Muslims the Hindus' national team. The bitter political animosity then raging between the two communities was reflected in the soccer ties between Mohammedan Sporting and Muhun Bagan, which became the annual classic of the new era.
131. Das, *Communal Riots*, 170.

132. Sarkar, 'Communal Riots', 309.
133. *Note on Volunteer Organisations dated 11 September 1946. GB SB 'PM' Series. File No. 822/46II*, quoted in Chatterji, *Bengal Divided*, 235–6.
134. Das, *Communal Riots*, 170. Also see *Amrita Bazar Patrika*, July 8, 1946, 4; *File-5/27/46 Poll (I), the IB Daily Summary Information* of 8 July 1946, referred to in Das, *Communal Riots*, 170.
135. Nandy, 'Calcutta Soccer', 318.
136. Ibid.
137. Ibid.
138. Sultan Ahmed, present Secretary of the Mohammedan Sporting Club, has argued that the club's representative character always acted as a bar in any long-term efforts to revive its fortunes. Giving a contemporary example, he pointed out that the club could not find a viable sponsor since the late 1990s because it represents the Muslim community, and in effect a Muslim identity. Following Ahmed's argument, it can be inferred that most of the better Hindu Bengali footballers in post-colonial period might not have preferred to play for the club for its exclusively *Muslim* character until the 1980s when the club offered them a lucrative financial package. Interview with Sultan Ahmed, July 15, 2004.
139. The club next won the IFA Shield in 1947.
140. Majumdar and Bandyopadhyay, *Goalless!*, 102, argue on this line.

References

Ahmad, Sufia. *Muslim Community in Bengal: 1884–1912*. Dacca: Asiatic Press, 1974.
Chatterji, Joya. *Bengal Divided*. Cambridge: Cambridge University Press, 1994.
Das, Suranjan. *Communal Riots in Bengal*. New Delhi: Oxford University Press, 1991.
Dhaka Mohammedan Sporting Club er Sankhipta Itihas (A Brief History of the Dhaka Mohammedan Sporting Club). Dhaka: Mohammedan Sporting Club, 2004.
Gallagher, John. 'Congress in Decline: Bengal, 1930–1939'. *Modern Asian Studies* 7, no. 3 (1973): 589–645.
'History of the Club'. In *Mohammedan Sporting Club. Calcutta League Champions 1934-35. A Souvenir*. Calcutta: Mohammedan Sporting Club, 1935.
Ispahani, M.A.H. *Qaid-E-Azam Jinnah – As I Knew Him*. Karachi: Forward Publications Trust, 1966.
McPherson, Kenneth. *The Muslim Microcosm: Calcutta, 1918–1935*. Wiesbaden: Franz Steiner Verlag, 1974.
Majumdar, Boria, and Kausik Bandyopadhyay. *Goalless! The Story of a Unique Footballing Nation*. New Delhi: Penguin/Viking, 2006.
Mohammedan Sporting Club. Calcutta League Champions 1934–35. A Souvenir. Calcutta: Mohammedan Sporting Club, 1935.
Mohammedan Sporting Club Souvenir. Calcutta: Mohammedan Sporting Club, 1939.
Mohun Bagan Club Platinum Jubilee Souvenir. Calcutta: Mohun Bagan A.C., 1964.
Momen, Humaira. *Muslim Politics in Bengal: A Study of Krishak Praja Party and the Elections of 1937*. Dacca: Sunny House, 1972.
Nandy, Moti. 'Calcutta Soccer'. In *Calcutta: The Living City, 2: The Present and Future,* ed. Sukanta Chaudhuri, 316–20. Calcutta: Oxford University Press, 1990.
Ray, Prafulla Chandra. *Life and Experiences of a Bengali Chemist,* Vol. 1. Calcutta: Chuckervertty, Chatterjee & Co., Ltd., 1932.
RB. 'Indian Football and Boots'. *IFA Shield Souvenir 1977*. Calcutta: IFA, 1977.
Report of the Indian National Congress. 1–39, especially 24. New Delhi: Nehru Memorial Museum and Library, 1896.
Ritan, Lutfar Rahman. *Football*. Dacca: Bangla Academy, 1985.
Sarkar, Tanika. 'Communal Riots in Bengal'. In *Communal and Pan-Islamic Trends in Colonial India,* ed. Mushirul Haasan, 302–19. New Delhi: Manohar, 1985.
Sen, Shila. *Muslim Politics in Bengal*. New Delhi: Impex India, 1976.
Sengupta, Achintya Kumar. *Kallol Yug* (The Age of Kallol). Calcutta: M.C. Sarkar & Sons, 1950.
Shamsuddin, Abul Kalam. *Atit Diner Smriti* (Memories of Olden Days). Dacca, 1968.

Colonial legacy, minorities and association football in Kenya

Wycliffe W. Simiyu Njororai

Department of Physical Education, Wiley College, Texas, US

Historical back ground

Kenya is a country that has a good reputation earned through her sportsmen and women, especially the athletes in middle and long distance running.[1] However, it is association football (soccer) that captured the imagination of the nation as the number one sport. To understand the context of football in Kenya, one should have an idea of the country's ethnic composition, geographical/regional distribution and colonization. The country has an estimated population of 37,953,840 (July 2008 estimates),[2] comprising 42 ethnic groups with the dominant ones being Kikuyu 22%, Luhya 14%, Luo 13%, Kalenjin 12%, Kamba 11%, Kisii 6%, Meru 6%, other African 15%, non-African 1% (Asian, European and Arab).[3] The history of emigration shows that cushitic-speaking people from northern Africa moved into the area, now known as

Kenya, beginning around 2000 BC. Arab traders began frequenting the Kenyan coast around the first century. Kenya's proximity to the Arabian Peninsula invited colonization, and Arab and Persian settlements developed along the coast by the eighth century. During the first millennium, Nilotic and Bantu peoples moved into the region and Bantu now comprise three-quarters of Kenya's population. Nearly all Kenyans are black Africans, divided into about 42 ethnic groups belonging to three linguistic families: the Bantu, the Cushitic and the Nilotic. Language is a major characteristic of ethnic identity in Kenya. It is also through language that one's closeness to power is determined. Bantu-speaking Kenyans are divided into three different groups: the western group (Luhya), the central or highlands group (including the Kikuyu, the Kamba and other subgroups) and the coastal Bantu (Miji Kenda). Among Kenya's Nilotic speakers, the major groups are the River-Lake, or Western, group (Luo), the Highlands, or Southern, group (Kalenjin), and the Plains, or Eastern, group (Masai). The Cushitic-speaking groups include the Oromo and the Somali. The Kikuyu are Kenya's largest ethnic group and have utilized their numeric advantage to dominate the political and economic life in the country.

For much of Kenya's history, her ethnic groups were loose social formations, fluid and constantly changing. In the late nineteenth and early twentieth centuries British rule solidified ethnic identities among Kenya's people. Colonial administrators associated ethnic groups with specific areas of the country by designating zones where only people with a particular ethnic identity could reside. This pattern of ethnically based settlement and regionalism continued to persist in Kenya since it became independent, even though economic and political development increased mobility and urbanization among the country's inhabitants. The majority of Kikuyu live in the central province as well as central part of the Rift Valley; the majority of Luhya live in western province with others in northern western part of Rift Valley province; the Luo live in Nyanza province which is to the south western part of Kenya; the majority of Kamba live on the lower side of eastern province, and the majority of Kalenjin reside in Rift Valley province of the country.[4] Ethnicity was a vital instrument of divide and rule over the indigenous people by the colonial power and the same tactics were an important factor in Kenyan politics as well as football management.

Kenya's official languages are English and Swahili. Both are widely used for communication between members of different ethnic groups.[5] However, given its Bantu background, other people, especially the Nilotes, find it hard to master the language. This has made them a butt of humour and other political satire as Luo people find it hard to articulate themselves in the language. Nearly all of the African ethnic groups in Kenya also have their own languages, making for considerable linguistic diversity within the country. Many Kenyans speak three languages: the language of their particular ethnic group, Swahili and English. The social structure that evolved in Kenya during the colonial time emphasized race and class. The dominance of whites over blacks was reinforced through segregation of the races and, within the black African population, through various ethnic groups. Within each ethnic group, status was determined largely by wealth, gender and age. After Kenya gained independence in 1963, race ceased to be an important indicator of social status, but wealth, gender and ethnic identity remained significant. Today, a number of Kenya's problems result from disparities in wealth. These problems include pervasive urban and rural poverty, overcrowded and substandard housing in urban areas, and a relatively high rate of unemployment. In the 1990s, the country also witnessed periodic clashes between ethnic groups, particularly between Kalenjin and Kikuyu peoples in the Rift Valley province of Kenya. These two ethnic groups are to date the only ones to have produced a president[6] for the country. Hence the clashes between them have had a lot to do with political incitement and repossession of land.

Football is Kenya's most popular sport although it is the runners who have gained worldwide renown for their excellent performances in middle and long distance races around the globe.[7] Just as it is easy to analyse Kenyan politics along ethnic lines, the same applies to sport especially football. Given the regionalization of the different ethnic groups, it was easy for football to follow a similar pattern. However, a look at the evolution of football in the country should reveal the minority and regional orientation versus the dominant political class who had no time for the sport.

An overview of football development in Kenya and colonialism

Association football has always been the most popular sport in Kenya and its popularity cuts across ethnic, regional as well as class lines. This passion is not unique to Kenya. Football scholars have pointed to the widespread and popular nature of football across the globe.[8] Darby, for example, argues that, 'Since its inception in 1904, following an initiative by seven European nations, FIFA and the sport which it governs have taken on an almost universal significance and appeal.'[9] He argues that FIFA has more affiliates than the United Nations and the majority of the world's population takes a greater interest in the former than the latter. This demonstrates that football is a universal sport that is followed passionately by people from diverse backgrounds, nationalities and social classes. Mazrui has argued that football is popular in Kenya because it appeals to people of all socio-economic classes and cultures, unlike sports such as golf, tennis and swimming that are still not as universal in popularity.[10] Kenyans follow national and international football both in the print and electronic media with the World Cup being looked upon as the climactic event. During the World Cup, Kenyans flock to their favourite recreational sites en masse to root for their favourite teams. Kenyan fans are also known to be very passionate about their favourite local teams especially the national team, Harambee Stars. Important matches involving the national team always attract crowds of close to 60,000, with millions more watching on television. In the villages and urban areas, children can be seen playing with bundles of rags (fondly referred to as 'Lifundo' in Luhya and 'Ajwala' in Dholuo)[11] that are routinely improvised for a ball as others walk with radios to monitor the latest football news across the globe.

Kenya National Football League (renamed the Premier League) draws teams from Nairobi (the capital city), Nyanza, Western, Central, Central Rift Valley and Coast provinces and is played all year round. The premier division consisted of 20 teams for a long time, but currently FIFA has insisted that the country reduce the teams to 18 and later 16. Each year two teams are promoted from the provincial Leagues to the Premier League while the two teams with the worst record in the premier league are relegated to the provincial leagues. The League winners from the inception of the league to the present reveal the dominance by teams whose identity is rooted in Luhya (AFC Leopards formerly Abaluhya United FC) and Luo (Gor Mahia) ethnic groups. The two teams have won the league 12 times each. Other winners are Tusker (8), Ulinzi (3), Luo Union (2), Oserian (2), Nakuru All Stars (2), Sony (1), Utalii (1), Feisal (1), Sony Sugar (1) and Mathare United (1).[12]

Gor Mahia and AFC Leopards are traditionally Kenya's most popular club teams.[13] Matches pitting the two regularly draw huge crowds. Supporters of both

teams are among the most passionate in the world. The rivalry is somewhat comparable to that between Celtic and Rangers in Scotland, Boca Juniors and River Plate in
Argentina, Barcelona and Real Madrid in Spain. This passion for football and ethnic
identity has its roots in colonial times when there was huge rivalry between Elgon
Nyanza and North Nyanza regions. Elgon Nyanza comprised the Luhya, who eventually formed AFC Leopards, and North Nyanza was occupied by the Luo who formed
Gor Mahia. Football itself was introduced to Kenyans at the beginning of the twentieth
century by British settlers. Kenyans naturally took to the sport due to the simplicity of
its nature. The game was introduced by missionaries, administrators, teachers and
farmers.[14] The game of football, which is simple to follow and easy to play, was a
vital instrument used by the British in their efforts to assert imperial hegemony and
racist discrimination. The British often imposed over-arching constraints on the
organization and control of the game in the country and elsewhere in the colonial terri-
tories.[15] The game was enthusiastically adapted by Kenyans of Luhya, Miji Kenda
and Luo origins even as the dominant Kikuyu ethnic group shunned the sport.
Competitive football, however, started in 1923 with the formation of the Arab and
African Sports Association. This marked a major departure by the indigenous people
to assert their authority in the management of sport. Football was a major beneficiary
as by 1924, a Kenyan team toured Uganda for the first international assignment.
However, the team comprised of players from different races including the minority,
but politically dominant, White Settlers. The select side's tour of Uganda in 1924 set
the stage for the inauguration of the Gossage Cup in 1926 involving both the countries. Tanzania and Zanzibar joined the annual competition in 1945 and 1947 respectively. In 1966 the cup gave way to the East Africa Challenge Cup and eventually in
1973 to the East and Central Africa Senior Challenge Cup.[16] This competition continues to be held on an annual basis involving countries in the East and Central African
region comprising Eritrea, Djibouti, Ethiopia, Kenya, Tanzania, Uganda, Rwanda,
Sudan, Burundi, Somalia and Zanzibar.[17]

In the 1940s and 1950s, the Kenya national team had outstanding players in their
ranks such as Shem Chimoto, Elijah Lidonde and Peter Oronge. Club teams competed
in the Remingtone Cup organized by the governing body of soccer, the Kenya
Football Association (KFA). Teams from Coast Province, in particular Liverpool
(later renamed Mwenge) and Feisal, dominated the local scene, producing classy players like Kadir Farah, Ahmed Breik, Ali Sungura and Ali Kadjo. Joe Kadenge was
arguably Kenya's most accomplished player of the 1960s. To date most of the
outstanding players to ever come out of Kenya have their indigenous origins among
Luhya and Luo and others from the Miji Kenda from the Coast Province, and Kisii
from Nyanza province. The dominant Kikuyu and their distant cousins Meru, Embu
and Kamba, Kalenjin, Cushites, Masai, Turkana, Teso, Pokots, Taita and others have
not had a significant presence on the Kenyan soccer map. The adoption of soccer by
the Luhya, Luo and Miji Kenda has therefore to be understood from the perspective
of colonialism, ethnicity/regionalism and political marginalization.

It is hard to discuss the popularity of association football without referring to
colonialism, ethnicity and the reaction of the indigenous people to the sport. The
coming of the colonialists in the late nineteenth century greatly influenced the physical
activity orientation of the indigenous people in Kenya. Prior to colonization, most local
ethnic groups had distinct cultural beliefs and physical activity patterns that they reli-
giously followed. Some of the outstanding and universal cultural activities included
dancing, wrestling, hunting, boating and spear throwing. The coming of the white

settlers and missionaries discouraged the local dance and physical activities by declaring them pagan. They therefore opened schools and churches where the emphasis shifted to European-approved leisure pursuits including sports. The introduction of European sports in the school curriculum quickened the pace at which foreign sports were adapted including football, volleyball, netball and track and field. However, what attracted the imagination of the local people were soccer and track and field. Phyllis Martin's *Leisure and Society* offers a rich account of football's place in the colonized countries using Congo Brazzaville and Leopoldville. According to Martin, as noted by Straker, the spontaneous positive appraisal of football was due to the fact that 'Sport as physical, organized, and competitive exercise was not completely foreign to the young workers who watched Europeans play football.'[18] This is because certain values such as courage, endurance and individual skill were also qualities admired in village recreational activities. A similar observation has been made in the case of soccer diffusion into South Korea.[19] Thus the major differences between traditional physical activities and western sports were in the latter's structure, plethora of rules and time frame which reflected the industrial society in which they were born.[20] Thus the introduction of football, though a foreign sport, found a willing and enthusiastic African population whose athleticism perfectly fitted the new sport. Peter Mählmann, too, argues on the same line while looking at sport and modernization in Kenya.[21] He examined the role of traditional 'movement culture' in Kenya, which was closely connected to daily life and was differentiated according to age-groups and gender. He argued that patterns of movement also differed regionally according to topographical surroundings or climatic conditions. He goes on to argue that the introduction of a 'modern sport culture' in Kenya during the colonial period was superimposed on the traditional movement culture, but in the process, the former was modified to include traditional norms and values. The Africans were not therefore passive recipients of the new sports. They were active in appropriating the new form of recreation and, with their natural athleticism, were able to turn football into their own.

Paul Darby argues that football developed in a relatively unplanned, haphazard fashion and was enthusiastically embraced by indigenous populations in remote African towns and villages.[22] However, the introduction of the game in urban areas was more deliberate. According to Darby, the European colonialists utilized their hegemonic position to impose football for their own ends. Thus the settlers and missionaries introduced the game particularly for the 'training of African bodies in pursuit of moral and physical health … but above all of Christian character'.[23] The missionaries were particularly uneasy with the local traditions rooted in vigorous dancing. They, however, believed strongly in the civilizing and industrial mission of the British Empire. A missionary had to carry both the Gospel and modern culture to the Africans, who had an equal right to them. Modern culture entailed modern sport including football, netball, volleyball, cricket and rugby among others. Some of the missionaries and settlers had a tradition of sporting excellence in their student days and found Africa an ideal place to champion their sports ideology.[24] Thus sport, particularly football, was introduced to the Africans as a useful way for newly arrived athletic missionaries to establish positive contact with the African pupils. Testing of muscle and skill on a football field could, in the words of Hokkanen, 'contribute to or reinforce a notion of physical equality between African and Scottish "Lads", rare during a time when both missionary and imperial propaganda ethnocentrically exaggerated the physical differences between the Europeans and the Africans, to the latter's disadvantage'.[25]

In colonial Kenya, centres of academic excellence such as Alliance High School, Maseno, Kagumo, Cardinal Otunga- Mosocho, Saint Mary's, Yala, St Patricks and Iten, among others, were also pioneer centres of sports excellence as well as religious discourse. The missionary leaders felt strongly that the civilizing mission include an inculcation of the British passion for sport and discipline.[26] Thus, throughout Kenya, most schools were established with a mandatory provision of sports infrastructure including football, volleyball, netball for girls and track and field. The inclusion of physical education in the curriculum via physical training and gymnastics added to the athletic ideology that characterized British hegemony.[27] To add to the athleticism ideology, the school curriculum also emphasized industrial education for acquisition of crafts and technical skills. Mählmann further writes that Britain promoted exclusive and prestigious sports because they were cheaper to run in Kenya than in the home country.[28] Football and athletics were thought to be fit for 'natives'. Sport in the formal education system was used chiefly as a means to achieve order and discipline. Practicing Western sports helped to internalize norms of Western superiority and values connected with sports.

Outside the school system, the role of football came to represent a site for generating resistance to colonialism and promoting nationalist aspirations. On the whole, therefore, the British introduction of football to indigenous Kenyans can be aptly summarized in the words of Darby as 'Eurocentric, patronizing and missionary style'.[29] But regardless of the British motive for introducing football, the indigenous people enthusiastically appropriated the game to promote not only their nationalistic identity but also engendered a regional and ethnic orientation by the time of independence. One of the characteristic features of modernization which compelled the indigenous people, especially males, to move from villages to urban centres was the issue of taxation. The introduction of taxes, especially the poll or hut tax, forced men to migrate in search of jobs in urban areas and plantation farms, owned by the settlers in the central highlands.[30] While away from their rural homes, the male youth found plenty of free time to engage in the exotic pastime of playing football leading to the formation of teams on the basis of regional and ethnic origins as they had a common language.

In an attempt to explain the enormous enthusiasm for football in Africa, Straker appropriately argues that football constituted a domain of action where players and referees shared a common knowledge of clear-cut, universal rules. He goes on to say:

> Whereas the daily and seasonal routine of the urban wage-seeker was dictated by fluctuations in investments and initiatives completely beyond his[31] control, football constituted a space where the individual player could deploy his energies as he saw fit. The sport presented a possibility of reclaiming control over one's body and time. Teamwork and discipline were ineluctable aspects of any game, but what a difference to give and take commands in relation to a goal one has willingly chosen to pursue with fellow African players, rather than according to the externally imposed hierarchies of the workplace. In football, radically unlike the workplace, one wilfully directed one's pursuit of the mission at hand at every moment.[32]

Football, therefore, provided a medium that brought out the free expression of the African players. It was a freedom they found curtailed elsewhere including work and in the community where the colonial rules were strict. The difference in approach to the game was captured by Straker, who argued that Africans played the game for fun and were unwilling to be regimented by whites in training sessions. The Europeans, on the other hand, emphasized inculcation of values such as team spirit, perseverance and fair play. It is interesting to note that the approach to the game by Africans in the colonial period has persisted to the modern day where African players are accused of being naive tactically and playing to entertain rather than to win. Versi describes how Joe Kadenge, one of the best dribblers to ever emerge from Kenya, received a pass, eluded defenders including the goal keeper but instead of scoring he retreated to outside the penalty area and proceeded to dribble past the defenders again before scoring. When he was asked about it, he said the fun was not in scoring, it was in beating an opponent hands down.[33] That experience resonates with many African players who place emphasis on free expression as exemplified by J.J. Okocha and many African players who are now in high demand in Europe and elsewhere. A BBC dispatch on Okocha highlights the unique African approach to football play:

> There's always a sense of anticipation among Nigeria fans whenever Austin 'Jay-Jay' Okocha touches the ball. The sublime skills of the Paris St Germain midfielder have drawn favourable comparisons with the very best of South American football. He is the man whom his fellow countrymen believe can really deliver African success at the World Cup finals this summer … the television cameras loved to dwell on his spectacular moves. Okocha has it all, from his exquisite back heels and dummies to stylish passing. Few would deny he is the most gifted player Nigeria has seen for many years … The 28-year-old is sometimes criticised by his coaches for being too ambitious with his dribbling and is sometimes accused of playing to entertain the fans. But that is the essence of 'Jay-Jay' Okocha.[34]

To the African player, therefore, the joy of the game was, and continues to be, in the self expression as opposed to the instrumental role of imposing discipline desired by the Europeans. Straker elaborates on this struggle over whether football constituted a vehicle for the extension of colonial power or whether it was a space where that very power would be revised, subverted or altogether suspended. According to him, the more practice of football generated distance and difference from the rhythms and clearly restrictive and more ambiguous laws of the colonial order, the more pleasure it could return to the African players and spectators. This was indeed a fascinating aspect of football in the colonial period and to some extent continues to play out in stadiums where unpopular politicians in government are jeered and opposition leaders given standing ovations. Thus it is interesting that a rule, which governed sport, created and imported by Europeans became a means for Africans to create spaces in which the onerous powers of European imperialism were deflected.[35] The soccer stadium is a vital medium for expressing dissent and displeasure against the political class, administrative control and power. Football is, therefore, the medium and symbol of resistance as well as freedom. The stadium remains the ideal site as there are no restrictions on self expression. The large gatherings at the stadium were an alternative to the political rallies which were subject to intense security restrictions and vetting by agents of the state and the political class.

The free expression against the colonial powers was however channelled in a new direction with the onset of international football. As a nation, Kenya had to play against other countries starting with Uganda and later Tanzania and Zanzibar in the East African challenge Cup.[36] The formation of the national team necessitated the pulling together of resources to face a common opponent from a different country. As a nation, Kenya struggled to dominate the East African region as Uganda posed a huge challenge.[37] Given the rivalry of the two countries on the soccer field and the free social and economic ties, there were passionate debates and conversations over the outstanding players of the day. Indeed, radio broadcasts of Gossage football matches were widely followed into the independent days. Due to the emigration of the labour force into urban areas and the coffee plantations around Nairobi, a lot of the Luhya and Luo people found themselves playing the game in their free time. They formed teams based on their ethnic and even sub-ethnic groupings including Maragoli, Samia, Bukusu Brotherhood, among others. In the cities, football provided an avenue for freedom and identity. The balkanization of the teams on ethnic and sub-ethnic lines was tacitly supported and encouraged by the colonial government. The tacit colonial support was consistent with their imperialist strategy of divide, conquer and rule. This meant that it was easier for the colonial government and her agencies to govern when the indigenous people were divided rather than united. However, most local trade union leaders and emerging politicians identified with the teams by providing material support. For the indigenous politicians, such an association was critical in articulating not only their ethnic nationalism but also political activism against the imperialist Government and her discriminatory policies and practices.

Colonial governance therefore heavily relied on a system of divide, conquer and rule. According to Raila Odinga, colonialism and the earlier slave trade were closely linked as the fundamental philosophy underpinning both was to divide and segregate human beings by skin colour and race.[38] Under this philosophy, the Caucasians were assumed to be the 'superior' race and the Africans, or the so-called Blacks, were considered to be an 'inferior' race at best. This racist notion informed everything the colonial administration did in Africa, especially in Kenya. Accordingly, at the top of the chain were the Caucasians who consisted mainly of the colonial administrators, the settlers, business people and missionaries. In the middle were the Asian communities mostly brought to Africa as indentured labour. And at the bottom were the indigenous communities whose job was to work the farms and provide for the comfort and wealth of the colonialists. The indigenous communities were dictated to about work or the profession to follow and where not to venture. For instance, they decided which communities would be recruited into the armed forces and the police force and which ones would work in their farms and homes. Odinga further argues that all the artificial divisions of African communities into little silos within their own countries were meant to serve the political, military and economic interests of the colonial powers.[39] They were also meant to breed mistrust and resentment between communities to make it harder for them to join forces to reclaim their countries or to liberate themselves. In Kenya, for example, with the start of the war for national independence, popularly known as the Mau Mau war for national liberation, the Kikuyu community who formed the bulk of that uprising were virtually separated from other Kenyans and mostly held in massive concentration camps. Tens of thousands of Kenyans of Kikuyu nationality were rounded up from the urban centres and taken to those camps. These were very deliberate acts of division aimed at weakening communities and stopping them from uniting for the common purpose liberation.[40] This separation of the Kikuyu meant that the Luhya and Luo, who had a considerable presence in the city and plantation farms, were encouraged to engage in western-approved recreation pursuits especially football. Additionally, the colonial government, which did not encourage political parties, supported formation of ethnic-welfare associations such as Abaluhya and Luo Union of East Africa. These welfare associations eventually found space for expression through the football clubs they sponsored.

By the end of the colonial period in 1963 when the country gained independence, Kenya had already established a formal football structure at national level. Kenya Football Association was formed in 1956 and actively promoted local competitions including the Remingtone Cup and participation by the national team in the Gossage cup at the regional level. The formation of the national federation was the result of a joint initiative by the local football leaders and colonial settlers.

Thus it can be argued that the British introduced football as a medium of strategic cultural imperialism, which elicited enthusiastic acceptance by a wide majority of youth in school and urban areas and at the same time fostered new found ethnic identity via team formations and nationalistic feeling towards the national team by the ordinary citizenry. Through the colonial policy and practice of divide and rule, and the political suppression of the day, football became an alternative avenue for ethnic identity, nationalism and resistance especially for the Luo and Luhya, who were encouraged by the colonialists. What was a colonial strategy was therefore capitalized upon to voice resistance and cement ethnic loyalty through football club formation.

The minority question and football at Independence

This essay approaches the definition of minority from an American dictionary's perspective. The dictionary meaning is: 'an ethnic, racial, religious or other group having a distinctive presence within a society; a group having little power or representation relative to other groups within a society'.[41] This is slightly different from the known practice where 'minorities' are defined as ethnic, religious or linguistic groups, living among a 'majority' group in considerable and justified fear of persecution. Examples of the latter definition include Jews and Gypsies in Europe, blacks and Asians in America. This is also the situation of non-Muslims living in any Muslim-majority country, such as Coptic Christians in Egypt, Christians in Lebanon, and Hindus in Bangladesh and Pakistan. These real 'minorities' have always been the target of ruffians from the 'majority' group. A good populist test of a group's minority status is how the world, including the national media and international opinion, perceives their oppression. If they are brutalized, and nobody cares, then they are clearly a minority. This is what has happened, for instance, in Sudan's Darfur region: blacks being terrorized by Arabs. This was also the case for a long time with South Africa's blacks under apartheid: they were really a 'minority' even though they were numerically a majority.[42]

However, in this essay, 'minority' is conceptualized as an ethnic group having a distinctive presence within a society yet having little political power relative to other groups within a society. The Penguin English Dictionary further defines 'minority' as the state of being the smaller of the two groups constituting a whole or a group of people who share common characteristics or interests, differing from those of the majority of a population. Related to the concept of minority is that of ethnicity. Kenya, as already pointed out, is a nation of many ethnic groupings each with a distinct language and cultural practices. Amir Ben-Porat has extensively explained the place of ethnicity in football.[43] I will therefore borrow heavily from Ben-Porat to illustrate the place of ethnicity and the perceived notion of minority in Kenyan football. Ben-Porat argues that the entire debate on ethnicity is epitomized by the demarcation of inter-ethnic borders or by an ongoing struggle between at least two ethnic groups to specify their social territory. There is thus a clear distinction between 'us' and 'them'.[44]

Ben-Porat advances a four point clarification of the concept of ethnicity.[45] It is quite reasonable to suggest that the struggle on ethnic boundaries may, in a certain historical context, be intertwined with elements of nationality. This appropriately referred to the minority Arabs inside Israel. Ethnicity exists in a state of competition. This is an essential element in any definition of ethnicity. In practice, this competition occurs between definite ethnic categories over issues such as neighbourhoods, economic resources and political hegemony. Competition can be of consensual or conflictual mode. The third meaning of inter-ethnic relationships is made concrete by dependency relations behind which lurks a tension that is a constant potential for conflict. In this set up, there is a persistent process of consensus-construction by compliance or exploitation. The fourth meaning is where inter-ethnic boundaries are marked by distinctive identification of each group marked by a whole set of symbols, signs and practices.

In the context of Kenyan football, the point of departure that is relevant is that of ethnicity in the face of competition and inter-ethnic boundaries marked by administrative identification of each group, which again is marked by a set of symbols, signs and practices. For a long time, the Luhya and Luo have competed as to who ranks next to the dominant Kikuyu as the most populous group. Additionally, the fact that the dominating club sides are either Luhya or Luo in ethnic affiliation brings out the obvious contest as to who is the dominant force in football. Thus, to further assert themselves, there is the added distinctive trait of belonging and identifying with either AFC Leopards for the Abaluhya or that of Gor Mahia which represents the Luo ethnic group. The struggle for football dominance has sociological significance. Indeed sport is considered by many as an arena of inter-cultural struggle. Sports competition opposes 'us' to 'them' and participates in the reproduction of boundary demarcations on the basis of factors such as ethnicity, religion, nationality and even colour.[46] Through sports competition, certain collective identities are reinforced. According to Ben-Porat:

> Soccer is considered to be the most popular spectator sport in the world and it incorporates some characteristics that can be used for purposes other than mere sport, such as, maintaining/reproducing ethnic-national identification within a society in which ethnicity, nationalism and citizenship do not fully converge.[47]

Some key assumptions include that of adaptation and assimilation on the one hand and that of protest and conflict on the other. According to the adaptation and assimilation assumption, ethnic minorities are highly willing to integrate by adopting the society's values and certain practices which symbolize nativity. The assimilation-adaptation assumption allows for both the togetherness and the loneliness. By participating and proving their excellence in football, the Luhya and Luo became assimilated and adapted to the colonial modernization strategy. However, through the formation of ethnic football clubs, they managed to sustain their autonomy. The second assumption relates to protest and conflict. Football is considered to be an instrument for protest and for maintaining a particular ethnic identity. Thus, according to Ben-Porat, ethnic-based soccer clubs are an effective means of maintaining a voluntary seclusion which keeps the ethnic group together.[48] Being a worldwide phenomenon, the existence of such clubs represents something profound in the social system such as class structure or ethnic division of labour. Thus one can argue that ethnic soccer clubs are a symptom of a cultural or political division of labour. Furthermore, this division reproduces the inter-ethnic boundaries; different social identities are formulated and reproduced on the opposite sides of these boundaries.

Given the above scenario which conceptualizes ethnic football teams as a medium of identity and integration, football in Kenya took on a different dimension by the early 1960s. The formation of the teams was rooted in ethnic identity and even when each sub-ethnic group could not bring about the desired impact, a merger of sub-ethnic groupings was instigated to form one solid team especially in the case of Luhya and Luo ethnic groups. The Luhya, Luo and the Miji Kenda share characteristics that place them in the minority class. These characteristics include the following:

- They all hail from the outlaying parts of the country far removed from the capital city and the seat of political and economic power which is dominated by the Kikuyu ethnic group and foreign-owned industries.
- They are less in numbers compared to the numerically strong Kikuyu.
- They have not held the reigns of power and therefore perceive themselves to be marginalized politically and economically during the colonial period as well as in the successive independent governments of Jomo Kenyatta, Daniel Arap Moi and later of Mwai Kibaki.
- They all had dynamic and vigorous physical activity-based recreational lifestyle before the onset of colonization and hence were best suited for the athleticism demanded by the game of soccer which explains their adoption and subsequent dominance of the game.

Whereas the Luhya and the Miji Kenda originally belonged to the Kenya African Democratic Union, which was a party for minority ethnic groups just before and immediately after independence, the Luo teamed with the Kikuyu in Kenya African National Union which formed the first government but was soon marginalized when the Vice President, Oginga Odinga, a Luo, resigned from the government over ideological differences and formed a new political party but was subsequently detained.

National League and team formation

Although football had been immensely popular in Kenya for several decades, the Kenya Football Association could not yet establish a nationwide national league by the time of independence. The idea to start a countrywide league was mooted at a meeting held at the Railways Club and attended by football leaders in Nairobi in the early 1960s. The historic meeting was attended by Jimmy McFarnell (Convenor), Isaac Lugonzo, Williams Ngaah and Tony Pinto, among others.[49] A committee, headed by Lugonzo as founder-chairman with Pinto as secretary, was formed to work out the logistics of inaugurating and running the league. It was not until April 1963 that the idea became a reality when 10 clubs lined up for the inaugural championship. Nairobi with seven teams – Luo Union, Maragoli United (later renamed Imara United), Marama, Nairobi Heroes, Bunyore, Kakamega and Samia Union – had the lion's share of the teams taking part in the league. Coast Province provided two sides – Liverpool (which was later renamed Mwenge) and Feisal – while Rift Valley had one team, Nakuru All-Stars, to complete the original line-up. No teams were drawn from Nyanza, Western, Central and Eastern Provinces at that time. Luo Union, which represented members of the Luo community from what was then the North Nyanza district, was the brainchild of Mr Oginga Odinga, Vice President of Kenya. It is also worth pointing out that other than Luo Union, all the six others from Nairobi belonged to the Luhya ethnic group and appropriately named after the respective ethnic sub-groupings.

The league started with four matches – two in Nairobi and two in Mombasa. The legendary Joe Kadenge, who turned out for Maragoli United, scored the fastest goal of the league. Nakuru All-Stars, coached by Ray Bachelor, colonial Rift Valley provincial sports officer, won the first league title. Luo Union, inspired by some of their talented stars such as Daniel Nicodemus, Stephen Yongo, Fred Siranga and James Siang'a, became the second winners of the league in 1964 and capped a glorious season by beating the Ethiopian national team. Their strength lay in the fact that it was the only team sponsored by the Luo community compared to a fragmented Luhya who had several sub-ethnic sponsored teams.

The dominance exhibited by Luo Union, which drew players and supporters from the Luo community, posed a challenge to the Luhya community who had several, but weaker teams. The Luhya leaders therefore came together to oversee the formation of Abaluhya United Football Club (later renamed AFC Leopards FC)[50] by merging the Luhya clubs, including Bunyore, Kakamega, Marama, Bunyatso, Samia Union and Bukusu Brotherhood. The motto of the team was 'Obulala na amani', i.e. 'unity is strength'. This was an appropriate rallying call for all the Luhya to identify with and support the football team. This was a significant departure given that the different Luhya sub-ethnic groups were merging to form one solid team under the Abaluhya umbrella. This represented the majority of football fans from the Luhya ethnic group.[51] However, one sub-ethnic group, Maragoli, who represented members of the Maragoli community, refused to dissolve. Abaluhya debuted in the league in 1965 and finished fifth. Feisal from Mombasa won the league with Luo Union second on goal difference. In 1966, Abaluhya, with gifted and outstanding players like Jonathan Niva, Joe Kadenge, Anthony Mukabwa, Daniel Anyanzwa, Moses Wabwayi, Charles Makunda, Livingstone Madegwa and John Nyawanga, clinched the league title and went on to retain it the following year.[52]

In the mid-1960s, when the historic political rivalry between two Luo giants, Tom Mboya and Jaramogi Odinga, came to a head, it split Luo Union right down the middle, giving birth to a splinter group called Luo Sports Club, sponsored by Tom Mboya. Due to Tom Mboya's overwhelming popularity and influence in Nairobi, the younger and much weaker Luo Sports club – not the mother-club Luo Union – was the one included in the Kenya National Football League (KNFL) programme. Thus excluded, most of the great Luo Union names decamped to Kisumu Hot Stars to be able to participate in the Kenya National Football League. They included William 'Chege' Ouma, the goal wizard; John 'Hatari' Owiti, a great defender; James Siang'a, the national goalkeeper, and Chris Obure. Travelling to Kisumu every Friday for practice and competition, however, proved to be too taxing. Luo leaders such as Tom Mboya, Bethuel A. Ogot, Zack Ramogo and Peter Anyumba, persuaded all former Luo Union players to form a single club. Thus in 1968, Luo sports club and Luo Union merged to form Gor Mahia under the sponsorship of Luo Union of East Africa, which was an umbrella welfare organization bringing all Luo people of East Africa together. It was a move in the right direction as Gor Mahia made a dream debut, winning the league title on their first attempt. The late 1960s also saw the formation of Ramogi FC which represented the large Luo community then residing in Mombasa.[53]

Nakuru All-Stars won the league and folded up soon after clinching the title in 1969. Abaluhya regained the league title in 1970 – with an unbeaten record. The years between 1970 and 1998 saw the dominance of both Gor Mahia and AFC Leopards teams with the occasional threat from Kenya Breweries, later renamed Tusker FC. But regardless of the number of teams, players who dominated the various teams tended to come mainly from the Luhya and Luo communities. The dream of every player growing up was to eventually play for either Gor Mahia or AFC Leopards. The sheer dominance of the Luhya and Luo reflected the celebration of regionalism and ethnicity. The formation of these teams constituted a pivotal space of collective social action and differentiation marked with intense allegiances not seen in other clubs. The merger of Luhya and Luo teams to form large ethnic-based football clubs had enormous social ramifications. The Psychological Continuum Model (PCM) advanced by Funk and James in 2001 may be used here to explain the awareness, attraction, attachment and team allegiance of the members of the Luhya and Luo communities towards AFC Leopards and Gor Mahia respectively.[54]

The PCM outlines a developmental progression that describes how an individual goes from initial awareness of a team, to attraction, to attachment and ultimately to team allegiance. The progression represents the formation of a connection with a sports team and identifies various facilitators including demographics, community events, advertising and individual motives that influence continued formation and loyalty. As such, this framework is useful in understanding how ethnically inspired team formation and the success in competition served to sustain team loyalties that were fiercely guarded.

The initial awareness level within the PCM is achieved primarily through an awareness process that describes how and when an individual first learns that certain sports teams exist, but does not have a specific favourite. According to Funk *et al.*, awareness outcomes reflect the level of general knowledge of sport and teams created by socializing agents such as parents, friends, school, media and events.[55] The level of awareness is even more prominent given the value of the sport and particularly the team in the society. Given the ethnic orientation of the teams (AFC Leopards and Gor Mahia), the awareness was created by the parents, siblings and peers as they talked of their favourite 'local' players. A growing Luhya or Luo kid was made aware of the family loyalty very early in life. The success in the league and regional competitions made it even easier to identify with the respective teams.

Given the family and peer socialization into team loyalty, attraction followed as a matter of course. Having already been christened in the team by family members, peers and school environment and reinforced by team heroes or role models from the community, it was a matter of time to desire to not only passionately follow the team but also to dream of playing for them. According to Funk *et al.*, attraction is reached when an individual forms an emotional response towards a team based on positive or negative evaluation of features associated with it. Thus the attraction to AFC Leopards or Gor Mahia was solidified through their success stories in the league at national and regional level. Spectators follow a team for various reasons: achievement, escape, drama, social interaction, attachment to players, and communal identity. All these factors combine to make an individual commit himself/herself to a favourite team. At this point, the loyalty is such that regardless of the results, an individual is attached to the team. Several studies have looked at the construct of attachment. Preliminary evidence suggests that the level of psychological significance and value connected to a team accounts for how attraction proceeds into attachment. According to Funk and James, attachment develops when the team elicits responses and tendencies from memory that strengthen internal links between the team and other important attitudes, values and beliefs (core characteristics related to self-concept).[56] This attachment is continually activated by more exposure which serves to strengthen the connecting links and embed the team firmly within the individual's larger associative network, eventually creating a more complex network and stronger relationship. Furthermore, a multitude of associations linked to the team would probably be accompanied by increased levels of team-related knowledge, more direct experience with the team, and certainty of one's evaluation of the team. For AFC Leopards and Gor Mahia, the attraction of players who often came from the neighbourhood made individuals become attached to the team as they came to be associated with success, nostalgia or community pride. These teams fostered movement to the attachment level by playing matches at strategic locations in their regional strong holds, bringing star players close to the people/fans, so as to encourage direct experience with the team (e.g., attending games rather than listening on radio, meeting the players), and developing an image that is valued within the community (e.g., hard work, giving back to the community). According to Funk and James, attachment may result from a collective strengthening of various physical and psychological features linking the team to other important attitudes, beliefs and values. Apart from countrywide visits, especially in areas of strong support, media publicity and promotion of the local derbies between the two giant clubs AFC Leopards and Gor Mahia also drew fans closer, thus enhancing team identity and attachment. To affirm team attachment and therefore allegiance, one chose to pay to be a member or attended matches whenever the team played in the vicinity, and even bought team scarves and kit to identify oneself fully with the team.

Allegiance represents the ultimate level of team support, loyalty or devotion to some one, group, cause or the like. As Funk and James argue, the notion that allegiance represents loyalty to a group is important because the PCM focuses on an individual's loyalty to a team. Allegiance therefore is understood as a reflection of the extent to which an attitude is persistent, resistant and influences cognition and behaviour. These four strength-related consequences are critical indicators of a strong, stable and continuous relationship with a football team and are viewed as determinants of loyalty. The allegiance perspective still encompasses the composite approach to understanding loyalty, but places emphasis on a reciprocal relationship that exists between how attitudes and behaviours shape strong, stable and continuous involvement with a team. The behavioural component could involve critical behaviour (e.g., purchase of ticket or merchandise, attendance at a sport event), or a behaviour that is expressed with some duration in a situational context (e.g., watching the team every Sunday on television).[57] In the context of AFC Leopards and Gor Mahia, the level of allegiance or loyalty was evident in passionate and committed following to live matches and in the purchase of basic merchandise as scarves, gaps and T-shirts. However, the administrative side of the teams never capitalized fully to institute a merchandizing portfolio that was strong enough on the market.

Thus the PCM conceptual framework explains the deep and passionate fan base of the two football teams that dominated the football landscape in Kenya for decades till about 1997 when they began to collapse.

Conclusion

Association football was introduced by the colonialists in Kenya where the game found an enthusiastic indigenous people of mostly Luhya, Luo and Miji Kenda origins who quickly turned the sport into their own. The game found easy acceptance as it demands athletic abilities and movements, which found resonance with a well established pattern of rigorous indigenous physical activity. Additionally, the local migration patterns in reaction to colonial rule that demanded taxes forced the youth to move to cities to find employment. Within the cities, the need for social cohesion found football as an appropriate medium for people from varied ethnic groups to come together and play the game. This encouraged ethnic-based team formation which characterized post-independent Kenya till the 1970s when corporate sponsored teams surfaced. The football success and dominance of the politically marginalized Luhya and Luo in terms of political authority and geographical distance from the seat of power in Nairobi can therefore be analysed in the light of a multiplicity of colonial legacies such as region-alization, urbanization, schooling, Christianity, divide and rule as well as political and demographic status as minorities. Football was therefore an imperialist tool that the indigenous people adopted and appropriated to solidify their ethnic and national orien-tation. The social cohesion and identity that coalesced around the ethnic-based teams is in line with the PCM conceptual framework which explains the deep and passionate fan base of the two football teams that dominated the football landscape in Kenya.

Notes

1. Njororai, 'Analysis of Kenya's Performance'; see also Sobania, *Culture and Customs*; Entine, *Taboo*.
2. See CIA World Factbook (2008). Kenya Demographics Profile. http://www.indexmundi. com/kenya/demographics-profile.html (accessed 17 September 2009).
3. See the population distribution map of Kenya at http://mapup.com/africa/kenya.html. Also see Crandall, *Culture Grams*, 77–80.
4. See *World Fact Book*. Also see Sobania, *Culture and Customs*.
5. Sobania, *Culture and Customs*.
6. The first President was Jomo Kenyatta, a Kikuyu; succeeded by Daniel Moi, a Kalenjin, and who was in turn succeeded by Mwai Kibaki, another Kikuyu.
7. Njororai, 'In Pursuit of Performance Excellence'.
8. Darby, 'Africa's Place'; Lee, Jackson and Lee, 'South Korea's "Glocal" Hero'.
9. Darby, 'Africa's Place', 36.
10. Mazrui, *The Africans*.
11. Improvised balls are made out of clothing, paper and wrapped tightly in a polythene paper and reinforced by a sisal string all around to form a mesh like appearance. When nicely done, the improvised ball can bounce and can withstand different weather conditions. The improvised ball is slightly larger than a tennis ball and is useful in the initial mastery of dribbling, juggling, control and kicking skills, which are fundamental in the technical evolution of a football player.
12. This is according to an account posted at http://kenyapage.net/football and retrieved on 19 April 2007.
13. Sobania, *Culture and Customs*; Versi, *Football in Africa*.
14. Versi, *Football in Africa*.
15. Hokkanen, 'Christ and the Imperial Games Fields'.
16. Njororai, 'Analysis of Technical and Tactical Performance'.
17. See compiled results since 1926 at http://www.rsssf.com/tablese/eastcentrafr.html.
18. Straker, 'Popular Culture', 745.
19. Lee, Jackson and Lee, 'South Korea's "Glocal" Hero'.
20. Straker, 'Popular Culture'. Also see Martin, 'The Social History'. This paper was part of the project 'African Expressions of the Colonial Experience'. The main focus of this paper is recreational activities and in particular sport in colonial Brazzaville (Congo). The author discusses the origins of football in Brazzaville, its development in the 1930s, individuals and the role sport played in their future life as politicians, and the influence sport has on identity.
21. Mählmann, 'The Role of Sport'.
22. Darby, 'Africa and the "World" Cup'.
23. See Hokkanen, 'Christ and the Imperial Games Fields', 748.
24. Ibid.
25. Ibid.

26. See for details Mangan, *The Games Ethic*.
27. Mangan, *Athleticism*.
28. Mählmann, 'Sport as a weapon'.
29. Darby, 'Africa and the "World" Cup', 885.
30. See Sobania, *Culture and Customs*.
31. Note that the writer uses the male reference here to capture the male dominance of football at the time. However, football has now progressed even among the women.
32. Straker, 'Popular Culture', 10.
33. Versi, *Football in Africa*.
34. 'Wizard Okocha Casts his Spell'. BBC Sport, Thursday, April 11, 2002.
35. Straker, 'Popular Culture'.
36. W.W.S., 'The Diversity of Sport'.
37. The results at http://www.rsssf.com/tablese/eastcentrafr.html show that Uganda has been more dominant followed by Kenya in the East and Central African regional Senior Challenge Cup.
38. Odinga, 'What Role does Ethnicity Play'.
39. Ibid.
40. Ibid.
41. American Heritage dictionaries retrieved from http://www.answers.com/topic/minority?.
42. Alegi, *Laduma!*, 152. Also see a review of Alegi's book by Leslie Hadfield, *Impumelelo – The Interdisciplinary Electronic Journal of African Sports* 1 (2005) at http://www.ohiou.edu/sportsafrica/journal/volume.
43. Ben-Porat, 'Biladi, Biladi', 24.
44. Ibid.
45. Ibid.
46. Ibid. Also see Rhoden, *Forty Million Dollar Slaves*.
47. Ben-Porat, 'Biladi, Biladi'.
48. Ibid.
49. This is according to an account posted at http://kenyapage.net/football.
50. AFC Leopards was coined as 'All Footballers Club, Leopards', which in real sense matched with Abaluhya Football Club. Gor Mahia temporarily changed to 'Gulf Olympic Rangers' so as to retain their favourite 'Gor' tag. However, the President of Kenya, Hon. Daniel Arap Moi, later allowed Gor Mahia to revert to their name as it was the name of an individual and not an ethnic group. The change of name in 1980 was a result of a Presidential decree for all organizations with an ethnic name to drop and replace it with a more national or ethnic-neutral one. The President was asserting his political control and authority as by then the Kikuyu (Gikuyu), Embu, Meru and Kamba (Akamba) ethnic groups, who dominated power during the Jomo Kenyatta reign, had coalesced together under the acronym GEMA. The body had a lot of political and economic leverage and some powerful leaders were opposed to President Moi, a Kalenjin, succeeding Kenyatta, a Kikuyu when the latter passed away on 22 August 1978.
51. See http://kenyapage.net/football.
52. Ibid.
53. Ibid.
54. Funk and James, 'The Psychological Continuum Model'.
55. Funk *et al.*, 'The Impact of the National Sports Lottery'.
56. Funk and James, 'The Psychological Continuum Model'.
57. Ibid.

References

Alegi, Peter. *Laduma!: Soccer, Politics, and Society in South Africa.* Scottsville: University of Kwazulu-Natal Press, 2004.

Ben-Porat, A. 'Biladi, Biladi': Ethnic and Nationalistic Conflict in the Soccer Stadium in Israel'. *Soccer and Society* 2, no. 1 (2001): 19–38.

Crandall, D. *Culture Grams World Edition: Africa,* Volume 3. London: Axiom Press, 2004.

Darby, P. 'Africa's Place in FIFA's Global Order: A Theoretical Frame'. *Soccer and Society* 1, no. 2 (2000): 36–61.

Darby, P. 'Africa and the "World" Cup: FIFA Politics, Eurocentrism and Resistance'. *The International Journal of the History of Sport* 22, no. 5 (2005): 883–905.

Entine, J. *Taboo: Why Black Athletes Dominate Sports and Why We're Afraid to Talk About It.* New York: Public Affairs, 2000.

Funk, D.C., and J.D. James. 'The Psychological Continuum Model: A Conceptual Framework for Understanding an Individual's Psychological Connection to Sport'. *Sport Management Review* 4, no. 2 (2001): 119–50.

Funk, D.C., M. Nakazawa, D.F. Mahony, and R. Thrasher. 'The Impact of the National Sports Lottery and the FIFA World Cup on Attendance, Spectator Motives and J. League Marketing Strategies'. *International Journal of Sports Marketing & Sponsorship* (2006): 267–85.

Hokkanen, M. 'Christ and the Imperial Games Fields in South-Central Africa- Sport and the Scottish Missionaries in Malawi, 1880–1914: Utilitarian Compromise'. *The International Journal of the History of Sport* 22, no. 4 (2005): 745–69.

Lee, N., S.J. Jackson, and K. Lee. 'South Korea's "Glocal" Hero: The Hiddink Syndrome and the Rearticulation of National Citizenship and Identity'. *Sociology of Sport Journal* 24 (2007): 283–301.

Mählmann, Peter. 'The Role of Sport in the Process of Modernisation: The Kenyan Case'. *Journal of Eastern African Research and Development* 22 (1992): 120–31.

Mählmann, Peter. 'Sport as a Weapon of Colonialism in Kenya: A Review of the Literature'. *Transafrican Journal of History* 17 (1988): 152–71.

Mangan, J.A. *Athleticism in the Victorian and Edwardian Public School.* London: Cambridge, 1981.

Mangan, J.A. *The Games Ethic and Imperialism: Aspects of the Diffusion of an Ideal.* London: Frank Cass, 1998.

Martin, Pyhillis. 'The Social History of Leisure and Sport in Colonial Brazzaville'. Paper presented at the Seminar on *Popular Culture and Performance*, Boston University, May 11–12, 1989.

Mazrui, A.A. *The Africans: A Triple Heritage.* London: BBC Publications, 1986.

Odinga, R. 'What Role does Ethnicity Play in Africa's Elective Politics?' September 12, 2007. http://africanpress.wordpress.com.

Rhoden, W.C. *Forty Million Dollar Slaves: The Rise, Fall, and Redemption of the Black Athlete.* New York: Crown Publishers, 2006.

Sobania, N. *Culture and Customs of Africa: Culture and Customs of Kenya.* Westport, CT: Greenwood Press, 2003.

Straker, J. 'Popular Culture as Critical Process in Colonial Africa: A Study of Brazzaville Football. Impumelelo'. *The Interdisciplinary Electronic Journal of African Sports* 1 (2005). http://www.ohiou.edu/sportafrica/journal.

Versi, A. *Football in Africa.* London: Collins, 1986.

Njororai, W.W.S. 'Analysis of Technical and Tactical Performance of National Soccer Teams of Kenya, Germany and Argentina.'. PhD diss., Kenyatta University, Nairobi, 2000.

Njororai, W.W.S. 'The Diversity of Sport in Kenya'. In *Sport in Contemporary African Society: An Anthology,* ed. L. Amusa and A.L. Toriola, 199–229. Mokapane, South Africa: AFAHPER-S.D, 2003.

Njororai, W.W.S. 'Analysis of Kenya's Performance in Middle and Distance Races at the Olympic Games, 1956–2000'. *Nigerian Journal of Emotional Psychology and Sport Ethics* 6 (2004): 102–7.

Njororai, W.W.S. 'In Pursuit of Performance Excellence in Middle and Distance Running in Kenya'. *The Sport Supplement,* United States Sports Academy, February 15, 2007.

Not just for men: Israeli women who fancy football

Amir Ben-Porat

Department of Behavioural Sciences, Academic Studies, College of Management, Rishon Letzion, Israel

Introduction: his game, her game

The TV camera zooms in on the football crowd. Exultant and twisted male faces and frantic limbs fill the frame. Occasionally, one observes a soft face; a woman or young girl that the camera's eye honed in the vociferous crowd. The Israeli spectator at home is convinced that he is witnessing a gimmick or an anomaly. The (male) Israeli spectator is likely to believe that football is a man's game and the presence of 'the other sex' in the terraces is unnatural: 'What the hell is she doing in the stadium?' The English, Spanish or European spectators react differently. The presence of women in the football stadium is not bizarre for them. Indeed, female attendance at football games has always been much lower than that of men; however their presence is no longer occasional or unique. It appears that female attendance in the football stadium is growing concurrently with the emerging presence of middle-class fans in the football crowd, while the attendance of the lower class still remains dominant. It appears that the remains of the 'men's territory' – the football game – is being gradually encroached upon by women. These are not women in the ascribed status of a player's mother, daughter or girlfriend, but women as devoted and passionate fans of the game. It appears that throughout the western part of the globe as well as in some other parts of the world, women have become involved in football as players in their league and as fans in the terraces. At present they do not intend replacing men: they show no ambition of hegemony or domination in this game, but merely to be part of the game by their attendance in the stadium. The 'other sex'[1] is settled in the stadium's terraces, and by means of interaction-assimilation with the 'opposite sex' it creates its own identity as a football fan, clearly indicating that 'this game is not just for men'.

Considering both the descriptive (the narrative) and the explanatory aspects, women's relations to sport are basically the same as men's. These relations could be concretized at two levels: at the participant level, namely as athletes, and at the spectator level as fans. However, historically and sociologically, the accessibility of women to sport is not equal to that of men. Men had and still have the dominant position. In the past, the participation of women either as athletes or spectators was dependent on men's permission, namely the permission of men from the proper (higher) class. Based on this, it is justly assumed that women's 'relative autonomy' in sport, that is loosening their dependence on the opposite sex, and the creation of their own holding in sport (a process which also involves ethnic and class factors) was a consequence of women's liberation battles, mainly in politics.[2]

The point of departure of this essay is that everything that happens to women in sport is determined by certain parameters that set definite degrees of freedom for women in the present era. These parameters are controlled by males. Practically, although in general the domination of males over these parameters is weakening, in sport men are still in a dominant position, particularly regarding the game of football (soccer), thereby relegating women to a minority status. In many places worldwide, women's attendance in the football stadium is welcomed but regarded with suspicion and even as threatening. Men are still convinced that this game is theirs, they are the hosts and women are just guests. Women who support football clubs are more often required to demonstrate that their sympathy is genuine: not because of their boyfriends, not because of a family connection, and also not because of eroticism. Women in a 'men's game' must provide good reason for their attendance and fandom.

The status of women as sport spectators more or less parallels their attained status in the capitalist societies in Europe. In Victorian Britain, asserts Birley, 'In sport women's role was that of handkerchief-fluttering spectators'.[3] But from the middle of the nineteenth century some noticeable changes began to emerge in the status of the young generation of women. The acquisition of education 'produced girls of independent spirit'.[4] These girls refused to concede the place imposed upon them by men regarding (their) roles outside home, for example, their participation in sport, in school and in leisure.

Indeed, already in the Victorian era, women took (limited) part in a few of what were considered men's sports, such as hunting. Women of the upper classes in the USA and Britain rode bikes in public areas. Women played croquet. Women played field hockey and lawn tennis. Women from the upper classes escorted by men watched boxing contests.[5] In essence, sport was dominated by men of the upper classes and they set the limits on the participation/presence of women and also of men from lower classes.

Football became a coded game during the second half of the nineteenth century in Britain. At the same time it became a mass consumption sport for the lower classes, predominantly for males. Football was considered – by men and also by women – inappropriate for women. Males considered this game as their stronghold.

As noted above, the relationship between women and sport was formed concurrent to a parallel process of transformation in women's status in the entire social context in Europe and America.[6] The Feminist struggle for women's liberation spilled over to sport, most importantly to sports such as football, which were monopolized by men.

Since men refused to accept them in their clubs, women established their own sport clubs, including football clubs.

The feminist struggle accelerated during the second half of the twentieth century. The focus moved from Europe to the USA and the struggle became even more effective. Attempts to hold back female athletes in the Olympics were abandoned. The legislation of Title IX in 1972 enhanced the extensive process of female participation in high school and college sports. The model that was posed by the Communist states at that time was imitated in part by a few of the Western states. European and non-European states conceded to the changing status of women in sport.[7] Moreover, women began to participate in sports that were considered 'inappropriate' because of the aggression and physical elements inherent in these sports which included football, rugby and boxing.[8]

The bottom line is that toward the end of the twentieth century, women – mainly in the modern states – no longer needed a 'gender permit' to participate in sport. Equal but separate organizations had been formed. Nevertheless, domination was still in the hands of men: they set the parameters and the degrees of freedom in sport.

The history of the relations between women and football is similar in most of its features to that of women and sport in general. But some differences are observed. Football is a physical game. The physical side of football is not only reserved for the players participating in the game, but it is also effective regarding the crowd whose demographic composition are most vulnerable to aggression and militant behaviour.[9] Even after the 'Taylor Report' that required the stadiums to convert the standing zones into sitting areas, football spectatorship involves body contact and militant behaviour. In practice, the football stadium is a 'permission zone',[10] which allows certain norms of behaviour unacceptable outside the stadium, such as body gestures, rough language, etc. The permission zone became a hindrance for female participation or attendance. Hence, it is not accidental that female participation in football as players in their own clubs was/is their first priority: playing the game by means of their league enabled them to form and control their life as athletes and spectators. Playing football was a kind of assertion of independence in order to make the point that the game is not for men only. Probably unintentionally, with the establishment of women's football clubs a process of 'encroachment' – one of 'conquering men's territory' in the pitch and the terraces – began. Two factors are responsible for this: change(s) in the realm of history and the feminist struggle.

It has been argued that women's football emerged and expanded partially because during the First World War women replaced men's football with their teams and tournaments.[11] However, they continued after the War; and in 1921 women's football clubs in England numbered 150, organized under the Women's Football Association. But the English Football Association (dominated by men) refused de facto and de jure existence of the above clubs and Association: 'The game of football is quite unsuitable for females and should not be encouraged.'[12] The English Football Association declared a boycott on women's football. Nevertheless, the English women did not give up and they carried on with their clubs and league. At about that time female participation as players crossed the boundary of Britain.[13] At present women's football is played in various national leagues, in the Olympic Games and in the World Cup.[14] The final game of the world cup in Los Angeles USA 1999, attracted over 90,000 spectators, both women and men. It appears that women have captured their own football territory: next to men and most importantly, not subject to them.

Yet, based on research and popular sources of information (newspapers, television), it is possible to state that women's football as well as women in the role of football spectators, is still dependent on the permission of males. FIFA, the international football association, is dominated by men. Despite President Joseph Blater's declaration that 'the Future is feminine',[15] the present is overwhelmingly male dominated. The leading hypothesis that underlies this study is that not only is women's football dependent on men, but also women as spectators haven't totally come out of men's clutches. This is elaborated upon in the following section through a case study of Israeli women soccer fans. Albeit being independent and committed fans, the relationship of Israeli women to football is intermediated by the gender effect.

Conquering a territory

Until recently, fans had to be present in the stadiums in order to watch football. The typical stadium in Britain (and also in other countries) was quite a simple ground,[16] divided into a sitting zone and a standing zone – the end zones. In the nineteenth century and the beginning of the twentieth century, women who wished to be present in the crowd faced different obstacles. Most critical was the 'normative obstacle': considering the ethic of gender division at that time, the presence of a lady in the football ground was stained with a reputation of licentiousness. Nevertheless, some women watched football (or even boxing) while escorted by a family member or other 'appropriate' male company. Women were probably present mostly at the stadiums of the senior clubs in the big cities,[17] which could offer a minimum of private services to their more affluent spectators. But the picture of the football crowd was changing: even before the Second World War, women of the middle and lower classes attended football games not only in England but also in other countries: France, Italy, Germany, Sweden and more.[18]

It is not possible to specify the exact date when women began to watch football as fans in the stadium. It is possible however to suggest that becoming female fans is metaphorically a process of conquering a piece of land in 'men's territory': the football ground has always been 'male's land',[19] the image of the macho male dominates the terraces. Also, women did not create women-only colonies in the stadium, such as the family balcony that is available today in Britain.[20] But the statistics very clearly indicate that women fans are permanent and no longer a negligible presence in the football crowd in many football stadiums worldwide. They are forbidden in states that are run by traditional religious regimes but they are quite conspicuous in the modern state, where football is heavily commercialized.

In tracing the evolution of the female fan, Dunning offers some points of interest: Many women came to the English Cup finals in 1927 accompanied by their husbands or friends. Mothers and their children were also present at that game. Two years later, half of the train passengers to the Cup finals were females.[21] Studies conducted over the last decade reveal that the percentage of women fans in the English league game remains between 10 and 13%.[22] While watching football matches in Germany, Spain, France or Argentina on television, the presence of women in the crowd is prominent. One gets the same impression while watching international football matches. Sometimes it appears that even the formal statistics are too conservative.

The division of sports between 'men's sport' and 'women's sport' is one of a number of mechanisms by which those of the dominant gender, men, formulate its identity, resets the boundaries with the 'other sex' and concurrently strengthens its privileges.[23] In the context of the present essay, it is of relevance to consider two related yet non-identical concepts: hegemony and domination.[24] Regarding sport, men have until recently been both hegemonic and dominating. As hegemonic, they set the 'proper' values (including the restrictions on women), which were considered so even by women until recently. As for domination, men control everything related to sport: the game, the arena, the rules and the institutions. For many years the male hegemony and domination coexisted. At the end of the twentieth century, this coexistence weakened: women contested men's hegemony in sport by participating in football or even in rugby. Their presence as athletes and as supporters was looked upon as a defiant act concerning men's hegemony.

The conceptual and, more important, the practical distinction between hegemony and domination has an effective meaning concerning female participation as football spectators/supporters. As noted above, this participation was welcomed but with a feeling of threat although female domination in the stadium is yet to become a real possibility. However, they do undermine male hegemony by challenging the values, symbols, verbal practices and the physically aggressive gestures men use during the game. In fact, female presence in the terraces was encouraged in part by the English Football Association in order to deal with hooliganism.[25] The presence of women supporters in football games is a direct, even bold, contest regarding 'men's territory': 'here we are, here we stay, football is (also) our game'.

However, the reference to women and football either as players or supporters is still related to the hegemony or more often to the domination of men in sport. The presumption of those scholars who deal with this subject is that in sport, as in other instances of modern society, gender is still a significant factor: the weakening of male hegemony has (meanwhile) little effect on their domination. The primary gain of female fans is the extension of their relative autonomy. Relative, because men are still in control of the terraces: they set the rules and the limits.

Becoming fans

The study of women and football draw attention to factors responsible for the creation of athletes and fans. Basically, becoming an athlete or a fan is an end product of socialization.[26] A few studies that deal with the process of becoming American athletes specify four involved factors: family, peers, school and community. Yet the order of importance of the impact of these factors is different for boys and girls. For boys the order is: peers, family and school. For girls the order is: family, peers and community.[27] Some studies specify the impact of Title IX: after its legislation by the American Congress the influence of colleges on women's sport increased dramatically.[28] In the same context, it has been argued that family and peers are most important for a girl under 12 years of age. Parents take the girl (and the boy) to watch games and in doing so ignite the process of becoming an athlete or fan. The continuity of this process depends on other factors such as peers later on. Over the age of 12 the agent changes: the influence of the family decreases while that of peers and teachers increases. These agents encourage and channel the young girl's attachment, either as an athlete or as a fan.

Socialization of a young girl into a football fan is dependent on the same factors noted above: family, teachers and peers. However, being a female fan is not a fait accompli. Female attendance at football games invokes certain inter-gender tensions whose roots are external to the stadium. Women are accepted in the terraces without overt opposition, but men doubt their 'kosher' motives and authenticity.[29] A woman fan is required, implicitly or explicitly, to demonstrate her genuine loyalty to the club. Sometimes women fans are accused that their motivation is not genuine, but is related to eroticism.[30] The study of fandom indicates that women fans feel that men perceive them as 'honorary males', not a very flattering compliment.

But there is another perspective concerning the status of female fans in the stadium. A study of Liverpool female fans[31] and an observation of the changes in the general atmosphere prevalent in British football[32] suggest that football has become friendlier to women. One of the reasons for the change in atmosphere is the economic potential of women: they purchase tickets, they are customers of the club shops, and they watch television. In sum, they constitute a concrete economic segment for commercial football.

Attendance in the football stadium is a special experience for women – mainly for young women. They are not required to behave like men, or to adopt macho gestures in order to be accepted. Crolly and Long argue on the basis of interviews with women Liverpool fans that they feel at home in their stadium.[33] The Liverpool football crowd is not divided on gender lines. In fact, male and female supporters intermingle freely and frequently. Women seem to accept men's culture in the stadium, but they do not follow their every gesture, such as using foul language.[34] Thus female fans do not always act as the passive/silent participant. There is evidence that women participate as members in the notorious Italian Ultras. In some Ultra groups they even act as spokeswomen.[35] Passive, active, initiating and so forth – female presence in the football stadium is an undisputed fact.

Israeli football fans

This study focuses on the very basic question of the status of female football fans in Israel. Given the paucity of any worthy study on the subject, this essay, instead of attempting to derive new questions or posit specific hypotheses, raises three basic questions: 1. the process of socialization to the game; 2. fandom as a way of life; 3. the autonomy of women at football games. These questions have a common denominator: the (presumed) presence of male agents who act as escorts, protectors and also as symbolic agents: men create and maintain the atmosphere in the Israeli football stadium. Apparently, men set the degrees of freedom for their female fan companions.

The study and method

During the months of March–May 2004, the author conducted a study of football fans in Israel. Fans of five clubs of the Premier League were interviewed: Maccabi Haifa, Hapoel Tel Aviv, Beitar Jerusalem, Maccabi Netanya and Bnei Sachnin – an Arab club. One hundred and forty three (fanatic) fans, male and female, over the age of 18, were interviewed at their homes, of which 17 were women. Only one of the women interviewed was an Arab. Arab women do not generally watch a football match in the stadium, except on rare occasions.[36] The number and the rate of those who were interviewed do not reflect the actual situation in the stadiums. It is approximated that female attendance in the stadiums of the major clubs is around 10%, but no concrete facts (i.e., a survey of fans in the stadium) can support this estimation. It is worth noting that the study was aimed at revealing patterns of Israeli fandom, the fan's football consumption, and attitudes toward various football-related issues (management, violence, commercialization, etc.). A standard, semi-constructed questionnaire was administered during the interviews with the fans.

Two years earlier, the author also conducted a nationwide survey of football fans in Israel. The results of that survey indicate that women who are interested in football amounts to 27% of the entire population interested in football in Israel. However, this value (27% females interested in football) does not reflect the traditional 'fanatic' fans: those female fans who are present at their club game every (other) week. The above rate is reflective of the fact that football in Israel is not solely a man's game. The women who were interviewed in this study are indeed traditional 'fanatic' fans.[37] Their profile – as follows – is indicative of their status.

Profile of the Israeli female fan

The typical fan was born in Israel. Her parents are also Israeli born. Thus her entire socialization took place in Israel. She is single and in her 20s. She possesses a university degree or is in the process of obtaining one. She is employed. Some of the women work odd jobs, but many are settled in a stable job – in business, management and public services. She earns an average Israeli income – about 5,000 Shekels per month ($1,200). Few, because of their position in the organization, earn high salaries. It appears that the typical female fan belongs to the middle class. This is an important characteristic, because as will become evident, their class status affects their behaviour in the stadium and their general and specific attitudes regarding football and fandom.

Results

The following sub-sections deal with the three questions already raised in the order of their appearance.

Socialization to the role of fan

It is suggested above that socialization to sport, football included, begins at a very young age – the first years of schooling. The information gathered by the present study indicates two time periods during which one becomes a football fan. The first is during the very early stage of socialization: 'when I was born'. Most of the fans specify the first years in primary school (age 8–11) as the period when they were introduced to football. The second, as some fans suggest, is following their army service (age 20–21). The difference is not accidental; those who belong to the first were introduced to the game by a family member. The second lot was mostly introduced to the game by boyfriends. It is worth noting that except for a very few, the male fans who were also interviewed in this study were introduced to the game at a very young age. One factor is common to all the female fans in this study – the male agent. Those who were introduced to the game as young girls were done so by a male family member (father, brother). Those who were introduced to the game in their 20s were done so by a boyfriend or male friend.

In fact, the fans identified the male agent as the mediator: 'I went with my father to watch Hapoel FC.' 'My brother "smuggled" me.' 'My brothers were fans of Hapoel FC They attracted me to football.' 'My father, the whole family liked football, my father is a fanatic.' 'At home, my father is a Beitar FC fan.' The status of the father as an agent of sport socialization is well documented. More often, Israeli fathers who love football take their sons and daughters to the game. It is his (modest) contribution to his children's education.

A male friend or a boyfriend is another agent. He introduces the latecomer female fan to the game: 'In order to keep the peace (at home) I go the Hapoel FC games … my boyfriend says that now I support the club more than he does.' 'My ex-boyfriend "bewitched" me, and we attend many games.' 'My boyfriend was a Beitar FC supporter, so I switched from Maccabi to Beitar FC, I fell in love with Beitar fans.' 'When I realized that my husband and my son are fanatics, I joined them.'

Regarding male fans interviewed in this study, their socialization to the game occurred in the family. Family and peers were most important in this process. Every single agent of their socialization to the sport was male, while only one female fan was attracted to the game by her female peers. Hence, the introduction and the attachment of Israeli women to football are mediated by male figures. It appears that there are two reasons for this. First, many more men are attached to this game than women. Second, introduction by a male family member or a male friend facilitates the attachment to the game and attendance in the stadium – males provide physical and symbolic protection. Even today, a young Israeli woman is not encouraged to come by herself to a football stadium. Third, a football match can be used for courting/bonding. Finally, it is a family event – the wife and children join the head of the family in the stadium.

Supporting evidence to the function of the male-figure as a mediator is offered by the responses to the question 'with whom do you go to the home games?' For the traditional fanatic fan these games are extremely important events. S/he would not miss a home game. The literature cited above indicates that it is not 'proper' for a woman to be present in the terraces by herself, but better with somebody, preferably a man. But a group of females is also a possibility. Unofficial double standards regarding men and women remain in effect in football all over the globe, including Israel.

The responses to the above question are almost uniform: A young woman does not go to the game by herself. In the past – when she was a little girl – she used to go with a family member, mainly her father. When the father was not involved, a brother was a substitute. Now she also goes, stays and leaves with male company, but this figure is a friend, boyfriend or husband. One could speculate about the reasons but the facts are that a young girl or a woman prefers male company in the football stadium.

It is worth noting again that the female interviewees in this study love the game of football. They love it *not* because of their male/boy friends. With regard to their (self) attachment to the game, males are instrumental. Regardless of their initiating motive of attachment to this game, they now feel and behave like a genuine football fan. For them, this game is 'a way of life'.

Fandom as a way of life

Recent studies that deal with football fans suggest that fandom is a way of life.[38] In other words, football is the central event in the life of a fan. Since a way of life includes many events and patterns of behaviour at different levels and importance, it is suggested that football as a way of life means that the fan's daily and weekly agenda is determined by 'her' club's league and cup schedule. Consequently, football fandom dictates fans' patterns of consumption and social relations. Football fandom is therefore concretized by consumption of related media: the broadcasting of the matches of the regional league, the champions' league, the English league and so forth. Consumption of various media that deal with football is also a practical way of keeping in close touch with the game as well as with the football community, which is often an important reference group to the fan(s). More importantly, consumption of football specifies the importance of football to the fan's (male and female) identity.

The focal interest in the interviewee's way of life is her club's matches: home and away games. Home games are the most important. A fanatic does not miss them because being there is most significant and a demonstrative act of fandom. Most of the interviewees in this study reported that they attend almost 'every domestic game' of their club. Away games are more difficult to attend regularly: only a third of the fans reported that they attend 'most of them'. However, it is important to mention here that usually female fans who attend domestic games and most critically, visitor games – which require more manoeuvring than domestic games – are accompanied by a male figure.

Football as a way of life also refers to the fan's behaviour outside the stadium. The fan is constantly alert to information about the game and 'her' club. The Israeli female fan is an ardent consumer of information regarding her club. At the time of this study, a football fan in Israel could consume a lot of information on football from various media. The fans of this study report the following: They regularly read the sports section of the newspaper. They watch the Israeli Premier League games on PPV. They watch the Champions League on television. They also occasionally watch the second division league games, which are available on different Israeli television channels.

The football menu of the above is far from being all encompassing: besides attending every domestic game, she consumes almost every bit of information available in the media and on the internet. The female fan invests about 10 hours per week on 'her' club (watching games, news specials on TV and in the newspapers, etc.). She spends on average 200 shekels (about $45) per month on football. This is not as much as the male fan because in most Israeli stadiums women are allowed entry free of charge.

Football as a way of life is demanding: The fan is required to show her loyalty to the club. Football as a way of life also involves tension: tension between the fan and significant others. She is often required to choose between football games and family events or friends. This issue is more real than hypothetical: 'Suppose a family event coincides with one of your club's games, what are you going to do?' The league schedule is predetermined for the entire season. A fan could plan his/her daily, weekly and monthly football life in advance. Although family events are also anticipated, some may interfere with the fan's football schedule. In such a situation the fan faces a concrete, often critical conflict of loyalties; that of being a fan and that of being a family member. She undergoes the most difficult exercise of choosing the right option in such a context.

A conflict of loyalties is a fan's nightmare. The traditional fanatic conspires to avoid a direct conflict with family and friends. But the club's priority is almost unquestioned. However, this situation is perceived as a dreaded and threatening situation: 'This is like a movie. I'll have a problem if the game is critically important. I'll have to weigh both sides; which is more critical? I don't know which it'll be. If it's my brother's Bar-Mitzvah, I'll freak.' In most cases, loyalty to the family comes first but with some specified pre-conditions: 'I'll do everything to listen to the game but I'll go to the [family] event … Me and my father listened to the game through a mobile radio.' 'If this is an important game I'll try to combine (both the game and the events).' 'Depends on the event. If it's a wedding of an important family member, I'll be at the event but I'll make sure I get an SMS on my mobile phone. If the family event is not very important, I'll go to the game.' 'Combine both, but leave early from the family event.' 'I left my nephew's circumcision party.' 'Usually I check beforehand that a wedding won't happen on the date of a game.' 'I videotape the game.' 'I'll probably come late to the family event.'

Some of the interviewees hesitate, but a priori lean towards the game: 'Usually I'll go to the game, but if they [the family] force me, then I'll go to the event.' 'I'll go to the game. It's happened 20 times in the past. The family disowned me. I missed a wedding and Bar Mitzvah.' 'I watch the game. Not be present at the event.'

Two intermediate conclusions are derived from the above responses to the not-so-hypothetical question: one, it appears that the interviewees in this study are indeed traditional fans. Football indeed is central to their life. Second and related, football is their way of life; it is the major issue that projects heavily on their intimate social relations. In other words, fandom is a critical element of their identity. Apparently exhibiting a club's identity is almost inevitable to the traditional fan – 'this is the real me'.

Indeed, recent studies point to the likelihood that sport fans and in particular football fans will demonstrate their fandom.[39] Football fans tend to demonstrate their fandom not just during the game and in the stadium, but also (more so) through their daily routine while interacting with others. Football fans are very keen on being seen and identified as such by others. 'How do you feel when others identify you as a fan of (your) club?' While responding, the word 'proud' is mentioned by almost every interviewee. 'I feel proud of myself. It's fun to belong to Hapoel FC ... it's nice that somebody smiles at you just because we have something in common.' 'Cool, I am proud to be a fan of Hapoel FC. I don't hide it. Every day I wear a red item.' 'I'm proud of the club and I love its badge.' 'This is part of me.' 'At work, everybody knows that I support Haifa FC. My car is covered with stickers. I'm absolutely proud.' 'I'm proud to be a supporter of Bnei-Sachnin FC.' 'I'm "Yellow Pride"', states a Beitar fan, whose club colour is yellow.

Football has become an important component of a female Israeli football fan's identity. There is also a new facet of their fandom, a facet of relative autonomy. While a mediating male figure remains in the background, the creation, management and consolidation of her way of life does not need the support or the immediate aid from the male gender. She does not need male mediation concerning her fan identity. She is responsible for the dilemmas and tensions that stem from football. It is possible to suggest that the socio-economic profile of the female fan explains, at least in part, her extended relative autonomy. Besides the issues related to her status in the stadium, she does everything else by herself.

Behaviour during the game

As a socio-cultural phenomenon, the game of football is a zone of permission.[40] Certain behaviours that are not acceptable (or even legitimized) outside the stadium are considered normal inside the stadium, such as using coarse language, cursing, body gestures, etc. This zone of permission has no formal legal basis. It has been created during the history of football ever since football became the game of the masses. The limits of this zone are established and re-established through an ongoing negotiation between the fans, the club and the state authorities. The fans are aware of that zone and its fluctuating limits: they know that certain behaviours are permitted and they follow suit.

The ongoing study of female fan behaviour in (and outside) the football stadium points to certain inhibitions on the part of the female spectator. They are less aggressive verbally and with regards to body language. It is suggested that their presence in the terraces has a relaxing influence on men, such as de-radicalizing men's dialogue with the game. It is therefore recommended to increase the number of women in the terraces[41] in order to decrease the level of aggression. Nevertheless, a female fan in the zone of permission might behave like a football fan more than anything else.

Upon request, one of the interviewees described her behaviour during the game in her own words. It appears that many of them do not fit the image of a relaxed and a mediator-moderator fan that the conventional literature attributes to female fans. While in the terraces, they let go some of the restraints:

'Venting frustrations in the stadium. Non-stop speaking, cursing, shouting … Letting out my hooliganism.' 'Emotions play a very powerful role.' 'I cheer [the team], I sing to the players, I curse the referee's assistant and the referee, also the players of the visitor club … I stand during the entire game. I feel tension and excitement.' 'I constantly criticize the players of Hapoel (my club). I get irritated with them.' 'I shout, I sing, I jump, I curse. I coach the team from the terrace.' 'I am highly wound-up. Screaming endlessly. Booing the opposite team. Cursing the referee and his assistant.' 'From the beginning until the end of the game, we sing our songs. Sometime cursing. I sometimes "help" the coach.' 'I'm tense. Sometimes I cry, whether we win or lose. When a goal is scored I shout. I dance. When we lose I'm quiet. I don't curse.'

Some of the interviewees report restrained behaviour: 'I don't belong to the cursers. I always cheer. This helps me to vent the tension.' 'I sit or stand, sometimes cheer.' 'I sing, I jump, I chat with the fans. I enjoy the experience.' 'I'm highly focused on the game. I stand when everybody else stands. I don't curse and I don't shout, but I'll get irritated when the referee calls a foul.'

Fandom during the game is a collective phenomenon. In practice, fandom is a crowd behaviour that squeezes the autonomy of the individual to almost nil. In the stadium the football crowd comes before the individual participant.[42] Basically, it is possible to discern two typical responses out of an individual fan: one, succumbing to and going with the flow (crowd) until a certain point when the crowd behaviour tends to get extremely aggressive. The statistics show that militant-aggressive behaviour is carried out by a minority in the stadium. Two, passive-pragmatic participation. The individual fan stands when everybody stands, he cheers to his team, etc. but he is not highly exhibitionist. He follows the moderate flow of the crowd. There is, however, a third option: an attempt to restrain the over-excited crowd and to keep behaviour within the limits of the zone of permission. This could be concretized, even in part, only by an organized group of fans that are focused on encouraging their club and avoid taunting the visitor team, the referee and so forth. In practice, this option is rare. Even the female fans studied here do not take this option; they opt for the type of behaviour that brings them close to the majority in the terraces.

The specific and anomalous behaviour of the fan in the stadium could also be examined from a different angle – her behaviour outside the stadium. The question regarding specific behaviour in the stadium was followed by 'Do you behave in this way in your daily life?' 'No. The football ground is more open. It has an atmosphere. Everybody behaves like that, not only you. There isn't as much tension in my life as in football.' 'No. The hard effect. Everybody does it on the ground, so it's OK to do it. It's not abnormal.' 'No. Everybody [on the ground] is the same … I'll join them. To drift with the fans.' 'No. This [the stadium] is a more emotional place. Let off steam. Feeling free to behave.' It appears that the female fan in this study refuses to carry the role implicitly imposed upon her, of an instrumental moderator of the crowd's behaviour in the stadium. She shows no tendency to concede or fulfil this role. She maintains a certain amount of relative autonomy in and outside the stadium.

In fact, most of the men interviewed in this study reveal the same pattern as the female fans. In the football stadium, they feel like different people and act accordingly. However, it should be noted here that these fans, save a few, considered themselves ardent but not over-aggressive supporters of 'their' club. Hence, women fans succumb to the atmosphere in the stadium: quite gladly they tend to adopt the major characteristics of crowd behaviour. This behaviour, as noted numerous times above, is created and managed by male fans. Thus, also in this situation, men play a mediating role: they still set the stage and the roles that (most of) the female fans adopt while maintaining relative autonomy over their behaviour.

Conclusion

This essay has focused on three questions: becoming a football fan, fandom as a way of life, and the relative autonomy of behaviour in the stadium. Based on literature that deals with female fans, it was assumed that a male figure is involved in every one of the above questions. The male figure plays the role of mediator: between the state of pre-fandom to a state of becoming a fan. Male figures mediate between female fans and football as a social event still dominated by men. Fathers, brothers, friends and boyfriends socialize and escort the girl, and later on the young woman to the football stadium.

Today, the football stadiums in Israel welcome women. This was not so in the past when football was almost completely men's territory. Not any more. But still men dominate this game: they set the rules in the terraces, they devise the atmosphere, and they consider themselves as offering patronage to female fans, allowing them relative autonomy.

Finally, the essay demonstrates that Israeli women are genuine fans. Football for them is an important, even critical, element in their identity. Although they enjoy only relative autonomy in football fandom, and although men run the show, women in Israel have become immanent on the football scene. Football is not 'just for men' anymore.

Notes

1. De Beauvoir, *The Second Sex*.
2. Hargreaves, *Sporting Females*; Dworkin and Messner, 'Just Do … What?'; Costa and Guthrie, *Women and Sport*; Cashmore, *Making Sense of Sports*.
3. Birley, *Sport and the Making of Britain*, 246.
4. Ibid., 246.
5. Ibid.
6. Cahn, *Coming on Strong*; Hargreaves, *Sporting Females*; Hall, 'The Discourse of Gender'.
7. Cahn, *Coming on Strong*.
8. Dunning, *Sport Matters*.
9. Dunning, *et al.*, *Fighting Fans*.
10. Ben Porat, *Football and Nationalism*.
11. Williams, *Game for Rough Girls?*; Lopez, *Women on the Ball*.

12. Birley, *Playing the Game*, 204.
13. Murray, *The World's Game*.
14. Mangan and Hong, *Soccer, Women*; Williams, *A Game for Rough Girls?*; Scraton *et al.*, 'It's Still A Man's Game?'.
15. Williams, *Game for Rough Girls?*, 1.
16. Inglis, *The Football Grounds*,
17. Coddington, *One of the Lads*.
18. Williams, *Game for Rough Girls?*
19. Hargreaves, *Heroines of Sport*.
20. King, *End of the Terraces*.
21. Dunning, Murphy and Williams, *Roots of Football Hooliganism*.
22. Waddington, Dunning and Murphy, 'Research Note'.
23. Bryson, 'Challenges to Male Hegemony'; Messner and Sabo, *Sport, Men*; Dunning; 'Sport as a Male Preserve'.
24. Ben Porat, *Football and Nationalism*.
25. Pelak, 'Negotiating Gender/Race/Class Constraints'.
26. Crawford, *Consuming Sport*.
27. McPherson, 'Socialization'.
28. Wann *et al.*, *Sport Fans*.
29. Williams and Woodhouse, 'Women and Football'.
30. Crolly and Long, 'Sitting Pretty?'; Crawford, *Consuming Sport*; Guttman, *The Erotic in Sport*.
31. Crolly and Long, 'Sitting Pretty?'.
32. Coddington, *One of the Lads*; Giulianotti, *Football*.
33. Crolly and Long, 'Sitting Pretty?'.
34. Back, Crabbe and Solomos, *Changing Face of Football*.
35. Dal Lago and De Biasi, 'Italian Football Fans'.
36. Sorek, *Playing With Identities*.
37. Giulianotti, 'Supporters, Followers'.
38. Sandvoss, *Game of Two Halves*; Crawford, *Consuming Sport*.
39. Crawford, *Consuming Sport*; Wann *et al.*, *Sport Fans*.
40. Ben Porat, *Football and Nationalism*.
41. Dunning, Murphy and Williams, *Roots of Football Hooliganism*; Williams, *Game for Rough Girls?*
42. Ben Porat, *Football and Nationalism*.

References

Back, L., T. Crabbe, and J. Solomos. *The Changing Face of Football*. Oxford: Berg, 2001.
Ben-Porat, A. *Football and Nationalism*. Tel Aviv: Resling (H), 2003.
Birley, D. *Sport and the Making of Britain*. Manchester: Manchester University Press, 1993.
Birley, D. *Playing the Game*. Manchester: Manchester University Press, 1995.
Bryson, L. 'Challenges to Male Hegemony in Sport'. In *Sport, Men, and the Gender Order: Critical Feminist Perspectives,* ed. M. Messner and D. Sabo, 173–84. Champaign, IL: Human Kinetics, 1990.
Cahn, S. K. *Coming on Strong*. Cambridge, MA: Harvard University Press, 1994.
Cashmore, E. *Making Sense of Sports*. London: Routledge, 1990.
Coddington, A. *One of the Lads: Women Who Follow Football*. London: HarperCollins, 1997.
Costa, D.M., and S.R. Guthrie. *Women and Sport*. Champaign, IL: Human Kinetics, 1994.
Crawford, G. *Consuming Sport*. London: Routledge, 2004.
Crolly, L., and C. Long. 'Sitting Pretty? Women and Football in Liverpool'. In *Passing Rhythms. Liverpool PC and the Transformation of Football,* ed. J. Williams, S. Hopkins, and L. Long, 195–214. Oxford; Berg, 2001.
Dal Lago, A., and R. De Biasi. 'Italian Football Fans: Culture and Organization'. In *Football, Violence and Social Identity,* ed. R. Giulianotti, N. Bonney, and M. Hepworth, 73–89. London: Routledge, 1994.
De Beauvoir, S. *The Second Sex*. London: Penguin, 1972.

Dunning, E. 'Sport as a Male Preserve: Notes on the Social Sources of Masculine Identity and Transformation'. In *Quest for Excitement: Sport and Leisure in Civilizing Process,* ed. N. Elias, and E. Dunning, 267–84. Oxford: Basil and Blackwell, 1986.

Dunning, E. *Sport Matters.* London: Routledge, 2001.

Dunning, E., P. Murphy, and J. Williams. *The Roots of Football Hooliganism.* London: Routledge, 1992.

Dunning, E., P. Murphy, I. Waddington, and A.E. Astrinakis, eds. *Fighting Fans.* Dublin: University College Dublin Press, 2002.

Dworkin, S.L., and M.A. Messner. 'Just Do … What? Bodies, Gender'. In *Gender and Sport: A Reader,* ed. S. Scraton and A. Flintoff, 17–29, London: Routledge, 2002.

Giulianotti. R. *Football: A Sociology of the Global Game.* Cambridge: Polity Press, 1999.

Giulianotti. R. 'Supporters, Followers, Fans and Flaneurs'. *Journal of Sport and Social Issues* 26, no. 1 (2002): 25–46.

Guttman, A. *The Erotic in Sport.* New York: Columbia University Press, 1996.

Hall, A. 'The Discourse of Gender and Sport: from Femininity to Feminism'. In *Gender and Sport: A Reader,* ed. S. Scraton, and A. Flintoff, 6–16. London: Routledge, 2002.

Hargreaves, J. *Sporting Females.* London: Routledge, 1994.

Hargreaves, J. *Heroines of Sport.* London: Routledge, 2000.

Inglis, S. *The Football Grounds of Great Britain.* London: Collins Willow, 1987.

King, A. *The End of the Terraces.* London: Leicester University Press, 1998.

Lopez, S. *Women On the Ball: A Guide to Women's Football.* London: Scarlet Press, 1997.

McPherson, B. 'Socialization into the Role of Sport Consumer: A Theory and Casual Mangan, J.A., and Fan Hong, eds. *Soccer, Women, Sexual Liberation.* London: Frank Cass, 2003.

Model'. *Canadian Review of Sociology and Anthropology* 13 (1976): 111–19.

Messner, M., and D. Sabo. *Sport, Men and the Gender Order.* Champaign, IL: Human Kinetics, 1990.

Murray, B. *The World's Game.* Urbana. IL: University of Illinois Press, 1988.

Pelak, C.F. 'Negotiating Gender/Race/Class Constraints in the New South Africa'. *International Review for the Sociology of Sport* 40, no. 1 (2005): 53–70.

Sandvoss, C. *A Game of Two Halves.* London: Routledge, 2003.

Scraton, S., K. Fastig, G. Pfister, and A. Bunuel. 'It's Still a Man's Game?' *International Review for the Sociology of Sport* 34, no. 2 (1999): 99–111.

Sorek, T. *Playing With Identities. Arabs Soccer in Jewish State.* Jerusalem: Magnes Press, 2006.

Wann, D.L., M.J. Melnick, G.W. Russell, and D.G. Pease. *Sport Fans: The Psychology and Social Impact of Spectators.* New York: Routledge, 2001.

Williams, J. *A Game for Rough Girls?* London: Routledge, 2003.

Williams, J., and J. Woodhouse. 'Can Play, Will Play? Women and Football in Britain'. In *British Football and Social Change: Getting into Europe,* ed. J. Williams, and S. Wagg, 85–111. Leicester: Leicester University Press, 1991.

Waddington, I., E. Dunning, and P. Murphy. 'Research Note: Surveying the Social Composition of Football Crowds'. *Leisure Studies* 15 (1996): 215–19.

INDEX

Abdenpost 108
AFC Leopards 172-3, 179, 181,
    182, 183
African football style: Kenya 175-6
Agergaard, S.: and Sorensen,
    J.K. 70-84
Alagich, C. 130
Alagich, J. 130
Alagich, R. 130
Albion Sports: Bradford 17
Alemannia Aachen 65
Ali, Z. 9
Allison, L. 33
Almithak 15-16
Almunia, M. 52
American Soccer League (ASL)
    103, 106
American Youth Soccer Organization
    (AYSO) 115-16
Arab and African Sports Association 173
Aragones, L. 29
Arif, I.G.H. 148
Asamoah, G. 64-5, 66
Assauer, R. 64
Australia: Victorian minority football
    127-46
Aziz, A.K. 150
Aziz, S.A. 152

Bairner, A.: and Sugden, J. 46
Bandyopadhyay, K. 147-69
Barker, M. 34
baseball 104
Basque nationalism 138
Bayern Munich 59
Beckenbauer, F. 60

Beckham, D. 87, 95
Beitar Jerusalem: women and
    football 192
Belfast 46
Ben-Porat, A. 178-9, 187-200
Bend It Like Beckham 10
Birley, D. 188
black amateur football clubs: Britain
    12-18; and cultural resistance 14-16;
    early post-migration years 12-14
Blatter, S. 190
Bnei Sachin: women and football 192
Bonilla-Silva, E. 34
Borjas , G. 80
Borussia Dortmund 64
Borussia Mönchengladbach 65
Bourdieu, P. 71, 73, 74, 76, 80, 81
Bourne, J. 34
Boyd, M. 55
British Asian amateur football clubs
    12-18, 29; club growth 16-18; early
    post-migration years 12-14; ethnicity
    and identity 18-20
Buller, J.R.: and Collins, M.F. 71
Burdsey, D. 8-25, 28, 37
Burin, F. 137, 139

Calcutta Monthly 148, 149
Caribbean Cricket Club (CCC):
    Leeds 14-15
Carrington, B. 14-15; and
    McDonald, I. 29
Castells, M. 27, 33, 35, 39
Catalan nationalism 138
Chadha, G. 10
Charlton, J. 47, 50, 52

Chatterji, J. 156
Cheska, A.T. 86
Chicago area soccer 99-126;
    All-Star games 102; attendances 101;
    commercialization 119;
    cultural Otherness 110; ethnic
    identity evolution 118-20; ethnic
    newspapers 108; ethnic period
    (1938-71) 105, 106-11; ethnic pride
    107-8; exhibition games 100-2;
    Great Depression 104; high schools
    116; Hispano-American Soccer
    League 112, 113, 114; immigration
    restrictions 104; indoor soccer 106,
    110; international games 102-3;
    isolationism and xenophobia 104;
    Jabat FC 121-2; Latin Premier
    United Soccer League 114;
    latinization 111-14; Mayor's
    Cup 102, 103, 109; Metropolitan
    Soccer League (MSL) 117-18, 120;
    Mexicans 112-13; National Soccer
    League (NSL) 117, 120; player
    payments 119; rise and decline
    (1921-37) 100-5; social/cultural life
    108-9, 119; suburbanization 114-18
Chicago Daily Tribune 100, 103, 104,
    108, 109, 111
Chicago Latin American Soccer
    Association (CLASA) 112-14
Chicago National Soccer League 103
Chicago Soccer League 103;
    establishment 100
Chicago Tribune 108, 110, 116, 118
civilizing processes: race domination
    35, 36-7
Collins, M.F.: and Buller, J.R. 71
colour-blind racism 34, 35, 37
Crepeau, R. 104
Critical Race Theory 10
Croatia Melbourne 138-9
Croatian immigrants: Victoria 135-9
Crolly, L.: and Long, C. 192
Cronin, M. 47; and Mayall, D. 90
cultural capital 73, 74, 75, 76-7
cultural incompatibility: race
    domination 35, 36

Danish football 70-84; cultural capital
    76-7; economic capital 78-80; ghetto
    area sports participation and mobility
    71-2; physical capital 76-7; social
    capital 77-8; youth football 75
Danish Football Association (DBU):
    ethical code 75
Darby, P. 172, 174, 175
Das, S. 164
Day, R.D. 86
Denni Hlasatel 108
Derry City FC 49
Dhaka Mohammedan Sporting Club 155
Drennen, A. 135
Dublin 46
Dublin, D. 15
Dunning, E. 190
Dutch immigrants: Victoria 139-41

East Africa Challenge Cup 173
East Bengal 153, 156-7, 162, 163
East and Central Africa Senior Challenge
    Cup 173
economic capital 78-80
Eitle, T.M.: and Eitle, D.J. 71
Eitzen, D.S. 36
embodied capital 73, 74
Energie Cottbus 64
England: British Asian/black amateur
    football clubs 12-18; ethnicity and
    identity 18-20; minority ethnic
    football clubs 8-25; politics of
    multiculturalism 18-20; race equality
    initiative resistance 26-43; racism 21
English County FA: and English local
    football governance 29-38
English local football governance:
    English County FA 29-38; and
    participation numbers 28; race denial
    34-5, 39; race derision 37-8, 39;
    race domination 35-7; race equality
    initiative resistance 26-43; race and
    racism 27-8
Ethics and Sports Equity Strategy: FA
    27, 32, 33
ethnic capital 80, 81
ethnicity 178-9

FA Cup 8-9
Farina, F. 131
FC St Pauli 63-4, 65
Finn, G.: and Guilianotti, R. 46, 47
Fishwick, G. 115
Fleming, S.: and Tomlinson, A. 16
Football Association (FA) 27, 30;
  equity strategy 32, 33, 38; Football
  Development Strategy (FEDS) 31-2
Football Association of Ireland (FAI) 44,
  47-8, 51, 52, 53, 55
Football Development Strategy (FEDS):
  Football Association (FA) 31-2
Fulton, G. 48, 49
Funk, D.C.: *et al* 182; and James, J.D.
  182, 183

Gaelic Athletic Association (GAA)
  46, 47
Gayle, H. 16
Geelong 128-9, 131
Geertz, C. 102
German football: Asians 62; black
  players 63, 64; Brazilians 63, 64;
  and combating racism 60-2;
  discrimination 58-69; England
  friendly (1938) 60; extreme right
  groups 63-5; Jews 59; national
  demographic profile 61; national
  identity 60; and nationalism 58-60;
  and racism 62-6; Scandinavians
  62; and Turks 64; World Cup
  (1954) 60; World Cup (2006) 65-6
Ghuznavi, A.H. 154
Gibson, D. 50-5
Giulianotti, R. 62, 63
Gladstone, W. 36
Gor Mahia 172-3, 179, 181, 182, 183
Great Depression 104
Greek-American Athletic Club: San
  Francisco 89-95
Guilianotti, R.: and Finn, G. 46, 47
Guru Nanak 17

Hall, S. 89
Hallinan, C.J.: and Krotee, M.L. 86
Halm, D. 64

Hamburger Sport Verein 63
Haner, J. 110
Hapoel Tel Aviv: women and
  football 192
Hassan, D.: McCullough, S. and
  Moreland, E. 44-57
Havemann, N. 65
Hay, R.: and Guoth, N. 127-46
Hellerman, S.: and Markovits, A. 105
Henry, T. 29
Heskey, E. 15
Hesse, B. 14
Highfield Rangers 15, 19
Hispano-American Soccer League 112,
  113-114
Hitler, A. 59
Hokkanen, M. 174
Holt, R. 37
Hylton, K. 10-11; and Long, J. 35

India: communal Hindu-Muslim rivalry
  150, 155-7, 162-5; football and
  communalism 162-5;
  IFA-Mohammedan Sporting Club
  conflict 156-62; Mohammedan
  Sporting Club success 150-6
Indian football: Muslim involvement
  147-69
Indian Football Association: and
  Mohammedan Sporting Club 156-62
Indian Workers' Association 13
International Soccer League (ISL) 104-5,
  106, 112
Ipswich 21
Irish Football Association (IFA) 46, 49,
  51, 52, 53, 54, 55, 56
Irish soccer: Darron Gibson case 50-6;
  FIFA and eligibility 45, 47, 51-6;
  Good Friday Agreement 45, 51;
  history 45-8; and Irish nationalism
  47; northern nationalists 48-50; and
  player eligibility 44-57; state-based
  identity 47
Israel: fan behaviour 196-8; fandom and
  way of life 194-6; female fan profile
  193-8; socialization and fan role
  193-4; women and football 192-8

Jacobson, M. 115
James, J.D.: and Funk, D.C. 182, 183
Jarvie, G. 86
The Jewish Daily 108
Jews: German football 59
Johal, S. 16
Jugoslav United Soccer Team (JUST),
　Victoria 137-8, 139

Kadenge, J. 173, 176, 181
Kassimeris, C. 58-69
Kay, T. 78
Kenya 170-86; African football style
　175-6; assimilation-adaptation
　assumption 179; colonial divide
　and rule strategy 177, 178; cultural
　activities 173-4; ethnic clashes
　171-2; ethnicity and minority football
　178; European sports 174; football
　development and colonialism
　172-8; historical background 170-2;
　international football 176-7, 178;
　languages 171; National League
　180-3; nationalism 175;
　Psychological Continuum Model
　(PCM) 182-4; resistance and football
　176; team formation 180-3; wealth
　disparities 171
Kenya Football Association 177-8, 180
Kenya National Football League 172
Kernoghan, A. 52
Kewell, H. 131
Khalsa Football Federation 17
Kick It Out 21, 34
King, C. 36, 37
King, D. 19
Kivel, B. 28
Krishak Praja Party 156
Krotee, M.L.: and Hallinan, C.J. 86
Kumilla Mohammedan 155

Latin Premier United Soccer League 114
Leeds Metropolitan University 28
Leicester 15
Leicester City 15
Leicester Nirvana 17
Leisure and Society (Martin) 174

Lennon, N. 50
Lever, J. 86
Linfield FC 52
Liverpool 15-16
local football: importance 28-9
Lokomotive Leipzig 65
London APSA 8-9, 17-18
Long, C.: and Crolly, L. 192
Long, J.: *et al* 27, 28, 29, 32, 34; and
　Hylton, K. 35
Los Angeles Galaxy 87
Lowy, F. 130
Lugonzo, I. 180
Luo Union 181
Lusted, J. 26
Luton United 17

Maccabi Haifa 192
Maccabi Netanya: women and
　football 192
MacClancy, J. 89-90
McCullough, S.: Hassan, D. and
　Moreland, E. 44-57
McDonald, I.: and Carrington, B. 29
McKay, J. 86
McKiernin, W.H. 133
Maguire, J. 49, 81, 82
Maharaja of Santosh 153-4, 157-8, 160
Mählmann, P. 174, 175
Mahon, E. 49-50
Major Indoor Soccer League (MISL) 87
Major League Soccer (MSL) 87, 92, 95
Marin, I. 139
Markovits, A.: and Hellerman, S. 105
Martin, P. 174
Martinez, D. 95
Mason, T. 129
Mayall,D.: and Cronin, M. 90
Mazrui, A.A. 172
Mercer, K. 19
Merkel, U.: Sombert, K. and
　Tokarski, W. 65
Midwest League 103
minorities: definition 178
Mohammedan Sporting Club 147-69;
　Board of Trustees 151; conflict with
　IFA 156-62, 163-4; early history

148-50; football boots 152; football and communalism 162-5; impact of successive league wins 152-6; and Muslim identity 154-5; Muslim player recruitment 152; patronage 152; revival and success 150-2
Mohun Bagan: IFA Shield victory (1911) 148, 149, 156, 165
Moller, V. 75
Moreland, E.: Hassan, D. and McCullough, S. 44-57
Morgan, G. 39
Mosely, P. 137
Murray, B. 135
muscular Christianity 36
Muslim Sporting Club 155

Nasiruddin, M. 155
National Soccer League (NSL) 106, 109, 111-12
National Socialist Workers Party of Germany (NSDAP) 59, 60, 67
New Muslim Majlis 150
New York Cosmos 87
Nooruddin, K. 150, 154, 158, 160
North American Soccer League (NASL) 86-7, 116
Northern Ireland: northern nationalists 48-50; player eligibility 44-57

O'Connor, M. 54-5
Odinga, R. 177
Okocha, J.J. 176
Osiander, L. 92
Owomoyela, P. 66

Pescador, J.J. 113
physical capital 73, 73-4, 74, 76-7
Pinto, T. 180
Planck, K. 58-9
player eligibility: Irish soccer 44-57
Pooley, J.C. 86
Portes, A. 78
Powell, E. 13
Price, M.: and Whitworth, C. 114
Psychological Continuum Model (PCM) 182-4

Quite India Movement 165

race denial: English local football governance 34-5
race derision 37-8
race domination: civilizing processes 35, 36-7; cultural incompatibility 35, 36; English local football governance 35-7
race equality initiative resistance: England 26-43
Radojevic, J. 130, 139
Radojevic, V. 130 Rally, J. 93
Ramadan 10
Rashid, S.A. 148, 149, 151
Reiss, S.A. 138
Republic of Ireland: Charlton era 50; player eligibility 44-57
Riordan, J. 9
Roediger, D. 115
Roth, J. 109
Rummenigge, K.-H. 60
Rust, B. 59

San Francisco Soccer Football League (SFSFL) 88-95; ownership 93; support 93
Sarkar, N.R. 153, 162
Sarkar, T. 164
Schalke 64
Schilling, C. 73-4
Scottish immigrants: Victoria 132-5
Sengupta, A.K. 149
Shaheed Uddam Singh Games 13
Shittu, D. 20
Simiyu Njororai, W.W. 170-86
Simunic, J. 139
Sivanandan, A. 14
Skandinaven 108
Soccerhead 109, 110
social capital 77-8
social identity: key types 33; legitimizing 33; project identity 33; resistance-based 33
social mobility 73, 74, 80
Sombert, K.: Merkel, U.; and Tokarski, W. 65

Sorensen, J.K.: and Agergaard, S. 70-84
South Korea 174
South-East Asian immigrants: Victoria 141
Sporting Bengal 8-9, 17-18
Star of India 152-3, 158-9
Straker, J. 174, 176
Sugden, J.: and Bairner, A. 46
Suhrawardy, H. 154

Thompson, E. 131
Tkalcevic, M. 137
Tokarski, W.: Merkel, U. and Sombert, K. 65
Tomlinson, A.: and Fleming, S. 16
Trouille, D. 99-126
Tull, W. 10

United States of America (USA): Chicago area soccer 99-126; ethnic subcultures 85-98; San Francisco Soccer Football League (SFSFL) 88-95; soccer and Americanization 86-9; soccer decline (1920s) 104-5
Unity Cup 21
University of Brighton 9

Van Rheenen, D. 85-98
Victoria 127-46; Croatia Melbourne 138-9; Croatian immigrants 135-9; Croatian Soccer Club 136-7; Dutch immigrants 139-41; Greek community 129; Hadjuk Melbourne 138, 139; Italian community 129; Jugoslav United Football Team 137-8, 139; Juventus 129, 134; religious organizations 129; Scottish immigrants 132-5; South-East Asian immigrants 141
Vucica, J. 136, 137

Westwood, S. 16
Wharton, A. 10
White, A. 32
Whitworth, C.: and Price, M. 114
Williams, J. 11, 19, 28, 29
Windsor Park 53
women: and fan behaviour 196-8; fandom and way of life 194-6; feminist struggle 188-9; football attendance 190-2; Israel 192-8; male hegemony and domination 191; socialization and fan role 193-4; Victorian era 188; World War One 18
Worthington, N. 52

Young, J.N. 88-9
Young Sportsmen Soccer League (YSSL) 116

Zidane, Z. 81